DIARY OF THE TERRA NOVA EXPEDITION
TO THE ANTARCTIC 1910–1912

Edward Adrian Wilson (1872–1912)

EDWARD WILSON

DIARY OF THE TERRA NOVA EXPEDITION

TO THE ANTARCTIC

1910-1912

An account of Scott's last
expedition edited from the original mss.
in the Scott Polar Research Institute
and the British Museum
by H. G. R. KING

LONDON

BLANDFORD PRESS

First published in 1972
by Blandford Press Ltd, 167 High Holborn, London WC1V 6PH
© Scott Polar Research Institute, Cambridge

Text filmset in 11 on 12 pt Monotype Baskerville
Printed on blade coated cartridge paper and bound in Great Britain by
Jarrold & Sons Ltd, Norwich

CONTENTS

LISTS OF ILLUSTRATIONS AND MAPS

All the sketches and watercolours listed are by Edward Wilson. The list does not include illustrations which are an integral part of the diary, nor a number of drawings of birds added to embellish various pages. Original pictures and other material marked 'SPRI' are in the collection of the Scott Polar Research Institute. Titles in inverted commas are those provided by Wilson. Titles not in inverted commas have been supplied.

Maps

Contemporary place-names have been retained
throughout. Present day equivalents will be found
in the index.

Half of the royalties received by the Scott Polar Research Institute from the sale of this book will be used to provide Wilson Memorial Grants to help young men and women to undertake field-work in Polar regions. The remainder will be used to assist the work of the Institute.

ACKNOWLEDGMENTS

The publication of Wilson's *Terra Nova* diary would not have been possible without the willing cooperation of my colleagues on the staff of the Scott Polar Research Institute and the enthusiastic support of numerous individuals elsewhere.

First and foremost I would like to thank the Wilson family for their continued support for the Institute's policy of drawing the attention of the general public to the life and works of Edward Wilson. In particular we are grateful to the Reverend Jim Wilson and his nephew, Patrick Wilson, for depositing essential material in the Institute's archives.

Among the staff of the Institute, I would particularly like to thank the Director, Dr. Gordon Robin, for his constant encouragement. Dr. Brian Roberts, with his unmatched knowledge of Antarctic birds, has checked the English and Latin names of sea birds and provided, where necessary, alternative names commonly in use today. Dr. Charles Swithinbank has read the proofs from a glaciological viewpoint, and Dr. Terence Armstrong has given editorial advice. Mr. Gregory Cole has drawn the maps. I am particularly indebted to Miss Kristin Hollick, my senior library assistant, who has helped me with the minutiae of editing—reading proofs, listing and checking illustrations, typing drafts and so on. Thanks are also due to Mrs. Eva Robinson for her accurate typing of sections of the original manuscript. Finally comes the pleasure of acknowledging a debt to Ann Savours (Mrs. Lawrence Shirley), now on the staff of the National Maritime Museum but still closely associated with the Institute. Her spadework on Wilson's *Discovery* diary resolved most of the editorial problems with which I was confronted, allowing me to follow in her footsteps.

One of the most pleasurable aspects of editing the *Diary* was the opportunity it gave to correspond with some of the junior members of the *Terra Nova* expedition—today all leading senior citizens. I refer, of course, to Major Tryggve Gran, Sir Raymond Priestley and Sir Charles Wright. They have all been badgered with my unending questions and all have responded helpfully and without demur. To Sir Charles Wright we are all indebted for his fascinating preface to the book.

Among the others who have helped in so many ways I thank Les Quartermain of Wellington, New Zealand, who provided historical information relating to Wilson's New Zealand visit. Mr. D. R. Mullis, Director of the Migraine Trust and Dr. J. D. Gomersall of the Department of Mental Health, University of Aberdeen, commented on Wilson's attacks of migraine. Dr. Allan Rogers of the Department of Physiology, University of Bristol, provided notes on blood chemistry and diet. Dr. F. C. Fraser, formerly of the British Museum (Natural History), commented on references to whales and dolphins throughout the diary. All my notes on this subject are derived from the information he has so kindly provided. Mr. W. Greenfield of Christian Salvesen Ltd. commented on Wilson's visit to the Shetland Islands. Lastly my thanks go to the Librarian and staff of the

Central Library Cheltenham for information on the firm of Sharpe who manufactured the expedition's snow goggles.

For permission to publish Wilson's sledging diary I am grateful to the British Museum. Mr. Peter Scott has also allowed us to reproduce a number of illustrations from *The South Polar Times* Vol. III in the British Museum. The Royal Geographical Society lent two of their Wilson watercolours for reproduction. To Dr. George Seaver and Messrs. John Murray I am grateful for permission to quote in my introduction extracts from Wilson's correspondence taken from *Edward Wilson of the Antarctic*.

Finally I should like to thank the publishers and the printers for their unrelenting efforts on the book's behalf. I should like to mention in particular Terence Goldsmith and John Chesshyre, of Blandford Press, and Desmond Field of Jarrold.

FOREWORD

by SIR CHARLES WRIGHT K.C.B., O.B.E., M.C.

There must come a time in the life of every mature person when he re-estimates the characters of the men who have most influenced his career and for whom he holds the highest respect. Looking back over my 84 years there were three men who seem to be pre-eminent in this respect. All three have now departed this life. Two of them, Admiral Sir Henry Sommerville and Admiral Sir Roger Backhouse, both stood high in my esteem for their respective qualities. The third was on a still higher plane. He was Edward Adrian Wilson, affectionately known to all of us on Scott's last expedition as 'Dr. Bill'.

If any explanation is needed as to why an author like myself, unknown except for his scientific papers, should be charged with a reminiscence of Bill Wilson it is because I am, with my brother-in-law Sir Raymond Priestley, one of two surviving shore party members of the *Terra Nova* expedition. Of the two of us I am by far the less competent as a writer, but while Raymond was in the Northern Party I had the advantage of being in the Main Party and so got to know Dr. Bill well, as he was the expedition's Scientific Director.

In this capacity Dr. Bill had to supervise a staff which included biologists, oceanographers, geologists, a physiographer, a petrologist, a senior meteorologist and geomagnetician, and a glaciologist. Indeed it is fair to say that this was the first scientific expedition to the polar regions which attempted to cover so wide a field of activity. Inherent in these responsibilities was one great disadvantage—there was correspondingly less time for Bill to pursue as fully as he would have wished his supreme talents as an ornithologist and as an artist. This explains why his sketches, especially of penguins and other Antarctic birds, were less numerous on Scott's last expedition than on the *Discovery* expedition of 1901–4, on which Wilson served as second surgeon, artist and zoologist.

Bill's attitude to his scientific staff was quite informal. He played no favourites and was always willing to give advice to the scientists or help them out with their own sketches, even to the extent of putting aside a sketch on which he himself was working. He was always unselfish and seemed to look for opportunities to help others, making it his business to keep himself informed of the progress we were making in our individual investigations. We all loved him.

I think Bill personally chose all his scientists. The way I myself appeared on the expedition may possibly be of interest. Griffith Taylor, the physiographer, and I were research students together at Cambridge. He was an Australian working on palaeobotany on the Great Barrier Reef and I was a Canadian doing research at the Cavendish Laboratory. 'Griff' was a friend of Douglas (later Sir Douglas) Mawson who had accompanied Professor Sir Edgeworth David to the South Magnetic Pole during Shackleton's expedition of 1907–9. Taylor persuaded Mawson to come and talk to a small scientific group at Cambridge. At that time I was doing some research on penetrating radiation which I thought might be quite different in the Antarctic. I naturally at once applied for the post of physicist. I was promptly rejected. Griff Taylor then persuaded me to walk with him to London next day to see Captain Scott and Wilson and, at the same time, to see if we could walk the fifty miles in ten hours. The upshot was that I was accepted by Scott on Wilson's advice. Later, when the whole party was aboard the *Terra Nova* on her way south from New Zealand and met with the Antarctic pack ice, I found myself taking a great interest in the flat-topped icebergs of the south so different from the majority I had seen in the north. To cut a long story short, Dr. Bill engineered my re-appointment as the expedition's glaciologist which meant that I became eligible for field work away from headquarters.

But all this is by the way. Undoubtedly Dr. Bill's most important function on the expedition was as prop and adviser to Captain Scott. Some of the younger members, including myself, used him as our go-between to Scott. I think it was because we had little knowledge as civilians of the naval system. I for one stood in some awe of Scott.

One case which I remember so clearly, because I felt very strongly about it, was the apparent neglect in Scott's plan to make the maximum use of the meat of the ponies, the survivors of which were to be shot at the foot of the Beardmore Glacier on the way to the South Pole. I spoke earnestly to Dr. Bill that the use of this meat should be part of the plan even though it would mean giving up something else to make room for the extra fuel needed to cook the meat. Even Atkinson's party returning from the top of the Beardmore Glacier would have been very glad of additional food. I, for one, was very hungry by then.

Returning to the subject of Wilson's character, I have yet to refer to his strong sense of duty. I have in mind the occasion on the lower part of the Beardmore Glacier when Dr. Bill stayed out sketching the topographic features of the glacier's west bank below the Cloudmaker, completely disregarding an attack of acute snow-blindness following several gruelling days of man-hauling in deep snow. This same fortitude coupled to sound judgment and an equable temperament was especially in evidence when he acted as leader of the winter journey to Cape Crozier to collect Emperor Penguins' eggs at different stages of development. All these special traits endeared him to the scientists and the naval staff alike. I think it was in conversation with Cherry-Garrard that we agreed that Dr. Bill's character could almost be described as 'Christ-like'. I was myself never a tent mate of Dr. Bill, but I feel certain that if I had been one when a major catastrophe occurred —such as the spilling of all the evening hoosh on the floor cloth—I would have suppressed in Bill's presence even the most modestly expressed 'damn'. It was not until many years later, when I found myself Director of Research at the Admiralty, that I really came to appreciate how much I owed to Dr. Wilson's example. The step from research worker to Director of Research is not an easy one to make.

The last time I saw Bill was in November 1912 when as navigator on Dr.

Atkinson's search party I found the bodies of Scott, Wilson and Bowers just eleven miles south of One Ton Depot. 'Atch', 'Cherry' and I had the duty of ensuring that the diaries and papers belonging to the dead men were taken from their sleeping bags. Cherry did this service for Dr. Bill while I did the same duty for 'Birdie' Bowers. All, of course, showed signs of the dreadful journey but the end was obviously peaceful.

Amongst the papers were Bill's South Pole diary and Captain Scott's journal, which eventually found their way to the British Museum in London. Scott's journal, of course, was published and became a classic. Now, sixty years on, Bill's own account appears in print for the first time. I welcome this not only for the pleasure I personally derive from this opportunity to re-experience the expedition through Bill's words, but because it is a major contribution to Antarctic history. I am confident that it will continue to inspire future generations not simply with a love of adventure and discovery for its own sake but also with some insight into those basic qualities which went to make up the character of Dr. Bill—loyalty, selflessness and a sense of divine purpose in all things.

CHARLES WRIGHT

Ganges,
Saltspring Island,
British Columbia.
October 1971

INTRODUCTION

EDWARD WILSON's diary of the British Antarctic Expedition 1910–1913, also known as the 'Terra Nova expedition' and 'Scott's last expedition', concludes a journal which its author had disciplined himself to keep since his boyhood days. A part of this diary, describing Wilson's experiences in the Antarctic with Captain Scott on the British National Antarctic Expedition of 1901–1904, was published in 1966, edited by Ann Savours, then Curator of Manuscripts at the Scott Polar Research Institute, Cambridge. The warmth of its reception by the public encouraged the Institute and Blandford Press to consider publication of Wilson's *Terra Nova* diary as a companion volume. As will become evident from the *Notes on text and illustrations* which follow, the problems involved in editing this journal were more complex than those relating to the *Discovery* diary. The latter was a coherent whole bound in three stout volumes, whereas of the former only a part was held by the Institute; and though a typed transcript of the entire diary was available it appeared to suffer from too many inaccuracies to enable it to stand on its own as a definitive manuscript. By one of those incredible strokes of good fortune which historians dream of but scarcely ever experience in real life, a substantial section of the missing manuscript journal unexpectedly came up for auction in June 1970 and was successfully bid for by the Institute. When the British Museum agreed to make available Wilson's field diary, covering the sledge journey to the South Pole and the return to the Barrier, publication of the complete *Terra Nova* diary was assured.

Like the earlier *Discovery* diary, Wilson's account of the *Terra Nova* expedition for the period 1 June 1910 to 30 October 1911, the day before the departure for the Pole, was intended essentially for family reading. It was written in pencil and a carbon copy made, presumably to form part of the expedition's official record. The diary is a daily chronicle written weeks or even months after the events described. It is of course by no means the only first-hand account of the *Terra Nova* expedition to be published. Several of its members published their own narratives. Of these, Scott's diary, edited posthumously by Leonard Huxley and published in 1914, is the fullest and has deservedly become a world classic. Of those who accompanied Scott to the South Pole—Bowers, Oates, Wilson and Petty Officer Evans—all except Evans kept diaries. Bowers's diary, still unpublished, is in private hands; Oates's diary was destroyed at his mother's request after her death; Wilson's diary has been quoted in extracts by Leonard Huxley, by Cherry-Garrard in *The worst journey in the world* and by George Seaver in biographical studies of Wilson. It has never been published before as a whole, though, and it deserves to be. For although Wilson lacked Scott's powerful literary genius, there is a quality about his style which holds one's attention throughout. His intense faith in the divine purpose, the minute accuracy of his observations of nature and the golden vein of humour which runs throughout the pages of his narrative, these perhaps explain its appeal.

Of those who were close to Scott on this expedition none was closer than Wilson. He was, as Sir Charles Wright has reminded us in his Preface, 'his prop and adviser'. The late Frank Debenham once described Wilson as 'the perfect foil to Scott'. Without Wilson's support, he suggested, it is unlikely that Scott would have considered going south. This unique relationship does not manifest itself within the pages of the diary—Wilson was never a man to betray personal confidences. But that Wilson's diary is as remarkable for its optimism as Scott's was for its pessimism, a comparison of the two accounts will readily reveal.

In short Wilson was a remarkable man whose work—literary as well as artistic —deserves wider recognition than it has generally received. It is particularly fitting, therefore, that his *Terra Nova* diary should be published in the year that marks both the centenary of his birth and the sixtieth anniversary of the achievement of the South Pole by the party of which he was a member.

Before considering the train of events which involved Wilson in Scott's second and final expedition to the Antarctic, a brief outline of his early background may be helpful to readers not already familiar with his career.

He was born on 23 July 1872 at 6 Montpellier Terrace, Cheltenham, the son of Dr. Edward Thomas Wilson, a leading and much respected local physician. At the age of four 'Ted', as he was known to the family, was beginning to show signs of artistic talent, inherited no doubt from his paternal grandmother's family. In 1874 his parents moved into a larger house, Westal, and a year later his mother rented and farmed The Crippetts, an estate three miles outside Cheltenham on a spur of the Cotswolds. It was here amidst the beauties of the Gloucestershire countryside that Wilson, encouraged by his father, began his life-long practice of recording nature in notebook and on sketch pad. In 1886, at the age of fourteen, Wilson entered Cheltenham College and here began to keep a journal which was to become the habit of a lifetime. In 1891 he went to Gonville and Caius College, Cambridge as an exhibitioner and read for the Natural Sciences Tripos and the medical examinations, taking his B.A. degree in 1894. In 1895 he joined St. George's Hospital, most of his spare time being given to the Caius College Mission in Battersea. But overwork combined with the austerity of his daily life led to a breakdown in health which was diagnosed as tuberculosis. He was ordered to take a complete rest and spent part of the years 1898 and 1899 recuperating in Switzerland and Norway. He was able to live an out-of-doors existence developing his talents as an observer and artist. In December 1899 he returned to England and in June 1900 successfully passed his M.B. examination at Cambridge.

It was about this time that Captain R. F. Scott was looking for a likely candidate to fill the post of junior surgeon and zoologist for the National Antarctic Expedition which was to leave England in July. On the recommendations of Dr. Philip Sclater, President of the Zoological Society of London and Sir Clements Markham,

President of the Royal Geographical Society, promoter and 'father' of the expedition, Scott accepted Wilson because of his singular combination of qualifications. Wilson, who was practising at Cheltenham Hospital, unfortunately contracted blood poisoning and was very nearly prevented from joining the expedition. Three weeks after his marriage to Oriana Souper, whom he had known since his Battersea days, he sailed on *Discovery* for the Antarctic on 6 August 1901.

For a detailed account of this expedition the reader is referred to Scott's *Voyage of the Discovery* and Wilson's own *Diary of the Discovery Expedition*. It was the first scientific expedition to carry out an extensive exploration on land in Antarctica. A sledge party, consisting of Scott, Wilson and Ernest Shackleton, achieved a record southern latitude of 77°59'S. and discovered King Edward VII Land.

On his return to England in September 1904 Wilson was at first fully occupied in writing up his work on the expedition. As to his future, this at the time seemed uncertain; he felt no immediate urge to return to medical practice. Then in 1905 he was invited to accept the post of field observer to the Board of Agriculture's Commission on the Investigation of Grouse Disease at £150 per annum plus travelling expenses. Travel there would be in plenty to the Scottish and English moors collecting grouse for dissection in the laboratory and searching for the cause of an unknown disease that was killing the birds in large numbers. The work was exactly in tune with Wilson's training as a doctor and field ornithologist in the Antarctic, and he accepted the offer without hesitation. The task occupied him so fully over the next four years that he was still engaged on it half way to the Antarctic in 1910.

About the same time an old friend from his Cambridge days, Gerald Barrett-Hamilton, who had, incidentally, competed for Wilson's post on *Discovery* in 1901, asked him to illustrate his new edition of Bell's *British mammals*. Wilson not only accepted this considerable undertaking, but also agreed to paint a series of illustrations for William Eagle Clarke's proposed edition of Yarrell's *British birds*. It was in the nature of the man to take on far more work than he could comfortably manage—comfort was something which Wilson actively eschewed. But though he denied himself a proper holiday during the whole of the period between the two expeditions, there were the occasional moments of relaxation, shared with his beloved wife Oriana, at the Scottish shooting lodge of their close friend Reginald Smith, the publisher. Here, in the summer of 1907, they were joined by Captain Scott, who was already making plans for a return visit to the Antarctic, plans which as yet he had revealed only to his closest friends.

Meanwhile, after a long lull, interest in Antarctic exploration was reawakened by Ernest Shackleton, Wilson's old sledgemate of *Discovery* days. Shackleton, who had been invalided home after a breakdown on the southern sledge journey of 1903, had vowed to return as leader of his own expedition. Now, with the financial backing of the Scottish industrialist William Beardmore, he had ambitious plans for an Antarctic expedition which would plant the Union Jack at both the South Pole and the Magnetic Pole. But Shackleton desperately needed a reliable second-in-command and that man, in his view, was Edward Wilson. On the very day of his announcement to the press in February 1907 that he was to lead an expedition to Antarctica, Shackleton wrote to Wilson: 'My dear Billy, you will have seen in the press that I am going south again . . . Will you come as second-in-command—you know me well enough to know that we can work together. I want the job done and you are the best man in the world for it, and if I am not fit enough to do the southern journey there could be no one better than you . . . Come, Billy. Don't say no till we have had a talk. Don't say no at all . . .' Letter after letter followed in a similar vein and each time Wilson was constrained to refuse. He had in fact already intimated to Scott that he would stand by to return south with his old leader should the opportunity present itself.

Scott's reaction to Shackleton's announcement was one of irritation. It seemed that his former subordinate now intended to make use of his old winter quarters at Hut Point, Ross Island. This Scott regarded as a breach of professional etiquette. In fairness to Shackleton it must be stated that he was entirely innocent of Scott's unannounced intentions, and had acted hastily because of rumours circulating that the Belgians and Americans were planning activities in the very same region. It fell to Wilson to play the part of mediator, a role in which he excelled by nature. Wilson and Shackleton met at Westal and it was agreed by the latter that he would not use McMurdo Sound as a base nor operate west of longitude 170° unless he found himself compelled to do so—a difficult decision to make under the circumstances, since the main strength of Shackleton's position, in the eyes of his wealthy sponsor, was his intimate knowledge, gained on the *Discovery* expedition, of this very region. In the event Shackleton had to break his word; unable to set up a base in King Edward VII Land he reverted to Ross Island and set up his headquarters at Cape Royds. Shackleton's very presence in the Antarctic had the effect of accelerating Scott's own plans. He wrote frequently to Wilson seeking his advice and cooperation. 'If I should go South again', he wrote, 'you know there is no one in the world I would sooner have with me than you, though I should perfectly understand the ties which might make it impossible.' Scott's first firm offer to Wilson of a post was made in September 1908. In a letter to his mother Wilson confided his reasons for accepting: 'For my own part I have long been convinced that the first principle of right living is to put one's life into the hands of God and then do the work He gives one to do. . . . There has been no choice, and therefore no difficulty to my mind in deciding, and I am to go as "Leader of the Scientific Staff", a high sounding title with the disagreeable duty attached to it of having to reply to toasts on behalf of the scientific staff at the send off dinners.'

In June 1909 Shackleton returned from the Antarctic the hero of the moment, having ascended the newly-discovered Beardmore Glacier and attained latitude 88°23'S., ninety-seven geographical miles from the South Pole. Scott, magnanimously, was prepared to overlook his rival's broken pledge. At a public dinner in Shackleton's honour he declared that, 'The Pole must be discovered by an Englishman.' In September a *Times* leader opined that, 'It would be deeply regrettable if for want either of men or of money, the brilliant recent record of Antarctic exploration were at this point to be checked, with the inevitable probability in such a case that the Pole would first be reached by an explorer of another nation.' With strong rumours circulating that American, French,

German and Japanese expeditions were planning to head south, Scott, now with a shore post at the Admiralty, hesitated no longer. On 13 September 1909 he opened an office for the British Antarctic Expedition at 36–39 Victoria Street, London and on 16 September sent a telegram to Wilson asking him to lead and organise the scientific staff. Wilson promptly accepted. 'As Scott's only companion on the previous voyage', he wrote to his father, 'I shall have a good position in the expedition from the first, and Scott is a man worth working for as a man . . . I shall more than double my chances of some billet by going on this expedition. When we come home, and as leader of the scientific staff I shall have wider opportunities of making a success in that way if possible, so that no one can say it has only been a Pole hunt, tho' that of course is a *sine qua non*. We *must* get to the Pole, but we shall get more too and there shall be no loopholes for error in means and methods if care and preparation can avoid them.'

During the months that followed Wilson worked daily round the clock. He had the entire responsibility for choosing the scientific staff which involved him in numerous interviews—'We want the scientific work to make the bagging of the Pole merely an item in the results.' And all the time he was being consulted on every aspect of the expedition's organisation including the calculation of food values and quantities, and on the selection of scientific instruments of all kinds. By the end of the year he was badly in need of rest. He forced himself to 'sit absolutely still for four hours on end for 3 or 4 days running' in the studio of the portrait artist Alfred Soord. Prophetically Wilson wrote to him, 'I too learned a lot in our conversations. You have done more good than to paint a picture which will be a great comfort to a "grass widow" . . . My character is weathered or ought to be as you have painted it and as I pray God it may be increasingly to the end. It isn't enough to suit one yet but it will be some day and the more the better for "here we have no abiding place and this is not our rest" are two lines from our book of instructions which keep me moving on always.' The finished portrait was exhibited at the Royal Academy exhibition in 1910 and now hangs in the museum of the Scott Polar Research Institute.

By the end of January 1910 Wilson had dealt with the selection of the scientific staff and was able to return to the task of completing the report on grouse disease. 'My work is endless', he wrote to his father, 'it seems as if I could not possibly get through it all, yet bit by bit it gets done.' Fortunately for his health, though not for posterity, the *British birds* book, for which he had completed a considerable number of illustrations, had been abandoned by the publisher. *British mammals*, however, still remained to be finished. The stress under which Wilson laboured, though it showed in his face, as can be seen in contemporary photographs and the Soord portrait, never expressed itself in his personal relationships and is only hinted at in his correspondence. The secret of his self control and moral strength lay in his deep religious faith. In a letter to his father, dated 18 May 1912, he reflects on the principle tenets of his faith:

'I am sure there is more for me to do when I come back than I've ever done yet and all the past has seemed to be like an education for something more useful than as an end in itself, even the disappointments and the apparent checks are all in their proper place and have been first-rate schooling, and even as long ago as the Battersea days I felt that willing intention was everything in this life, and not achievement,—for it so often happens that, after making up one's mind with some difficulty to do something which appeared difficult, it has been made impossible after all. Well, it only means that free will in the eyes of God means the willingness to do one's best at whatever comes in our way and however difficult it may seem; but tho' He does not like us to look back after putting our hand to the plough, He often takes the plough away as soon as He knows we mean to carry through. Nothing can disappoint one if one sees things in this way because everything has been done in the eyes of God if the intention was there to do it . . . In this way one lives a long life in a few years.'

Examples of Wilson's application of his philosophy to the exigencies of Antarctic exploration will be found throughout his diary. The successful accomplishment of the midwinter journey in July–August 1911 is perhaps a perfect instance of the mastery of mind over matter.

We take up the diary on 1 June 1910 with Wilson *en route* to the Shetland Islands where he was to study the techniques of whale catching with a view to applying them in the waters of the Antarctic. This forms a prelude to the expedition diary which begins on 15 June, when the *Terra Nova* sails from Cardiff docks bound for the Cape via Madeira. With the exception of a few weeks in September 1910, while he was travelling independently to Tasmania on R.M.S. *Corinthic*, and for periods while he was travelling in Australia and New Zealand, Wilson managed to keep his diary up to date.

The South Pole diary stops abruptly on 27 February 1912. Why, the reader may ask, does Wilson so suddenly break with the habit of a lifetime? Scott, after all, kept his account going until nearly the very end. The answer lies in Wilson's adherence to his own maxim 'to become entirely careless of your own soul or body in looking after the welfare of others.' On the journey down the Beardmore Glacier Oates, and in particular Evans, had needed his constant ministration. Later, on the Barrier, with temperatures falling and food and fuel in short supply, all his dwindling energies were needed to keep the others going. Evans was dead and now it was Oates, his feet horribly frostbitten, who was to make the heaviest demands on Wilson. The agonies of those last few weeks—the final self-sacrifice of Oates, the last bid to drag the heavy sledge, with its precious load of rock samples, to One Ton Depot and safety, the tent pitched for the last time within eleven miles of that depot—are described best in the pages of Scott's journal. In a last letter to Oriana Wilson Scott wrote of his companion: 'His eyes have a comfortable blue look of hope and his mind is peaceful with the satisfaction of his faith in regarding himself as part of the great scheme of the Almighty. I can do no more to comfort you than to tell you that he died as he lived, a brave, true man—the best of comrades and staunchest of friends . . .'

The end came on or about 29 March 1912. Only three weeks previously Cherry-Garrard and the Russian dog-driver, Demitri, had reached One Ton Depot to

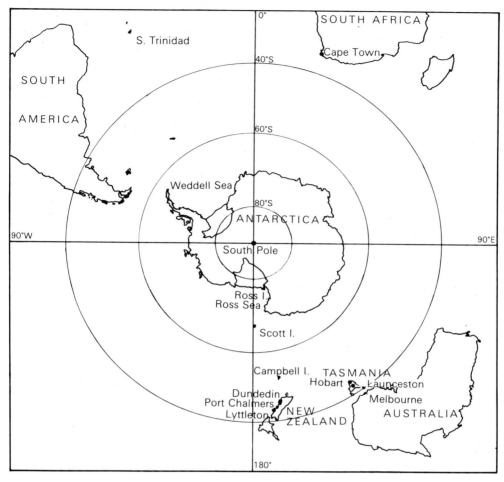

Map of the Southern Hemisphere showing the main ports of call of *Terra Nova*

relieve the Pole Party. After waiting a week, beset by blizzards, they were obliged to return to Cape Evans. Eight months later, on 12 November, Charles Wright, one of the search party which had set out under the leadership of Lieutenant-Surgeon Atkinson, discovered, by a miracle, the top of the tent now nearly drifted up by snow. The tent was dug out and in it was found the body of Scott lying in his sleeping bag with Wilson and Bowers flanking him. The Norwegian, Tryggve Gran, was one of the last to see Wilson before the tent was finally covered by a cairn of snow: 'Dr. Wilson was sitting in a half reclining position with his back against the inside of the tent facing as we entered. On his features were traces of a sweet smile and he looked exactly as if he were about to wake from a sound sleep. I had often seen the same look on his face in the morning as he wakened, as he was of the most cheerful disposition. The look struck me to the heart and we all stood silent in the presence of this death.'

NOTES ON TEXT AND ILLUSTRATIONS

The text of the *Diary of the Terra Nova Expedition* comes from two entirely separate journals. One describes a whaling trip off the Shetland Islands, the voyage of the *Terra Nova* to the Antarctic and the expedition's activities prior to Scott's departure for the South Pole. The other is Wilson's sledging diary, kept during the journey to the South Pole and found with his body by the Search Party in November 1912.

The main diary, like the diary kept during the *Discovery* expedition in 1901–4, was written primarily for his wife and family. Wilson compiled it from his field diaries, none of which has been traced, in his rare moments of free time. As with the *Discovery* diary, Wilson made a carbon copy. It is fortunate that he did so; had he not, we should lack today all the entries for the period 24 January to 31 October 1911, of which only the carbon copies survive. These were deposited with the Scott Polar Research Institute by the Trustees of the Scott Memorial Polar Research Trust in 1920 (SPRI ms. 234/3). As late as the summer of 1970 three sections of the original diary (the top copies, not the carbons), contained in Winsor and Newton sketch books ('Black and White Series'), were offered for sale at a London auction and successfully bid for by the Institute. These three sections (SPRI ms. 900/1–3) cover the following dates: 5 July (part) to 27 August 1910, 12 to 27 October 1910 and 26 November 1910 to 15 January 1911. There exists also in the Institute's archives a typed transcript of the whole diary from 1 June 1910 to 27 February 1912 (SPRI ms. 715/2), which was presented in 1965 by Wilson's surviving brother, the Reverend James Wilson. Unfortunately it contains a number of small errors of transcription and cannot therefore be used as a definitive source. Nevertheless, it has proved to be an invaluable guide to the editor and has enabled him to provide material for the following dates: 1 June to 5 July 1910, 28 to 31 August 1910 and 28 to 29 October 1910. It also contains the only available version of the scientific report, written on 24 October 1911, but removed from the original manuscript by Wilson. Since the typed transcript supplies no entries for 1 to 11 October 1910, 30 October 1910, 1 to 25 November 1910 and 16 to 23 January 1911, it must be assumed that no diary existed for these dates.

The sledging diary was returned to Mrs. Wilson after the expedition and lent by her to the British Museum in 1926 for public display alongside Scott's diary. After her death in 1945 it was presented to the British Museum in accordance with her 'wish-book', and catalogued as Additional Manuscript 47459. The diary, which covers the period 1 November 1911 to 27 February 1912, is written in a 'Wellcome's Medical Diary and Visiting List' for 1910. It is a very concise day-by-day account of events, with here and there rough sketches of cairns, parhelia, snow crystals, landforms, etc., most of which have proved impossible to reproduce satisfactorily in this book. In addition to the daily entries, there are notes on rations, a list of cairns south from One Ton Depot and a memorandum—'paint 2 Pole pictures "The Queen's Flag at the British Pole" and "The South Pole for King George"'—followed by two minuscule sketches. None of these has been reproduced here.

The sledge diary is accompanied by two small sketch books, now in the Institute's archives (SPRI ms. 797/1–2). They are remarkable firstly for the series of panoramic sketches of scenery which Wilson made as the Pole Party laboured up the Beardmore Glacier, and secondly for the geological notes they contain, which are very detailed, especially on the Mount Buckley region. A selection of the panoramic sketches, an example of the geological notes and some sketches made on the Barrier and at the Pole have been used to illustrate the South Pole diary.

In editing the Diary, the basic rules laid down by Ann Savours in her edition of Wilson's *Diary of the Discovery Expedition* (London, Blandford Press, 1966) have been followed. The two diaries have been treated as one and the manuscript divided up into chapters where natural breaks in the narrative occur. In the case of the main diary, paragraphs have been introduced, spelling and punctuation corrected, capitalisation rationalised and abbreviations expanded. The Pole diary, it was felt, called for a slightly different approach. This is not a retrospective and considered narrative, but an immediate and dramatic logging of events. Too strict an adherence to the editorial rules might easily have destroyed its flavour of spontaneity. It has been transcribed, therefore, with a view to reproducing the original as closely as possible.

Illustrations

In contrast to the Pole diary which, as we have seen, contains its own marginal sketches and is complemented by the two sketch books, the main diary is virtually lacking in illustrations. The editor has therefore made a representative selection of Wilson's pencil and watercolour sketches to embellish this book. With the exception of two watercolours which hang in the Royal Geographical Society, the originals of all the coloured illustrations are in the collection of the Scott Polar Research Institute. The majority of the black-and-white illustrations are also in the Institute's collection. As on the *Discovery* expedition, a series of monthly parts of *The South Polar Times* was issued, with illustrations by Wilson in both black-and-white and colour. A few of these have been reproduced here in black-and-white from the original manuscript in the British Museum. Although it had been the editor's intention that the *Terra Nova* diary should be illustrated solely by Wilson's own work, it was eventually decided that, to add to the interest of the book, a few of Herbert Ponting's beautiful photographs, which Wilson himself so much admired, should be included.

In his diary entry for 28 October 1911, Wilson states that he packed up 118 watercolours in two parcels to be sent home to his wife on the *Terra Nova*. He appears not to have been entirely satisfied with their quality: 'They were all done by artificial light—acetylene— and so they look queer by daylight—the blues and the yellows are apt to go wrong.' Probably he was being too strict with himself, for after the expedition his comrades unanimously proclaimed his pictures to portray the colours of the Antarctic scene exactly as they remembered them. Readers of the *Discovery* diary will not need to be reminded of the difficulties under which the artist laboured; freezing, or near freezing temperatures made it impossible to use watercolours out-of-doors for much of the year. Fortunately Wilson had a remarkable memory for colour and had taught himself over the years the technique of making rapid pencil sketches in the open air, identifying the shades of colour in note form. An example of this technique is illustrated on p. 180. The watercolours he would then work up in the comfort of the hut. 'I have sketches enough to occupy me for months when I get back to a paint box' he writes in his diary for 19 April 1911. It was, as Brian Roberts has observed in his book *Edward Wilson's birds of the Antarctic* (1967), one of the tragedies of his early death that he never had an opportunity to apply this technique to most of his *Terra Nova* sketches.

1

SHETLAND PROLOGUE

At 5 p.m. the *Terra Nova* left the West India Docks and reached Greenhithe at 8 p.m. Ory[1] was on board but not I, and Ory's initials may be seen in the *Terra Nova*'s log as one of the officers on watch. I did not put them there or suggest it, but there they are. For myself, on June 1 I sailed from Aberdeen on the *St. Sunniva* at 10 a.m. By 7.30 p.m. we were abreast of the south islands of the Orkneys, constantly passing steam trawlers, steam drifters, herring boats with their high brown sails, the ships we so often watched passing through Lough Ness and the lochs at Fort Augustus and the Caledonian Canal for the fishing of the west coast, after having fished the herring southward from the Orkneys down. Steam trawlers are steel ships with a deep waist, high funnel and two masts, about 115 ft long and 80 tons register. They are all registered as low as possible because they pay harbour dues according to their registered tonnage. Tugs may be just as big as trawlers and yet register no tonnage and so pay no dues. For this reason some harbour-masters charge every tug 1/6d. each entrance. Tonnage is registered according to the *space* given up to cargo and so double as many tons *weight* can often be carried as tons registered.

The trawlers fish with long sack or bag nets fixed to two heavy boards which keep the net just off the bottom. The old beam trawl was superseded as too heavy. The steam trawlers go also to Iceland and fish for cod there, putting the livers into casks and the cod into salt and ice, to be sold as fresh fish when it comes in. The livers used to be the men's perquisite, but now they are salted into casks. Each trawler carries its number and port initials. G.Y. for Grimsby, B.F. for Banff, and so on. Steam drifters fish for herrings by drift nets—twelve sheets of net hung vertically in long lines in the sea with buoys on the surface, which appear as rows of black bladders, or one sees a line of a dozen large red and green bladder buoys. The herrings run into these nets and get caught by the gills, the mesh being just the size to ensure this. No fishing is allowed to these boats within the 100 fathom line. The lighthouse watchers at Fair Isle are allowed to take all the fish caught by drifters that transgress this law. The transgressors are caught by cross bearings and their numbers taken and cabled to their ports where the fish are confiscated and sold for the Fair Isle people. In a case where a transgressing boat hung a tarpaulin over its number, the Fair Isle people made a sketch of the patches on the jib, and after many months' search brought the ship's owner up and had him fined after all. On the *St. Sunniva* I made friends with a Dutchman who was up there as an inspector of the herring fisheries. He tells me that the Caa'ing Whale[2] is good eating. He described the hunting of a school in the Faroe Islands just as they hunt them in the Shetlands, but he added that their first object was to draw blood with a harpoon, and that when once this is done the other whales all keep within the circle of bloody water so that the whole school can then be driven inshore and killed on the shallows. More probably the blood in the water prevents them from seeing which way to go and makes them flustered and so more easily driven.

Arrived at Kirkwall just in time to get a view over the Cathedral which I had seen three years before. It is a beautiful building and especially a gateway door on the north into the unused nave. It is proposed to open up the whole church soon; at present the choir only is used. The building is of red sandstone much weathered but beautifully worked and of late Norman. In the nave is a monument which I liked before and determined to sketch this time; a full length figure of 'John Rae M.D., L.L.D., F.R.S., F.R.G.S., Arctic Explorer. Intrepid discoverer of the fate of Sir John Franklin's last expedition. Born 1813. Died 1893. Expeditions 1846–7. 1848–9. 1851–2. 1853–4. Erected by public subscription in 1895'. That is the whole inscription—and the man is a life-sized figure lying asleep wrapped in a buffalo sleeping bag, with moccasins on and a gun and a book open by his side. The whole thing looked rather natural and nice, and although the 6d. guide-book claims credit from McClintock[3] for John Rae, there is no suggestion of it in the monument itself. He was a member of the Hudson Bay Co. and so was probably in a position to help a good deal, and sleeps soundly in this little out-of-the-way Cathedral of Kirkwall—honoured by his own people and caring nothing about the rest. This is what the monument suggested to me in the darkening nave of Kirkwall Cathedral at about 10 p.m. that evening just before the verger turned me out.

The evening so far north was very light and very peaceful. All the inhabitants were out loafing round to see the arrivals by the *St. Sunniva*. A few shops were open and the people in them very pleasant, and it was a great joy to walk round the Cathedral close in the waning light and to see the few bluebells, sturdy plants, and primroses and delphinia, which seem best to repay the care taken of them in the small sheltered gardens of the narrow walled-in streets, and alley ways. They seemed infinitely valuable, these small but simple and successful efforts to introduce something beautiful into such a barren stony place. The people obviously value them. There is only one tree in the Orkneys and none in the Shetlands. This one tree is a rich green sycamore in the shelter of the houses of the main street, not far from the Cathedral.

Thurs 2 June It was still light when I turned in about midnight on the *St. Sunniva* to the music of two donkey engines removing some tons of goods on to the quay. At 6 a.m. I was awakened by the stopping of the engines and the ringing of the engine-room telegraph, and I went on deck just in time to see a clergyman hoisted on board from a boat which was filled with hairy Fair Islanders, a most cheery, but rough looking, lot of briny men who kept the lighthouse watch year in year out, and who have interbred there so many years that many of them go mad and throw themselves over the cliffs. It was a glorious sunny morning, and a most beautiful view of Fair Isle with its immense rocky cliffs crowded and whitewashed by birds, wherever there was a ledge of rock sufficiently wide to hold an egg. We passed both lighthouses and Sheeps Crag, which is annually visited by climbing first 400 ft of cliff, and then by chains, for the purpose first of changing the old stock of Shetland sheep for new, secondly, for the purpose of collecting thousands of the young sea birds which are used for food. Nelson[4], who has known the Shetlands all his life, and will some day own half of them, tells me that if the whole stock of sheep on this crag is not changed at one time, the old stagers push the newcomers over the cliffs, a clear drop into the sea. He also told me about the madness among the lighthouse keepers. The minister who boarded us was a nice looking man with a beard, about 58 years old and evidently a favourite with the boatmen, who all shouted out something pleasant to him as we got up steam and left them rowing back to their isolation. Fair Isle is probably the best island in the country for migration varieties. Eagle Clarke[5] has worked there systematically for years, and now the Duchess of Bedford has taken a croft and a cottage and lives there from time to time while her yacht puts into Lerwick.

By 8 a.m. we had breakfasted and got into Lerwick. I counted over 100 steam trawlers and drifters coming in with us under full steam and loaded with fish. Crowds were also going out. The harbour was crammed with life and movement. No ship waits for room but just jostles her way out amongst the standing crowd. Gaily coloured Dutch herring boats gave an air of animation to the whole; the herring season was in full swing, and a good one. Herrings had been caught very early by people who were out for bait. Once found every available ship pours out on the area where these herrings were found, all full of roe and about to spawn; these make the most valuable catches. The business is a regular gamble with the dealers. Small owners of a boat or two will make £1,000 in a night with luck. Packing and salting sheds are continuous along the beach for about 5 miles, and on the shore opposite are saw mills and carpentry sheds making boxes by the tens of thousands for the millions of herring crans. It is a very lively scene, and on Saturday night and Sunday, when no fishing is done, all the fishermen and Shet-landers, men and girls, crowd into the cobbled road, the High Street of Lerwick, until one can scarcely move amongst them. Dutchmen, Norwegians, Swedes, and Shetlanders all laughing, smoking, singing and talking late on into the sunlit Saturday night. On Sunday, in some of these places, the minister encourages the Dutchmen to come at a certain point in the service and sing a hymn or two of their own. They come in with their pipes and sing, and then go out again, while a surreptitious suck or two has kept the pipe alight. As for the islanders themselves, it is well known that they are largely Scandinavian, and at one time the island was possessed by Norway and inhabited mainly by Norwegians, so that in the Scottish now spoken one finds quite a number of pure Norwegian words, and on the map they are really thick.

After breakfast I took a room at the hotel and shopped until 11 a.m., then by dog cart drawn by a fine young black horse, and a Shetlander named Hunter, was taken to Lochend, a matter of 36 miles over a barren moor road, the length of Shetland, at one spot crossing a neck where one could at once almost throw a stone into the North Sea on the right and into the Atlantic on the left. We passed Sand-water without stopping, and came on to the whaling station at Olnafirth, where I called on the manager[6], a Norwegian, who was very polite and gave me all the information he could as to the finding of a whaling gunner to go with us to the Antarctic. As a matter of fact the men one might like to take are not available; they are all drawing high salaries and are under contract for the season, which only ends about the middle of August, when no more whales are to be found off the Shetlands. The only thing to do is to wait till the return of the Norwegian Bottle-nose whalers who come from the Faroes and from Iceland in sufficient time, if necessary, to have one picked out at Christiania in July and sent on to join us in New Zealand, but the probability is that we shall have to do without. We wanted a man sufficiently good and experienced to be put in full charge of a boat's crew of Royal Navy Petty Officers, and this is impossible with our present choice, unless one pays very heavily for it. However, Mr Lange promised to make inquiry. He told me that this station, the Olna Co., at Brae, Olnafirth, had 4 whaling boats, each 96 ft long with gun complete, belonging to Salvesen Bros[7], and all British capital, was now the only Co. which was allowed to have more than one boat. The one boat bye-law came in since Salvesen had his 4, so he was allowed to keep them. Here they had already killed 49 whales up to June 2nd, all 'Finner' or Seihval, the Northern or Rudolphi's Rorqual, the Finner having black and white baleen and the Northern Rorqual black, with white bristles and fringe, making the mouth pure white inside. Mr Lange told me also that Seihval is found at the Falklands exactly resembling the North Sea species, but that no Seihval is to be got at Belgian Strait in South Shetlands of the Antarctic where the Norwegians have a large factory and where they get chiefly Humpback, Finner, Blue Whale, Sibbalds and the Atlantic or Southern Right Whale[8]. He told me, too, that a new gun was in use here with an improved recoil into a cylinder of glycerine instead of the old method of rubber pads. Salvesen's men are all Norwegians although the Salvesens' father and 3 brothers all own stations and call them British as well as themselves. They own Olna Co.'s station in the Shetlands, and others in the Faroes, Iceland, Falkland Islands, and South Georgia stations. Of the whaling stations in the Faroes, there are 6, every one Norwegian except Salvesens', and his men are all Norwegians. In the Shetlands there are now 4 stations running 8 gunboats between them, as follows:

1. Alexandra Co.,[9] at Lochend—manager Capt. Mathesen, 2 boats, one run by my friend Eric Henriksen, the other by Capt. Knuppen, both true Norwegians and first class gunners. 2. Shetland Co.[10] at Rona's Voe, not 2 miles from Lochend, manager Capt. Bernstein, 1 boat only. $\frac{1}{3}$ Norwegian capital, the rest British. 3. The Norona Co.[11] at Rona's Voe with one boat, Capt Abrahamsen, manager. $\frac{1}{3}$ Norwegian capital, the rest British. 4. Olna Co.[12] at Bovar, Olnafirth, under Alex Lange, manager, 4 boats, capital all British. Then there are 2 stations on the Irish coast, both Norwegian, and one at the Isle of Harris in the Hebrides, called the Bunvanrader Co., under Capt. Herlopen[13].

The Queen Alexandra Co. is the one I was to join to go on the North Sea, but I visited all the other stations on the road to Lochend. The Alexandra factory is about a mile from Haldane's[14] house. When we reached it late on Thursday evening the first thing I was told was that Haldane had gone to Edinburgh that morning to meet his son who had returned from Africa. I found that one of the whaling ships was in at the time, and that it was ready for sea, and would start the moment I got on board. I had my luggage taken up to the room given me at Mathesen's house, a regular Norwegian wooden erection, the veriest detail of which was Norwegian, even to the pictures and picture frames, clocks, pianos, table, furniture, foods, drinks, bread, butter, manners, and language. The stoves were Norwegian, so was the cook; so was the beer; the only British thing was the whale steak which was grilled with onions, and the whale meat rissoles which were excellent. I had a huge supper and then hurriedly put a thing or two into a kit bag and went on board. Happily I took my sea boots and a thick Norfolk jacket, both of which came in very useful later. I expected to be out for a day to 3 days at a time, and to see at least a whale or two killed.

That night the light was quite good even at midnight. We made our way out N.E. **Fri 3 June** to the North Sea, and as the law requires that a whaler shall be outside the 40 mile limit between June 1st and July 5th before firing at a whale, I turned in as we began ploughing into heavy weather the moment we were clear of the Shetlands and outlying rocks. We steamed straight away at from 10 to 11 knots. I slept very fairly being dead tired by the night journey from Cheltenham to Edinburgh, a day's work there which was satisfactory as I squared up the mammal book[15] with Oliver and Boyd finally, and they not only paid me £60 over the amount agreed upon, for extra drawings, but told me to count upon 4 copies, to be sent part by part to anyone I named and to Ory in New Zealand. I went the same evening to Aberdeen, and next morning on the *St. Sunniva*. Well, the first day on the steam whaler *Haldane* was an experience I shall not soon forget. I slept all right while we got 40 miles out, and I dressed and went on deck and there found we were ploughing along through very heavy seas and with a pretty fair gale. There was no chance of seeing a whale as the water was too broken and the wind swept the 'blow' away with the scud the moment it came above the surface. Whaling was for the time impossible, but it was for me to realise what a whaler could do by way of turning one inside out. I felt so fit in the early morning that I made a good breakfast on sour brown bread, margarine, very third-rate small Norwegian tinned herrings, some anchovies raw in vinegar, and excellent coffee. After that I was dreadfully sick, and remained so for the rest of the day without intermission. I had no more Norwegian food that day till evening, when we at last got into less violent weather under the lee of the Shetlands, having made for the nearest port, which was Baltasound, to stay until the gale blew over. The motion of that whaler all day was the worst I have ever experienced. I lay down in my bunk in the afternoon during intervals when I hung my head over a save-all, wishing devoutly or otherwise that it would drop off and stay there. The blessed boat lay first on one side then on the other, then moved like a screw and with a jerk came round to try a reverse. In the procession I was occasionally shot off the mattress to touch the covering roof, but much more frequently one was landed on the leeboard of the bunk which was intended to keep one from landing on the cabin table. A can of powder came adrift in large black grains, like nuts, and strewed the cabin floor. Sea water poured down through the scuttles and skylight and wetted everything. The jump and the jerk of the ship smashed the lamp and unshipped the compass card of a cabin skylight binnacle, and generally made me feel sick unto death. But joy came at Baltasound, where I crawled upon deck to breathe air instead of concentrated chief engineer and whale oil which alone filled the space below. The engineer was one of the fattest and oiliest men I have ever seen and was constantly coming down to shut himself into his tiny cabin for a sleep. Every time the door was opened to allow him out again, whale oil smell came out with him like a wall which enveloped me as I lay there, just outside his cabin door in my bunk space.

Sat 4 June However, we anchored in Baltasound on Saturday morning, and remained as the gale continued. The harbour was full of fishing boats many of which were Swedish. Henriksen and I went on shore together and up to the Post Office, and then to the one hotel, which was kept by an old whaling skipper. On the way we had the good fortune to find two whaling boats hauled up on the beach, one of which had all the equipment for Bottlenose whale-fishing. Henriksen showed me exactly in this boat how all the men and lines and harpoons and guns were to be arranged, and I picked up many points which I couldn't have learned otherwise. At the Post Office there was a crowd of all nations—Swedes, Norwegians, Dutch, Shetlanders, and Britishers. The place was a general store as well. I was feeling the results of my sickness, and was glad to get a quiet few hours at the hotel. We also had two excellent meals and then went on board the whaler again after supper. It was still light enough, even at midnight, to read the paper.

Sun 5 June I turned in early, and the whaler started out again northeast at about 2 a.m. on Sunday morning, as the wind had dropped and the weather promised to be better. When I turned out in the morning we had got over the 40 mile limit from the coast and had sighted whales, and the chase began. It was a most awfully exciting and interesting show. Henriksen was on the firing platform in the bows with the heavy gun loaded; the harpoon and forerunner and line and everything all in place—and then appeared the whales. There were two of them swimming together and blowing every now and again a cloud of spray. We constantly saw their broad heads appear and the blow-holes open and close—they were a dull brown colour and had a dorsal fin. They showed but little of the body above water, a characteristic of the species they represented which was *Balaenoptera borealis*, the Northern Rorqual[16], or, as the Norwegians call it, the Seihval. We turned our boat here, there and everywhere when the whales were sighted, but I think it was very nearly an hour and a half before we were sufficiently close on top of them when they rose to blow, to get a certain shot. Then Henriksen fired, and the explosion was terrific. Amid a perfect smother of smoke and cotton waste and tow I saw the coils of the forerunner fly up in the air and very little else. I was too close to the gun, but as the smoke cleared I saw that the whale was not far from dying. It was slowly flopping about on the surface with less and less power in its blows while the blood all round showed it was well struck. The flukes were powerless as the shell had burst in the lungs and had shattered the back bone from within. Then it sank and the line ran out from the locker. As soon as the whale was at the bottom they hitched the line over the blocks which took the jerk of the winch on very powerful springs. Then the winch reeled in and soon the whale appeared up alongside of

6

the bows. The moment it appeared Henriksen shouted to let the line out again, and go astern with the engines, for the whale was still moving and flapping its pectorals, and as we were in an iron ship, which one of these whales could stave in with a blow, it was the only thing to do. Meanwhile Henriksen seized a long lance of about 20 ft and ran it into the whale's heart from over the bows two or three times, and then it died, bleeding profusely from the wounds and from the blow hole. The next move was to get it close up again, and to pass a line under it, then a rope and a chain which was slipped along to the tail, and then shackled. Then, by means of the winch, the huge tail was hoisted out of the water and the flukes, 5 ft on each side, cut off with a cutting spud about 12 ft long. The flukes dropped off and sank, and the whale came gradually right alongside fastened to the bow end by the tail so that it towed tail first. The flukes were cut off as being valueless and stopping the way of the ship. The next thing was to prod a length of iron piping ending in a perforated point into the whale's abdomen, then to attach the free end to a force pump by means of which the engine forced air into the whale's belly and so blew it up that it floated alongside without assistance. Meanwhile we had sighted other whales blowing, and now we made for them towing our first alongside. We had a hasty breakfast having fasted till very nearly 11 o'clock. I had had no more sea-sickness, and was desperately hungry, nor had I any further qualms after that first day. This morning I thoroughly enjoyed my sour bread and third-rate herrings and margarine, and the coffee was simply splendid. The sea by this time was rapidly going down, and although very cold in the wind it became really enjoyable and very exciting to watch for another blow. We had not to wait long, and were soon going full speed ahead to come up with another couple of Seihval that had been seen, and up they came again quite close ahead. The gun boat is made in such a way that it can be turned almost in its own length; it is used in that way turning and twisting in every direction, following the tack of the whales under water. As soon as one is anywhere near a whale it is easy to see in which direction it is swimming by the swirl of the water on the surface above the spot where the whale has used his fluke. This swirl is to be seen every 10 or 20 yards, a smooth oily looking flat circle on the surface, plainly visible from the deck, and much more so from the crow's nest, where three or four could be seen clearly indicating the movements of a whale at a depth of 5 or 6 fathoms. The whale is, of course, quite invisible until it comes to within a few feet of the surface, unless it happens to be right under the side of the boat, when one can look down vertically. We were following these two Seihval in this way, and they came up and blew, but again just out of range, Henriksen standing upon the gun platform all the time with the stock and the string in his hand ready to fire, but never taking a risky shot. After about thirty minutes of this kind of chase up came one of the monsters about 20 yards ahead, and crossing our bows and Henriksen banged off. This time I stood on the bridge well back and saw the harpoon fly out with its forerunner in coils. I saw it strike the whale almost in the back, through the ribs at the foremost one third of the body, the only part which showed above water. The distance was such that the gun required elevating to allow the harpoon almost to drop on to the small part which showed above water, and it dropped on to it right enough, and was lost in a hole which then showed only the rope coming out, and at once a column of smoke-like steam cloud issued from the same hole, showing that the shell had burst and done its work. This whale was killed at once, a few blows high at first and infrequent, but rapidly increasing in frequency and decreasing in force, while the poor beast slowly flapped its fins on the surface and lazily, as it appeared, wallowed there unable to swim away or to sink, until at last the blows died down, and the dead whale sank. The same process was carried out as in the last, tow plugs being placed in the holes to prevent the air escaping. We now were towing a whale each side, 40 ft each in length, belly upwards, white and grey, with innumerable scars made by some parasite, oval marks the size of a penny, with lines radiating from a central line. There were none of these marks on the tail, or on the flippers, or on the head. After killing the two whales, one of which was a bull, and the other a cow, we again made for a spot where other whales had been seen to blow, and they also were Seihval. The Seihval's blow is bushy, and easily distinguished from the Finner's and the Blue Whale's, which are high and thin and vertical. The Blue Whale has the highest of all, and this whale shows himself much more out of the water in blowing, and is of a bluish grey colour instead of dark brown, as is the Seihval. All these whales can be recognised by their blows in still weather. In rough weather the blow is dissipated by the wind. Each whale, too, has distinctive whalebone, and some of them are peculiar. The Finner e.g. almost invariably has all the whalebone on the left side of its mouth black, while that on the right side is always half black and half white. The foremost part being always the white half. The whalebone of the Seihval is black altogether on the outside and pure white inside, i.e. the plates are black and the bristles pure white. The whalebone of the Blue Whale is always streaky black and grey, and white, while that of the Humpback and the Atlantic Right Whale is wholly black, and that of the Lesser Rorqual[17] wholly white. The blows are as under.

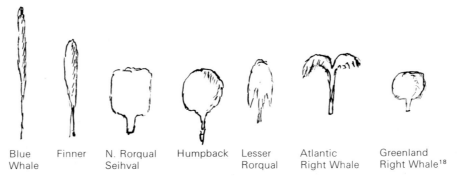

| Blue Whale | Finner | N. Rorqual Seihval | Humpback | Lesser Rorqual | Atlantic Right Whale | Greenland Right Whale[18] |

The third whale we killed was also a Northern Rorqual, and it was killed dead almost instantaneously.

After this we spent an hour or two chasing another couple and several times came almost within range, yet Henriksen would not fire. The patience of this man was quite extraordinary, and it accounts for the fact that a miss is almost unknown. Unless the whale is within range and in a position to be hit in such a way as to be probably killed, the gun is not fired. Each shot, using as it does a very large and heavy harpoon, and a shell made of cast iron, and a patent detonator, all of which are useless after the shot is fired, is quite a costly business. Today it became evident that the towing of 3 whales so reduced our speed, and power of rapid turning, that we could not hope to overtake the whales we chased. In dead calm the whales might have been cast adrift to float, with a flag flying, while the gun-boat killed a fourth, and perhaps a fifth, and the first three would then have been picked up again; but the sea was not quiet enough, and there was danger lest the air forced in to float them might be beaten out with the result of sinking the whales, which would have been a great loss. So in the afternoon we decided to hurry homewards for the whaling station. Instead of 8 knots we were now going 3 to 4, and we had 60 to 70 miles to cover.

We got in at breakfast time of Monday morning and the whole of that day I spent **Mon 6–Tues** in collecting details of the business. The second gun-boat came in with one Seihval **7 June** only. Both boats coaled at once, and were away again in the afternoon. That day I lunched with Mathesen's family, and called at Haldane's house, but found he was away. I then walked up to N. Roe and sent a wire to Ory, came back to Lochend, and slept at the whaling station. At 6 a.m. I turned out to see if my pony trap had arrived from Lerwick to take me there to catch the evening boat to Aberdeen. I found the same driver and cart and horse had arrived at 2 a.m. and at 9 a.m. would be ready to start. We had a fine day, sunny and cold, and so on Tuesday, June 7/10 after a 30 miles' drive, I caught the *St. Giles* and got away for Aberdeen direct, without touching at the Orkneys.

A perfect day and as there were no first class passengers except one lady who turned **Wed 8 June** out to be related to Nelson, our biologist on the *Terra Nova*, I enjoyed the passage. It was a great bit of luck that a small party of 3 or 4 White-beaked Dolphins, *Lagenorhynchus albirostris*, should have come and sported under the bows just when I happened to be watching the bow wave. This is a rare dolphin, and the opportunity a rare one, so I went below and wrote a note on what I had seen for future publication. It was strange that four years ago I should have had the rare good fortune to see a school of Caa'ing Whales breeching one after another on this identical journey to Scotland. We reached Aberdeen in the afternoon of Wednesday, and I slept there; then on to Edinburgh by the first train on Thursday, June 9th.

In Edinburgh I had some business at the museum where I saw Eagle Clarke, and **Thurs 9 June** also drew whales' skulls, until I was turned out at 4 p.m. Then went up to the Castle Mount to see Leslie[19] about grouse business, and to call on Mrs. Leslie. Leslie was alone, so we set to work at the correction of papers, and when dinner time came I dined there as Berry[20] had also turned up. We formed a festive trio, until it was time for me to bolt and catch my train. I had to run the whole way as my bags were still unpacked at the North British Hotel. However, I caught the night train, and packed in the carriage from pockets and slept until turned out to change at Leeds and Derby and Birmingham.

At 9 a.m. arrived at Cheltenham, where Ory met me, and after a good bath and **Fri 10 June** breakfast, a long day's packing and sorting at Westal[21].

9

Sat 11 June   The same thing, packing books and clothes and implements for the next 2 or 3 years' needs, and we got them sent off by 'goods'. The leather snow-goggles, which Sharpe[22] had made for us after a pattern of my own, are being exhibited in the shop window in the Promenade, and Sharpe has put a letter about them in the *Cheltenham Examiner*.

Sun 12 June   To St. Philip's[23] at 8 a.m., the last chance for some time to come, probably August in South Africa. Dad, Mother, Ida, and Biddy[24] were also there. We had a very pleasant Sunday together, though we had to do some packing in the forenoon, but in the afternoon we all drove to the foot of Leckhampton, and walked up to say goodbye to the Whishaws[25], Aunt Sophy supposed to be dying. We met Aunt Adini Cattley, and an Aunt Blessing, and Berns and Mary Whishaw. Either today or yesterday I had a lot of drawing to get finished—first a number of grouse skins to paint for coloured plates to a paper[26] on the plumage changes of grouse, to be read at the Zoo meeting on Tuesday next, Ogilvie-Grant[27] having undertaken to read it, as I was due at Cardiff. I had also drawings to finish for the British mammal book, as tomorrow I have to meet Barrett-Hamilton[28] and square things up with him. I don't know when these drawings were done, but they were done, all but a residue to be sent from Madeira or the Cape. These were days of very hard work for Ory, as she has had all the London packing to do, while I was really making holiday in the Shetlands. She has had no holiday, and the weather has been very hot for London packing, and this was no joke for it meant all the grouse work apparatus, grouse skins, books and bookcases, and various pieces of furniture which had accumulated in our four rooms in London. Somehow she got clear of 19 Holland St. while I was up whaling, and I had not to go back there at all. She also had got all my clothes ready for the whole voyage, and had them packed for Madeira, the Cape, Australia, New Zealand, and the Antarctic. I left all to her, and she managed it perfectly. Then, when I got back and had to work late every night writing and drawing, she would not be sent to bed until I was near coming, and so we both got tired out with very short sleep, but happily not irritable with it, and I shall always remember these days as days of perfect companionship, the best of all good things that a wife can bring at such times as these.

Mon 13 June   Ory and I were up at 5.30 and caught the 7.20 for Paddington. We had breakfast before leaving, and I wrote at my grouse plumage paper the whole three hours' journey, but could not get it finished, which was awkward as I had undertaken to hand it over to Ogilvie-Grant to look through today before reading it at the Zoo meeting tomorrow. However, Ory and I went first to the South Kensington Museum at 10.30 for an hour with Barrett-Hamilton, who had come over from Ireland, to square up the British mammal book with me. Ory went to Harrods and then joined me at the museum. I saw Ogilvie-Grant and told him he could not have my paper till the evening; also saw Fagan[29], who was full of some letter re whaling he had received from Norway, and he was interested to hear I had just been whaling, and very keen that I should take the matter up, so I told him nothing would suit me better and I would miss no opportunity down south of seeing whaling stations and learning all about whales. He said Nansen was interested in starting some international movement to go into the science of whales before they were all killed out by the present boom for whaling stations. Ory and I then hurried off to the Reginald Smiths'[30] in Green St. where we lunched, and they lent us their car for the rest of the day. We first called at Greener's the gunmakers and learned that the whaling gear had just reached London and by spending money might be got to Cardiff before the ship sailed, so I told them to spend money and get it there, which they did; it was therefore a little annoying, on arriving at Cardiff two days later, to find there was no room for it on the ship and that arrangements had been made to send it on later by New Zealand Shipping Co. However, I succeeded in getting the complete equipment for one whale-boat on board, the heavy swivel gun, the shoulder shelling-gun, the whale lines, harpoons, and flensing knives, so that if we want to go for a whale we can do so. I don't expect, however, to touch any work of that sort until the ice is reached, then we shall have two boats fully equipped, and the risk will be much reduced. After visiting Greener we went to the Alexandra Hotel and saw Aunt Maude Pike and Aunt Emma Beaumont and Gladys, just returned from India. Then to Goerz, Holborn, about glasses, then to various booksellers, then to Smith in the Strand to get the 3 guinea aneroid[31] given me by the Grouse Disease Commission with a cheque for £30, and also to get the chronometer watch which had been on Henriksen's northern journey. Next we called on Sir Clements[32] and Lady Markham and had tea with them, and then we came off to Paddington, and after dining there sat in the waiting room till 9.20, writing hard to finish my paper on grouse plumage, which I managed to get done, while Ory went out for a messenger boy who took it to Ogilvie-Grant's house as we caught our train down to Westal. On the way I wrote an epitome of the paper for Grant to read at the Zoo meeting the following evening. We were both tired and very sleepy when we got home, had supper, and went to bed at 2 a.m.

Tues 14 June Worked hard until noon finishing off the colouring of 15 grouse skins which were posted off just in time to reach the Zoo Society's meeting. Then we turned to the packing of Grouse Commission papers, and got all finished by about 8 p.m. when we left Cheltenham for Cardiff, travelling first class for the sake of a rest, and writing to the home folks on the way. Dad and Mother had gone down by an earlier train and met us on arrival, also Hodgson[33], who had come from Plymouth to see us off, and was at the same hotel, the Royal.

Wed 15 June In the morning we packed up and took all my gear on board the *Terra Nova* by 10 a.m., and then began a scrambling sort of hunt for various packages which had been sent by post, train and 'goods' at various times during the past fortnight. Also there was such a crowd on deck one could hardly move. Ory, Dad, and Mother remained on board to the last. We all had lunch on board. The weather was perfect, and it must have been about 4 p.m. when they all went off in a tug provided, and we were started for the Cape via Madeira.

2

CARDIFF TO CAPE TOWN

I BEGAN shifting cases and unpacking gear, and continued doing so till it was dark, and then turned in. We were in sight of the coast all along to the Land's End, and saw Ilfracombe. The send off from Cardiff was very enthusiastic, enormous crowds having collected at every available spot to cheer and fire guns and detonators, and to make a perfectly hideous din with steam sirens and hooters, of which Cardiff seems to possess an infinite number.

Thurs 16 June Slept soundly—no seasickness. Got to filthy work right off, shifting cases and hunting for my gear, stowing and un-stowing, to find my boxes which had got buried in every part of the ship, as there was no one on board when they arrived to see to them. Cherry-Garrard was invaluable as he had kept an eye on the whereabouts of all that had been sent to the docks when he was down there. Several of the 'Afterguard'[1], i.e. the Wardroom Mess, were very seasick, but stuck gamely to their work. Cherry, looking very green, continued manfully to type-writing notices and general orders for Evans. We got a fair breeze and made good way under plain sail with a good deal of motion. The only bird seen today was a shearwater in the offing.

Fri 17 June The breeze dropped and we went ahead under steam, 6–7 knots. Fine with a good deal of rolling, therefore a noisy night as things had not settled in yet and seasick people are not always careful to make gear fast against motion. The worst roll as yet was 28°. The *Discovery*[2] reached 52° and the *Morning*[3] reached 58°, Evans tells me. The only birds seen were a few Mother Carey's Chickens[4], *Procellaria pelagica*, in the wake of the ship towards evening.

Sat 18 June Steam all day, no wind, hot sunny weather. Nelson got several interesting things in a townet haul; one was a beautiful Doliolum[5] with blue muscle bands and orange coloured stomach contents. A good many Mother Carey's Chicks in our wake, small black and white birds, like House Martins. A large Sunfish passed the ship, showing its great black flippers above water just like the Brögde[6] which I saw in the North Sea when whaling. It swam on its side flat, not upright as one might expect.

Sun 19 June Under steam only. Turned out 7 a.m. Breakfast 8 a.m. Slept on the ice-house part of the night, but the breeze was cold. Evans read prayers—2 hymns and the

Psalms. Nearly everyone had a prayer book but few had books of hymns. Glorious hot weather. Ship rolling too much for any careful work and one is unconsciously tired out by the uneasy motion, the fatigue of unwonted exercise trying to keep one's balance from morning to night and from night till morning. Nelson got a trawl in the full speed townet—*Peridineas tintinnerdoe*, copepods and nauplia. We saw a Northern Rorqual going N.N.E. close enough to see the brown colour and fairly big dorsal fin. A Turtle-dove settled on the rigging looking very tired and ruffled. It stayed with us an hour or two, and then flew away north. We passed 2 full-rigged sailing vessels, one the *Pacifique*, a French ship from Dunkerque, bound for Valparaiso, had four masts full rigged.

Mon 20 June Late turning in last night as I remained on the bridge till midnight for cocoa with Levick who was on watch, and Nelson who is always late. At 4 a.m. I awoke below, and it was very stuffy, so went on deck and saw the sunrise at 4 a.m. Then saw 2 whales moving north at a great pace and from the invisible blow and the height of the dorsal fin, I judged they were Killers (*Orca gladiator*)[7]. Soon after we saw a school of dolphins, and they made for the ship, and the sea seemed full of them everywhere, leaping right out of the water for about half an hour. They were the Common Dolphin (*Delphinus delphis*) and there must have been 100 or more of them. They appeared off and on during the day, but none came near enough to harpoon. Spent the forenoon writing and hunting for packets of scientific books of reference which are in the ship but seem to have gone astray. Same job all afternoon. Sun very hot, breezy towards evening under sail. Again the only birds were Mother Carey's Chicks in moult, and a common swift which flew with us all the afternoon.

Tues 21 June Up at 4.30 a.m. and got a sunrise, the sky a regular Trade Wind sky. Fair breeze S.E. Trades. The sunrise was very beautiful, very ethereal pale grey and misty, soon changing to white broken clouds all trending the same way in a blue heaven, the water the most wonderful blue imaginable. Breakfast 8, lunch 1, tea 4, and dinner at 7. All these days have been taken up with search for gear, unpacking and sorting and stowing, to make room, and make things shipshape against the arrival of bad weather. As yet nothing but sunshine, no spot of rain. We discussed snow goggles today after dinner, Campbell having had a good deal of experience on snow in Norway. The only birds a few *Procellaria pelagica*. Saw several Common Dolphins. Overhauled all the whale gear and found everything on board for one boat if necessary.

Wed 22 June Slept sound all night on top of the ice-house in a greatcoat and Jaeger sleeping bag. Tried the bag alone, but the wind came through too cold. Gran calls me 4 to 4.30 with some good cocoa which I have with Campbell on the bridge every morning; he taking the morning watch, having Gran as midshipman of the watch, from 4 a.m. to 8. Gran is a delightful young Norwegian giant, a great expert at ski running and jumping. Speaks very good English and is the most obliging soul on earth, most good-natured, and enormously strong, but a trifle slow with it except when he gets excited. He is from Christiania University and sublieutenant in the

13

Norwegian Royal Navy, where they have a funny combination of both services, and as there are few men-of-war the Royal Navy cadets have to do all their sea-time in merchant service ships. Gran is 21 years old and is wealthy for Norway; has a mother and sisters and is building a very strong wooden ship at his home for further exploring work in the Antarctic when he returns from this expedition. For his ski jumping he says he has been offered £800 by German hotel-keepers in certain places if he will go and jump as an attraction for a few months in the winter; but the Norwegians are as yet so far jealous of their simplicity that they refuse professional offers of this kind. Every Norwegian is an expert on ski, but very few jump or even try to. Saw a shearwater some way off.

Thurs 23 June Up 4 a.m. no sunrise. Sighted Porto Santo about noon, got a sketch, then almost at once we sighted Madeira, but as Funchal is on the south side, it was 5 p.m. before we got in. Cherry and I went aloft for a view of the islands which is grand. There seems no inch of ground which is not under cultivation. Blandy came on board and brought out mails. I remained on board and wrote letters home. We were anchored a long way off Reid's large new hotel where they had a bad out-break of typhoid not long ago, with 16 or 17 deaths. We are not taking water from here though the mail steamers do now again, and it is said to be quite safe. Before coming in we saw a shearwater, and some of Leach's Storm Petrel[8]. Mother Carey's Chicks have left us. Our leak now instead of making $4\frac{3}{4}$ inches in the hour, as it did at Cardiff, is only making 1 inch—quite a welcome difference. I had 2 letters and a wire from Ory, whereas poor Campbell and Evans did not hear from their wives at all.

Fri 24–Sat 25 June Among my mails was a long letter from Ogilvie-Grant, who had read my paper[9] before the Zoo Society and agreed with it all but one point where I have unwittingly upheld Millais against Grant. Here, of course, Grant says I am all wrong, but as a matter of fact I believe Millais is right. After breakfast packed up my paint-box and my box of choice grouse skins and went ashore. Titus Oates, Atkinson, and Lillie insisted on carrying my gear, and I took a room with 2 or 3 good tables at the Monaco Café just by the Golden Gate. Here I worked at my grouse end on till 2.30 a.m. Then up again at 6 a.m. and worked till midnight on Saturday, then went on board and wrote letters till 4.15 a.m. From Friday breakfast time to Sunday breakfast time I had something like 7 hours sleep, and I fear some of the 25 letters written from here will have read like it too, for I was latterly quite unable to keep awake for more than a line or two at a time. During the daylight I succeeded in finishing all the coloured grouse skin plates that were wanted for my paper on plumage changes. I knew Funchal pretty well and I had done the orthodox toboggan rides down the cobbled streets and been in the bullock waggon and visited a fine house and gardens on the upper heights, so I had not much to miss. As it was I enjoyed my time working in a room from which I overlooked the lazy Portuguese enjoying their sunny life, cigars, umbrellas, sunshades, flowering shrubs, loquat trees, loud cries to the bullocks, and general air of idleness and foreigner. There are few people here except Portuguese and the whole place has a smell and atmosphere of flowers and heat and unsanitariness and onions. Very few whites, all dark Portuguese, and the changing guard at the barrack entrance was a standing joke—dirty, slovenly blue uniformed soldiers; the one on sentry duty at sundown gives a long drawn weird unearthly cry, suddenly and without warning, and then is relieved—poor creatures not a bit smart, and utterly bored. Figs were delicious here, already red and green as were the loquats, a sort of golden medlar, which has large pips, 3 or 4, and not much flesh round them, but they make delicious jam, expensive because sugar duties are so high. They grow on large trees which have a large white flower just like a medlar, and an over-ripe and sleepy loquat is very like a sweet medlar. The small Madeira banana is excellent and so are the passion fruits; other varieties of fruit come on later in August. The place swarms with lizards and a very minute ant, which covers everything within and without. I slept one night only on shore and caught a bug which had fed off me in the morning. Yet there was no old furniture and the whole place looked very clean, without carpets, and with white-washed walls everywhere. After sundown mosquitoes were the chief nuisance, and they made work very difficult.

I was not sorry to get done and on Sunday to get to sea again. Gran had been to the top of the island with a Portuguese to photograph him at the top. We never understood why he took with him a large rucksack containing his Norwegian naval uniform and a hammock and a Japanese umbrella made of paper. Apparently he reached the top naked, having dropped his clothes one by one on account of the heat. No one to this day knows why he took a hammock. One of the chief innovations here since 1901 are public motor cars which make a ghastly noise over the cobble stones, but which the natives seem to use with pride. I lunched at the English Club with the Consul and several business people, but otherwise avoided entertainments. I found that precisely the same jokes and amusements were provided for Campbell and Evans by Reid, the big man of the place, as were provided for us 9 years before—old stock chestnuts, and by no means choice.

Weighed at 5 a.m. and swung ship, then returned, and sent in our mail at 10 a.m., **Sun 26 June** the weather was perfect and I fell on sleep.

And onwards now for a long time life became sheer enjoyment with plenty of air, **Mon 27 June** food and exercise in a sort of routine. Saw few birds, except a sand-martin which followed the ship the day we left Madeira. We began to see flying fish every day and simply enjoyed life.

Flat calm, very little way on the ship, and some current. Cherry-Garrard and I **Wed 29 June** now always sleep on the top of the ice-house with blankets and a coat, and the hard deck for a mattress, to which one gets accustomed almost at once. The weather is warm, with hot sun, and no rain as yet. I get myself called every morning for the sunrise, and we all turn up to pump out the hold at 6.30 a.m. Pennell is the only other early bird taking sights for navigation, stars and planets before sunrise. After breakfast there was a call for volunteers to help with the coal trimming, and Cherry-Garrard and I went below on the job. Coal trimming in the bunkers is a dirty business. It means transferring coal from the main hold, where the bulk of it is stored, into the two bunkers, one on each side of the engine-room stoke-hold. The bunkers hold about 50 tons each and have to be filled periodically, so that coal can be got for feeding the furnaces. The work lasts from 9 to 12, and from 1 to 4, and we take it in three hourly spells. There was no room to stand up in the main hold until we had dug out a few tons and shovelled it into the bunkers. It is hot work, and in 10 minutes one is streaming with sweat and black as Kaffirs with dust. The heat is, of course, from the engine-room and stoke-hold as well as from our proximity to the tropics. It is also a back-breaking business as one cannot straighten up at all. One works in black darkness, except for a small oil lamp, and the air in the coal hold is always tested first to be sure that it is breathable, and the hold aired to prevent any collection of fire-damp from making an explosive mixture. A good deal of care is needed with coal on board ship. Nearly the same precautions as are taken in a mine. One wears as little as possible—a pair of boots, a thin vest, and a pair of rowing or football shorts. At the end of our 3 hours we are pretty tired and quite black from head to foot, and one is allowed an extra ration of fresh water to bathe in on the upper deck. One may look fairly clean after it, but everything one puts on for the next day or two gets black from the coal dust working out of the pores. From lunch to tea painted at sunrises, then stowed taxidermist stores and scientific library, then pumping from 6 to 7 with seven others, then dinner and bed, wholesomely tired out. No bird or beast seen by anyone today.

Thurs 30 June Up at 4.30 a.m. Cocoa and sunrise now a regular routine, and when we are under sail alone the bilge has to be pumped out by hand. Each watch, i.e. every 4 hours, the bilge has to be pumped dry, and that means from half to three quarters of an hour at the pump for 8 men. We, the 'Afterguard', undertake to pump her dry during the morning watch, and to this end I haul everyone out at 6 a.m. to a large cup of cocoa and the pump. Most of them turn up in pyjamas and bare feet. When the pumping is finished everyone bathes on the upper deck by means of a bucket over the side and throwing water over one another. If the engines are going we use the fire hose, which is much more effective. We have 5 large flat hip baths, but they are only used for cleaning the coal trimmers, and stokers of the Afterguard, and are therefore always black. At 8 a.m. we breakfast, an excellent meal with porridge, treacle, milk, coffee, tea, fresh bread made aboard, margarine, marmalade, and generally scrambled eggs (stored eggs) and bacon, or tinned fish, which is generally excellent. Then work from 9–12. Today Cherry and I were again coal trimming all the afternoon, the exercise is splendid. I see myself getting more flesh on every day and feel as fit as can be. In the forenoon we were working out sledging programmes, Evans, Campbell and I, arranging all the weights, and their distribution on sledges, ponies &c, for the depot journey, which is to be the great effort of January, February, and March 1911, as soon as we can get off to lay out provision for the following year, when the main effort will be made, and when Evans and I both hope to be with Scott on his longest trek. We lunch at 1, except on baking days at 12—and it is a meal with one hot or cold meat and vegetables, both excellent, and often fresh stuff from the ice-house, and a pudding of sorts. That is a two-course lunch. Then work again till tea at 4, which carries biscuits with it, or a common cake, and then dinner at 7 when we have soup, meat, vegetables, and a pudding. Nothing besides, just 3 courses, and as long as it lasted beer and ginger beer—after that was gone, lime-juice and water. There is nothing luxurious about the meals, but they are well cooked always, simple, and the men have exactly the same. After dinner every one is so sleepy and tired that there was an hour or so of diary writing and then a general exodus for sleeping billets on the upper deck, either in hammocks, or on the ice-house, or below in the cabins, which are getting terribly stuffy, not to say unbearably hot as we get into warmer weather. We got a flying fish 10 inches long on board today with perfect wings, and the funny tubular mouth which is so characteristic. It was a lovely blue colour with opalescent tints. I spent an hour or two drawing it to scale today.

Up at 4 a.m., reading and writing, no sunrise. Lillie, who has been ailing for the **Fri 1 July** last few days, has now come out with unmistakable measles. He had been coal trimming, and we put his throat and discomfort down to coal dust and the heat. His sore eyes, too, we put to coal dust, as it always gives sore eyes, especially the dust from patent fuel, and so much so that in the Navy the coal trimmers have to wear goggles when they work at it. He must have caught the disease at Cardiff. We have put him in the photo lab. on deck, where he will be quite comfortable, and he will also be away from the men. All the forenoon I was again coal trimming with Cherry and Titus Oates. After lunch painted till tea-time. We passed a barque, the *Inverclyde* of Aberdeen, sailing from Glasgow to Buenos Ayres, and now 17 days out. We spent an hour signalling various inanities. She looked very beautiful in the trade wind skies and blue seas, with crowds of flying fish flashing in and out and dropping into the deep blue water with little white spits like bullet splashes. No birds—skies cloudless blue with a sudden overclouding every night at sundown. After tea, painting and writing till supper, then talk and writing, and a little reading, and turn into the sleeping bag on the ice-house, with a ship's biscuit and some lumps of sugar to chew, before dropping off to sleep under the starlight. Generally by 9.30 or 10 most of us have turned in.

Turned out soon after 4 by Pennell for a sunrise. After breakfast operated on **Sat 2 July** Atkinson's finger for a whitlow. Worked all forenoon in the coal bunker. Had a sleep in the whaler in the afternoon trying to write up my journal. Sure as I begin to write I fall asleep unless I am actually standing up—then painted, but had to pump again in the evening. Another 10 inch flying fish came on board; both this and the last have been infested with parasites, the first with trematoda in the stomach and this one with parasites in the gills.

Up 4.30 sunrise and some reading and writing. Prayers on the upper deck and **Sun 3 July** 'rounds', inspecting all the living spaces and the men's quarters for'ard. Painted all afternoon as long as there was any light. Saw several dolphins today (Common) which were moving fast, but none came under the bows.

Mon 4 July Up 4.30. No sunrise. All day working out and weighing sledge rations and making models of bags for provisions of various kinds on the ship. Then writing and drawing. Saw Portuguese man-of-war, and flying fish.

Tues 5 July Up at 4.30 a.m. Again had a day at sledging weights and while we were at this, Hooper the servant opened the cover of the hatch leading to the present use store, just outside the wardroom door. We three, Campbell, Evans and I, were sitting at the wardroom table, and when Hooper opened the hatch, out of which came a great volume of smoke, he shouted that the ship was on fire. He then shut the hatch down again as Evans told him, and Evans and Campbell both ran up on deck to call everyone to fire stations, which we all knew in a vague sort of way, and every one began to close down every window, skylight, door, and hatch-way, to stop all possible draught. I got a fire extinguisher and went down into the hold where the smoke was coming from, and then round a corner I saw where the bonfire was, so turned the extinguisher on to it and had it out in a jiffy—happily it had not caught very much, for there was a large stock of wine in straw packing within a foot of the paper which had caught alight. A whole stack of paper was alight, but it went out almost at once. Evans had followed me, and we soon found the cause of the fire, for the carpenter had left a lamp alight down there with his cap, and the roll of the ship had upset the lamp, while the hatch was closed as though no one were going down again at all, and it was a very lucky thing that it was found out before the fire had got real hold. As the carpenter had left his cap, there was no doubt as to the culprit, and he was 'logged', a very serious punishment in the Navy, which would frighten him more than any other at sea, even on this ship, for it means that he is brought up before the Captain and the First Lieutenant on the bridge, and generally reprimanded, and then the offence is written down in ink in the official log-book, and signed by the offender himself on the spot. In this case he was also fined a pound to cover the damage resulting from his carelessness. As a matter of fact the man is as good and careful a worker as any on the ship, and the punishment will not be insisted on in the end. The fright to everyone is a very great safeguard, for it is a warning which will make everyone more careful. We had the same thing on the *Discovery*, and Campbell, who has been many years at sea in all sorts of ships, says he has never been in a ship in which there has not been one fire scare of this kind. It is rather like letting off a gun by accident for when it has once happened the individual is infinitely safer than he ever was before. This time it came off successfully, and the culprit was frightened without much damage being done.

There are any number of flying fish about us now, and they seem all of the smaller blue species, with silver white bellies and glittering fins, the front pair of which are brown and white and transparent, the hinder ones transparent with black veins. As usual in the North Atlantic there are no birds at all. Or at the most of all a bird or two, small Stormy Petrels, or Pomatorhine Skuas[10], are the only species one ever sees. Afternoon again on the pump and then a long argument on socialism, politics and degeneracy of the nations. Simpson is our only real socialist, anti-everything and a firm believer in the *Manchester Guardian*. We had a selling auction sweepstake on the chances of our date of arrival. I drew and sold my number for

62/– and bought in the 10th of August for a first place and the 23rd for a second, which gave me also the 13th for a ten days either way second prize—but I won nothing. Teddie Evans and I, however, had clubbed together for good or ill to share profit or loss and he also won nothing but sold his draw to so much profit that neither of us lost.

Pumping as usual, and then all the forenoon at sledge figures with Evans and **Wed 6 July** Campbell. Afternoon trimming coal as usual for three hours in the bunkers.

Sledging figures all forenoon. Diary all afternoon. Discussions on things in general **Thurs 7 July** —this time on tonnages. There are many ways of reckoning tonnage. The *Terra Nova* has a registered tonnage of 745 tons, registered tonnage taking in the space only which can be given to cargo; i.e. pure carrying space apart from dwelling spaces. About 60 cubic feet mean a ton of average goods. In the Navy ships are always measured by their water displacement and this means an equivalent for the dead weight of a loaded ship—in the *Terra Nova* it is about 1,100 tons displacement. Nett tonnage is yet a third ship's measurement and includes only the capacity useful for non-consumable material, and by this the *Terra Nova* is 400 nett tonnage. Gross tonnage is yet a fourth and this includes holds and coal bunkers and engine-room spaces and living spaces. The ordinary one used in speaking of the *Terra Nova* is the 400 nett tonnage.

Quite the hottest day we have had so far and a tropic sun and as luck would have **Fri 8 July** it one of the stokers had to be put on the sick list and volunteer stokers were wanted from the wardroom. Cherry-Garrard and I were the first to go down, and we had to take on the morning watch from 4 a.m. to 8 a.m. It was very hot and hard work and working at three furnaces in a thin vest, trowsers and boots only. We were streaming with sweat in less than five minutes and in 3 hours I had so far had my fill of it that I was glad to go up on deck when Nelson came down at 7 o'clock and offered to do the last hour for me. Cherry-Garrard stuck to the job for the full four hours but it was very exhausting, though one recovered in a few minutes on the upper deck, where the air was fresh and cool in comparison.

Procellaria sp.   S.P.R.I. 1647

All the forenoon was spent in hunting up the names of birds and fish. We were seeing heaps of bonito, flying fish and Portuguese men-of-war. The bonito, or a kind of Horse Mackerel, were leaping clean out of the water catching the flying fish in their mouths in mid-air. We saw three or four gannets today flying around the ship from time to time the nearest land being [   ] from which they must have come as they are not ocean going birds. Some looked adult or even moulting. They were brown all over some having no white on the breast, some having white under breast and wings. The bill and skin about the eyes and face creamy white and bluish white. The sunsets just now are beautiful but always with gentle greys and golden yellow tints. After tea writing diary and various odd jobs, trimming sail, bracing up. Towards nightfall, as we are under steam, we overhauled a sailing ship.

Sat 9 July All the others in the wardroom are now taking turns at stoking. Two hours at a time is considered enough, however, for every one now. Evans has proved the strongest of all, and has carried through a complete four hours watch by himself and without help. Rennick came up after an hour and nearly fainted on the upper deck, but went down again and finished his two hours' watch with Birdie Bowers. The heat increases every day now in the stokehold, every day two or three degrees, and it is really trying work there. One has enormously heavy tools to use, prickers and devil rakes, about 12 feet of solid iron to reach the back of the furnaces with. One has to throw coal into each of the three furnaces every ten to fifteen minutes, and this in the front of a heat and glare that scorches one's eyes and makes them burn. One has then to spread the fire in the furnace and keep each one bright over the bars which run back 7 or 8ft and are about 3 to 4ft across the front. The fire has to be glowing about 6 inches deep all over this. Then one has to break up the clinker with a 'devil', an iron rake with three teeth which one can barely lift off the ground after two or three hours in the heat. While one is shovelling in coal one gets stung by what are called 'stokehold flies', which make one jump for the moment. They are drops of hot oil off the engines working over one, which catch one on the back of the neck as one stoops to shovel coal into the furnaces. Between the shovelling, which takes 7 or 8 minutes in every quarter of an hour, one has to get the coal out of the side bunkers, breaking up the large lumps with a sledge hammer, and measuring it all into a three foot bucket of solid iron. This has to be dragged across to each furnace in turn—and the floor is of hot iron plates—then one has to rake out the ashes and from time to time send them up in a hoist after wetting them with water from a hose as they are often red hot. If between all these odd duties one finds a minute to lean against or sit back upon a stationary part of the engines, it either scalds or burns one. Everything is too hot to touch and one works in so little clothing, except for thick soled boots and thick leather gloves. I think that three hours of this at 4 a.m. on a cup of cocoa only was the hardest work I have ever put myself to. One has to get accustomed to the sweating in trimming coal for the bunkers are all of iron and almost as hot as the engine-room. Perhaps the most trying part of stoking is the noise which is continuous and so excessive that one has to shout to one's mate at the work, and as the noise is all a clanging and clatter of iron and metal and a roar from the furnace and from the working of the engines all round and above one, it is somewhat trying. We saw no birds at all today. As usual the North Atlantic is almost deserted in that respect. No birds are ever seen on this side of the Equator. The other side always crowds, at any rate south of 30° lat. We saw some whales today, a whole school of them but at some distance.

Church as usual and rounds, rounds being the weekly inspection of the ship in **Sun 10 July** which the Captain, First Lieutenant, Senior Medicals, myself and Levick, and all the other officers and warrant officers take part. A tour is made all round the ship, round the men's quarters, round the engine-room, and so on. Everything having been cleaned up and tidied down on Saturday. This morning from 4 a.m. to 6 a.m. Atkinson and I took on the stoking and though the temperature was 105°, we found two hours quite a manageable quantity. We were relieved by Cherry-Garrard and Simpson for the next two hours, 6 a.m. to 8 a.m., but Simpson came up faint in half an hour and was too sick to go down again. Wright finished the watch with Cherry-Garrard. Sunday afternoon from 12 noon dinner to 7 p.m. cold supper I always get in at painting, the only interruption occurring when we are under sail and have to turn up on deck to haul and help with the men.

Up every morning for the sunrise, and cocoa, generally between 4 to 5 a.m., so **Mon 11 July** that gradually my collection of sunrise sketches increases in number much faster than I can work at them in colour. Sunsets I also get down roughly pretty nearly every evening between tea and dinner time. From lunch to tea often writing in a boat on deck or painting stripped to trowsers only down below—but this is very difficult as the perspiration literally runs from one's face and fingers. The heat in the wardroom and in our cabins is most trying when we are under steam, as at present, for the engine-room is only separated from us by a thin bulkhead with a door into the nursery cabin. Several of the cabins have not got names. One is the 'Rogues Retreat', another the 'Abode of Love', and yet a third is the 'Wine-bin'. We have also quite a number of nicknames from Teddie Evans downwards. Five of us are 'Teddies' in the ward room. Myself is 'Bill'. Campbell as the 'President of the Purity Brigade' wears a halo, but it has been broken so often it hardly holds together and has a permanent cant. Pennell is 'Penelope'. Rennick is 'Parny'. 'Max and Climax' are the inseparable Atkinson and Titus Oates. Nelson is the 'Immaculate', for he wears a clean collar at dinner time. Wright is 'Jules Verne'. As I am the oldest of the party now on board, I am known as 'Uncle Bill'. Saw some dolphins, the splash they made was quite like a whale's blow for the moment. We saw also a Leach's Petrel.

After a tropical sunrise with heavy squalls round the horizon we were suddenly **Tues 12 July** struck by one and in a moment we were out of the sultry heat of the doldrums into a delightful storm of wind and drenching rain. We were very busy on deck until nearly 11 a.m., setting sail and then washing clothes in the sudden abundance of fresh water, for we are on an allowance of fresh water half a gallon a day since leaving Madeira where we refused to take any water on account of the typhoid outbreak which they had a few months back. Most of us enjoyed the change in pyjamas on deck which got washed as they stood. It continued to pour torrents all day off and on and the wind went round so that we had to take in sail again. I did some drawing and painting at sky pictures in the afternoon. We again saw a few dolphins and two Leach's Petrels.

Wed 13 July Slept on the ice-house until 4 when a rain squall sent us all below. We set sail again after breakfast, then clearing my lab. on deck which has to be the sick bay while Lillie, who has the measles, occupies the photo laboratory. After lunch painted a bit and wrote up my log on deck in one of the whalers. We are now sailing close-hauled to a good breeze from the S.W. and making 8 or 9 knots. Steam as well, straight for Cape Town. Several people are seasick again, but not me ever in this ship, tho' she has a very funny confused motion today, pitching and tossing in addition to the usual roll. Cherry-Garrard was aloft furling sail again today with the seamen. Any number of flying fish about and 2 came in board and were picked up on deck in the morning. They generally fly in at night and are found dead in the morning; the ship's lights attract them. I saw one as big as a mackerel fly right across the old *Discovery* once, hit the top of the rail on the opposite side and go into the water. There were 6 or 8 bonito, deep crimson or bronze red fish, chasing the flying fish and catching them at the surface. Some-times the light caught the bonito in such a way as to make them a deep peacock green or most vivid blue. They are about 2 feet long and they keep pace often just under the bows of the ship when she is running at 8 or 9 knots, but of course they can dart ahead at times with twice the speed or more.

Thurs 14 July Up at 4 a.m. A most glorious sunrise and a regular trade wind sky, lemon ochre, grey clouds, and massive cumulus with the most delicate and beautiful greys and tints of colour in the west. Sleeping on the ice-house last night we were caught in heavy rain squall at midnight and we had to finish the night in our very hot bunks below. Forenoon on deck writing up log and enjoying the sun. Afternoon helping in preparation for crossing the Line tomorrow. We are to have the full show and a holiday and there are 10 men on board that require initiation. The show begins today in the evening by Neptune's messenger, Triton, coming up out of the sea over the bows and hailing the officer on the bridge to say that Neptune and his Queen Amphitrite will be visiting the ship tomorrow. Then he goes back into the sea again.

Fri 15 July We crossed the Line at 10 p.m. this evening, but Neptune came on board with Amphitrite and his whole retinue at 11 a.m. These are:

Neptune, King of the Ocean	— Petty Officer Evans.
Amphitrite, his Queen	— Petty Officer Browning.
The King's Doctor	— Paton.
His Barber	— Cheatham.
His two Policemen	— Crean and Williamson.
Barber's Assistant	— Heald.
Four sea bears in the sail bath	— Oates, Atkinson, Keohane and Johnson.

All went exceedingly well. Neptune's address was presented to the Skipper and then he was brought to the platform where his court was held, provided with seats, one of which was a stool, and was put at the very edge of the platform about six feet above the sail bath. On this stool the individual had to sit who was to be initiated and he sat with his back to the bath and his face to Neptune and his court. After being brought along by the policemen he was asked if he had ever crossed the Line before, if not he was to be medically examined first and then was handed over to the ridiculous doctor who had a small handbag containing pills and a megaphone for a stethoscope, and a serving mallet to percuss with, and a large wooden thermometer which had to be held under the tongue. The doctor's report was always that a pill was wanted which was as big as a golf ball and made of soap and tallow, and a draught which was of vinegar and cayenne. Then the Barber had a go, and he had a latherer with a bucket of whitewash and another of soot and grease and whitewashing brushes. With these the unfortunate was plastered from head to waist and then shaved with a three foot wooden razor all over his head and face and chest, most of the novices being stripped, as they say at sea, to a gantline, which means altogether. Some had trowsers. Anyhow, when the man's eyes and mouth and ears were all full of soot and whitewash, his stool was unexpectedly tipped backwards and he fell into the sail bath underneath where the four Tritons were waiting to catch him and hold him under till he swallowed enough sea water to wash the whitening out of his mouth. It was a very amusing show, and as I had had my turn on the *Discovery* I enjoyed it all the more! Nelson created a diversion by taking the Barber into the bath with him quite unexpectedly. Gran was also initiated. He was not expecting it and the two Policemen seized and undressed him and put him on the chair, and he suddenly seized Paton, the Doctor, and threw him into the bath with his pills and megaphone and spectacles and all. After this there was a procession round the ship, and a splicing of the main brace with port wine and then the show was over. Everyone took it in good part and there were no tempers lost, though one or two of the mess deck hands were initiated pretty roughly. After tea we had a sing song on the fo'csle, and as it was going on we had one of the most gorgeous sunsets imaginable. I sang at the show. We had Feather, the bo'sun, Cheatham, the second bo'sun, and Archer, the chef, to dinner with us in the wardroom—an awful crowd it was in such heat—and after that we had another sing song and so the day ended and everyone was pleased as possible.

Sketching at sunrise. Wrote and read till breakfast, as this is our wedding anniver- **Sat 16 July** sary. We set sail again today, very hot, no cloud at all—a beautiful clear cloudless tropic day. Odd jobs took up all the forenoon. All the afternoon I sat in the sun on deck and wrote up my Shetland notes on whaling. It is strange that I have only browned in the sun, never skinned at all, and never had a hat on through the tropics. The sun at sea is very different, for one couldn't do this on land in the tropics for a day without risk. I remember that it was the same on the *Discovery* where neither Michael Barne[11] nor I ever had a hat on and we were none the worse, even when we slept in the sun in the afternoon, but it has taken all the curl out of my hair. After tea Cherry-Garrard and I put up some shelves in our lab. on deck.

The sunset was a very beautiful one. In the evening did some writing. Slept on the ice-house and again a rain squall came on and soaked us, but we slept on there and dried again by the morning.

Sun 17 July Up at 4.30 a.m. Sunrise and cocoa. Church and rounds at 10 a.m. Spent the whole day painting. Fresh breeze all day. A few heavy rain squalls. Have been under steam and sail all day, doing $9\frac{1}{2}$ knots but generally 7. We saw two dolphins yesterday, and a whale blow today. We saw also a White Tern (*Cygis candida*)[12] and a Black Tern or Noddy (*Anous*) and one small Petrel (*Cymodroma grallaria*)[13]. Fresh breezy day with few heavy rain squalls. Wrote up my diary and sketched at sunset.

Mon 18 July Up at 4.15. Splendid sunrise. Spent the forenoon oiling and rubbing over 5,000 fathoms of steel wire which had to be wound off one reel on to another for sounding. We have some 20,000 fathoms on board for deep sea sounding. Afternoon went through all my Antarctic correspondence. After tea sketching sunset and writing. A gannet came on to the ship from the open ocean today and remained with us for the night.

Tues 19 July Sailing only now. Engines stopped yesterday as we have a fair wind. So far we have made 9 knots under steam and sail together and our best run so far has been 191 miles in 24 hours. This morning, having no engines, we began the hand pump again which means turning all the Staff of Science out at 6 a.m. Every four hours the pump has to be worked for about half an hour. The leakage is still about an inch an hour which is not much for a ship like this. In the afternoon I painted. We saw whales again today.

Wed 20 July Up at 5.30. A stormy sunrise. Breeze stiff and steady, under sail only. Atkinson and I having had suspicions about one of the seamen, examined him and found he had phthisis. Funnily enough he was one that had been taken on at the last moment in London and had not been examined by either of us, so we were not to blame. We arranged to send him home to a sanatorium from the Cape. Cherry-Garrard and I spent the afternoon carpentering putting up shelves on my lab. on the upper deck. We also overhauled all the whaling guns and harpoons and other whaling gear and found it all right. Sunset was magnificent, gorgeous colouring, and a very well marked green flash as the sun disappeared, a thing often seen at sea in the tropics, and understood by no one. We had a very lively evening after dinner, playing games chiefly. 'The Priest of the Parish'[14]. Fines all go towards buying luxuries at the next port, and luxuries include paint for the ship and gold leaf and gilding as well as beer, cider and ginger beer and so on.

Thurs 21 July Up at 5.15 a.m. to a very fiery, grand, stormy sunrise, fiercely red and purple. Two rain squalls in the night through which I slept—on top of the ice-house. I awoke once and found my pillow wet—turned over and slept through all. At the pump three times today, splendid exercise which everyone enjoys. We passed through a long line of orange yellow sea today, the colour altering most conspicuously from deep blue. It was caused by fish ova—one easily caught them in

July. 17. 1910. Sunset. E.

Sunset, 17 July 1910

a bucket thrown over the side with a line attached. They coloured the sea for a long band about half a mile wide stretching S.E. by N.W. The ova were like small sausage-shaped masses of jelly cram full of orange yellow dots and otherwise transparent. There must have been many millions of them to colour the sea as they did. They seemed all to float near the surface.

Fri 22 July Up at 5. Pumping at 6. Again a very fine sunrise of which the antecedent glow is perhaps the most beautiful part, appearing at sunrise in the west before the sun appears. Again carpentering all the afternoon, and arranging plans for South Trinidad in the forenoon.

Sat 23 July My birthday, and now I am 38. Up at 5 to a lovely sunrise and antecedent glow in which the moon hung in the west. Pump at 6. Carpentering at shelves all the forenoon. Cherry-Garrard trimming coal in the bunkers all the forenoon, and painted our lab. out and the new shelves in the afternoon. I worked at whales till tea time. Still very hot below. It was 84° F. in our cabin. Quite cool at night sleeping on deck in the open. Costume all day is still a simple one, a canvas shirt, a pair of white duck trowsers rolled up to the knees, bare legs and no socks, but a pair of canvas shoes. Quite impossible to be clean except at dinner—but we dine in shirt and trowsers only. One could comfortably wear nothing. We are still under full sail, no steam. We expect to reach South Trinidad[15] on Monday night. The swell has been very heavy today and yesterday with an unusual one coming up ahead of us. One or two shearwaters today and no other birds.

Sun 24 July Up at 4. A heavy squall prevented our having service as we were all wanted and had to change quickly into dirty rig and help to shorten sail. My birthday was celebrated last night between 12 and 1 when Evans, Rennick, and Birdie Bowers came and danced and sang on the main hatch dog kennel and turned everybody out of bed to come and wish me many happy returns of the day as I slept in my bag on top of the ice-house. This was done to make up for having forgotten to celebrate the event at dinner. I was glad that no one minded being turned out for such a purpose, but I saved some of them by going round myself. Happily everyone is overflowing with good nature. On the *Discovery* I was always 'Bill'. On this ship I am always 'Uncle Bill'. I got a corner prepared today in a sort of baggage room cabin where I could stand and write and do some work in quiet from 4 a.m. to breakfast. It becomes more necessary every day now to get my grouse papers finished off to send home from the Cape. The place I have is liable to be wet and coal dusty, but apart from this it is a great thing to feel that one can get the work done there. No one has a table to write at and I purposely do all mine standing as I invariably fall asleep at once if I sit down. A few hours of sleep at sea goes a long way—and 5 or 6 hours in the 24 is ample—but one is always capable of sleeping if one sits down, so one has to stand to one's work. We began steaming again this morning and with sail we reached 9½ knots. Heavy sea and high wind. We are making for South Trinidad, but it may not be possible to land. All the afternoon I painted but we are rolling and pitching very awkwardly for such work. Saw some Trinidad Gannets[16] today and 2 or 3 Great Shearwaters[17].

Up at 4 to sunrise, reading and writing. Wind dropped light but we did 201 miles **Mon 25 July** in the 24 hours under steam and sail. Trimmed patent fuel in the bunker all the forenoon. Afternoon with Rennick, remounting a sounding machine, when South Trinidad was sighted at 3 p.m. The island was beautiful at sunset 6 p.m. We furled sail, several of the scientific staff assisting, Cherry-Garrard and Nelson among them. Some White Terns *(Gygis candida)* came off to us from the island also Gannets and Petrels. I had a lot to sketch as we came round three sides of the island nearly, and when darkness came we hung off and on all night till it was light enough to see what we were doing again.

Up at 4 to sketch and see the sunrise. We then went in on the southwest side and **Tues 26 July** anchored 4 cables off the breakers on shore—4 cables=$\frac{4}{10}$ mile, or about 700 yards. We were in the same bay that contained the pier of rough rock where we landed from the *Discovery*. As daylight appeared we saw the outline of the island and Campbell and I were on the bridge when on the very highest peak there appeared a brilliant light like a bonfire, and both at once thought of the *Waratah*[18]. But in a minute or two this flickering bonfire rose off the mountain top and we realised that it was Venus. It was very beautiful all the same. We had breakfast early and Evans went off with a party to choose a landing place. The landing here being always a difficulty owing to the swell which breaks on the very rocky shore and endangers the boats. We, Cherry-Garrard and I, shot two Frigate Birds[19] and some terns from the ship. Having found a place which looked possible for land-ing, Evans returned and then we all went off loaded up with collecting gear. We had arranged that no one should go less than two together, that each party should collect some definite group of things and that a rocket from the ship should recall every one. Cherry-Garrard and I took the birds, so I had my gun and he had his. Pennell and Bowers undertook insects and earthworms. Lillie undertook the botany and geology of which there was enough for everyone to observe what they could. Nelson with two or three helpers worked along the coral pools on the shore and caught many of the brightly coloured fish that lived there eating crabs. Cherry-Garrard and I shot a good series of birds, especially the Trinidad Petrel[20] which has two phases, a black one and a light one. This bird has been given no less than three specific names but I am sure they all interbreed and are really the same species. Besides being called *Oestrelata trinitatis* it is also called *Oe. arminjoniana* and *Oe. wilsoni* after me—but we found every phase together nesting along cliff ledges, dark and pale—young and old. We got young ones in down, large and very fat. Also many young full fledged, having just left the nest, with downy points still attached on the head. They were flying round us everywhere and at every height, being as abundant at the summit which we reached at about 2,000 ft as they were on the beach and off the land by the ship. They made a most delightful noise between the drumming of a snipe and the bubbling note of a cuckoo,

27

arranged rather like the spring song of a Common Sandpiper. It was in the throat —not made by the feathers. The White Terns *(Gygis candida)* also made a very nice chattering noise on the wing. These terns were wonderfully confiding, especially if one came near their single eggs or young downy chicks, perched anywhere on a rock or boulder, or on one of the dead skeleton tree trunks. The young were to be found in every stage, some fully fledged and able to fly. One could catch the old ones in a net as they fluttered round our heads, and last time I was here one actually settled on my sunhelmet as I sat sketching. They are very clever in sitting on the egg which balances often on a smooth rounded boulder. The chick has very sharp claws and a tremendous grip of the smooth rock on which it lives— probably saving itself from being blown away. These birds appear to take no notice of a land crab, and I saw them close together. There were numbers of handsome gannets which evidently have no enemy on land at all as they slept so soundly on the tree trunks and bushes that one could crawl up and catch them by hand. This seemed to annoy them, however, and they made a great noise. Sometimes they heard one approaching and out came their heads from under the wing, but often so dazed and surprised that one could catch them by the neck before they thought of flying. These gannets are chiefly morning and evening feeders, I think, and therefore were all resting at noon. Some were sitting on their old nests but none had eggs or young. All we saw were fully adult, white all over the body, and none were speckled or dark. The gannets were abundant only on the higher parts of the island, and at 1,500 ft one often found 5 or 6 of them asleep on a large evergreen bush—a kind of laurel, I think—with a berry, very acid, which the land crabs crawled up to eat. We saw nothing of Frigate Birds after landing, though quite a number were to be seen always just off the shore. Both species live here, and we got one of each, the Greater with his great scarlet pouch, and the Lesser with a less conspicuous pouch, and smaller measurements.

Pennell, Cherry-Garrard and I kept together up to the top where we got into thick bush full of land crabs and thick with tree ferns and living laurel trees, and various flowering plants. I found an interesting parasitic plant growing freely on the laurel. The climbing was most difficult as everything gave way on the steep sides, and slid downhill under one's weight. There were large locusts and numbers of red-legged, black-bodied running flies, and innumerable spiders. Land crabs were larger and more abundant in the bush at the top than on any other part of the island. If one sat down one heard them stealthily creeping all round amongst the dead ferns and lichenous growth and before long one could count a dozen or more and one or two would come and pick at one's boots to see if they were eatable. If disturbed by a rock they ran quickly for a few inches and then stealthily crept away or up again.

It was a very hot day but on the top, where we looked down to the beach on the northeast side of the island and away to the Martin Vas Islands on the horizon, we had a fine breeze and a grand view. Some of the rocky volcanic boulders on the summit were weathered into water holding basins of a wonderfully regular shape. These held water too. There was also a small, almost dry, watercourse running down the gully up which we had climbed. The climb was a very hot and difficult one, everything loose and often a chaos of large angular blocks of loose

'South Trinidad'

rock which over balanced and shifted at every step. Higher up was loose volcanic ash and earth and fine tussocky grass which came away with one downhill at a touch. We all had constant falls and my gun suffered a terrible dent in one barrel which was rendered useless. The other was all right, however, and we continued collecting. Cherry also dented his gun. The vegetation was on the whole un-interesting. A cyperus [sic] was abundant and so was a creeping willow, and a pea which had been introduced by some Dutch settlers, whose attempts to settle were to be seen on the northeast side, where was an exposed beach and some flattish grass land. It is on that side also that treasure has been supposed to lie buried and hunts have been organised from time to time for it.

At about 4 p.m. we had begun the descent from the tree fern zone when we saw the recall rocket go up from the ship at anchor in the bay. It took us a very long and tiring climb to get down and when we reached the beach several of us were getting cramp in the thighs from the unwonted exertion on land. We then saw that a heavy swell had come in and made it quite impossible for a boat to come inshore and take us off. The sun sets rapidly here and we had to get something done before dark at about 6 p.m. The surf was magnificent, the swell coming in on the rocky shore where we landed and breaking up to an immense height. Every now and then it nearly washed individuals off the rocks where a moment before they were 12 or 14 feet above its reach. The swell came in in two or three immense rollers every now and again, and before people could get out of reach they were up to the neck clinging by their nails to the cracks of rocks to hold on. It was necessary for Evans and one or two others to be at the water's edge to try and secure a rope which had been floated in from a boat anchored about 50 yards out where the rollers were not breaking. Theirs was a dangerous job and most of us were high up on the rocks looking on and expecting to see someone swept in every time they were lost for a moment in the immense surf. The actual surf broke often as high as 25 to 30 feet, and they had to be in it. In fact we were all in it before we had finished. That morning from the ship we had counted 14 sharks inspecting the anchor cable. The water was so clear we could see every fish and the anchor lying on the white sandy bottom. Happily one forgets one risk in dealing with a more pressing one, for I confess that I quite forgot the sharks when my turn came to dodge those breaking rollers and run in between them to swim off to the boat. One by one we all swam off helping ourselves from being sucked back to the breaking surf and the rocks by clinging to the rope. The suck back was very strong, but only one of the whole party on shore—about 15 of us—got brought back on to the rocks. This one was the wardroom servant who lost hold of the rope and was at once carried back on to the rocks in the immense surf. He was then carried out again and again brought back. It was quite impossible for anyone to help him and we all thought he was done for, but the third time he was carried against the rope and caught it and hung on and though he was under water for what seemed an impossible length of time to us who were watching him, he succeeded in swimming out and got to the boat. He happily was only grazed and bruised a bit about his legs; had his head or ribs been carried against the rocks he must have been killed, and it seemed a miracle that he wasn't pulped in amongst the rocks both times. It was quite dark enough when Evans swam off as the last one that night. We left two men on shore for the night, one a sick seaman and the other Atkinson to look after him. They were not troubled by the crabs, and they had matches and food and some spare clothing, but they found it pretty cold.

It was hoped that the swell might have abated a bit by this morning, but it was **Wed 27 July** rather worse. When we all swam off yesterday we had to leave all our collections on the beach, and this was bad for all of them and fatal to some as the heat had been excessive all day, Trinidad being in the tropics. This morning we hoped to be able to bring them all off to the ship with Atkinson and the seaman. With our collections, of course, we also had to leave everything that would have been damaged by sea water. I had left my gun, cartridges, Goerz field glasses, an aneroid, and my silver watch, happily not the chronometer watch. All these lay in a heap with my boots and clothing, for most of us had swum off to the boat with not much more than a belt and a sheath knife. Had I thought of the sharks I should perhaps have kept my boots on as white feet are apt to be attractive to sharks— but I forgot their existence. To get all these collections off a boat went from the ship and tried again to get in touch with the two men on shore. And once the boat got in so close that the sick seaman succeeded in jumping in with two guns. But my Goerz field glasses, I am sorry to say, were dropped in the water and lost. After this the seaman and the guns were sent on board and then the boat tried again for Atkinson. This time it was less fortunate for it was caught by a swell and thrown up high and dry on to the rocks and the two officers in it were thrown out also on to the rocks. It was a marvel that no one was hurt, for the next wave took the boat back and it was only by a most plucky piece of management that one of the officers, Bowers or Evans or Rennick, got into it as it came in again and saved it from being broken to pieces. It was judged then too risky to try further to get within a jump of the shore, so the boat was taken out and anchored outside the breaking surf and all our gear—aneroids, watches, clothing, boots, specimens of birds we had shot, plants, insects, cameras, &c, &c—were all dragged through the surf on a line. And of course nearly everything was damaged, and much was done for altogether. My own losses were considerable, for my gun looked a perfect wreck— salt water had got into lock and barrel and it was bright red all over. Sea water corrodes off the browning of a gun in a few hours in flakes, and had a dreadful action on the metal underneath. Moreover, one barrel was put out of action by a hopeless looking dent which had resulted from a fall on the rocks the day before. I took the lock to bits and soaked the gun in paraffin and vaseline and when we reached the Cape I had it overhauled and the dent hammered out and it is safe as ever again. Not so my watch, or the aneroid, which I had bought just before leaving for 3 guineas. Both were impossible and had to be thrown away when we reached the Cape. My field glasses (Goerz prismatic), a present from the firm, were lost, and so were my heavy nailed boots. Yet the whole show was very excellent sport and quite worth the loss. I regretted most of all that the large collection of birds we shot there having been dragged through salt water and having been delayed in that heat, made only very second rate skins. This was especially regrettable on account of the doubt concerning the specific position of the petrels. However, Nelson's shore collections suffered even more for they were nearly all dead and rotten by the time he recovered them. Lillie's plants came off pretty well and so did Lillie's observations in respect of the island's dead trees. The whole of the island is covered with bleached skeletons of a previous forest and no one has ever explained why they all died. Lillie suggests that they are really all gradually making their way down the slopes and gullies from the tops where there is still a very thick bush and that none of these trees have really grown on the slopes at all, and that the probability is that the island has not long been as high above sea level as it is now. There is much to uphold the view besides its simplicity, for there are evidences of raised beaches which Ferrar himself saw and described ten years ago on the *Discovery*. All today I have been painting the heads and feet of some of the birds we shot while Cherry skinned them. Cherry-Garrard was so keen to save them too that he continued skinning all night till breakfast. The men have been getting very successful catches of fish with lines and hooks, some of the fish very handsomely marked, large 10 lbs fish of 5 or 6 kinds and now and then a shark and a lot of black Trigger Fish with beastly dangerous spines in the dorsal fin which lie flat along the back until the fish is irritated when the spine springs out as though released by a trigger. There were also spotted Conger Eels and beautiful peacock blue fish and others of all colours in the coral pools. Everyone is worn out with two very hard days of work and excitement. We have also taken the opportunity to repaint the ship for our approaching arrival at Cape Town. We spent a second night at anchor here and had the following forenoon to finish work.

Thurs 28 July Up at 5 a.m. and got in a few hours on my grouse reports work before breakfast. Then skinned and painted the birds again and continued skinning until midnight, teaching two seamen. We weighed anchor at noon and went off round the southeast end of the island getting sketches and a good view of the part where the Dutch settlement had once been. Three Frigate Birds followed us and pecked at our wind vane until we were 10 miles off, and then they returned to their island. They are strange birds like great kites, and it was interesting to see them hunting other birds, such as terns and gannets, and making them disgorge, just like skuas. These Frigates are very clever at picking up scraps in the water without settling. They have a very wide spread of wing and long swallow tails.

Fri 29 July Birdie Bowers is 27 years old today. Turned out at 6 a.m. just in time though for a gorgeous tropical sunrise. From breakfast until 7 p.m. I was making up bird skins with Cherry-Garrard. We had some rain squalls during the night, but having got used to sleeping through them on the top of the ice-house they don't hurt one at all. One's bedding (blanket only) dries before morning except for a little puddle underneath. We saw two whales blowing today, they were probably Humpbacks (*Megaptera*).

Sat 30 July Up at 5 a.m. to moon and stars. Sunrise appears only about 6 a.m. We are now under steam and sail. We have now made skins, some quite decent ones, of 15 Trinidad Petrels, 1 or 2 *Gygis candida*, 2 Frigate Birds and there are yet 8 or 9 to do. We saw *Oestrelata mollis*[21] today for the first time.

Up at 4 a.m. to read and write. Sleeping always on the ice-house where 5 hours is **Sun 31 July** more good for one than 8 hours below. Magnificent sunrise at 6 a.m. Have got a few painted but under difficulties. The Soft Plumaged Petrel (*Oestr. mollis*) is abundant today. After breakfast spent an hour or two with Simpson over his instruments and over his special hut which I believe to be a superfluity. Believe it can be done without and without hindering any of his work. He is an obliging good tempered old thing and takes himself very seriously.

Up at 4 a.m. and got some drawing and writing done by breakfast. Prepared some **Mon 1 Aug** albatross traps and lines. After lunch trimmed coal (patent fuel) from 2 till 4.30 and then 5 to 6 with Birdie Bowers. We shifted 1,200 blocks = 7 tons from the hold into the bunkers—ship rolling so heavily that we were continually dodging avalanches of coal in the dark there. Patent fuel burns your eyes with its dust and often gives you a splitting headache. We come up black as niggers. We saw our first Wandering Albatross[22] today, a young one, and very nearly caught it on a tarpon line.

Up at 4 a.m., the ship rolling to a very heavy swell with no wind. Drew some **Tues 2 Aug** whale's skulls which have to be sent home from the Cape for Barrett-Hamilton's book.
Oussa, one of our white Samoyede pups (we have 4 on board), had fits today, evidently from parasitic worms, and died. They were all given a run on South Trinidad and one had fits there from sheer excitement and the heat as well I think. Wet paint now everywhere on the upper deck, for Cape Town. Everyone helping, officers and scientifics.

Up at 4 a.m. to finish off my grouse reports. Painting sunrises all afternoon and **Wed 3 Aug** evening. We saw a very marked example of zodiacal light this evening. A white pyramidal shaft of light high up from the horizon above the spot where the sun had set and lasting long after it had set even to when it was pretty dark. We saw Cape Pigeons today for the first time. Cherry-Garrard caught a nice Soft Plumaged Petrel on thread. Eight or ten were flying round the ship.

Up 4.30 for grouse reports. Grand sunrise, flat calm with swell—no wind, beautiful **Thurs 4 Aug** day. We saw 5 or 6 whales making a rapid passage to the N.E. They were *Megaptera*, Humpbacks, I believe, but we also saw one *Balaenoptera borealis*, Northern Rorqual, close in by the ship. Also an adult Wandering Albatross and a young brown one, as well as a Grey Head Mollymawk[23]—probably Gough Island Albatross. Lillie has been caricaturing various members of the mess. Today a very good one appeared of Nelson. Another appeared not long ago of Birdie Bowers, also one of Sunny Jim Simpson whose, I think, was the best of all. Lillie has a wonderful talent in this line and he does them all after long observation from memory. He cannot do them with the person before him. He will be a great help in the *South Polar Times*[24].

Up at 4 to a good sunrise—and grouse reports. Spent the forenoon, after setting **Fri 5 Aug** sail, in working at birds with Pennell who is wonderful in the way he picks new things up and in the accuracy with which he tackles them. There are now more birds following us than we have seen the whole voyage. A breeze sprang up today with a fair sea and a grand sunset. The sea dull lead grey with green topped combers which begin lopping over into the waist of the ship. We are now making headway to Cape Town. Evening writing and drawing.

Sat 6 Aug Cool enough now down below and too wet with breaking waves to sleep on deck. Slept below today for the first time. Up at 4. Wrote till 6 and then, whenever we are under sail only and the steam pump is therefore not at work, I have to turn out all the wardroom people to man the hand pump and pump out the bilge. Owing to a leak the *Terra Nova* makes about an inch an hour and we have to pump her out every watch—i.e. every four hours. We in the wardroom undertake the morning watch pump out and the evening one. It means pumping for about half an hour at a time. We have cocoa when we turn out early. It began to blow early today and we shipped a good deal of water and had to take in topgallant sails. The weather remained dirty and wet all day, high and heavy seas and almost impossible to do any work.

Sun 7 Aug Up at 4. Pumping at 6. Otherwise doing grouse reports. Heavy weather with rain squalls all day. Saw a Northern Rorqual quite close. Also Sooty Albatross[25] for the first time and a Giant Petrel[26].

Mon 8 Aug Up at 4. Writing grouse work till 6 then pumping, which we continued till 8, for a drum of oil has run out in the hold and has percolated through the patent fuel to the bilge. Our pump in consequence gets absolutely plugged with an oily compound of pitch, resin, oil and coal dust. It was lunch time before we had reduced the bilge to 1 ft 3 ins. The drum contained 48 gallons of heavy Colsa oil and we have to pump this out now as it slowly carries coal dust into the bilge. Heavy squalls last night, but sunny breezy weather. After lunch did grouse work.

Tues 9 Aug Pretty big seas. Up at 4. Grouse work till 6 then pumping till 7.30, then a sea water bath on the upper deck. Ship rolling very heavily under sail. Work at labelling of bird skins all the forenoon, then an hour on deck watching birds and after that grouse reports until 7 p.m. dinner. Got a lot done—all standing and without a table. Can't sit as I always fall asleep. Work under these conditions is awkward. The cabin is minute and full of gear—no table, no chair, no room to spread papers, very little light and less air, with a heavy roll which spills one's balanced papers on to a wet and greasy, dirty floor. It will be a miracle if what I am now writing will be acceptable to the Grouse Committee, for I feel as though I had left the grouse work behind me years ago; the surroundings are not conducive to such work. Still it has to be finished and has to be sent home from the Cape. Then adieu with every pleasure.

Wed 10 Aug Up at 4.30. Grouse work till 6.30 then pumping and a bath. Pumping again after breakfast till 10 a.m. Wind falling light so we are rolling very heavily. On deck nearly all the forenoon and then at grouse from lunch till dinner at 7. Had a splendid view of the green flash at sunset which appeared about 15 seconds after the sun had been covered by a large distant swell on the horizon. We expected to see the sun again but saw the green flash instead—most distinctly. Great Grey Shearwater appeared today for the first time. The birds are most interesting and quite abundant.

Up at 4.30. Grey and rainy generally dark and starlight till 6.30. Gran always **Thurs 11 Aug** makes me cocoa. Pumping at 6.30 for which the Afterguard or Wardroom is always turned out. Today we are again getting up steam, however, so we shall have the steam pump. Today I was on the pump three times otherwise at grouse reports all day. In the evening we had a tremendous rag or 'scrap'. Campbell, Cherry-Garrard and I held the Nursery, which has two doors, against the rest of the Ward-room. The struggle lasted an hour or two and half of us were nearly naked towards the finish, having had our clothes torn off our backs, but all in excellent fun and splendid exercise in this heat. We thought at the end of it that a cinematograph exhibition of the leisure hours of the officers and scientific staff of a great national enterprise for the discovery of the South Pole would surprise the audience of the Albert Hall and would fetch an audience at the Empire.

Friday we were under steam again so no hand pumping. Was up at 4.30 for grouse **Fri 12 Aug** work. All day painting ship and scrubbing paint work. After lunch I was trimming coal below—filthy work but good exercise—for 3 hours. We were in a very chilly white fog when it was necessary to wash the coal off on deck. Afterwards went on with my grouse work, which is gradually nearing completion. I generally turn in before 10 p.m., but am often called at 12 or thereabouts for cocoa by Nelson and Evans. After which I sleep again at once and am called again for cocoa between 4 and 5 a.m. A very good, fattening routine which gives me a very nice long day—but I couldn't keep it up on shore. Sea air, while it keeps one ready to go to sleep the moment one sits down to anything less interesting than one's meals, seems at the same time to enable one to get fat with 4 or 5 hours sleep in the 24. Moreover, the only hours one can get to oneself with anything like peace are the early ones when no one is up except the officer on the bridge and Gran, his 'drumstick'[27], to make cocoa, and Pennell, who is always up before sunrise to take stars for purposes of navigation. Pennell is at work from 4 a.m. as a rule until past 10 p.m. and I have never yet known him sleep in the afternoons. He gets through a perfectly extra-ordinary amount of work every day—always cheerful and genial and busy, but never too busy to talk birds and to be interested in other work than his own. Today in smoother water we have had fewer birds. We are gradually nearing South Africa.

Up at 4 a.m. Grouse work till breakfast. We have been under steam all night, **Sat 13 Aug** $7\frac{1}{2}$ knots. Water dead calm, birds keeping a long way off compared with rougher weather. Grouse work all forenoon. After lunch painting deck houses with the others on the upper deck. Great energy cleaning up for port.

Up early and spent the day at grouse work chiefly. **Sun 14 Aug**

Mon 15 Aug Blowing a very heavy gale again all night from the northwest. High seas and exceedingly heavy squalls. Had to take in all sail except foresail and lower topsails. Between the squalls the topgallant sails and topsails (upper) were reset—nine times in 10 or 11 hours, which means plenty of work for the watch. Was up at 4.30 and worked at grouse till 8. Was called up at 1 o'clock to see a huge white rain bow thrown by the moon in the squalls. The bow was almost a perfect semi-circle. After breakfast I joined Nelson for a day's work at the wardroom paintwork. We washed every inch of it clean and then scrubbed the floor and got done by 4 p.m. when we were within signalling distance of the *Pandora* and the *Mutine*, two naval ships lying in harbour at Simon's Bay. The *Pandora* was a cruiser—the *Mutine* a surveying sloop. It was just getting dark when we tied up to a buoy in Simon's Bay and I could see Ory and Mrs. Evans on the bridge of the *Pandora*. Our passage from London to Simon's Bay was just one day quicker than the *Discovery*. A number of ocean birds accompanied us to this last day. Ory soon came on board and so did Mrs. Evans. Captain Scott and his wife are up at Pretoria with the Governor and the Admiral, Admiral Egerton[28], and Lady Egerton. We all came off the ship in the dockyard launch and dined together at the British Hotel; and were there interviewed by a *Cape Times* reporter; and then turned in very tired after a long day.

3

CAPE COLONY

AUGUST 16 and onwards we remained in Simon's Town, Ory and I, and had a good many luncheon parties and calls to make and dinings out—but we enjoyed life too. Some of the people are very nice and all are very kind. The nicest of all, we thought, were the two Commanding Officers, Captain Hardy of the *Mutine* and Captain Evans of the *Pandora*. Both had very nice wives and Captain Hardy was a keen ornithologist. The naval medical men also were very good to us and we were shown over the naval hospital here by the surgeon in residence there with his wife, with whom we lunched. Then there was also a Captain Ackerman, a gunner in charge of the forts, who was keenly interested in scientific work, but chiefly physics and optics with a special interest in microscopes and photography. He had quite the most elaborate microscope I have ever seen. We, of course, had our mails here and indeed the home people were very good in writing so often and so fully. During our stay here at Simon's Town I got my grouse work completely finished and all the illustrations in and the paging and all, which was a load off my mind, though I must of necessity leave the whole of the proof correcting and proof reading to be done by others; and this leaves room for very abundant error as my papers are all in ms. written under difficulties, often in a heavily rolling ship and always standing with no table to work at but a ship's washstand and the top of a suit case and all necessarily in pencil. However, Shipley[1] and Leslie will be equal to the occasion, I am sure, and both of them are happily real bricks. Shipley sent each of us Cambridge people that had been his friends a special little parcel of choice literature for the voyage, which I thought was exceedingly nice of him. But mentioning his kindness makes me feel I ought to mention all the others who were equally thoughtful, but there were so many! Ory was looking fit and well. She was with Mrs. Teddie Evans. Constance[2] was staying away with some friends. Ory and I remained on here until the ship left for Melbourne. Captain and Mrs. Scott turned up in 4 or 5 days and then I got leave to go to Saldanha Bay[3] to see a whaling station; and then it was that Scott asked me to go on ahead of the *Terra Nova* to Melbourne while he came on in the *Terra Nova* in my place. Our life on board had been so happy that Ory was really sorry that I couldn't go on as before instead of coming in the *Corinthic*, White Star, Shaw Saville Co. steamer. But it was a great thing to be able to go on with Ory, of course, and the only loss was the impossibility of keeping as fit living an idle life on a liner as one was living a harder life with heaps of hard work on the *Terra Nova*. Also I had to look after Mrs. Evans and Mrs. Scott. As a matter of fact Mrs. Evans was exceedingly nice and a very pleasant companion to Ory as well as being always ready for active games all the voyage. On the whole I was very glad to get to know her so well, for she is a real brick and is devoted to her husband, Teddie Evans, who is equally a thoroughly good brick and a very great friend of mine. Mrs. Scott was a bad sailor and I saw a great deal less of her than of Mrs. Evans. The remainder of what there is to say about our voyage on the *Corinthic*, however, must come later and as a matter of fact has probably already gone home in Ory's letters from Hobart and Melbourne. We neither of us enjoyed anything on the voyage very much except being together. It was a very cold, wet journey and the crowd of ocean birds was our chief interest all the way. My diary is simply a record of what we saw in the bird line to compare with what Pennell noted in the same way on the *Terra Nova* at the same time about 7° further north. We in the *Corinthic* went as far south as 47°S.lat. The *Terra Nova* came no further south than 40°.

At Simon's Town we had some long days together writing letters and papers and occasionally a walk up the hills to watch Sunbirds, and Colys and small Fly-catchers with long tails and other wonderful little Cape Colony birds and flowers we never tired of admiring, they are so wonderful here.

Wed 17 Aug Very heavy downpour of rain from time to time making everything steam in the hot sun which came between. Simon's Town is the port where we stayed in the *Discovery*, only then I lived on the ship. Admiral Moore[4] was in command here then. Now it is Admiral Egerton. Admiralty House is very pretty with gardens. Violets in profusion now and a deep red Bougainvillea all over the house. Gum trees in the garden are full of Weaver Birds' nests hanging and swinging in the wind with dozens of chattering orange yellow Weaver Birds. They make very neat clipped hedges here of Plumbago; cactuses—or as they are commonly called, Prickly Pears—grow everywhere on waste ground like nettles and look very untidy as the old stocks die and fade. They are horrid to touch for if you carefully pick a fruit, avoiding all the more obvious spines, you will find your skin tingling with fine, sharp, and all but invisible spines innumerable. The whole plant is one to avoid for these imperceptible spines become very annoying afterwards, just like small glass splinters. We have lost two of our seamen here through illness—both nice men—one an exceedingly nice young chap who has developed phthisis on the voyage; really must have started with it and we find that he was the one man who was taken on with one other at the last moment in London and so escaped being medically examined. However, we have got excellent men in their places from the *Pandora*. Constance turned up today but we did little more than writing all day on the hotel verandah. Dined in the evening with Capt. and Mrs. Hardy of the *Mutine* and there met Capt. and Mrs. Evans of the *Pandora*.

Thurs 18 Aug Again a walk with Ory before breakfast and a long uninterrupted day writing up grouse reports and finishing off business. No early hours in these days. We are seldom at breakfast before 9 a.m. and rarely late at night.

Fri 19 Aug Ory and I went into Cape Town by train to call on the curator and see the museum and some whales' skeletons recently obtained from the whaling station at Saldanha

Bay. We enjoyed the botanical gardens too, which were full of beautiful plants and a good many birds. Arum Lilies are a weed here and cover acres of ground all along the line. Mimosa and Bottlebrush with its yellow flowers and sweet scent is in blossom everywhere. The sea is also always peculiarly beautiful in this bay, with shades of green and blue and yellow and always a mistiness which obliterates the line of junction between the mountain range opposite, some 50 miles across the bay—a range which was snowcapped every day we were there. I met Hodgson's brother today; he is in business out here.

A birdie walk with Ory, then a day's writing in the verandah and dined with the **Sat 20 Aug** Ackermans in the evening.

With Ory at 8, in the small English Church near by, but having nothing to do with **Sun 21 Aug** Admiralty House. It was an exceptionally nice service. We lunched with Fleet Surgeon Chambers at the naval hospital and supped with the Dennys's, who also were naval surgeon and wife. The hospital is very compact and prepared for war. Enormous medical stores ready at a moment's notice.

After a day of business on the ship and writing, for our sins we were entertained **Mon 22 Aug** by the Cape Town 'Owl Club', a sort of colonial Savage Club and one of the worst we have ever had the ill fortune to attend. We were all seated at small tables and apparently two members were told off to look after two guests. My two hosts first of all made offensive remarks about teetotallers when I said I didn't drink, and then quarrelled about the payment for a bottle of soda water which I was given and half a glass of sherry which had accidentally been poured into my glass by the waiter while I wasn't looking. The quarrel was not who should pay for it, but who should *not* pay for it, and eventually as both refused to pay for the sherry, and as the old waiter said if *they* didn't *he* would have to, they said he might! Imagine my joy when I found that one of these delightful people, the most amusing if the most vulgar of the two, was a relative of Ruskin's[5]. No, I think strictly only a connection by marriage—not a relative happily. The evening was truly one of the most awful penalties of being a member of such a public expedition. There was no redeeming feature about the whole thing.

Writing grouse reports all day in Simon's Town. **Tues 23 Aug**

Again grouse work all the forenoon and got off a large package home by post. **Wed 24–Thurs** Ory and I then went to Cape Town, saw Pérignay, the curator, and met Tiny **25 Aug** (Florence) Stokes[6]. Also obtained a free railway pass to Hopefield for Ory and self. Hopefield being the furthest point towards Saldanha Bay by rail. We returned to Simon's Town for the night, and then Scott told me he wanted me to go to Melbourne by a liner while he went in the *Terra Nova*. I was to arrive at Melbourne a week or ten days before the *Terra Nova*. Was to choose a third geologist there, see Professor David[7] and do what was possible to stir up interest in the expedition and ask for £5,000 from the Federal Government if possible, but if not—and they have already warned Scott in the papers that he would get nothing—then to see if private subscriptions could be raised. In Cape Town Ory and I had visited the new Cathedral, which was nice and quiet and cool. They are building it without any debt.

Fri 26 Aug We were up at 5 a.m., made tea, and caught the 6.30 for Cape Town. Then had breakfast in the station and started off for Hopefield at 8.30 a.m. The line was lovely—narrow gauge—not too fast to see flowers and birds by the way. As we got further up country and Table Mountain began to disappear, the accommodation at the various stopping places got more doubtful, but here and there we came to respectable towns with hotels. We were travelling mainly with Boers—farmers—great big Dutchmen who all spoke broken and rather ridiculous English in preference to Dutch, hoping, I have very little doubt, to be taken for Englishmen. It seemed to me everywhere that Dutch talk was considered a sign of low class amongst the Cape Colony Dutch and only the poorer Boers spoke it. In this, however, I may have been mistaken. As we got more into open country we saw the flowers getting more and more beautiful and when we got on to actual veldt it became a perfect carpet of colour. We passed Darling where there was a church and where we had refreshments at the station—a great variety. Darling was quite a sizeable place. At 4 p.m. we reached our terminus, Hopefield, and put up in a funny old Dutch inn near the railway and adjoining the veldt. Here we had a large dark wooden-walled room, stained wood floors, very large and dark and bare, but the windows made up for all, for as we lay in bed we could watch a colony of orange coloured Weaver Birds building their compact grass nests swinging at the very ends of long gum tree branches. They were ridiculously funny in their chattering eagerness and the cocks were continually being scolded for bringing the wrong stuff for the nest, or for gadding from one nest to the other to visit friends. Our room opened into the dining room where we had an excellent supper which we shared with several English men at work on the line—engineers and so on. One huge fat red man took such a fancy to Ory that he brought her a lovely bunch of very rare scented lily only to be found in one place there, when we left in the morning.

Sat 27 Aug We are surrounded by Boers and Kaffirs everywhere. Here the blacks are all the Kaffir type, but in Simon's Town there was a very great mixture, Kaffirs, Bushmen, Malays, Chinese, Turks and a great many Indians. I saw nothing like Zulus, but the Admiralty has a great number of west coast Kroo boys, who are very ugly with black, shining flat faces—very strong and reliable and very respectful and proud of being in white uniform or blue jackets—all working in the dockyard here. The Cape Colony Kaffir is a very degenerate man, dirty, lazy and unreliable, I am told; and certainly the mongrel looking lot that one sees in Cape Town and Simon's Town have the appearance of hopeless riff-raff, most unattractive indeed, but one feels that their degradation has been the direct result of our occupation. Perhaps the worst side of it by far is to see white derelicts wallowing in the idleness and dirt of these degenerate Kaffirs on equal terms. There is a respectable looking black village half a mile from Simon's Town where they have built about a hundred small houses on a sandy slope above the sea.

40

To return, however, to Hopefield. We slept well and things were clean. We had a good English breakfast—all the food here is on the English régime—and then we hired a Cape cart with two horses and a Kaffir boy who spoke no word of English at all. The horses all over Cape Colony are perfectly dreadful to see—thin, un-groomed, small, but hard fleabitten animals that seem capable of any amount of distance, lame or not lame. We had 30 miles of sandy veldt ahead of us and 30 miles to return. We had a grand day of sunshine and neither Ory nor I could have believed that any country in the world could produce such a wonderful display of beautiful flowers. There was not a yard that wasn't beautiful the whole way. Hopefield, the place where we left the rail, was a typical Cape Colony town—chiefly blacks and Boers—very wide open streets, and only two or three of them at right angles to one another. Everywhere low spreading houses, a few shops, generally one or two stories high. A very wide sandy river with wide irregular banks and not much water, but what there is the colour of porter from veldt peat. Smaller and larger enclosures in which various grains are grown and where flocks of small cooing turtle doves are seen always on the move. Wonderful little birds appearing now and then of the most gorgeous colours—a flaming crimson finch with black velvet head and waistcoat. Another like a small Bird of Paradise quite tame and like a fat thrush for size, was brilliant gold or lemon, gold yellow, and velvet black. Then Weaver Birds everywhere, chattering and building nests, and most wonderful of all, the lovely flitting Sunbirds—the African Humming Birds—glittering emeralds and rubies and sapphires with yellow touches, and long delicate curved bills, and long thin tail feathers. How one admired these wonder-ful little creatures, so full of energy that they couldn't stop their chippering little squeezy song, as they flew from bush to bush, always settling on the topmost twigs to glitter and glance with their metallic colours in the sunshine. We immensely enjoyed our few hours at Hopefield, rambling along the river banks and watching the black and white Shrike, and the other larger Shrike.

Wilson and his wife left Hopefield in 'a Cape cart with a Kaffir boy to drive' and arrived eventually at Hoetjes Bay where they put up at 'a little low white-washed house . . . labelled "Hotel"', whose proprietor arranged for them to be rowed to the whaling station at Saldanha Bay the following morning[8].

We got a large sea-going fishing boat rowed by 6 Kaffirs, 4 oars, long sweeps, one **Sun 28 Aug** man steering and one off by turns sat in the bows. They were delightful, cheery boys, all coloured, but only 3 looked pure Kaffir, the others had Dutch blood in them. Only one spoke broken English, but all were respectful, always 'master' and 'misses' with every word. They rowed us across to Saldanha Bay, close past Marquis Island, that we might see the penguins[9] already collecting for nesting in small groups among the stones, crowds of dyker (cormorants)[10] of two species, one dark all over and under, the other much larger with white breast and neck. Dominican Black-backed Gulls[11] were abundant and a much smaller Red-billed Grey-backed Gull[12] with legs and bill nearly black still, probably turning red in the breeding season a little later on. There was also a bird like a Black Tern or Noddy on the rock. One met with penguins in the bay off and on and they were not shy.

The island on which they breed is a low one, almost bare white broken rock all over and very rocky on the shore. The Atlantic rollers came in from the N.W. and broke over the rounded granite shore to an immense height, sometimes 40–50 ft, and they looked splendid on such a still, clear blazing day while the sea apparently did nothing, for there was no sign of wave, except those long rolling swells which were 10–12 ft high and entirely hid the land from our sight when the boat sank in the trough. Marquis Island was nowhere more than 30 or 40 ft above sea level. On it was a square stone house inhabited two months in the year only by the egg collectors. Near by is a notice board forbidding anyone to land without a government permit. On the ground between the boulders everywhere was a buff coloured guano which contrasted with the white weathered granite rocks. These rocks were of immense size all along the coast and worn smooth and round by the heavy breakers. We saw on the way other interesting birds which I was glad to be able to identify for Ory. We saw the fine Black-browed Albatross (*Diomedea melanophris*) on the wing and sitting on the water quite close—also the Cape Hen (*Majaqueus æquinoctialis*), a large black Petrel with yellow bill—also 2 Black Oyster Catchers[13] which the Kaffirs called 'Devip'. They called the Cape Hen Petrels 'Batjorn'. Then there is an island just in sight called Malagas Island as it swarms with gannets (malagas)[14]. We saw one catch and swallow a largish fish close by and as he could not fly up with it we caught him and had a good look at his buff head and whitish bill and beautiful blue rings round the yellow eyes. His feet were very pale greenish white with a black line down each toe to the nail, a very quaint and characteristic marking. We then let him go again. We saw several beautiful little caves, one a perfect picture with flowers and half a dozen graves and crosses. These were, I found, the remains of an isolation camp during an outbreak of smallpox and another of enteric in Saldanha Bay. We called at 2 fishing smacks anchored in these coves—one called Salamana Bay—and the Kaffirs all helped themselves to water from a tank on the smacks. The owner, an old Africander fisherman, was mending his nets as a Sunday occupation—a delightful old world picture. He was an old greybeard and spoke excellent English—perhaps was English.

And so by the end of 2 hours' rowing we came round a little point and were in to the whaling station. The buildings were all galvanised iron. There were 2 whaling gunboats there and only two at this station, exactly like the one I was in at the Shetlands. There were also 3 ships, one a barque in seagoing trim and very fair condition which was brought here from Norway to be converted into a floating factory and remain here. The other two were mere hulks, both very old and brought out from Norway and no longer seaworthy. The one in which the owner, Captain Steen, whom we met here, came out last year, a 50 year old ship whaling barque, began to sink at St. Helena and had to be towed in to save dry-docking expenses and tinkering up as she was past saving. Capt. Steen was a dour looking Norwegian, but we got him interested and dragged a smile out of him eventually. We had many whaling friends in common and we discussed polar matters; he disbelieves every one, even Nansen[15], whose story he calls nonsense story, a great joke! He does not believe he ever separated from the *Fram*—Peary and Cook[16] he entirely discredits. He however showed us all over the factory and gave us a large amount of information as to expenses, profits, the figures of which were most interesting. Working expenses at this factory come to about £1,000 a month. The season lasts 6 to 7 months, from May to near Christmas. They get an average catch of 5 whales a week. Sometimes they may have 8 whales on hand at once and then they lose a lot as the factory cannot deal with them before the heat renders them partly rotten and the oil is deteriorated. They get chiefly Humpback Whales up to 60 ft. They also get Finners and the Northern Rorqual and the Blue Whale (*Balaenoptera sibbaldi*)[17]. They get the Atlantic Right Whale[18] but very rarely and the Cachalot[19] never. They call *B. rudolphi* the Minke[20] and Steen says it is never got here. He also told me that there is a great difference between *B. borealis*, or Seihval, of Africa and the Seihval of the North Sea[21]. He thinks they are different whales, as the African one gives whalebone worth only £3 per ton, while the North Sea species yields whalebone worth £8 a ton. Also the quantity of oil is much less in the West African Seihval. Yet they look and behave very much alike and both are called Seihval. But the whale they rely upon here is the Humpback, and there were the remains of two at the station when we visited it, so that I saw the fore flippers and the head and mouth; cut barnacles off and also saw the whalebone of about a dozen just cut out of the mouth. Black plates with greyish black hair. Sometimes the bone is patchy, black and white, but all I saw was black. The flippers were black on one side, and white on the other, the edge crenate and the barnacles collected on each prominence of the crenation. The whalebone, Steen says, is hardly worth the labour required to clean and pack it. Each plate has to be separated, washed with soda, and dried and packed into barrels or sacks, but the scraping, washing, and cleaning which was necessary left too little profit. This whale's whalebone is not nearly so valuable as that of the Right Whale which fetches £1,500 a ton[22]. That of the Humpback fetches only £300 a ton and it requires 4 whales to make a ton. So each whale gives but £70 to £80 worth of bone. They get over 200 Humpbacks in the season and seldom have to go far. Saldanha Bay is the only harbour and they always come in for bad weather. As a harbour it is perfect except for a strong suck back which is able to drag a ship from her moorings. No sea or swell ever gets in though, and apparently the only reason why it has not been developed is because Cape Town is so afraid of losing her trade. Saldanha is a far bigger, safer, and better harbour than Table Bay, but the latter even now has too little traffic to make it pay—so the Government refuse to allow the railway to be completed to Saldanha and Hoetjes Bay. It stops at Hopefield, though it is still being built to Vridenburg, but only on a narrow gauge—very narrow, about 2 feet from Kalabas Kraal where everything has to be transferred to the broad gauge to get on the Cape Town line; and this is bad for live stock and costly for everything else. An enormous amount of money has been sunk in endeavouring to make Saldanha Bay Co. a success.

We are staying in the company's hotel, very clean and quite nice, but no other visitors, though two Cape mounted police, an Africander commercial traveller and the schoolmistress all board here and have their meals with us. The schoolmistress is the best of them, an Africander Dutch, speaks perfect English and is a Miss Retief. The one policeman is an undergraduate of Trinity College Dublin who was to have been a medical student but was sent down after a year, then was apprenticed to a chemist and then came out here. The other policeman is an Africander born out here.

Ory and I returned from the whaling station very quickly by rail. The swell was still rolling in and the breakers were immense on the rocky coast. We had dinner at 5 p.m. and then went for a walk up the hills amid a perfect wealth of flowers. Scores of new and beautiful ferns and colours such as I have never seen or dreamed of in hot-houses or anywhere else. We were in a sort of enchanted land where the commonest things were all new and beautiful and one's foot crushed new beauties at every step. Wherever we turn we find new flowers . The variety of lovely irises and small lilies and daisies and marigolds and heaths and geraniums and heaven knows what, was quite bewildering and unreal. It beat what we saw yesterday on the veldt, if it could ever be beaten. We were led up this wonderful hill side by the sight of a large black and white buzzard with a red brown tail at the top where we could see he had his eyrie on a rock like a monument—a regular column of granite about 40 ft high. When we neared it the bird flew off and then two others appeared and these three handsome birds circled round and round us as we sat there and watched them with our glasses—whether two cocks and one hen, or vice versa I cannot say, they all looked much alike. They screamed and circled and then settled on rocks near us while we got sufficiently above the monolith to see the nest of sticks in which we believed we could distinguish two reddish eggs when the hen flew off. We also saw a number of large black lizards, about $1\frac{1}{2}$ ft long which ran over the weathered rocks and sunned themselves; sometimes we saw four at once. Then we found the gem of the day in a small bush of lemon scented shrub, very fine little leaves growing quite low, a most beautiful domed nest made of white cotton just held together like a thin shell by grass threads, not one of which showed inside, and this was a Sunbird's nest. Ory put the hen off and in it were two delicate little bluish eggs with brown spots, new laid and looking lovely in the pure white lining of cotton wool. It was the prettiest nest I have ever seen and we had been watching the brilliant little Sunbird all the afternoon, just like a humming bird, quite small with a long delicately curved bill and metallic green head, neck and breast and back, with a band of vivid crimson across the breast and below this greyish white. Their song and twitter was very characteristic and recognisable and they seemed fairly abundant, flashing this gorgeous colour in the sunlight. The hens were sober little brown birds. We have seen 2 or 3 species. This today was the commonest and most widespread, for we have seen him from Simon's Town to this place, flitting from the top of one bush to flash in sunshine from the top of another. The other species was larger and apparently emerald green all over with a darker rich green metallic gloss and 2 long central feathers to his tail, which flicked up as he flew. This bird we have seen but twice. The most striking bird we have seen was like a Bird of Paradise as big as a fat round thrush, but as though made of richest black velvet all over except the back which was covered with a thick mantle of vivid lemon yellow feathers. The contrast was perfectly wonderful. We also saw and watched a pair of yellow Canary Finches making their nest in a spurge which grew like a shrub, large and succulent, with yellow flowers and milk white sticky juice. Then the sun went down and we came home to supper and to write and to go to bed at 10 p.m. after a perfect day, full of interest and of wonderful beauty. We had no service here as there is no church save an English church school run by a West India nigger missioner, no white parson, either Dutch or British, and no resident doctor or nurse; the nearest being at Hopefield, or Cape Town, the former being a 30 mile drive, and Cape Town 116 miles, taking 36 to 48 hours at least in reply to a telegram.

Woke up to an overcast grey day blowing up from the S.E. so we had our ponies **Mon 29 Aug** inspanned and got away soon after 10 a.m. for Hopefield. We were in a Cape cart, very springy, with a canvas hood, seating 4 and taking a moderate amount of luggage behind. With our coloured boy as driver we were three. No one drives less than 2 ponies or mules in this country as the roads are too rough, full of deep holes in many places made in deep soft sand. We passed Vridenburg and came to Grootfontein where the ponies got a rest and we were again taken in by the peasant wife of the storekeeper and given tea and cakes. She was an Africander, a Jewess, married to a Russian Jew. Both spoke excellent English and refused all return for their hospitality, so I bought a pair of quaint, but large and strong leather shoes such as the Kaffirs wear here, after a pattern of their own, for 7/–, large enough to hold 2 or 3 pair of socks and therefore useful for me later on in the cold. The S.E. gale was gradually getting up all day and we saw constantly huge clouds of fine sand and dust being swept across the veldt accounting for an immense amount of transference.

Scott told me yesterday that he wished I could come on the *Terra Nova* as well as **Wed 31 Aug** himself, but he must send someone on ahead to Melbourne and he thinks it will be best for me to go as Chief of the Scientific Staff. It is pleasant for me, and for Ory too, to know that the people on the ship have done all they could to persuade Scott to let me come and not bother about the geologists till we reach Australia, but Scott, although he gave me the choice, was so evidently anxious for me to go ahead and prepare the way that I have consented to go. I fear it is no easy job there as the government has already published its intention of giving no money at all to Scott's expedition. That is the result of the proposal to start an Australian expedition and Mawson[23], an Australian, having failed to get appointed to our expedition on his own terms, will no doubt have Shackleton[24] to back him. I have to get in touch with all these Australian people, and especially with David, and smooth out any disagreeables. I have letters to Dr. Fitchett[25], who is head of a big training college at Melbourne, and is the author of *Fights for the Flag*, &c. The happy family on the *Terra Nova* is still the happiest crew imaginable. It is marvellous that so many men shoved together at random into a ship in which comfort is almost absent, should have shaken down without a quarrel through the whole voyage. I think Scott felt that he was not getting to know his people well enough before reaching New Zealand and I think he was right in going on the ship for this next part of the voyage. I have to go and be diplomatic and tactful at Melbourne and find out how the land lies before the *Terra Nova* gets there. Admiral Egerton has given orders that everything needed for the ship shall be done and we have paid very little indeed for any work or stores or materials, and everything has been very well done. My grouse work is done and sent off—a very heavy job and most difficult at sea where the only possible work hours for me were from 4 a.m. to breakfast time—what with pumping the bilge out, trimming coal, re-stowing holds, occasional stoking, hauling on the ropes, in making or taking in sail and a hundred other jobs, there never seemed any opportunity for reading or writing.

On 11 September Wilson and his wife, together with Mrs. Evans and Mrs. Scott, boarded R.M.S. Corinthic *bound for Hobart, Tasmania. On arriving at Hobart they travelled by train to Launceston, thence by steamer to Melbourne. Wilson then went to Sydney to raise funds for the expedition. The diary resumes on 12 October with Wilson back in Melbourne awaiting the arrival of* Terra Nova.

Diomedea exulans   S.P.R.I. 1635

4.

R.M.S. CORINTHIC.

Wednesday. Sept. 14·10.   40°58 S.   34° 41′ E.   at noon.
10 a.m.   (300 miles)

D. regia – absent.

D. exulans. 7 or 8 fully adults or younger.

D. melanophrys. 1 or 2 adults. yell. bill, orange tip.

Thal. culminatus. Greyhead, black bill with broad
orange culmen + tip. + orange yell. stripe on
under mandible. broad black margin to the
underwing in front. narrower behind.

Diomedea sp. Smaller than melanophrys, +
with white head but black bill. unyielding
white under the wing. Though doubt
looks like an adult bird — though doubt
whether it is an immature melanophrys.

Phoebetria fuliginosa – dark grey type. 1.

Ossifraga gigantea. 1 black or grey which looks young.

Majaqueus aequinoctialis – 1 only.

Puffinus cinereus. 20 or 30. These birds travel
with us. When they come down to look at
stuff that routed be food – the feet drop & they
settle quickly along the surface, + they
decide the food is not suitable.

Daption capensis. 1 only.

Prion of. sp. good many.

Oest. macroptera – 1 or 2. One was astern to day
with a black Ossifraga or Majaqueus. the three
sizes were very distinct.

Cymodroma melanogaster 1 only.

Afternoon.

D. regia. At least 3 of these turned up –
all uniformly marked apparently –
pure white over back + wings
to the second joint.

D. regia. Several of the large Diomedeas have had a
scarlet mark on the side of the neck
like a red collar.

4

AUSTRALIA AND NEW ZEALAND

Wed 12 Oct WE had arranged to go for a long day's motor drive into the gumtree bush with the Charles Rendalls[1]. They called for us early at Menzies Hotel, bringing lunch with them, and I arranged that we should call at one or two villages with post offices on the way in order that I might ring up the hotel to know if the ship's arrival had been telegraphed in from the head of Melbourne Bay. We expected four hours warning, but had no notion where the *Terra Nova* would anchor or whether she would come into Port Melbourne and go alongside anywhere. I expected her to arrive today. We started off in the motor and had a very good forenoon run out towards Dandenong. We were going much further after lunch to a part where the 'bush' is still intact and full of tree fern. Most of the bush in Victoria is gumtree bush more or less open—but much more open than the gumtree bush of Tasmania. We also passed through a good deal of titree bush, pronounced 'teatree', a thick bush which grows up to 15 feet or 20 with a number of very small dark green leaves and small white flowers rather like jasmine. In some places the titree bush was half and half titree and wild jasmine—the jasmine being far more full of a creamy white flower than ours and growing as a thick bush instead of a creeper, wonderfully sweet and the two together looking in places like a snow sprinkled shrubbery with its abundance of small white flower. The gumtree bush is of course quite a different thing—tall gaunt white or bluish grey or buff grey trunks reaching up to a hundred feet with tattered bark dropping off in rolls everywhere and hanging down in long festoons. And amongst the taller trunks are young gumtrees of every imaginable size and age, but always gumtrees so far as one can see from a railway running through. One went through an immense amount of standing bush—but far more of clearings. The method of clearing seems to be the same everywhere. First the young growth is cut and the older trees are ringed some feet from the ground. The trees then die and are left standing until the leaves have all dropped off dead and the poor old tree looks like a gaunt white skeleton. Isolated trees are left at a fair distance apart from one another to give shelter to the cattle and sheep and to protect them from the sun. They also save the grass and prevent drought. It is not an unknown thing for a large tract of country which had an abundant supply of water when covered by bush, i.e. forest, to become absolutely waterless when the land is cleared for a sheep run. When the ringed trees are dead they are burnt and one sometimes passes through a tract of country where this is going on at night time and the effect is very fine. However, the bush that we saw in Australia and in Tasmania

48

was nothing like so grand or so interesting or so varied and picturesque as the bush of New Zealand or the Auckland Islands. We ought, however, to have gone further afield with the Charles Rendalls—we should then have seen more of the mixed Australian bush with tree fern which always increases the beauty and the interest. As it was, the very first place that we reached at 1 o'clock, with a telephone to Melbourne, gave us the news that the *Terra Nova* had been signalled entering Melbourne Bay and that she would be coming into port in about 6 hours. It therefore became necessary for me to return and so we lunched by the wayside and came back to Melbourne. We saw by the way a number of the Australian Pied Crow, or Crow Shrike, or as they often call it here the Australian Magpie. There are two birds of the kind which one sees constantly everywhere—the White-backed Magpie and the Black-backed Magpie, both conspicuously piebald black and white, and the latter often known as the Piping Crow, because it has a loud piping note and can whistle a tune. We also saw the Laughing Jackass out wild in the country. They call it here the Cuckooburrer, or the Bushman's clock, as it laughs loudly early in the morning and late at night, often on a chimney top. Then we also saw most magnificent parrakeets and wonderfully coloured lorikeets, which are much bigger. It is an epoch in one's life, I think, to see these beautiful long-tailed lorikeets on the wing in their own country. They fly with extraordinary energy and rapidity, but we had a good sight of them and their wonderful colouring—yellow, orange, crimson, blue and green. They seem very long and big in the head and neck compared with the rest of the body and wings. The tail is long. It may be that the weight in front necessitates a very dashing flight and that is what they appear to have. We saw other birds some of which I failed to identify. One was a sulphur yellow winged bird as big as a pigeon. Another was a kestrel, and another a much bigger hawk like a harrier. But perhaps the most fascinating little bird of the lot was the Blue Wren (*Malurus cyaneus*) which Ory and I watched for a long time and quite fell in love with at the botanical gardens at Melbourne. It is coloured with a sort of sapphire blue and jet black like velvet

and has a long tail, the whole bird being like a Long-tailed Tit, only the tail is carried right over the back and head like a wren's, while the little jewel-like bird hops about on the grass plots catching minute insects. We also watched one drying himself after bathing and he allowed us to watch him at a few feet. It was in these gardens also that we saw the large Australian Cuckoo and quite a number of the olive grey Honeyeaters which have brush tongues, i.e. tongues ending in a little frayed out paint brush for getting the honey out of flowers. We also heard their beautiful bell-like notes which are in one passage very like the full notes of a Nightingale. Here also we watched a number of lovely little blue and grass green parrakeets flying from the top of one tree to another chattering like thieves all the while. One other Australian bird struck me as being very beautiful—a Chat, rather the size and elegant shape of a Goldfinch, but pure white with a few jet black markings. This little bird settled on the ship while we were still in sight of Melbourne. The black and white Fantail Flycatchers were very fascinating also, and the Waxeyes, both of which I saw at Sydney. Also in Tasmania I saw a small flock, now and then, of Bee-eaters in the gumtree bush. We had so much business to do in Australia that it was only by accident that we saw any bird life at all, but it must be exceedingly interesting. In the zoo at Melbourne we saw a number of the rarer and larger birds of the north and west and centre of Australia, but they are not to be seen wild anywhere near Sydney or Melbourne. The Frogmouth (*Podargus*) is a quaint creature which has the habit of standing like a stick, and is coloured like a Nightjar, so that amongst tree trunks and branches it is quite inconspicuous.

There are other things to speak of at the zoo, but to return to the day in question, namely Wednesday Oct. 12/10, when we heard from Dandenong that the *Terra Nova* had been sighted. We drove straight back to Menzies Hotel, Melbourne, found Mrs. Scott and Mrs. Evans and went off—the four of us—with a sackful of mails to Port Melbourne by train. We got there about 5 p.m. No sign or word of the *Terra Nova*. So we had tea at an inn and waited at the petrol canning factory which is supplying us with Shell motor spirit for the motor sledges. It was pouring with rain, but we got a motor launch and went out into the bay to see if we could sight the ship. We got as far as the lighthouse and asked them and they told us that she was still four miles out. So we returned to shelter and waited and then went out again. It was now dusk—pouring rain—and ships' lights guided us. We went to several of them, but none turned out to be the *Terra Nova* so in we came again. All this time the sea was getting up and it soon became quite dark. We were all soaked through. Luckily it was not very cold, even out in the bay, but it was now so late that I thought the chances of our getting on board the *Terra Nova*, even if she came in, were small as the sea was distinctly more dangerous for our crank little motor launch each time we went out. So I tried to persuade the three wives to return to the hotel at Melbourne while I went out once more to make a final attempt to put my sack full of mails on board the *Terra Nova* that night. We were telephoning here, there and everywhere all the while to find out if anyone knew where the *Terra Nova* really was, but we couldn't get any definite news until about 9 p.m. when the lighthouse people in the bay telephoned us that she had just then anchored about half a mile outside their light. So once more we set out—the wives with me and the mail bag. It was pitch dark and the sea was very bad indeed for our beastly little boat. But we reached the *Terra Nova* and shouted. She was at anchor by the bows and had swung round to the wind, so that there was no lee side except under the stern, where we should have been smashed under the counter. So we first tried one side and got into a sudden rocking sea off her sides which all but upset us. It was quite impossible to go in close or to stop our motor there without being swamped or capsized, so we raced by her shouting our messages and receiving good news, and this we did three times without getting near enough for a line to send up the mail bag. The other side of the ship seemed exactly the same and we almost decided to leave the mails till morning. But it seemed worth one more try and so we ran in once again and found the sea was nothing like so bad on the other side. It was all pitch dark and we were dancing about like a cork up and down and rocking so quickly and so freely that everyone had to keep in the bottom of the boat and hang on to the seats to keep in the boat at all. However, they all thought we could come alongside, on the ship, so alongside we went. It was for them on board, Captain Scott and Lieutenant Evans, to say whether I should risk drowning their wives now, so as they seemed in favour of it I went in and they soon dropped down the side of the ship into our launch, and I went on board with the mails. They were all delighted and so were we to have succeeded at last. We didn't remain there long. Scott and Evans came off with us and by half past ten we were on our way back again. Everyone was well and we had a very jolly meeting. We got back to Melbourne by the last train and it was past 12 when we got to Menzies Hotel and, after some cocoa, turned in to bed. Ory behaved like a brick all through our difficulties in the bay, but in future I hope it will never fall to my lot to have more than one wife at a time to look after, at any rate in a motor launch, in a running sea at night time.

Was spent chiefly in business, giving Captain Scott all the information we had **Thurs 13 Oct** gained and handing over the reins to him. Up to date we had seen a good many of the Ministry and their Private Secretaries, the State Governors and their wives and aides, the Governor General, Lord Dudley, and his Chamberlain, Lord R. Neville at Sydney—the Prime Minister (Federal) Mr. Fisher[2] who I caught and had an interview with the day he left for the Cape, he being the Premier who had written six weeks before to tell Captain Scott to expect nothing from Australia. Hughes, the Chancellor of the Exchequer, took his place pro tem on his leaving. I also saw O'Malley, the Minister for Home Affairs, and his Secretary Colonel Miller, and the State Meteorologist Mr. Hunt. O'Malley told me of his experiences gold prospecting in Alaska. He was very American, a man with long dull red hair brushed back from his forehead, and a sandy beard, a large shirt front (or a dicky?) with an enormous fixing in the centre of five opals (this was

9 a.m. at his office) and a loose purple suit. He quoted 'Sockertes' to me and gave me a long account of how he scored off a mining friend of his who thought he had diddled him out of a silver mine with the help of a starving donkey, who really scraped up the silver and discovered the mine, and eventually got on to a semi-religious discussion, and declared that someone out here, the Opposition I imagine, was 'crucifying Christ afresh.' I then thought it time to go, and as he had given me about three quarters of an hour of Government time, for which of course all the Members here receive £400 a year, and his of course at a much higher rate than a Member, I think I was right. However, they are not all alike. I found the Federal Premier, Fisher, a very straightforward sort of chap, quiet and rather shy, looking uncomfortable in a frock coat and tall hat at a Governor's 'at home', but with the keenest brown eyes one could wish to see. I did all I could to persuade him we were a worthy object on which to throw away £5,000 of federal money. He said he had told Scott not to expect help from here, but I reminded him he had helped Shackleton. He said, only because Shackleton had come out there insufficiently equipped and unable to proceed further—in fact they helped him because he was 'stuck'. I told him I thought our position was more deserving of help for we were not 'stuck'. We were admirably equipped with a bigger staff of better workers than any previous expedition, and all we asked for was the funds to allow of an additional year's work. All he could say was that if two men were running a race and one fell and broke his leg, one's duty would be to help the one with the broken leg. But he knew he was talking rot and

promised to see what could be done to overcome their former decision. He allowed that Scott's appeal had come at an unfortunate time when they had just voted £10,000 for a British Association meeting some weeks ago. He thought he could see some people before leaving for the Cape to reverse the decision. So on the whole I was hopeful after seeing him. At the same garden party which Mabel and Ory also attended (Frank[3] was away in Tasmania) we met a number of interesting people—the Governor of Victoria and his wife, Sir Thos. Gibson-Carmichael[4] and Lady C., whom we met at Colinton, Edinburgh, some 5 years ago and who came to tea with us there with Dr. Inquair. It was funny to meet them here as 'Their Excellencies'. We also met Sir John and Lady Forrest[5] who did a good deal of exploring in central Australia. He is now an enormously stout and apoplectic looking man with a multitude of stars and garters, but still talked very enthusiastically of his methods of transport and relay work in central water-less deserts. He says never turn back for anything yourself but always have relays and depots coming on and on and on after you so long as you are advancing at all; relays must never stop coming on in your steps but you must never take a step back to fetch them but go forward again the moment they come up with you. His lady was a jolly old stout body too. We met also various university professors and their wives and a Doctor [   ] who was a very keen naturalist and was also Consul for Turkey and a friend of the Wilsons. Captain Boyle and Mrs. Boyle, an exceed-ingly pretty woman, was the Governor's Aide. We also met General and Mrs. Fitzpatrick, both very nice and friendly, and a Mrs. Reynolds, wife of Commander Reynolds, R.N.—all friends of Frank and Mabel. We owe Mabel an immense debt for her extraordinary kindness in introducing us all round and to such very nice people—far the nicest in Melbourne—and she took such infinite pains to help us in everything we had to do, besides entertaining us and making us feel at home there. We felt we always had a refuge to fly to in her house and a place to go to for tea, whether she and John[6] were at home or not. And it was delightful to see how all the officers on our ship appreciated her. John is a splendid little chap, cram full of fun. Campbell, our 1st Lieutenant, was very fond of him and sent word to say that unless Major Wilson brought John with him he wouldn't be allowed on board. John has the merriest way with him and always a twinkle in his eyes—he and his mother are very great friends.

It was very unfortunate that Frank should have had business in Tasmania the whole time we were in Melbourne. He met us at Launceston on our arrival from Hobart by train—and we saw him just for a few minutes as we went on board the *Loongana* to cross over to Melbourne. Frank returned to Melbourne the very day that we were sailing. And they all three came on board at the same time that the Governor's party, the Carmichaels, also came on board to see us off. They brought me a magnificent bunch of roses. John was wearing a *Terra Nova* ribbon on his sailor's straw hat. We were very sorry indeed to see the last of them all, but I knew that Ory would see more of them. We then weighed anchor and went off up the bay spending the day swinging ship and doing magnetic work. But this must come in its proper place. I ought to be writing about Thursday, Oct. 13th, the day after the ship's arrival. She was at Melbourne from Oct 12th to Oct. 17th. On the 13th, as I said, I handed over my business reins to Captain Scott and for the first time

53

here had the leisure to go for an afternoon with Ory to the botanical gardens which are very beautifully arranged round a sort of serpentine piece of water with Australian moorhens on it, much bluer birds than our own and with red beaks, plaques and feet, more like the New Zealand Pukeko. The gardens were full of interesting birds and native plants—palms, tree ferns and all sorts of weird flowering shrubs. In the evening we had a very jolly dinner at the hotel with all the *Terra Nova* officers.

Fri 14 Oct Partly business and partly with Ory. In the evening we went to a very grand Lord Mayor's ball given in honour of the Dutch men of war who were in Melbourne Harbour with a couple of cruisers and gun boats. They were not very impressive people, the older officers being stout, bald and ugly, and the younger officers, with one or two exceptions, being fairly on the way to becoming stout, bald and ugly. But their uniforms were smart, and as the Governor and his consort and aides and various ambassadors in their uniforms and decorations were there, and Ministers and civic dignitaries in sort of knickerbocker court suits and bows and ribbons at their necks and military uniforms of various kinds, many quite pretty ones of volunteer contingents and medical corps, as well as of the regular army a few, the show was altogether quite a good one. It was held in the Town Hall, which is a fine building. We didn't stay long after we had spoken to various people. We had a talk to the Governor and the Lady Governor and his court; Captain and Mrs. Boyle were the nicest of them. Also the Premier (Federal) Mr. Hughes, and the Turkish ambassador, who was a naturalist. Mabel came with us, and of course had many friends there. She is a good dancer, but there were so many people that it was impossible to find partners for introduction.

Sat 15 Oct Bernard's[7] birthday, and many happy returns. We did our packing and got my luggage down to the ship by teatime. In the evening I had to attend a dinner given us by the University professors. Some were very nice and the dinner was pleasant. Professor Baldwin Spencer[8] was president and Scott and I sat on either side of him and had to speak afterwards—but it was not a formidable business and we all enjoyed it.

Sun 16 Oct I had to go on board as the ship was leaving her moorings after the Governor's party had inspected her. As I said before Frank turned up with Mabel and John and we had a very jolly and quiet send off as it was Sunday morning. Ory went off with the Scotts and Mrs. Evans to Menzies Hotel. It was nice bright weather. Scott goes to Sydney and follows us by a liner, so I once again went on the *Terra Nova* from Melbourne to Christchurch N.Z. after a disagreeably businessful fortnight in Melbourne seeing so many bigwigs every day and agitating ministers for a grant from the Federal Government. As it turned out we got all we asked for, namely £5,000 in all; £2,500 from the Federal Government and £2,500 from a private individual[9]. So it was worth going to Melbourne for. The thing was really worked for us by Professor David and Professor Spencer and Lieutenant Evans as a Welshman with his arm around the Prime Minister's waist—his name being Hughes—and his nationality in accordance with his name. This got us the first half and the other half was given by a man who was disgusted with his Government for not giving us the whole sum at once. There is much feeling between Melbourne—the capital of Victoria—and Sydney, the capital of New South Wales. What Melbourne starts Sydney will have nothing to do with. Hence the absurd plan which is to be carried out at an enormous expense of building a Federal Capital at Yass, half way between the two—now nothing but bush. However, having got away from Melbourne itself the *Terra Nova* was next hung up by a request from the flagship *Powerful* that we should all dine on board that night and give the Admiral an opportunity to inspect the *Terra Nova* the next morning. So we had to do this, and at 7 p.m. we were fetched by a pinnace and all taken to the flagship. I had to sit by the Commander and had a major of marines on my left. The Admiral dined alone with Captain Scott in his cabin. We were all in a large wardroom very prettily decorated and we had a very good dinner, and then sat on the quarter-deck and smoked and went on board the *Terra Nova* late. Some of the officers were exceedingly pleasant and I like the Flag Captain particularly—can't remember his name. They all were very different in appearance from the Dutch officers. The Chaplain was a man from Pembroke, Cambridge.

We anchored for the night close under the flagship *Powerful*, 13,000 tons I think **Mon 17 Oct** she was. Our White Star liner was 12,000. The *Terra Nova* at the same rating about 700. We felt rather small but looked very neat. The Admiral and his officers came on board early and we were all introduced and trotted him round. He was a most intelligent questioner and seemed to go to the heart of every detail at once and was really very pleasant. Our cat was inspected. We have a small muscular black cat called Nigger who came on board as an almost invisible kitten in London or Cardiff. He has grown stiff and small and very strong and has a hammock of his own with the 'hands' under the fo'c's'le. The hammock is about 2 ft long with proper lashings and everything made of canvas. A real man o' war hammock with small blankets and a small pillow, and the cat was asleep in his hammock with his black head on the pillow and the blankets over him. The Admiral was much amused and while he was inspecting the sleeping cat Nigger opened his eyes, looked at the Admiral, yawned in his face and stretched out one black paw and then turned over and went to sleep again. It was a very funny show and amused the Admiral and his officers as much as anything. Nigger has learned to jump into his hammock which is slung under the roof with the others and creeps in under the blankets with his head on the tiny pillow. When the party left we all at once got into our old and dirty rig and prepared to make sail. It was a funny coincidence that Evans, now in command of the *Terra Nova*, had been told in the old days when he was a midshipman by this very man, now an Admiral, that he had better leave the service as he would never do any good in it! His manner was different now, and Evans took the opportunity of a fair wind to show that he could manage the ship he was in charge of anyhow. So it was all arranged that the moment the Admiral's party left us we were all to get into dirty rig and make sail and leave the flagship and Melbourne harbour under full sail. It came off beautifully and we got all sail set and sailed down the line of battleships looking most beautiful. We were vigorously cheered by each and when we passed the flagship quite close we all manned the rigging and gave them a huge cheer. It was quite a thrilling experience and was all done so quickly and neatly and successfully. Not such a very easy thing to manoeuvre our old sailing ship in enclosed waters, but the wind and weather favoured us and at last we were off and away at about 8 knots and, notwithstanding that it meant another fortnight away from Ory, we and I were jolly glad to leave the place.

Tues 18 Oct Made a splendid start with a fair wind and steam as well getting out of the bay and through the Bass Straits, the navigation of which requires care on account of the innumerable islands and the frequency of bad weather and fogs. We had land in sight off and on for a day or two and also a few land birds from Australia and Tasmania and a very strange flock of moths. The whole sea was covered with them and the ship was full of them, the air also was full of them. Wherever one looked the air was full of them—large and medium-sized, fat-bodied geometer moths, like yellow under wings but all brown and grey. When we shook out our jib-sails, which had been furled on leaving Melbourne, about a hundred moths flew out of the folds. The cat and our two dogs were eating them and choking over them all day and we were stepping on them everywhere. It was a huge flight, either blown off from the bush or migrating—but I never saw anything like it. On the ship they were with us for about three days.

Wed 19 Oct Our engagement day. And I began early hours again with cocoa at 4 a.m., which Cherry-Garrard now makes for the morning watch. The Norwegian Gran, who used to make it as midshipman of the watch, has been allowed to go forward by liner to ascend Mount Cook in New Zealand (It didn't come off). Gran had begun to object to making cocoa for the morning watch on the plea that Campbell treated him as a 'drumstick', which he didn't like. We found he meant a 'domestic', and so Cherry-Garrard volunteered to become the 'drumstick' and makes cocoa for me at the same time. We are again a *very* merry party. Captain Scott and Gran and Simpson are away, all going to N.Z. by mail steamers. Evans

Diomedea sp. S.P.R.I. 1629

'July 1. 1910. Sunset. Clouds beginning to form' S.P.R.I. 67/1/4

'July 22. 1910. 6.15 a.m. looking W. Moon and afterglow'

Diomedea exulans   S.P.R.I. 1634

and I are once more together and I find everything as genial and pleasant on the ship as it was when I left them all at the Cape. I dropped into the old routine at once without difficulty, except as to finding my clothing and gear etc., all of which had been moved once or twice. But it is all in the ship and will turn up. Meanwhile I wear other people's and they do just as well. We saw a large school of dolphins today and I got drawings. On the voyage from the Cape to Melbourne Cherry-Garrard has been busy collecting. They added to our bird collection a Sooty Albatross, a Great Grey Shearwater, a Black-bellied Stormy Petrel[10], a Banks's Whale Bird[11] and about half a dozen Cape Pigeons[12]. We were now onwards surrounded by albatrosses, petrels and shearwaters, and my diary becomes rather a record of birds than of other business, but it was a most enjoyable trip.

Thurs 20 Oct Up at 7 a.m. only. Glorious sunny day. Spent the forenoon trying to catch albatrosses with a bolas arrangement, but they were rather shy. We tie a weight— a bolt or piece of iron—on the end of a strong light line and throw it over the albatross's wing as he sails close by the stern of the ship. Some days one has great success in this way. We saw two distinct species of dolphin today, a very handsome pair, jet black and pure white, a species I cannot find described anywhere, and the ordinary southern Dusky Dolphin in large numbers. Many birds.

Fri 21 Oct Up at 4.30 a.m. and a grand sunrise. Cherry-Garrard had lines out and caught three albatrosses today, a Sooty Albatross, a Wandering Albatross and a Black-browed Mollymawk[13]. After breakfast we had them all photographed and they made good pictures. I spent the day painting their heads. We also saw some Northern Rorqual Whales today and a lot of birds. I counted 18 albatrosses following us at one time. The painting had to be done in sunshine on the upper deck, standing, and with the ship rolling everything about, myself included. It was very difficult. We saw another large school of Dusky Dolphins constantly breaking the surface all round the ship as well as under the bows, but not so often leaping clear of the water.

57

Sat 22 Oct Up at 5, reading and writing. And again spent the whole day painting the albatross heads with their mouths open. The different species have very different tongues and palates and colour in the mouth. Cherry-Garrard began skinning them and we have also taught Abbott, one of the bluejackets, to skin birds. Abbott is the seaman that has some friends in Stoke. He knows the Crumps and Jim[14] sent me a letter about him. He is an exceedingly nice gentlemanly fellow and a tower of

Diomedea sp.   S.P.R.I. 1629

strength. Heaps of birds today which I keep a special book for—but I will give a list later of what we saw on this trip. We also saw another Northern Rorqual, surely one of the most ubiquitous of all, as it is very abundant in the northern seas. Saw this one very close and heard his blow.

Sun 23 Oct Head wind all day. Up at 4 to read and write till breakfast in the foremost cabin which is at present full of books and gear which I therefore get to myself at this hour. All day went skinning albatrosses. We entered a belt of fog and mist at 5 p.m. and though we had a crowd of birds with us all day we lost nearly all of them except 6 or 7 Black-browed Mollymawks which followed us in the mist.

Mon 24 Oct Up at 4.45, reading and writing. Cleaning albatrosses all day on from breakfast till 8 p.m. Cherry-Garrard and Abbott also at the same job. These enormous birds take a great deal of time and have to be done on the upper deck with everything blowing and rolling about. We sighted the first New Zealand light this evening, but still have a long way to go round the Bluff and up the east coast. Lots of birds.

Tues 25 Oct Up at 4 a.m. Light enough to see Stewart Island ahead on our starboard bow above a fog bank, and on the port beam a chain of snow-topped mountains with the rosy light of a magnificent sunrise on them and on the snow. Sketched, read and wrote from 4 a.m. to 7 a.m., having had cocoa at 4. Then the seawater hose on deck over one at 7. Then dress and breakfast at 8 a.m. This has been the morning routine—and the sea water is none too cold to be most agreeable and refreshing. Generally I am in bed by 10 p.m. and am called regularly before 12 midnight again to a huge mug of thick cocoa—just to help me to go to sleep again. Nelson always makes this. They all declare that nothing wakes me now like a spoon being stirred in an enamelled iron mug—and I must confess it has a better chance than any alarum clock, and is much more fattening! We have now strong head winds which are delaying us, and fogs also, so we are steaming all the way. And today I spent trimming coal in the bunkers with Cherry-Garrard and Wright, till nearly teatime from 9 a.m. onwards. Hard work and headachy from the gas given off by the Australian coal. Have a nasty thumb from an albatross bite—one of them took a piece out about an inch long. Their beaks are like scissors and they are strong and quick to bite. But this has been quite a clean wound. We are now getting a lot of coastal birds. Black-backed Dominican Gulls, Giant Petrels, Diving Petrels[15], etc. Beautiful sunrises most of these days and land near enough now all day to see the bush with glasses.

Wed 26 Oct Up at 4.15 to a magnificent stormy sunrise, gorgeous with fiery rose and orange and purple and deep blue. Saw a party of Humpback Whales (*Megaptera*) going south. Very heavy swell dead ahead but at 2 p.m. the wind suddenly came round and blew fair till evening, right against the swell, making an unusually confused sea. We had a festive dinner for Evans' birthday and I had to propose his health with a speech. The table was decorated with flags and bunting and champagne and after dinner we had a general rag, which means turning individuals' clothes inside out for some imaginary offence. This is known as 'furling topgallant sails' and it generally ends in half the mess scrapping together with most of their clothes torn off—and sometimes all.

Thurs 27 Oct All the forenoon trimming coal in the bunkers with Cherry-Garrard—and the coal is now patent fuel which has a horrible burning action on one's eyes and skin as it is full of pitch and resin. The scalding comes on in an hour or two after one has bathed and lasts for many hours, sometimes till the following day. In the Navy they insist on goggles being worn by everyone who handles these patent fuel blocks. Was up at 4.30 a.m. to read and write and sketch. We have lovely sunrises and sunsets and lots of birds. No wind and a good deal of fog.

Fri–Sat 28– 29 Oct Up at 4 a.m. beautiful morning. All hands have been cleaning ship—painting and washing paintwork above and below. We are spick and span and trim and neat to come in to Lyttelton, and we were all in collars and blue suits by breakfast time, and then came out the harbour tug and the medical officers, and we entered the Heads and came alongside where Ory and Mrs. Evans and Mr. Kinsey[16], our faithful friend, were waiting. Constance and Lily Bowen came down later and we had our letters and then went up to Christchurch after having some tea at a teashop in Lyttelton. So happily ended our voyage to New Zealand and all safe. I found that Ory was staying with Lady Bowen[17] at Middleton Grange, Riccarton, 3 miles out of Christchurch—the place and the people I most like to be with of all here. Ory and I then called on the Kinseys, Papanui Road, and went out to Middleton with our luggage. Lady Bowen met us.

A month in Lyttelton was passed in a round of social and business engagements while the Terra Nova *was overhauled and equipped for the Antarctic. The diary resumes as the ship leaves Lyttelton for Port Chalmers, her last port of call before heading south.*

Sat 26 Nov The *Terra Nova* sailed from Lyttelton at 3 p.m. Ory and I had come from Middleton where we were staying with the Bowens and had lunched with Captain Forbes on the huge 13,000 ton steamer *Ruapehu*, where were also the Kinseys and the Scotts and about twenty other people, mainly directors of the shipping company, and their friends. I sat between Mrs. Wigram[18] and Mrs. Kinsey. Mr. and Mrs. Rhodes were there. After lunch we went to the *Terra Nova* and fetched Mrs. Evans and Ory and I then took her on to the bridge of the *Warama* from which we all watched the send off, which was very pretty and very exciting, for the harbour was crowded with people and every ship in the place was decked with flags, and sirens and hooters and gunfiring to say nothing of a number of tugs and small craft literally loaded up with friends and sight-seers from Christchurch and Lyttelton, all to accompany the *Terra Nova* out of the harbour and out to the Heads. Ory and I remained behind to follow the ship on Monday by train to Dunedin. Mrs. Evans went off that afternoon with Mr. and Mrs. Wyatt to join her husband at Dunedin by steamer. When Ory and I got back to Christchurch we went out to Middleton first to tea and then came back to supper and to spend the evening with the Kinseys at Warrimoo. We very much enjoyed the evening with them, they are dear good friends both to the expedition and even more to us. Mrs. Kinsey has been a real brick to Ory. Kinsey is our representative in New Zealand and has full powers to deal with everything that crops up there in connection with the expedition in Captain Scott's absence. We spent most of the evening examining their treasures—pictures, china, jewels, agates and books. Kinsey gave me a beautiful sheath knife for the south and a small axe, and various fur and felt mits. He is one of the best in the world—a man to be trusted with everything in the world that one most values, and he was good enough to tell me to tell Ory to realise that there was nothing in the world he wouldn't do for her if he could if she would only ask him. We got back to Middleton before eleven.

Advent Sunday. Holy Communion after the midday service at Riccarton Church. **Sun 27 Nov** Ory and I and Lady Bowen went to the forenoon service and remained to the Holy Communion. It turned out a rainy day, but after the drought of five months from which the South Island of New Zealand has suffered during this spring and summer, every living thing looked so grateful and smelt so delicious that we rejoiced in it quite as much as in the continual sunshine which we have been so enormously enjoying together ever since we came to New Zealand. Even though our time has been much taken up with work at the ship in the port and in business and in social duties, we have really had a very great deal of real happiness together up to the very last and the people we have to thank without a shadow of doubt are the Bowens. Dear old Lady Bowen and Lily Bowen—both have allowed us to live at Middleton the whole of our long stay in Christchurch, exactly as though it was our home. Even when we left Wellington and stayed with the Bishop Wallis and his wife there, our rooms were kept with all our things about exactly as we left them for our return. And this Sunday is our last quiet day here together, and we really did enjoy it. We wrote letters together all the afternoon, and got our packing finished and went to bed early as we have to be early up for the 8 a.m. express to Dunedin tomorrow.

We were up early but Ory was up the first and made me tea, dear girl! And then **Mon 28 Nov** we were given our breakfast at a quarter to 7, when dear Lady Bowen and Lily were actually up to see us off, which was a sad thing to remember too, for I don't think the dear old lady was a bit happy over it and I was made to promise to come straight back there first on our arrival back—and that surely was a promise I was only too pleased to make. After the Bowens, I have to go to the Wigrams on our return. They are all too good and kind to us—every one. We had a cab to catch the train at Christchurch and there we were met by other kind friends who came to see Captain and Mrs. Scott off as well by the same train. But one sweet old lady, Mrs. Anderson, came all the way from Opawa to see my Ory off and to give her some lovely flowers which were full of scent and reminded us of Dad's send off posies that I took out, all the lemon-scented verbena, and have it with me here on the ship dried. So full of reminiscences of Westal. Ory and I had a first class carriage to ourselves all the way from 8 a.m. till we reached Dunedin at 4 p.m. The Scotts had another to themselves. We enjoyed our journey and though there were only three or four stops on the way, we were met by friends at three of them and I also saw Peel Forest country where Ory will go for the first few days of her temporary widowhood to stay with the Dennistouns[19]. At another stop we were met by the Rhodeses—and at Rakaia Anne Hardy[20] waved to us from the store which lies close to the station. Arrived at Dunedin we were met by Nelson and Lillie on the platform, and while Lillie stayed to see Ory with her luggage up to the hotel, I had to go off at once with Nelson to Port Chalmers where the ship was lying. Ory knows, and knew then, why. I had to remain there until the 6.15 train brought me back, then I had a rush to the hotel to dress and go with Ory to the Moore's to dinner party at which the Scotts also were and several other friends of ours. Mrs. Moore is the Kinsey's daughter, and a good soul. After this we were driven to a dance given in honour of our officers and here we had to stay for an hour or two. It was a funny dance as none of our people had dress clothes and all turned up in clean tennis shirts, flannels, or whites, or any other clean garb they happened to have handy. Ory and I came away and back to the hotel, and there we were very happy together for the last evening for some time—poor dear.

Tues 29 Nov We were very happy together and after breakfasting with some of the *Terra Nova* people—Evans and his wife and others—Ory and I went to call on Professor Benham[21] at the museum and did some small shopping, and then by train to Port Chalmers writing notes to various kind people on the way in a very crowded train full of people, for Dunedin had been given a special holiday to see us off at 2.30 p.m. We were boisterously and very cheerily seen off and Ory was with us on board to the last when she had to go off on to a tug—and there on the bridge I saw her disappear out of sight waving happily, a goodbye that will be with me till the day I see her again in this world or the next—I think it will be in this world and some time in 1912. We had excellent weather for a start and a sunny day for the send off. Ory goes to the Dennistouns whom she likes—poor dear.

5

NEW ZEALAND TO THE
EDGE OF THE PACK ICE

Wed 30 NovINE weather and steady sea and all looks hopeful and happy. The horses and
dogs all in first class condition. The ship is dry though desperately heavy
laden. Several of our newcomers are exceedingly seasick—but they really
had no reason. Most of the day went in settling and stowing things away that are
no longer wanted. We are making splendid headway under steam and sail with a
fair light wind.

We were to have paid Campbell Islands a visit on our way south and to have **Thurs 1 Dec**
left the instruments there for a meteorological station and to have instructed some
of the 12 men shepherds, who live there, to take observations. But we have made
such a good pace south that by tonight we shall be there and as the wind is freshen-
ing we have decided not to stand off there till the morning but to leave them and
go right on and establish the station there when the ship returns with Pennell. This
decision was come to in the morning—by the evening the weather had so far
altered for the worse as to leave us no choice and we went right on—under steam
and full sail. So we had no sight of the Campbell Islands. I was rather sorry for
this as I had hoped to see albatrosses nesting there, but the barometer is very
threatening and we have no choice but to go on south as we could make no headway against the wind now to get into Campbell Islands under steam. There are
no lights and the harbour is impossible at night. At 9 a.m. we sent off two carrier
pigeons which had been brought by Paton from New Zealand. I believe he has
two more which will be liberated later—no, I find they were liberated yesterday
at noon. I watched the two go off today and they looked strong enough on the
wing. They flew round and round the ship in increasingly wider circles, rising to
a good height and gradually disappeared somewhere in a sort of circular direction.
It was impossible to say that they had gone in any particular direction. They
ought at any rate to reach Campbell Islands one would think.
We are today at noon in 50°44′S., 170°38′E. having made good 191 miles since
noon yesterday and the barometer keeps falling, falling constantly and the wind
and sea and swell rising all the forenoon and afternoon until it became force 8 on
the scale of *Conditions of the Sea*[1] which I will give presently. By 4 p.m. in the afternoon it was blowing so hard that both topgallant sails were taken in, and between 4
and 6 p.m. the main and outer jib were also taken in, as well as the fore and main
upper topsails, and at 6 p.m. the foresail also was taken in. The wind was W.N.W.
force 6 in the forenoon and by midnight had gone through S.W. by S. force 7 and

8 to W.S.W. force 9. The sea during the day rose from 5 to 8 and we were taking in green seas on both sides filling the waist of the ship and tearing everything adrift that could come. The ship wallowed in the water like a thing without life and it was evident that we were in for trouble with a barometer steadily falling and continuing to fall—and our heavy deck cargo. Besides all the ordinary ship's necessities on the upper deck we have added as permanent weights three deck houses on the poop, including all our laboratories, which are full of gear as they will hold, five boats and the ice-house. Then there are 162 carcasses of sheep in it and two of beef; three enormous cases containing the motor sledges chained down to the deck—about 128 cases of petrol, oil and paraffin, in two and three layers, tied down to the deck; 15 tons of horse fodder in compressed bales; 33 dogs, and stables all solidly built of heavy timber, and 19 horses in them; 30 tons of coal in sacks thrown in at the last moment, wherever there was space to take one. We have 1,700 gallons of petrol on the upper deck and it was this, in tin cans packed two together in heavy wooden cases, that caused most of the trouble. They were all arranged as a sort of floor on the upper deck and we walked over them and over the coal sacks and amongst the dogs and the coils of ship's ropes. We climbed over the heavy wooden props and stays and chains which kept all the motor car cases in their places—in fact there is no clear space on the whole deck on which to move—the deck itself being invisible everywhere. And yet the heavy green seas that came on board over the rail, both on the weather side and, still more disastrously, on the lee side as she rolled to leeward wallowing into a trough of the enormous seas, got under the whole of these cases and gradually loosened the ropes and wedges which held them down. It was rather appalling to see the whole floor of these rising and getting out of place until at last one or two got adrift and then the whole lot started moving about and breaking one another up. We had to plunge every now and then into the drowned waist of the ship, seize one of the broken cases and haul the two tins of petrol—10 gallon tins—up on to the poop to save them from being burst. Constantly one was caught in the act and a green sea would sweep along the whole deck, rail under, and over one's shoulders while the cases beneath all floated up anyhow, jambing one's seaboots and themselves in every possible direction, and forcing one often to drop everything and cling to the pin rail[2], or the ropes attached to it, instead of going over the side with tons of water. I had never seen a ship wallow so persistently or take such tremendous seas over the rail every time she rolled to leeward as this ship. Of course we were much too heavily laden and the storm was a very heavy one. I have already said that by 6 p.m. the only sail we carried were the lower topsails and the fore topmast staysail—but we were still under steam. Early in the afternoon the seas were coming in so heavily that 5 tons of the deck cargo of coal in sacks was thrown over the side to facilitate the job of securing the petrol cases again. By the evening the sea was tremendous, but whether it was really bigger than anything we saw in the *Discovery* I can't say. Certainly I never saw any ship so constantly swept from foc'sle to poop, or sometimes right on to the poop, by green seas. Then one of the horses went down and was got up on its legs again, then another, and another— and Oates and Atkinson worked like bricks helping them up. Then one refused to stand or be helped up, and then one died—and all this happened in the after-

noon of the forenoon when we were playing about with carrier pigeons and wondering what the barometer was falling so quickly to bring us. The one thing we didn't want was this heavy storm—but it came right enough and it came quickly, and when everything began to happen at once it looked as though it had come to save us a great deal of trouble and two years' work, for 24 hours after the storm began it looked to everyone who knew what was going on as though we must go to the bottom. The afternoon and evening had been wet and cold and fatiguing for everyone and we turned in for a bad night, as the ship's decks were so strained that she was pouring water into every cabin. Everything everywhere was wet and we were of course battened down—yet all through the night one heard periodically the thud of a sea on the decks overhead and a water cart full of water pour down upon the wardroom floor and table and then subside to a trickle and a drip. Seas were breaking over us, especially aft, and we were very much lower there in the water than further forward. I must say I enjoyed it all from beginning to end, and as one bunk became untenable after another, owing to the wet, and the comments became more and more to the point as people searched out dry spots here and there to finish the night in oilskins and greatcoats on the cabin or wardroom floors, or on the wardroom seats, I thought things were becoming interesting. This night, however, I had a dry bunk and a good sleep—until early dawn, when the storm was worse than ever. So far, however, it was only an unfortunate storm breaking on an overladen ship, and save for the horses, which were being thrown about in an unmerciful way in their narrow stalls, and for the dogs, which were miserably wet and constantly being nearly drowned by seas, things were shaking down in a fairly manageable way. The engines were working and the water in the well was kept well in hand by the steam pump, though the straining of the old ship was evidently helping her to take in water through the seams. Then dawn came and with it things began to go wrong again all at once.

We were now in 52°07′S. and 172°11′E. and since noon the previous day we had **Fri 2 Dec** made 101 miles S. 35 E. We were under easy steam and main lower topsail, and foretop staysail, and at 4 a.m. furled fore lower topsail and inner jib. Then we were all turned out to lend a hand on deck, those of us who were fit for it. Some of the staff were like dead men with seasickness. Even so, Cherry-Garrard and Wright and Day turned out with the rest of us who were not seasick, and alternately worked and were sick. I have no seasickness on these ships myself under any conditions so I enjoyed it all, and as I have the run of the bridge and can ask as many questions as I choose I knew all that was going on. The only breakfast this morning was some coffee and biscuits and whatever could be discovered dry enough to eat in the pantry; it was impossible to bring food through the seas from the galley. The waist of the ship was a surging, swimming bath, and one went there at the risk of being drowned alive in one's clothes before getting out again, or else of being broken up amongst the ruck of petrol cases, or else of mistaking the outside of the ship's rail for the inside in a green sea and not finding one's way back again by the end of whatever rope one happened to seize as the deluge engulfed one. It was really terrific and the alternative was to climb up by the pump on to a hayrick of forage, then on to the main hatch afloat with dogs, then up on to the ice-house, and so to drop down by the foc'sle—all the while with very little to hold on to, and some parts nothing, with the chance of being swept over any moment by a sea. It was all very exciting, but wet and very cold.

Between 5 and 6 a.m. the bunkers were leaking so much water down into the engine-room that we had to pass the coal down in sacks to the stoke-hold by hand from the upper deck. The water in the stoke-hold was gradually gaining on the steam pumps chiefly because the rolling of the ship so stirred up all the coal dust in with the bilge water that it clogged in great balls in the pump valves. This entailed a very unpleasant duty for the engine-room leading stokers. Lashly, for instance, spent hours and hours up to his neck in bilge water beneath the foot plates of the stoke-hold clearing these balls of oily coal dust away from the valves which could be reached no other way. The water gained and gained until at last it was impossible to reach the valves without getting under the bilge water entirely and that then became impossible. The moment this happened the valves became so clogged that no water could be pumped out by the main engine pumps at all and we had to fall back on a subsidiary pump which was much smaller but which worked for a very short time and then also got its valves choked, also out of reach on account of the depth of water already leaked into the ship. There was now a huge wave of water in the engine-room stoke-hold, washing backwards and forwards, or rather from side to side, with a rushing roar at every roll of the ship. In this water the stokers stood and worked at the furnaces to keep the engines going—and the noise and steam and clatter of iron and rush of water down there in the dark lamplight and glare of occasionally opened furnace doors was fearsome. It was the one place in the ship where the rise of water could be watched inch by by inch, and it continued to do so. The wind meanwhile was blowing its very hardest from the S.W. force 10, then S.S.W. 10 to 9, then to S. force 9. The sea was very high indeed. I don't think I have ever seen such a high sea and such an immense swell running at such a furious rate, and the old ship simply lay down in it and wallowed every time. The port whaler—the boat hanging high up on a level with the bridge rails—was constantly dipping into the water and was lifted in the davits and swung in under the bridge deck and there jammed. The weight of water in the waist of the ship began early today to take timbers out of the rail bulwarks, and at 8 a.m. we had one of the bulwark uprights carried away and all the planking so that there is now a big gap in the bulwarks. We lost today 60 gallons of petrol and about 20 gallons of lubricating oil carried overboard in cases by the heavy seas. We also lost a dog carried overboard with a broken chain—and we lost another pony which died of exhaustion after falling in its stall. They are all desperately tired of trying to keep upright in the roll of the ship which is pitching also in the most trying manner. They seem every now and again to forget and go to sleep and then the ship catches them unawares and down they go without room or strength enough to recover themselves.

If the old ship is opening up everywhere, as she is on the deck above our cabins, there is nothing to wonder at in her making water, for she is leaking like a sieve, and at 7 a.m. the wardroom officers and staff had to lend a hand to try and get some of the water out by hand as both the engine pumps were out of action. So the main hand pump handles were shipped in the waist of the ship where we were at one moment up to our knees and at another up to our necks in water, but no sooner had we started to pump than we found the valves there were also blocked with caked oil and coal dust. The water still rising in the stoke-hold and rushing about the foot plates in such an enormous wave and so close sometimes to the furnace gratings just above them that it was considered no longer safe to keep the fires alight for fear of an explosion of steam—so the fires were drawn and the engines stopped. This was a bad state of things as the water in the hold was rising all the time. The next thing we got at was a small hand pump for two hands which again failed as the lift in the pipe was insufficient for the depth of the stoke-hold, and indeed it was not made for such a lift or ever intended for it. And last of all at 7 a.m., as a last resource, the whole of the wardroom mess, not laid out with sea-sickness, was divided into two watches and started baling out the stoke-hold, that is the ship! For the stoke-hold was the only place where it could be reached with buckets! All Friday and Friday night we worked in two parties, two hours on and two hours off. It was heavy work filling and handing up huge buckets of water as fast as they could be given from one to the other, from the very bottom of the stoke-hold to the upper deck, up little metal ladders all the way. One was, of course, wet through the whole time in a sweater and trowsers and seaboots— and every two hours one took these off and turned in for a rest in a great coat, to turn out again in two hours and put on the same cold sopping clothes, and so on until 4 a.m. on Saturday when we had baled out between 4 and 5 tons of water and had so lowered it that it was once more possible to light fires and try the engines and the steam pump again and to clear the valves and the inlet which was once more within reach. The fires had been put out at 11.40 a.m. and were then out for 22 hours while we baled. It was a weird night's work with the howling gale and the darkness and the immense sea running over the ship every few minutes, and no engines and no sail, and we all in the engine-room black as ink with engine-room oil and bilge water, singing chanties as we passed up slopping buckets full of bilge, each man above slopping a little over the heads of all of us below him wet through to the skin, so much so that some of the party worked altogether naked like a Chinese coolie—and the rush of the wave backwards and forwards at the bottom grew hourly less in the dim light of a couple of engine-room oil lamps whose light just made the darkness visible. The ship all the time rolling like a sodden, lifeless log, her lee gunwale under water every time. All this time another effort was being made at Captain Scott's suggestion—and this was to reach the suction well of the hand pump through the bulkhead which divided it in the after-hold from the engine-room. It meant hours of work on top of and at the back of the boilers, which were hardly cooled, and as the bulkhead was of iron sheeting it took hours to cut a manhole through. Still it was done, and then a quantity of coal was taken out and the suction valve reached and cleared. It all took a lot of time and at this work Evans was for hours in water and in oil and coal dust, and Williams, the engineer, worked end on for hours till the thing was done by 9 o'clock on the Saturday morning.

We were all at work till 4 a.m. and then were all told off to sleep till 8 a.m. At **Sat 3 Dec** 9.30 a.m. we were all on the main hand pump, and lo and behold it worked and we pumped and pumped till 12.30 when the ship was once more only as full of bilge water as she always is—and the position was practically solved. We had been hove to all yesterday, just wallowing in the wet, and we had moved 23 miles to leeward S.77°E. We were now in 52°12′S., 172°48′E. At 2 a.m. the fore lower topsail and the main upper topsail were set as the wind had dropped to 5 or 6 from the S.S.W., though the sea was as bad as ever and the swell immense. At 6.15 a.m. the fore upper topsail and the foresail were set. The day went in pumping out the ship and securing gear and making all the moving deck cargo fast again. There was one thrilling moment in the middle of the worst hour on Friday when we were realising that the fires must be drawn, and when every pump had failed to pump, and when the bulwarks began to go to pieces and the petrol cases were all afloat and going overboard, and the word was suddenly passed in a shout from the hands at work in the waist of the ship trying to save petrol cases, that smoke was coming up through the seams in the after-hold. As this was full of coal and patent fuel and was next the engine-room, and as it had not been opened for the airing it required to get rid of gas—on account of the flood of water on deck making it impossible to open the hatchways—the possibility of a fire there was patent to everyone and it could not possibly have been dealt with in any way short of opening the hatch and flooding the ship, when she must have foundered. It was therefore a thrilling moment or two until it was discovered that the smoke was really steam arising from the bilge at the bottom having risen to the heated coal. This hatchway it was impossible to open as it had tons of water washing over it at every roll of the ship—and yet it was the only way to get at the suction inlet of the main hand pumps, which were choked with oil and coal dust and which, therefore, had to remain choked with coal dust until the manhole had been cut through the iron bulkhead from the engine-room into the fore-hold where the pump well was placed. Just about the time when things looked their very worst, the sky was like ink and water was everywhere, everyone was as wet inside their oilskins as the skins were wet without, and things looked very bad indeed in every way, there came out a most perfect and brilliant rainbow for about half a minute or less, and then suddenly and completely went out. If ever there was a moment at which such a message was a comfort it was just then—it seemed to remove every shadow of doubt, not only as to the present issue, but as to the final issue of the whole expedition—and from that moment matters mended and everything came all right. At 12.30 we set main top gallant sail, and at 1.30 the fore topgallant sail and inner jib. In the afternoon the two dead ponies were hauled up through the foc'sle skylight and passed overboard, and by night all the moveables on the upper deck were once more made secure. Air temperature 42°–44°F. Water 45°F. And as the change in these as we near the pack will interest some of you, I will put them in from now onwards.

Sun 4 Dec Air temperature 42·8° to 45°F., water temperature 45°–40°F. We are now in 54°31′S., 173°50′E. having made good 147 miles to the S. 20 E. Wind has been S.S.W. 7 to 5. S.W. and W.S.W. 5–7 and the sea 6 to 7 gradually going down. This Sunday was a quiet day and everyone rested. It seems queer to think that only a week ago Ory and I were walking to church in Riccarton with Lady Bowen in delightful summer weather; now everything is wet and damp and cold. Evans and I take turns in the bunk which is dry, the wire one in the Captain's cabin. Captain Scott sleeps in the big one. When Evans is in the bunk I sleep like a log on the floor. But on the port side everyone is worse off as the bunks are wet through and water still running through from the wet deck above. The occupants have abandoned them in most cases and are taking turns to sleep four hours at a stretch. Some of them have gone below to the next storey and are now sleeping in the chronometer room and the lazarette—below. Everyone is cheery and good tempered, notwithstanding the fact that an immense amount of property has been ruined. Books, papers, clothes and even instruments have been trodden on the floor of the nursery for instance, into an unrecognisable black pulp—but the nursery is the worst of all because it has been a high road between the engine room and the wardroom; the condition there was appalling. Probably the driest place in the ship has been the deck dark room where Ponting has been hors de combat on his back with seasickness for the last four days; throughout the storm he hasn't appeared. Priestley, too, is completely overcome with seasickness. All the others are up and about though several are very sick at times—but the conditions of life are improving very fast and though we had no service this Sunday, it was a very acceptable day of rest. There was a great writing up of diaries and sound sleep in the afternoon.

Air temperature 41° to 43° — 56°41′S., 176°23′E. our position today, having made **Mon 5 Dec** 154 miles S. 32 E. Water temperature 40° to 41°F. Wind W.S.W. and S.W. force 5 to 4. Sea fell from 6 to 3. Up at 5 with Cherry who made cocoa. We are all rather dirty as we have no allowance for washing at all beyond half a pint a day for our teeth. The horses and dogs want so much in addition to 60 men on board that no one is allowed to wash except in sea water which does nothing to remove dirt; but we have all a bucket bath on deck every morning. Last night I was on the floor in my clothes and a sleeping bag and very wet, but I slept the bag dry and after this had very little trouble with wet except when I migrated into Campbell's cabin and slept in the upper bunk where it leaks in on one's face whenever the deck gets wet, and it is the least windy place for bucket baths on deck so it is often wet. Priestley has been lying up as much with a cut foot as seasickness; he found a broken tumbler with his bare foot in the wreckage on the nursery floor during the storm and he stepped heavily on it. Everything is now looking bright and cheery again and settling down. I have been reading *The Illustrious Prince*, which Mrs. Wigram, you remember, gave me just before leaving New Zealand, a book I have thoroughly enjoyed—and the last novel, probably, that I shall read until we are well up in the warm sunshine on the way home. If I read novels habitually there would be no diary writing. As it is, the only quiet time in the day is from 4.30 a.m. or 5 a.m. to breakfast at 8 a.m.—and my writing is all done then. But I turn in by 9 p.m. every evening. This evening we saw a Fin Whale (*Balaenoptera musculus*)[3] and then a small herd of the unnamed dolphins[4] which we saw in the *Discovery* about the same latitude. They were very lively little dolphins with an hour-glass shaped mark down the length of each side and dark brown elsewhere. We failed to harpoon one and they very soon disappeared in the dark. Five of us saw them and I got each one to draw what they had seen independently, and have now got

5 drawings of the same animal, all different, from Scott, Evans, Bruce, Lillie and myself. We have been seeing a large number of birds—larger and small albatrosses, Sooty Albatross, various petrels of medium size such as Cape Pigeons, Lesson's Petrel[5], Black-bellied Stormy Petrel and Giant Petrel—in fact the birds have been abundant and worth far more time than the gale has allowed us to give them. There were numbers of Royal and Wandering Albatross and of various ages, changing from dark brown to pure white with black wing primaries. Also numbers of Mollymawks, the difficult smaller albatrosses which have black backs and wings all of them, but every variation from white to dark grey heads, and from black bills to orange yellow bills, with many of them black and yellow streaks in various arrangements according to their age and species.

Tues 6 Dec 5 a.m. cocoa and writing and reading till 8. Our position today is 59°7′S., 177°51′E. having made 153 miles S. 17 E. in the 24 hours from noon to noon. Air temperature 40·9° to 37°F and water 40·2° to 39°F. Most of the day spent in clearing up mess made by the gale and drying out clothes and books and papers. I had a big box of things in my laboratory on the upper deck and they have all been under sea water for about three days—and books and pamphlets take months to dry. All my collection of Antarctic pamphlets was in this mess, but very few were bad enough to throw away. We have all been on the look out for ice as we are in the region of bergs.

Wed 7 Dec Position 61°22′S., 179°56′W. having made 150 miles S. 25 E. Air temperature 36·8° to 29°—a sudden drop. Water temperature 36° to 32°. Wind N.W. force 2 to S.W. force 7. The ponies are recovering their spirits but are getting leggy from long standing and no exercise, and rather rubbed in places by the roll of the ship. We have now 17 ponies and 31 dogs. Today we were discussing our winter quarters nearly the whole day and we arrived at the conclusion that Cape Crozier[6] would be a preferable spot to Cape Royds[7]. We know a certain amount about the place for Scott and I both landed there one day and walked up a couple of thousand feet of the Mount Terror slopes above the rookery of penguins when we first arrived there in the *Discovery*. It was then that we first had a view over the Barrier[8] surface before we knew what sledging was like at all. This was in Jan. 1902. Then in Sept. 1903 I was there again for 3 or 4 days with Charles Royds[9] on a sledge journey and again for a month on a sledge journey of my own in Nov. 1903. So on the whole I know something of the place—and it has always struck me as an ideal place for wintering as one cannot be cut off from the Barrier surface by open water as one can and often is at Cape Royds and at Hut Point[10]. Moreover, we are in the middle of an enormous rookery of Adélie Penguins and within three miles of the Emperor Penguins' rookery and the Great Barrier, where it abuts on Cape Crozier, and has the great Cape Crozier pressure ridges piled up. It is sheltered, moreover, from all heavy winds and from the southerly blizzards absolutely, though one has only to walk half a mile from the hut to walk into the teeth of the worst blizzards we ever experienced. Add to this that we are at the foot of Mount Terror and Mount Erebus, also within 40 miles of Hut Point round good travelling south side of Ross Island, also within 60 miles by the same road of Cape Royds, also on the shore of open Ross Sea where we can make daily notes of the open pack ice and winter sea ice movements and changes which have never been watched before. Also heaps of food at our doors and lots of seals all along the coast—also heaps of other advantages and a clear run to the South Pole on the solid Barrier from start to finish. Moreover, it is new ground where no serious work has been done before, and it has a number of points to be examined in the shape of parasitic volcanic cones, raised beaches, old moraines, and erratic boulders a thousand feet above the present Barrier surface, old remnants of glaciers now dead and dying, new glaciers from Mount Terror and névé slopes ad lib., to say nothing at all about the Barrier and its movement which is a living thing at the junction with Cape Crozier where it raises ridges to 40 or 50 feet but yet leaves us a grand, hard roadway along the border of the island for our sledgeway on to the Barrier and away to the South Pole. Today the first iceberg was sighted from the crow's nest away on the horizon, and very small—almost invisible—but it was accepted as ice. This was at 7 p.m. We had the following birds with us today:

Diomedea melanophris, The Black-browed Albatross. Adults.
Phoebetria fuliginosa, The Sooty Albatross.
Prion sp. Whale birds in large flocks.
Priocella glacialoides[11], one only—the Southern Fulmar.
Megalestris maccormicki, one only—Maccormick's Skua.
Daption capensis, Cape Pigeons—several.
Cymodroma melanogaster, The Black-bellied Petrel.
Haloboena caerulea, The White-tailed Blue Petrel—one only.

Nearly the whole day went in discussing the possibilities of our making our winter quarters at Cape Crozier.

Our position 63°20′S., 177°22′W. Air temperature 28° to 33.9°F. Sea water temperature 29.8° to 31°. Wind S.S.W. 7, S. 5, S. by E. 5, S. 5, S.S.W. 4, and at 7 p.m. two very distant bergs were again sighted from aloft. In addition to all the birds seen yesterday, except *D. melanophris* which has left us, we saw today quite a number of *Thalassoeca antarctica*, the brown-backed Antarctic Petrel—also a Giant Petrel (*Ossifraga gigantea*)[12]—one Wilson's Petrel (*Oceanites oceanicus*) and at 10 p.m. one Snowy Petrel, the first (*Pagodroma nivea*). With so many indications of our approach to ice one was naturally most of the day on deck looking for more—if not for ice—but no more were seen and I turned in. Be it added here, perhaps, that I have a nightly routine as well as a daily one on which I am again growing very fat again and very fit. I turn in now always in the top bunk in Campbell's cabin which is seldom wet, though mouldy. This is about 9 to 10 p.m., and between 11 p.m. and midnight I am called by Nelson— commonly called 'Marie'—with a large mug of steaming cocoa, which I drink— and then go to sleep again. At 4.30 a.m. to 5 a.m. I am called again by Cherry, and again I have a large mug of steaming cocoa and some biscuits and turn out and dress and do my reading and writing squatted in my cabin door on the medicine chest, with Scott and Teddie Evans asleep at my elbow in their respective bunks. At 7 a.m. the servant comes into the wardroom and I again have half a

Thurs 8 Dec

71

mug of hot cocoa—then dress, and as it is now too cold for a bucket over one on deck, washing is postponed, as we are forbidden to use any fresh water for washing and one can only swill one's hands and face in the salt water to be obtained on deck. Even the salt water soap is no use, and only makes one dirtier—but every now and again there is found to be a certain amount in hand and we are each given half a gallon, hot, in a can—once a week at least—and in mine this week I not only bathed from head to foot but washed a vest and a flannel shirt and three handkerchiefs—all successfully—before helping it to get out of the basin. It was a great joy to feel clean once more.

Macronectes giganteus S.P.R.I. 1693

Tabular berg. 9 December 1910. 5 a.m.

S.P.R.I. 428

'Iceberg in the pack ice. Ross Sea. Dec.21.10. 10 a.m.'

S.P.R.I. 413

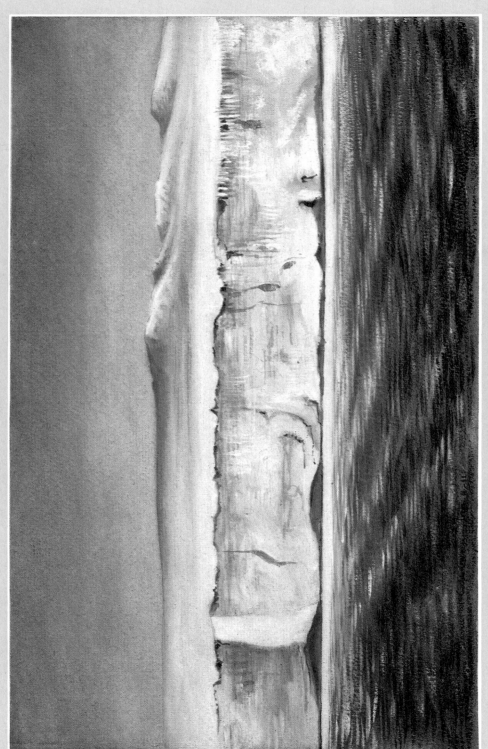

'Barrier at Cape Crozier. Jan.4.11.'

6

IN THE PACK ICE

UP at 5 a.m.—and at 5.30 we passed a tabular berg quite close which I drew, **Fri 9 Dec** and at 7 a.m. we ran into loose streams of broken pack ice at last little thinking at the time that what we had been looking for so eagerly we should be so jolly glad to see the last of in three weeks' time. However, here it was and we were today at noon in 65°8′S., 177°40′W. having made 109 miles to the S. 4 W. Air temperature 26·3° to 30·5°. Sea temperature 29° to 30°. Wind S.W. 4, S.W. by W. 3, W. 3. S.W. 1–2, W. 1 to 2. As we entered the pack we saw a large berg to the E. and we passed through great loose streams of open broken and water worn ice, much of which seemed to have come off the great bergs which soon surrounded us—but the ice was all so broken and water-washed that it may quite possibly have been sea ice which had been broken up and washed by heavy seas so near the open ocean edge. We were at once in still water on entering the ice belt and the soft seething noise of moving ice and an occasional bump and grating noise along the ship's side gave one a feeling of old times. At 8 a.m. we were in broken pack, obviously sea ice. 10 a.m. much yellow diatomaceous sea ice in bigger floes, and 27 bergs were counted at one time, some of which I got sketched. We met our first two Adélie Penguins on a floe today and left them in peace for their greeting. At 3 p.m. we saw an immature, but full-grown, Emperor Penguin[1] in its first year coat. Snowy Petrels[2], Antarctic Petrels[3], Southern Fulmars[4], and Wilson's Petrel[5] were all with us today. So were several Cape Pigeons. The Antarctic Petrels have a gregarious habit and we met with flocks of them often enough all asleep together on the top of some immense tabular berg as a rule—or else on a large floe. We also saw the enormous blow of a great many huge Blue Whales (*Balaenoptera sibbaldi*) and their great grey backs occasionally appeared with the little fin well aft; the blows were very high and looked almost like factory chimney smoke as they rose dark grey against the white ice blink of the pack ice sky. They were actually about 15 or 20 feet high from the water, a grey column of foggy, frosty breath.

Now in heavier pack 66°38′S., 178°47′W. having made 94 miles S. 17 W. We **Sat 10 Dec** stopped at 9 a.m. and tied up to a heavy floe with blue ice on it and watered ship. This means all hands turning out on the floe with picks to break out lumps of ice and throw them up into the ship where we have a tarpaulin laid out. The lumps are then by degrees melted in the steam tanks round the engine-room hatch. It is hard work and good exercise. While this was going on a deep sounding was taken and bottom found in 1,964 fathoms. The sample which was brought up was a light grey mud full of foraminifera, chiefly radiolaria shells visible to naked eye. Various nets and water bottles and thermometers were let down and samples taken while we also at 3 p.m. stopped and collected 4 Crabeater Seals (*Lobodon carcinophagus*) and took them on board where Cherry and I at once skinned them. Air temperature 27° to 32°. Sea water 29°–28·5°. In the evening we entered some very heavy pack—very thick ice and large pieces. Days in the pack seem to fly, one has so much to look at in the stillness. Seals turn up lying asleep on floes at all distances and I have to see them all to make certain what they are—as we would go out of our way to take a Ross Seal (*Ommatophoca rossi*) but not others, as they can be trusted to turn up in our proper course sooner or later. The killing of seals is a hateful business, but it is necessary—and having shot them with rifles from the ship we lower a pram and reach the floe they lie on and haul them in. So far we have only seen Crabeaters. The four we got were 8 ft 8 ins, 9 ft 2 ins, 7 ft 3 ins and 7 ft 3 ins, the latter two being young half grown specimens. All were frightfully scarred by the teeth of Killer Whales (*Orca gladiator*). We saw also a whale about 30 ft long with a small hooky dorsal fin and a yellowish mark diagonally running up on the side. Evidently a whalebone whale, I think, and the one I believe which I took to be *Neobalaena* in my *Discovery* report. Cherry-Garrard and I shot a number of petrels this morning for skinning. We got Snowy Petrels and Antarctic Petrels and one Wilson's Petrel. We also saw a Southern Fulmar and a Giant Petrel. We shot from the poop while Oates and Atkinson picked the birds up which fell among the floes. We saw also one or two Adélie Penguins, one of which was adult and the other a white throated one year old.

Sun 11 Dec The Third Sunday in Advent. Up at 5 a.m. Holy Communion reading and writing. Today we are fast stuck in the pack unable to make any headway. A large berg is in sight which is supposed to be Scott Island but really is a berg. We are not quite near enough to Scott Island to see it from here. We had service for all hands in the wardroom today at 10 a.m. Scott read the Church service from the prayer book given to the expedition by the Bishop of Wellington, Bishop Wallis. Afterwards we all got our ski out and had some exercise on a very large ice floe, and as the surface was good snow and our ski and ski-boots this time are the best possible, we had an enjoyable time. Gran, the Norwegian, was very useful in helping us to learn the new fittings and the use of two sticks. We are now within the Antarctic Circle. The sunlight at midnight in the pack is perfectly wonderful. One looks out upon endless fields of broken ice, all violet and purple in the low shadows, and all gold and orange and rose-red on the broken edges which catch the light, while the sky is emerald green and salmon pink, and these two beautiful tints are reflected in the pools of absolutely still water which here and there lie between the ice floes. Now and again one hears a penguin cry out in the stillness near at hand or far away, and then, perhaps, he appears in his dress tail coat and white waistcoat suddenly upon an ice floe from the water—and catching sight of the ship runs curiously towards her, crying out in his amazement as he comes, from time to time, but only intensifying the wonderful stillness and beauty of the whole fairy-like scene as the golden glaring sun in the south just touches the horizon and begins again to gradually rise without having really set at all. We have now broad daylight night and day, but the beauty of the day, with its lovely blues and greens amongst the bergs and ice floes, is eclipsed altogether by the marvellous beauty of the midnight when white ice becomes deepest purple and golden rose and the sky is lemon green without a cloud. No scene in the whole world was ever more beautiful than a clear midnight in the pack, and this we had on this Sunday night. We are now in 66°55′S., 178°51′W. having made 17 miles S. 4 W. in the 24 hours. The air temperature is 27·6° to 34·2°. The sea temperature 28·8° to 31°. Light winds off and on N. 2, N.E. 3, N.N.W. 4, W.N.W. 5–4, and then we banked fires and set sail but made very little headway in the heavy ice, though the floes, 4 ft thick and rectangular in shape, opened out a bit at midnight.

Position 67·5°S., 178°22′W. Made good 15 miles to S. 48 E. Air temperature **Mon 12 Dec** 28·5° to 35°. Sea temperature 29° to 30°. Winds N.W. 4 to 3 to W. 2 to 4. Pack unchanged but floes in motion. Much rotten snowfall ice in between, very thin and wet. Floes today have been getting smaller, but much thicker and heavier in character. Was out at 5 a.m. to read and write and cocoa. We have made very little way today. The birds are the same as yesterday, and nearly all the Adélie[6] and Emperor Penguins to be seen in the pack are in one year old plumage. They live here on euphausiæ reddish orange little shrimplike schizopods, and small fish. We see these little creatures thrown up on to the ice floes to freeze, by the wash of the water, in thousands. The petrels live by picking them off the ice. The penguins and the seals catch them in the sea itself. The amount of life in the pack is its most astonishing feature—and the diatoms which support it all simply colour the ice red orange and yellow everywhere underneath. It is white above, of course —but the white of the snow is relieved everywhere with fissures and hollows of a wonderful cobalt and prussian blue light, and along the edge washed by sea water the colour is peacock green. The diatoms feed the euphausiæ, the euphausiæ and such like, all living on lower life depending on the diatoms, feed not only the penguins and the Crabeaters and the other seals and fish, but also many of the biggest whales, while there are other whales such as the 'Killers' and other seals, such as the Sea Leopards[7], which feed on the seals and fish and penguins that have been living on the euphausiæ. It is difficult to say how the days go in the pack— one has so many odd things to do, such as examining distant seals, penguins, and birds with the glasses to say what they are, drawing icebergs at critical moments and various distances, putting in an hour now and then below to make a water colour sketch; then turning to the skinning of penguins because the bodies are wanted for dinner; then flensing seal-skins and cleaning the meat off skulls and skeletons, and a dozen other things. Everyone was at work—in fact all the scientific staff take hours on watch and are on the bridge with the officer of the watch in the crow's nest where all the ice navigation is done. These midshipmen of the watch manage the engine-room telegraph according to orders from the crow's nest. Wright is responsible for all the expedition ice notes and is helped by Priestley and Debenham. Rennick does the soundings. Nelson and Lillie manage the townets and water bottles and deep sea temperatures. Pennell, of course, does all the navigation and sleeps still on the bridge always in a sleeping bag whether it blows or snows or freezes. Bowers has his hands full of stores work, and preparations go on with the landing party stores for east and west. Titus Oates and Atkinson look after the horses, poor things, which are very tired and badly chafed and very swollen about the legs in some cases from long standing. Meares and his Russian boys manage the dogs, and we all pump out the ship when the ship is under sail. The ship is a busy centre and work is not lacking, though now we no longer trim coal or work in the stoke-hold. There is no illness on board.

Tues 13 Dec Position (at noon always) 67°30′S., 177°58′W. having made 27 miles to S. 20 E. Air temperature 31° to 33°. Sea temperature 29·7° to 30°. Winds W. 2, S.W. 2, S.E. 1 and calm. At 12.30 p.m. the fires were let out and the engines stopped as we were stuck in very heavy pack. We took a sounding and got bottom at 2,131 fathoms with the same radiolarian ooze, or white mud, as before. At 9 a.m. we again watered ship and so had some exercise picking at blue ice and throwing lumps into the ship. No birds beyond the Snowy Petrel, pure white all over except for its black eye and bill and feet—and the Antarctic Petrel, brown backed and brown and white like a domino, and the Wilson's Storm Petrel, black all over with a white rump. We saw also a few Adélie Penguins.

Wed 14 Dec Position at noon 67°28′S., 177°59′W. with a 2 mile set to N. 20 W. So now we are drifting back again fast in the pack. Air temperature 30·6° to 35°. Sea 26°, calm to S. 2, S.S.W. 1, S. 1, W.S.W. 3, S.W. by W. 1. The pack has been heavy but interspersed with thinly frozen leads. A few bergs have been sighted and there is a little swell which is unusual in the pack. We took current measurements and water bottle stations and temperature readings. We had a very large floe next to us and on it everyone again turned out with their ski, while Ponting took photos of the ship which turned out to be most beautiful pictures. Birds the same as usual.

Thurs 15 Dec Position at noon 67°23′S., 177°59′W. A set of 5 miles to the N. 2 E. Air temperature 27·5° to 26° to 26·5°. Sea temperature 28·9°. Wind S. 2, S.S.W. 3, N. 1. We took a sounding of 2,044 fathoms. At midnight there was a considerable swell and some movement in the pack. The ice-house was opened and aired. Today I was out at 4.30 a.m. and got my writing done and some reading. We are still fast in the pack and had again some ski running on the large floe which is drifting with us. Gran and Campbell, of course, are by far the best—there is not much to choose between the rest of us, but I think the Old Sport[8] will be very good in time. Again I cannot put down the hundred and one odd jobs that fill the long days in the pack. For myself I know that not one minute hangs on my hands from 4.30 or 5 in the morning until 9 in the evening, and though I sleep like a log at night without waking except to drink cocoa, I never even feel sleepy during the day and can work quite as well and comfortably in the afternoons as in the mornings. Only after dinner I am no good when 9 o'clock comes and get deadly sleepy. I am getting very fat again, eating huge meals, drinking large quantities of cocoa and feeling as fit as a fiddle from morning till night. It is a most wonderful air and the life is a healthy one. The spare fat will all come off in sledging. I am not afraid of it. I don't think I can ever have weighed so much. So much for me—and there isn't a man in the mess of whom one mightn't be saying the same except for one or two who will stick in doors too much—which is a very great mistake.

Position 67°23′S., 177°59′W. Air temperature 27° to 30° to 33° to 32·5°. Sea 29°. **Fri 16 Dec** Wind N.N.E. 2 to N. 4–5 to N.N.W. 3 to W. 3, to S.W. by W. 3–5. Pack growing looser with large leads[9] of water opening to the eastward. Swell and movement among the floes considerable and we moved a bit under head sails and fore topsails and topgallant sails. There are many signs of thaw in the ice owing to the wet snow and rain and high air temperature. Turned out about 5 a.m. and went up to crow's nest for a look round. Also did my reading and writing before breakfast. We saw a whale again today—there are lots about and one often sees the blow in the distance, but less often one sees the whale close in. This journey, however, we have been particularly lucky. They feed and blow in the leads between the ice floes, but whaling is out of the question in the pack ice—probably we shall do none before we reach our winter quarters. We have not had the ghost of a chance yet, and it looks rather as if it will have to be done from the ship's bows at all. So I

Oceanites oceanicus S.P.R.I. 1688

have had a socket fixed there for the heavy gun just in case we get a chance at a whale under the bows. We have seen a great many one year old Adélie Penguins round us lately, all kept away from the nesting colonies which are on the coast further south. These young birds have all white throats instead of black, otherwise they are much like the old ones. The Emperors we see in the pack are also nearly all young birds. Crow's nest again in the evening. One gets a grand outlook over miles and miles of pack ice from there and one can see penguins and seals, and occasionally whales, actively in motion in the water. Besides, one has the crow's nest to oneself and one is quite sheltered from the wind when the trap door at the bottom is shut so that one can with comfort read there, while Snowy Petrels and Antarctic Petrels fly a few yards from the edge of the barrel wondering what the creature is inside it. I like the crow's nest—and no day passes now without my going up there two or three times for an hour or so. If one remains there longer than that one gets very cold.

Sat 17 Dec Position 67°24′S., 177°34′W. Made 9·7 miles only in 48 hours to the S., 82 E. Air temperature 32·5° to 34·8° to 32°. Sea temperature 29·3° to 29°. Wind S.W. by W. 4, W.S.W. 3 to 4, S.W. 4, S.E. by E. 3, S.E. by S. 3 to 2. We are now in large floes of soft-looking one foot ice with wet areas, and their size and softness rather than their thickness is stopping the ship's progress. There are 3 or 4 bergs in sight drifting along with a very long open water lee. We remained fast in the ice all day.

Sun 18 Dec The 4th Sunday in Advent. Position 67°24′S., 177°34′E. Air temperature 28° to 31·8°. Sea temperature 29·1° to 29·3°. Church in the wardroom with all hands at 10.30 a.m. I watched a whale in the open spaces of the pack this morning from the crow's nest. Was up at 5 for cocoa with Cherry. Also read Holy Communion in the morning and wrote up my books. We watered ship at a tumbled floe. Sea ice when pressed up into large hummocks gradually loses all its salt. Even when sea water freezes it squeezes out the great bulk of its salt as a solid, but then the sea water gets into it by soaking again—and yet when held out of the water, as it is in a hummock, the salt all drains out and the melted ice is blue and quite good for drinking and for engines, etc. We are seeing a good many Crabeater Seals but no Ross Seal has yet appeared. We also got a small fish from an ice floe, thrown up on it by the wash of our bows. The air temperature was 28°–32°. The sea water 29°. Winds S.E. to W.S.W. The pack has been lighter and more rotten—floes close but breaking up, some 2 ft and 3 ft thick. We passed through lanes of water between sheets of low Barrier bergs of very large area and quite recent fracture. They stood 15 to 20 feet out of water and we had open water, like streets between rows of houses, where they had split.

Mon 19 Dec 5 a.m. cocoa with Cherry and Pennell, then to crow's nest and sketched for an hour. We were passing some fine bergs. During the night I was called up to see a supposed Right Whale, but it was only a Blue Whale. We are in some of the heaviest pack ever seen down here and we have had some terrific bumps. Some of the piled floes were 6 to 10 feet high and even more. All the forenoon we were hammering our way through very heavy pack like small bergs, and occasionally through thinner, rotten, and more recently frozen ice in large sheets, all heavily snow covered. We also passed through more and more leads of open water towards night as the pressure became less. Spent some of the day sketching and in the crow's nest before turning in. And in the afternoon I painted the head of a young Adélie Penguin. Position at noon was 67°54′S., 178°30′W. 37 miles made good to S. 34 W. Light winds south-southwesterly, easterly. Air temperature 25°–30°. Sea 32°–29·5°. One berg we saw today had a rounded flat top like an ice cap or an ice island.

Candlice Pacg. from its Crowsnest. Blue Littrates.
Pack ice Ross Sea   Dec 19.10. 7.am.

View from the crow's nest, 19 December 1910. 7 a.m.

'Ice island berg and pack ice from the crow's nest. Ross Sea. Dec.19.10. 6.30 a.m.'

'Berg in the pack ice. Dec.20.10. 10 a.m.'

Tues 20 Dec We saw two Sea Leopards (*Stenorhynchus leptonyx*) which were the first we had come across. We have as yet seen only Crabeaters, the common seal of the Antarctic pack ice, and of these we have only killed 4. Everyone appreciated the liver and the meat, as they have also appreciated the meat of penguins. One of the Sea Leopards was in the water swimming about amongst the ice floes and constantly raising his head high out of water to look over a floe and find his mate —who was fast asleep among some hummocky ice and took no notice of him at all. We had good views of isolated Crabeaters but saw none in numbers greater than two together. Our position today 68°41′S., 179°28′W. We have made 58 miles to S. 36 W. Air temperature 33° to 23°. Sea temperature 28·5° to 30°. Ice today thin and pitted below water. Open water leads and an open water sky to S. and S.W., but most of the leads here covered with tough soft ice hard to break or work through. Had morning cocoa at 5 a.m. and sketched all the morning. Spent the afternoon skinning Adélies and examined three for parasites etc. till dinner time. At noon we tied to a floe, banked fires as a southerly wind had come up, and all hands went skiing. We sounded also and got bottom in 1,800 fathoms. We also lost a large townet. Cherry-Garrard very busy skinning petrels and Adélie Penguins. We also lost a heavy ice anchor today down a crack in the floe, and the man carrying it nearly went too.

Wed 21 Dec 5 a.m. cocoa. Crow's nest several times night and morning. Ice all much looser. Many tabular bergs. Painting all forenoon. Skinning penguins and dissecting with Atkinson—and discovered a small new tapeworm in some numbers which was very interesting, and the hunt continued till dinner time. We saw a lot of the Adélie Penguins today, almost all young ones with the white throat, porpoising. They go at a tremendous rate using their wings under water and leaping out clear of the water, like dolphins, to get a breath without losing any of their pace. They are really bluish grey on the back, but they look brown in the water. I counted about a minute, rather less, for their usual deep swim in fishing for schizopod euphausiæ. They have lost none of their attractiveness—they are most comical and very interesting—as curious as ever, they will always come up at a trot when we sing to them, and you will often see a group of explorers on the poop singing 'for she's got bells on her fingers and rings on her toes, elephants to ride upon wherever she goes', and so on at the top of their voices to an admiring group of Adélie Penguins. Meares is the greatest attraction, and he has a full voice which is musical, but always very flat. He declares that 'God save the King' will always send them into the water and certainly it is often successful. Meares is a capital chap and the amount of active life he has seen is extraordinary. He has been in the fur trade in Kamchatka and Okotz and the north east of Siberia since he was a boy almost. Saw the taking of Pekin and the Russo-Jap war. Made

Macronectes giganteus S.P.R.I. 1693

a great journey into Thibet and the Lolo country when Brooke[10], his companion, was killed and he brought the body and all his Chinese companions back into safety. He knows Thibet, China, Japan, Burmah, India, and the N.E. of Siberia, speaks Russian—and generally has had a wild life. Then he joined the Scottish Horse under Lord Tullibardine, and was in the thick of the fighting in the Boer War for 15 months. Typically a man of action and a most entertaining messmate and full of fun. Today I got a Maccormick's Skua[11] for the collection. We have already seen several since we saw ice.

Thurs 22 Dec

Cocoa at 5 and crow's nest several times. We were fast jammed in the ice all day again, and have seen many more young Adélie Penguins—23 in one batch. We got some of them for our Christmas dinner and I was skinning them today for our collection. No engines, no sail, no movement. Blowing against us all day rather. Very cold but sunny. Same birds as usual in the pack and a Giant Petrel.

Fri 23 Dec

Cocoa and crow's nest at 5. Pennell's birthday, so after dinner we had a sing-song —and a rowdy evening. All day went discussing sledge programmes with the 'Owner', as Captain Scott is always called to distinguish him from Teddie Evans, who is called the 'Skipper'; Campbell is the 'Mate', Rennick is 'Parny', Pennell is 'Penelope', or 'Pennylope'. Bowers is 'Birdie', Atkinson is 'Fancy Atch', Oates is 'Titus' or the 'Soldier'. Oates and Atkinson together are known as 'Max and Climax'. Levick is the 'Old Sport', or 'Tofferino', Nelson is 'Marie' or 'Bronté' or 'Antonio', Lillie is 'Lithley', or 'Hercules', Griffith Taylor is the 'Skuagull', or 'Keir Hardie', Wright is always called 'Silas', Simpson is 'Sunny Jim', Day is the 'Frog-face'. Cherry-Garrard is of course 'Cherry', Priestley is always called 'Raymond'. Drake is 'Franky', Bruce is 'Jumbo', and I am 'Uncle Bill'. Gran is sometimes 'Willie', and the only unnamed as yet are Ponting and Debenham.

Sat 24 Dec

Cocoa and crow's nest at 5.30. Writing and reading and finishing off the seal flensing and skeleton making and skinning penguins, when Ponting got a cinematograph show of us both skinning, which he says is most successful. This is Christmas Eve and one's thoughts are naturally with you all at home, bless you all! I got several useful and independent drawings of a new whale today, which are very interesting. Evans and Scott and Pennell and I all saw it and agreed in all the main points of our drawings. Also saw several Blue Whales blowing.

Sun 25 Dec

Sunday and Christmas Day. ✝ Still in the pack ice and still immoveably fixed. Cocoa and crow's nest at 5 a.m. Read Holy Communion. Then we decorated the wardroom with all our sledge flags and mine was most handsome amongst the others. I also hung up my Caius flag, which Mrs. Roberts gave me[12], and the

Thalassoica antarctica S.P.R.I. 1655

small Jack and New Zealand flag, which Anne Hardy gave me. We also had Queen Alexandra's flag up and Lady Islington's[13] and everybody else's. Then Church service with all hands in the wardroom and three hymns. A big lunch—no tea. Discussion all the afternoon over dozens of problems and a Christmas dinner with penguins for turkey—and then from 8 on till after 12 we had a sing-song in which every member of the mess had either to play or sing a song, or tell a story—three rounds. I sang songs each time. Ponting plays banjo and sings well. Taylor plays the piano to some extent. It was a very festive Christmas. I reserved my plum pudding till the New Year as we had enough for Christmas unpacked. Everyone in the very cheeriest of spirits and good health notwithstanding our long delay in the pack. Our New Zealand rabbit, which has lived in the stack of horse fodder ever since we left Dunedin, has presented us today with a family—the estimate of its number varies. Some say there are seventeen.

Mon 26 Dec 6.20 a.m. cocoa and crow's nest. After breakfast salted my seal skins and finished flensing them, in fact had a blubbery day, and smelt in proportion. Birds as before very much—we are still in the pack with no apparent prospect of ever getting out of it. But even from the crow's nest one's outlook is very limited on the sea surface, probably one cannot see more than 6 or 7 miles ahead, though high mountains one sees over 100 miles away. We have had as many as 20 or 30 young Adélie Penguins in small companies round us today. We watched two or three immense Blue Whales at fairly short distance today; this is *Balaenoptera sibbaldi*. One sees first a small, dark bump appear and then immediately a jet of grey fog squirted upwards for 15 or 18 feet, gradually spreading as it rises vertically into the cold air. I have been nearly in these blows once or twice and had the moisture blown in my face with a sickening smell of shrimpy oil. Then the bump elongates and up rolls an immense blue grey, or blackish grey, round back with a faint ridge along the top on which presently appears a small hook like dorsal fin, and then the whole sinks and disappears.

Tues 27 Dec 4.30 a.m. cocoa and crow's nest. Today we got under sail and moved a little through some sludgy wet ice floes. It was a wet, snowy, blowy day. Easterly wind 5 to 6. We saw a lot of Crabeaters, but couldn't touch them as the ice they were on was all rotten. There were 12 on one floe. We examined our sheep in the ice-house. All good except one or two near the door which we removed and hung up in the rigging. Spent most of the day writing up diary and finishing off a seal skin and drawing seals and penguins.

Wed 28 Dec 4.30 cocoa and crow's nest. Ice everywhere all round, but thin floes which we can steam through, and as open leads are appearing in the right direction it was decided to get up steam again and try and force a way through. While the engines are not going we have to pump out the ship every four hours by hand. She is making less and less water now, however, and we have to pump only for 15 to 20 minutes. We got away under steam at 8.30 p.m. otherwise made no way through the ice. One of the horses began getting tired of standing up today and dropped several times, but eventually recovered and remained standing. It was given a

84

'Sea Leopard'   S.P.R.I. 67/4/3

rest out of its stall on the upper deck later and recovered its spirits any amount, leaning its head over the side of the ship it used to watch the pieces of ice moving along. Spent some time packing gear for the shore.

Thurs 29 Dec Cocoa and crow's nest at 5 a.m. Ice everywhere. Writing up diary. Under steam we are making very fair way through this ice. It is extraordinary that we have not seen a single Ross Seal and have only sighted two Sea Leopards without a chance of getting either. A regular sea came on in the open leads of water today and we have now a good water sky ahead of us, so there is every prospect of our coming into some open water at last. We saw two young Emperors, one year old birds, which had been in the pack probably for the whole year and a half. We also saw one adult Emperor. As evening came on we found more and more signs of the ice pack ending and the open water leads became more numerous and more and more extensive, and soon after midnight we passed through the last strip in Birdie Bowers' watch and were in open water in Ross Sea.

Fri 30 Dec We were out of the pack in open sea and passed a very beautiful berg in the morning, soon after cocoa and crow's nest at 5 a.m. On the top of the berg sat about a hundred Antarctic Petrels like brown dots. They reminded me of the group of fleas one sees round the entrance of a Sand Martin's nest in the sunshine. The lower part of the berg, which had been burrowed into by the sea, was a wonderfully rich blue. We had open water all day and made a very good distance, but towards night it began to blow and we once more saw pack ice ahead. We came up to it by the time it was blowing and snowing half a blizzard from the S.E., and so we decided to lie with banked fires under the lee of this line of pack until we could see where we were going to and how far the pack extended.

Sat 31 Dec We were hove to more or less all day under the lee of the same pack with which we drifted N. and W., but as it was very broken ice and kept very compact at the edge, and as it was extensive enough to completely damp the sea and the swell, which the wind had brought us and which was proving troublesome again to the horses, we were only too glad to have found so good a harbour in the open sea. I spent the day cleaning up two seals' skeletons and got them into sacks. One was D a young male Crabeater, the other C a young female Crabeater. The shining hour is improved generally when we are hove to or stopped in the ice, by taking soundings, deep sea temperatures, water samples at known depths, and by tow-netting. We are now getting into shallower water. From 2,000 fathoms we have now got 200 fathoms and mud bottom with bits of volcanic rock. This is New Year's Eve, and as the wind dropped and the weather cleared in the evenings, we gradually had a magnificent view of the Admiralty Range with the wonderful peak of Mount Sabine on our starboard beam at midnight—120 miles away. I went up last thing into the crow's nest and then turned in to be awakened by a general midnight hurrah party, and the steam siren with which the New Year was welcomed.

Sun 1 Jan New Year's Day, and a very glorious one for the sun shone and it was a clear open sea without a scrap of ice in sight. Cocoa and crow's nest and Holy Communion at 5 a.m. Church service at 10 a.m. with all hands and three hymns in the ward-room. In the afternoon the wardroom collected like rattlesnakes in the sunshine on the poop. I spent the day partly in writing up diary and partly in the crow's nest with a book. We had the best plum pudding I have ever eaten—which is saying a good deal—and it was the one which our good cook at home made specially for us and filled with shillings, sixpennies and buttons etc. I got a button which I hope I shall be able to bring along home as a souvenir.

Up in the crow's nest from cocoa at 5.30 to lunch at 12—except for breakfast. **Mon 2–Tues** Wrote up there and also looked for whales as we are in a calm sea and have bright **3 Jan** sunshine and can see to the horizon everywhere so that whales are visible at a great distance. Today I had luck for a new whale, as yet unnamed, came up alongside the ship and I saw it from end to end in the water as it appeared and rose to blow. It was a very well marked whale, 30 ft long, blackish on the back and white below with white paddles. The white showed as a border all round the black and outlined the whale most beautifully. It has only a small hooked dorsal fin like a Fin Whale (*B. musculus*). It seems fairly common down here. We have seen it half a dozen times and have now got a lot of drawings. It is quite distinct from the high-finned whale which I described in the *Discovery* report. We haven't seen those yet. In the afternoon I fired off the whale gun with a harpoon in to see if they knocked one over or burst or anything. The recoil was pretty heavy, but the harpoon flew well and straight carrying a line with it by which it was easily recovered. I had promised Atkinson a shot also. We were watching it to see how much drop to allow for in the sighting as the whole thing is so heavy that one can only hold it up to the shoulder for just long enough to fire. Atkinson got part of the recoil on his jaw and the harpoon flew, but the line alas! was no longer fast to it, so we lost the harpoon after watching it make a meteoric flight of about 30 yards as straight as an arrow. However, the engineer is going to make me another, and I also have a second one in hand, so we shall do. Not that I am very sanguine about getting a whale now, for it would mean far more delay making the attempt than we can possibly allow now. It might be possible on the way home, or we might have a chance in winter quarters.

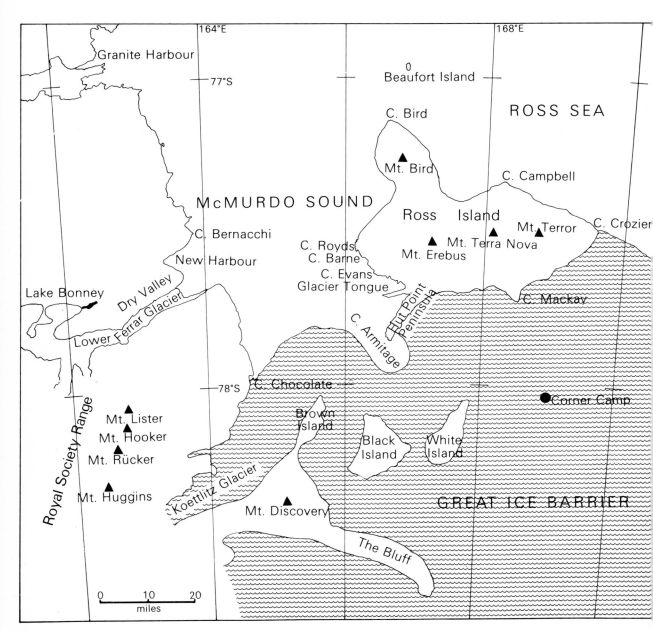

Map of the McMurdo Sound region

7

CAPE CROZIER TO CAPE EVANS

A

LL today we were busy on board with the approach to land. Mount Erebus **Mon 2—Tues 3** came in sight and we could see the double topped knoll which overlooks **Jan (continued)** the Emperor Penguins' rookery bay. We ought to be at Cape Crozier tomorrow and everyone is keen to see the place where we expect to winter during the coming year, but there is a horrible swell rolling in from the N.E. which will make a landing there impossible, at any rate today or tomorrow, and this may spoil our chance of wintering there as we have expended so much coal that we cannot afford to wait. We gradually came closer into the land and then made rather eastward with a view to examining the Great Barrier for some miles of the ordinary Barrier face before coming to the disturbed part where it abuts against Cape Crozier end of Ross Island on its way northward. It was a very beautiful day and a very beautiful sight as we saw first a brilliant white line appear on the horizon to the left of Mount Terror and then, as we came nearer, this white line developed into a long irregular line of white ice cliff standing out of the dark inky water. The water here at a distance has an inky blue look, but when one looks into it over the ship's side it is a dark sage green as the result of innumerable yellow and orange tinted diatoms floating in blue water. The water is thick with them and this accounts for the number of crustaceans, penguins, seals and whales in these waters—and they are abundant. As we came closer in the number of Adélie Penguins in the water became extraordinary. They were leaping in and out like little dolphins all round us in small schools. I was in the crow's nest nearly the whole time, and the water was as though hundreds of rifle bullets were dropping in around us everywhere. They swim extraordinarily fast, and though they live on euphausiæ (a schizopod crustacean) they often catch fish as well. In the water they look brown from above with white edges just showing on the sides and flippers. They don't use their feet but swim with their wings, and when they leap out and in to breathe in making a fast passage like dolphins, they leave the water and enter it again with wings spread out at right angles—and so make a good big splash every time. In the ordinary course of events when feeding they remain often less than a minute under water, but they can swim under very large sheets of ice in a very short time. Their chief enemies are certainly Killer Whales, of which more later. They are a perfect terror to all things in the water and on loose ice down here. Sea Leopards also eat penguins, but they are much less numerous than the Killer Whales.

As we came close into the Barrier we had a grand view over its surface which was

89

much curved, and we could see right away to White Island and Black Island—which were evidently what Sir James Ross called the Parry Mountains, only he had misjudged their distance, and therefore their height and position[1]. In the cliff just before us we had the usual wonderful green colour in the caves—a wonderful holly green—also cobalt blues and a line of emerald green along the water line. On the right, where the Barrier was jammed against Cape Crozier, we had a splendid view of the biggest pressure ridges known down here. There are five main ridges and they are a chaos of ice blocks and crevasses in ridges and hollows, 40 feet from the top of a ridge to the bottom of the hollow on each side. All these things are strangely familiar and it seems but yesterday that I was clambering over them roped up with Cross and Whitfield[2], or camped here with Charlie Royds. I was here three times and once was camped by these ridges for a month with the penguins on the sea ice, so I recognised every point and found very little alteration in any way. The Cape Crozier cliffs were as magnificent as I had always thought they were. More than a sheer drop they actually overhang at the top which is 400 feet above the sea beneath. There was a swell running in from the N.E. which proved an absolute bar to any landing here. The bay ice on which the Emperors habitually breed during the winter had, of course, all gone and in its place was open water to the foot of the ice cliff of the Barrier and to the foot of the Cape Crozier rock cliffs. Here, however, we brought the ship close in and then we lowered a boat in which were Captain Scott, Lieutenant Campbell, myself, Cherry-Garrard, Titus Oates and Taylor. We were to examine the possibilities of landing, but the swell was so heavy in its break among the floating blocks of ice along the actual beach and ice foot that a landing was out of the question—we should have broken up the boat and have all been in the water together. But I can assure you it was tantalising to me, for there, about six feet above us, on a small dirty piece of the old bay ice about ten feet square one living Emperor Penguin chick was standing disconsolately stranded, and close by stood one faithful old Emperor Penguin parent asleep. This young Emperor was still in the down, a most interesting fact in the bird's life history, at which we had rightly guessed, but which no one had actually observed before. It was however in a stage never yet seen or collected, for the wings were already quite clean of down and feathered as in the adult, also a line down the breast was shed of down and part of the head. This bird would have been a treasure to me, but we could not risk life for it, so it had to remain there with its faithful parent, asleep. It was a curious fact that with as much clean ice to live on as they could have wished for, these destitute derelicts of a flourishing colony now gone north to sea on floating bay ice, should have preferred to remain standing on the only piece of bay ice left—a piece about 10 feet square and now pressed up 6 feet above water level, evidently wondering why it was so long in starting north with the general exodus which must have taken place just a month ago. The whole incident was most interesting and full of suggestions as to the slow working of the brains of these queer people. Another point was most weird to see, namely, that on the *under* surface of this very dirty piece of sea ice, which was about two feet thick, and which hung over the water as a sort of cave, we could see the legs and lower halves of dead Emperor chicks hanging through—and even in one place a dead adult. I hope to make a picture of the whole quaint incident, for it was a corner cram full of imperial history in the light of what we already knew, and it would otherwise have been about as unintelligible as any group of animate and inanimate nature could possibly have been. As it is, it throws more light on the life history of this strangely primitive bird. We rowed round the bay trying at every likely spot for a landing but without success—the swell was too heavy for us. We rowed all along under the overhanging cliffs of Cape Crozier close in to examine the beautiful arrangement of the unusually fine columnar basalt which formed the face all along the lower half of the cliffs, and which was composed of hexagonal columns of a very unusually small size and regular shape which ran in curved lines forming fan shaped faces and caves as at the Giant's Causeway. Here and there the sea had undermined these caves deeply in, but only a foot or two above the sea surface. There was an ice foot all along hanging to and imbedded in a beach too steep to land on and very slippery, and undercut in places by the sea. Above us overhung thousands of tons of volcanic rock at about 300 to 400 feet and over this fell a waterfall of thaw water from a glacier at the top which was thawing out in the sun rapidly, owing to the amount of dark grit blown on to it, and owing to its proximity to so much dark rock. We were joking in the boat as we rowed under these cliffs and saying it would be a short lived amusement to see the over-hanging cliff part company and fall over us. So we were glad to find we were rowing back to the ship, and already were two or three hundred yards away from the place and in open water, when there was a noise like crackling thunder and a huge plunge into the sea, and a smother of rock dust like the smoke of an explosion, and we realised that the very thing had happened that we had just been talking about. Altogether it was a very exciting row, for before we got on board again we had the pleasure of seeing the ship shoved in so close to these cliffs by a belt of heavy pack ice that to us it appeared a toss up whether she got out again or got forced in against the rocks. She had no time or room to turn and got clear by backing out through the belt of pack stern first, getting heavy bumps under the counter and on the rudder as she did so, for the ice was heavy and the swell considerable. However, we got clear and were once more on board and then we proceeded round to the westward along the cliffs and then to the landing places with shelving beaches where the Adélie Penguins have their enormous nesting colonies. There must be two or three millions of birds here we think in this one colony. In the centre we could see the post which we put up ten years ago and on it the two cylinders, the lower one of which I attached myself when I was there in 1903, and read the contents of the upper one which had been left for us by the *Morning* in 1903 summer. There was no pack ice here, but there were several large stranded bergs—but alas no shelter of any sort or kind from the swell which rolled in straight from the north east and made our proposed landing here impossible, and the place as a winter quarters, admirable in every other aspect and beyond every other place interesting, out of the question.

It was now evening when we came unwillingly to this conclusion and wended our way along towards McMurdo Sound by way of Cape Bird. We made a running survey of the coast line up to midnight, all taking part with sextants, range-finders, altitudes, my own part being a running sketch as we went. I was very tired having been up since 4 a.m., and I turned in for two hours sleep, but was called up then at 1.30 to see the immense penguin rookery we were passing on Cape Bird.

Wed 4 Jan It was a lovely morning and I went up to the crow's nest and remained there—to go back to bed was out of the question for there were Killer Whales to watch around us, and the coast along Cape Bird I had never seen so close, and ahead of us was McMurdo Sound with all its familiar landmarks—full of pack ice and replete with possibilities, and the chances of a new landing place close ahead of us for our winter quarters. Fortune was with us for the morning was a glorious one, brilliant sunshine ahead all night and the sea as smooth as glass and the pack all loose enough to make a way through. These days are with one for all time—they are never to be forgotten—and they are to be found nowhere else in all the world but at the poles. The peace of God which passes all understanding reigns here in these days. One only wishes one could bring a glimpse of it away with one with all its unimaginable beauty. All that morning I was in the crow's nest or on the bridge. As we came along the coast and gradually approached Cape Royds—our old camping ground—lo and behold, the ice had all gone out and it was no longer a possible winter quarters for ourselves! So we proceeded further, having noticed on the way that the hut stood firm which Shackleton had built there and that no other change, but the mess around it, had taken place since the day when Captain Scott and I were camped there in January 1904, and the relief ships arrived, the *Morning* and the *Terra Nova*, just seven years ago.

We passed this place and worked our way on through the pack ice bit by bit until we were brought up by unbroken ice abreast of Inaccessible Island. I was all the time in the crow's nest—for we were seeing the new rorqual constantly around us and in such still water that it was possible to see the exact spot at which he would appear while he was still under water, and so one could see the detail of his head and blow hole and lips and back and fin again and again. Moreover, one of them was constantly rising out of the water at an angle of 45° to the extent of his paddles, so that one saw the long pointed rorqual-shaped head and shoulders all out of water. It was evidently done merely in sport as the throat was nearly always uppermost, and then he fell in backwards with a great splash. It was a lazy attempt at breeching. When we fetched up against solid unbroken ice, too thick to break, Captain Scott and Evans came up to the crow's nest and we had a consultation as to what it was possible to do. We had no choice but to abandon the idea of wintering where Shackleton had wintered at Cape Royds, because open water had already cut it off from the south. The next land point south is Cape Barne, and this was also isolated by open water. Then came Barne Glacier, and what we used to call the 'Skuary', a cape of moraine and rock standing out towards Inaccessible Island—and here we could winter with advantage. A new playground, a good position for relief, and separated from us now in the ship only by a mile and a half of hard sea ice over which we could easily transport our hut, motors, horses and stores. The alternative is to go to the west side of the strait, but we know that the road to the south from there is over very bad ice—the so called pinnacle ice[3] which comes down from Koettlitz Glacier[4]. Or we could wait and get further down towards Hut Point, which means an indefinite coal consumption

92

for a very doubtful benefit. So we all decided on the Skuary for our winter quarters and Captain Scott re-named it on the spot, Cape Teddie Evans instead of the Skuary. By this time it was breakfast hour, so we fed and then Scott and Evans and I walked over to find a suitable place for the hut and to see if there was good fresh ice for drinking purposes and stations for meteorology and so forth. We found all, and a most admirable sandy flat for the hut with a long snow drift for the horses and easy access from the sea ice. So the work of transhipment was at once begun. All the horses and the two of the three motors were got out first—without a hitch[5]. The horses were slung out in a small cage from the yard arm. So also were the motors slung out. The floe under us was about three feet thick. Everything went well and apace and the weather was absolutely perfect—baking hot sun, flat calm, clear sky and good surface for sledging. The hut pieces were next got out and taken over and then followed a week of uninterrupted hard work from morning till night during which every soul in the ship did his utmost and turned in dog-tired out every night at 10 to be called up to breakfast at 5 a.m. and work again till night. All today I was hauling over sledge loads with Campbell, Priestley, and Levick till 8 p.m. when we had food and turned in dead tired, having done about 12 miles, half of it heavy hauling and all on sea ice and snow.

Called at a quarter to 5. We had breakfast at 5 and then hauled over loads back- **Thurs 5 Jan** wards and forwards all day again until 7.30 when we dined and turned in. Our meals are breakfast 5 a.m., lunch at 12 to 1. Tea 4.30 to 5 and dinner any time after 7.30.

Turned out at 5 again and again sledge hauling till noon, then, as the sledge **Fri 6 Jan** runners were being cut up by the rough ice, Captain Scott turned me on to skin and flense seals to cover the runners of a sledge with seal skin. Finished at 8. Turned in after dinner.

Seaman Evans was turned over to me to help covering the runners with seal skin **Sat 7 Jan** as it was successful. I was therefore steeped in blood and blubber, killing and flensing from 5 a.m. when we turned out until 8 p.m. when we dined and turned in.

Turned out again at 5 a.m., all hands—a mistake. The hot sun we have had all **Sun 8 Jan** these days has rotted the ice. But nevertheless the third motor was got out and put on the ice floe and was being hauled for safety towards the shore by about 20 men, when it broke through and very nearly took two men with it. The ice was everywhere rotting fast. The motor went down in some 60 fathoms—R.I.P. We shall do all right without it, and it has warned us of the danger of running these things on unsafe ice. Had there been a driver sitting on it and a train of loaded sledges the whole lot must have gone together. There was great risk also in individuals falling through as two did, for the current at once dragged them under the ice. Happily in both cases they were helped out in a moment. Things were so unsafe in this way that work had to be stopped for the day and everyone had a rest. No one was allowed to go on the ice at all. I was on the ship all day and wrote up my diary. The motor is of course a big loss but happily we have two others, both of which have been working very well taking heavy loads over to the shore every day. From now onwards, however, they are not to be risked on the ice and they will therefore not be used again till after mid-winter when the sea is firmly frozen over. The ponies have been given very easy work and much rest to begin with after their trying time on the ship, but they have picked up quite wonderfully. There are some splendid animals amongst them, very vicious, and also some regular crocks, also vicious. They all bite and kick and run away without any warning. Campbell and Pennell and I went up to the crow's nest to find a better place for the ship to land stores on sounder ice, and we found it a little further north. Steam was raised and the ship was moved during the night to a place alongside very sound ice floe, also about a mile from the camp on shore.

Mon 9 Jan 5 a.m. to 8 p.m. sledging over stores and also taking pony loads over. I had Chinaman who ran away with me on sighting one of the motors. We had a tremendous flight over the sea ice, happily with an empty sledge, but I had a firm grip of his chin strap and I flew with him until on a very slippery piece of ice we all came down in a heap together, horse and sledge and I, and we slid in a heap for about 20 yards, and I was the first on my feet and still had hold of his head. After that he went like a lamb. Neither of us was any the worse for our run and I had the satisfaction of seeing Cherry-Garrard run away with in exactly the same way directly after—only the strap he was holding on to broke and his horse got away and went back to the pony lines on shore. These were the two initial efforts and they seemed to promise well for excitement, as we had begun with the quietest ponies of the whole lot. However, the next pony I took out went very well and so did the next, and I had one named after me that went like a brick with me and has gone well with me ever since. The ponies are good sport when they play up, but a little slow when they go too well. They carry a load varying from 600 lbs to a small pony to 1,000 lbs for a big one. Man haulage one allows only for 200 lbs per man—and dog haulage less than 100 lbs per dog. The motor sledges haul tons but we are not certain how many per motor on the Barrier, and the petrol is a heavy item.

Tues 10 Jan Shifting stores and transporting instruments 5 a.m. to 10 p.m.—a very long day— blowing a bit from the south and looks like blowing more.

Wed 11 Jan Up at 5.30 a.m. but it was blowing a mild blizzard and as the camp and ship were obscured from time to time no sledging was done and we had a rest. On shore they got on well with the hut and the stores. Evans and Bowers, Oates, Atkinson, Nelson, Day and the carpenter, Davies, have been working like bricks there. It is simply wonderful how quickly and how well everything has been got into order over there. They all live in tents and have their meals cooked on primus stoves in a very large general tent and the whole camp is extraordinarily well sheltered from all the troublesome winds. In the ship I had time for packing and writing up my diary.

Up 5.30 and turned in at 10, after a long day on shore at the camp, wet through **Thurs 12 Jan** the whole time from working with a pick with Teddie Evans and Nelson in the ice grotto—a cave we have made in a small glacier remnant to hold all our frozen mutton. It is now big enough to hold 120 carcases, but the work is difficult as it is only 4 ft high and one has to sit in a heap of ice chips all day long, very hot and therefore thawing all the little bits that touch one. When I got in to the ship my trowsers were lined with a smooth sheet of white ice and were able to stand up by themselves on the strength of it. It was a cold, wet job but the ice grotto is beautiful.

Up 5.30 and turned in at 10 p.m. after another long day on shore. We have now **Fri 13 Jan** got all our stores out of the ship and we have to ballast her as she is too light in the water. So all yesterday a gang of quarrymen was breaking out blocks of kenyte, a heavy volcanic rock, and the ponies were taking it on sledges to the ship. Today I joined the quarrymen and humped rock. The kenyte is very heavy and by Saturday—tomorrow night—we had 25 tons of it in the empty hold, a rare quarry for the New Zealand geologists to work over when the ship returns. We rolled the blocks along to the top of an ice slope on shore, loaded a heavy sledge with them and then let it run down on to the sea ice guided by one on each side, to where the ponies were waiting to carry it over the mile of sea ice to the ship.

Up at 5.30 a.m. to another day of ballasting the ship, and this time I did pony **Sat 14 Jan** wallah most of the time. It was lovely weather and it is to the continued fine weather that we are indebted for such great success in our landing and camp building. Everything has gone wonderfully well, and Captain Scott called me in after tea and showed me a long letter of some 12 sheets he had written home, and in it was absolutely nothing but the fullest appreciation of everybody's work —he is quite delighted with everyone and indeed everyone has deserved it. He also told me all his plans for the future, and that he has sent orders for 6 more ponies—more dogs—more sledges—more finnesko—more stores—in case another year is necessary for the reaching of the Pole, that is in case we fail next year. He also told me the plans for our depot journey on which we shall be starting in about ten days' time. He wants me to be a dog driver with himself, Meares and Teddie Evans, and this is what I would have chosen had I had a free choice of all. The dogs run in two teams and each team wants two men. It means a lot of run-ning as they are being driven now, but it is the fastest and most interesting work of all and we go ahead of the whole caravan with lighter loads and at a faster rate. Moreover, if any traction except ourselves can reach the top of Beardmore Glacier[6] it will be the dogs, and the dog drivers are therefore the people who will have the best chance of doing the top piece of the ice cap at 10,000 feet to the Pole. May I be there! About this time next year may I be there or thereabouts! With so many young bloods in the heyday of youth and strength beyond my own I feel there will be a most difficult task in making choice towards the end and a most keen competition—*and* a universal lack of selfishness and self-seeking, with a complete absence of any jealous feeling in any single one of the comparatively large number who at present stand a chance of being on the last piece next sum-mer. It will be an exciting time and the excitement has already begun, in the healthiest possible manner. I have *never* been thrown with a more unselfish lot of men—each one doing his utmost fair and square in the most cheery manner possible. Teddie Evans, Bowers, Oates, Meares, Atkinson, Nelson, Day, Cherry-Garrard, Wright, all are just as good a lot as one could ever hit upon. I say nothing now of the Eastern Party who are splendid, or of the Ship's Party led by Pennell, who is a most exceptional man. Nor can I say much of the geologists, except that they will do a power of work, but they don't come in the longer sledging competition. We are a very happy lot and so far have had the most unexpected good fortune with but few accidents and hitches, none of which, except possibly the loss of the third motor, could possibly have been foreseen or avoided, and the loss of the motor has been most useful as a warning against more serious loss, I think. As things are we stand very well indeed. No sickness, no serious accident, and in ten days' time we shall be away to the south to lay our depots and learn experience in horse traction and cold weather.

Sun 15 Jan   We were allowed to lie in till eight o'clock! And the day was given over to rest all hands or 'make and mend' as the saying is. We had Church service and thanksgiving hymns in the open sunlight on shore at our camp, just by the hut just built and now almost complete inside. It was a glorious day and everyone joined in— the Captain of course reading the service. After the service I came back to the ship and wrote up this diary and got some letters done as well.

'In the teeth of a blizzard'

8

DEPOT LAYING

A<small>T</small> Cape Evans in the new hut where we are now all living. We turned out early **Tues 24 Jan** to start off on the depot laying journey. Breakfast at 7. All the dogs, two teams, one of eleven and the other of thirteen, with their sledges and sledge loads, were put on board the ship last night. Meares and I, who are attached to the dog teams, did not go with them but led the horse party over the rough rock and snow of Cape Evans and down on to the sea ice of the South Bay and then across about 6 miles of sea ice to the Glacier Tongue. The ice here was on the point of breaking up and there were very large open water sheets round several bergs on the landward side of the Razorback Islands and also off the glacier snout north of Turk's Head Rock cliffs. We had good walking, however, on this ice and had no difficulty in avoiding the larger thaw pools, nor had we any trouble with the string of horses, no less than seven of them led by Oates, Atkinson, Bowers, Cherry-Garrard, Keohane, Forde and Gran. We heard on our return to the hut in April that the whole of this ice broke up and went out the very next day, so that we were only just in time. We reached the Glacier Tongue at the same time as the ship, which was bringing all our dogs, sledges and sledge loads for the ponies, and Captain Scott and Evans. We halted the horses on the sea ice under the Glacier Tongue while I went across with Meares to the ship to get instructions. The whole Tongue is much crevassed but there was no other way to get to the south side of the Glacier Tongue so we had to take all the ponies across it. We had no accident, though they were constantly putting their feet through crevasse lids and just not getting in. There was open sea right up to the end of Glacier Tongue, preventing us from going round it. In trying to find an easy way up to the top of the glacier Captain Scott and I both got into very rotten thin ice and he went through up to his knees. There was an Emperor Penguin standing near by but on unsafe ice. The rise up on to the Glacier Tongue is by a snow drift slope and one can get an easy road up the 15 or 20 feet which lands one on the top towards the end of the Tongue where we were. This snout is the peculiar tongue of glacier ice which runs out about 6 miles from the slopes of Erebus to the sea. It must be supported on a ridge of rock or it would long ago have broken away. It was now exactly as it had been in the *Discovery* days, but when we returned to Hut Point in March we found that about 2 miles of the end had broken up into icebergs and floated off to the sea. Some of these pieces got stranded on a reef of rock not far from Cape Evans and later on gave me splendid material for sketches. After crossing the Glacier Tongue we took the horses down on the other side and picketed them on the sea ice, not far

97

from where the ship was moored to the Tongue. We then lunched on the ship and after lunch started off with horses and dogs all loaded up with sledges for our march to Camp I abreast of Castle Rock. There was a great deal of photographing and a good deal of trouble and excitement with the dogs on the hard blue glacier ice, and with the ponies on the sea ice. One got into a crack and it was a very difficult thing hauling it out with an alpine rope! But it was got out all right and seemed none the worse for it. With the dogs the difficulty was that on the blue glacier ice it was quite impossible to check them and they took charge entirely, which was uncomfortable when one had ice precipices of varying heights up to 50 and 60 ft on one side down on to sea ice, and crevasses every 5 to 15 yds. But we all survived it and turned in to our tents and sleeping bags at 11 p.m. I will add a small map showing our route on this sledge journey and our various camps, and the outline of the open water and the sea ice over which we were hurrying our animals and very heavy loads for the depot laying on the Barrier which is to assist us materially in our journey to the Pole next year.

Wed 25 Jan Turned out at 7 a.m. Went back to the ship with all the ponies and the two dog teams and brought on more loads. I lunched again in the ship—she is still moored to Glacier Tongue and in the afternoon I returned with my dog sledge loaded up to Camp I and turned into my bag about 11 p.m.

Thurs 26 Jan Turned out at 7 a.m. Back to fetch remainder of loads with my dog team—lunched at ship and then bade a final goodbye to our friends on board and the Eastern Party who are to attempt to establish a station on King Edward's Land. This Eastern Party, which we learned afterwards became a Northern Party, consists of Campbell, Lieut. R.N., Levick, Surgeon R.N., Priestley, geologist who was with Shackleton, and Abbott, Petty Officer R.N., and Browning, Seaman R.N. I was sorry to lose Pennell's companionship—he is such an exceedingly nice chap and by far the most capable man on the whole expedition. However, we had a great send off and we all had our hands so full that we couldn't worry much about partings. Ponting took numerous photos—cinematograph and others—which no doubt you will see. I came in on one of the dog sledges which Captain Scott was driving for the first time almost—and for the last—for I had charge of that team and drove it throughout the coming 3 months. In the group—the only one I have seen myself—I see I am very fat! And indeed I was, and equally fit, which was necessary as in dog driving one runs alongside the loaded sledge for miles over the snow and ice every day. At the end of March when I had had two months of this running on the Barrier I wasn't quite so fat. It was interesting to watch a couple of rorqual whales (*B. musculus*) which kept feeding close round the ship alongside the Glacier Tongue. They showed themselves well—constantly coming up to blow close by and diving under the fast ice. While I was dog driving they would occasionally blow and show a dorsal fin in an open crack in the middle of what was apparently at a distance fast sea ice, and then nothing would hold the dogs—they were simply mad to get at it and they would tear off in the direction of the blow where I knew there was a great lake of open water which we couldn't see till we were within a few yards of it. I had awful trouble to stop them from going in with me and the sledge and loads and everything. Seals, too, and stray penguins are a constant source of trouble when one is on sea ice as the ice is so hard that the iron shod stick with which one puts on the break will not bite and one simply rushes along in a shower of ice chips. Well, we got away finally from the ship today and again slept at Camp I. In the tent with me are Captain Scott, Teddie Evans and Meares—4 of us.

Turned out at 7 a.m. and took on some of our loads to Camp II off Cape Armitage. **Fri 27 Jan** In the evening we all went over to Hut Point where we found the old hut simply filled with hard packed snow drift up to the roof. We had to get in through a window and then we began to dig and clear it out—a long job which we couldn't nearly finish. The last occupants had been Shackleton and his party on their return from the southern journey. His relief and depot parties had also spent a good deal of time there and had left it in a perfectly filthy condition besides having broken a window open and left it unboarded, so that every blizzard had poured more snow drift in and filled the hut. We found a lot of *Discovery* biscuit there, our own and dog biscuit, as well as some other stores which we had left there 7 years before—they were all quite good. It was sad though to see the place in such a state. The two asbestos huts used for magnetic work were mere skeletons, all the asbestos sheeting having been stripped by the winds, but the actual living hut structure was as sound as ever and only wanted cleaning out to be quite habitable, and this we are glad to see as we shall have to live here when we get back from this depot journey until the sea freezes over enough to take us back to Cape Evans— that is if the ice is going to break out to Hut Point this year. We slept tonight at Camp II. Atkinson has a badly rubbed heel which he showed me today—looks like knocking him out of the journey which will be awkward.

Meares took his dog team in to Hut Point and brought out some dog biscuit. One **Sat 28 Jan** of the horses went lame and was kept in camp. So was Atkinson, and I remained with my dog team to look after them all that night after making one journey to Camp III and back.

Fourth Sunday after the Epiphany. Up at 8 a.m. and Captain Scott read prayers **Sun 29 Jan** in the open after breakfast. Then made a journey to Camp III which is on the edge of the Barrier ice, and then back to Camp II, where Atkinson is lying up, and here remained with him the night.

Camp III is to be called Safety Camp because it is on the old Barrier ice, which **Mon 30 Jan** is not expected to break away under any circumstances. Here, therefore, a depot was made and the horses were all given a rest while Meares and I, with the two dog teams, were employed in bringing loads along to this camp from the very edge of the Barrier ice where they had been first dumped. Close to this point, and quite near the edge of the Barrier, we came across two of Shackleton's tents which had been abandoned there with all the sledging equipment belonging to a party. These were dug out and the primus still had oil in it which we used to cook a meal. The tents were two thirds buried in snow and were full of hard compact snow ice. The tent material had of course perished. We found also a complete cooker—and the two sets of male bamboo tent poles were very useful. Enormous numbers of seals, all Weddells, lay along the cracked sea ice where the sea ice joins the Barrier, and all along to Pram Point. There is a large pool of open water off Cape Armitage and another off Hut Point as in the old days. Between them is a good ice road into the ice foot by the hut though. I brought Atkinson along to Camp III on my dog sledge as he couldn't walk, and here I had to open up his heel and I got a lot of bad stuff out which relieved him a lot. The seals have been giving us a lot of trouble, that is just Meares and me, with our dogs. The whole teams go absolutely crazy when they get wind of them or sight them and there are literally hundreds along some of the cracks—many hundreds. Occasionally, when one believes oneself to be quite away from trouble of that kind, an old seal will pop his head up at a blow-hole a few yards ahead of the team and they are all on top of him before one can say 'knife'! Then one has to rush in amongst them with the whip, and then everyone of the team of eleven jumps over the harness of the dog next to him and the harnesses become a muddle that takes much patience to unravel, not to mention care lest the whole team should get away with the sledge and its load and leave one behind to follow on foot at leisure. I never got left the whole of this depot journey, but I was often very near it and several times had only time to seize a strap or a part of the sledge and be dragged along at full length helter skelter over everything that came in the way until the team got sick of galloping and one could struggle to one's feet again. One gets very watchful and wide awake when one has to manage a team of eleven dogs and a sledge load by oneself, but it was a most interesting experience and I had a delightful leader, Stareek[1] by name—the Russian for 'Old Man'—and he was a most wise old man. One has to use Russian terms[2] with all our dogs. 'Ki Ki' means go to the right, 'Chui' means go to the left. 'Eshte' means lie down—and the remainder are mostly swear words which mean everything else that one has to say to a dog team. Dog driving like this in the orthodox manner is a very different thing to the beastly dog driving we perpetrated in the *Discovery* days. I got to love all my team and they got to know me well, and my old leader even now—I am writing this six months after I have had anything to do with any of them—never fails to come and speak to me whenever he sees me, and he knows me and my voice ever so far off. He is quite a ridiculous 'old man' and quite the nicest, quietest, cleverest old dog gentleman I have ever come across. He looks in face as though he knew all the wickedness of all the world and all its cares and as though he was bored to death by both of them. I must get Ponting to photograph him with me—he's a dear old thing.

Tues 31 Jan Spent the forenoon transferring bales of Geelong horse fodder (compressed chaff with a few oats) from the depot at the edge of the Barrier ice to Safety Camp with my dog team. After lunch there was a general meeting as the horses had found the Barrier snow surface very heavy yesterday. They were rested here, and Atkinson also is laid up here. Only one pair of horse snowshoes have been brought—these were tried today and found to answer very well so it was decided that Meares and I should go back to Cape Evans hut, or try to do so, and fetch all the other horses' snowshoes. My team had been working all day, so Meares and I went with his team of 13 dogs. We had a long steady run, and it was bitterly cold with a biting wind and snow drift. We covered about 15 miles and reached the Glacier Tongue almost without a stop. We had a little trouble here and there with seals but we went at a very good rate and on nearing Glacier Tongue came to a crack which had opened too wide for the sledge to go safely over. I got off and ran along it to find a narrower place when the dogs suddenly took it into their heads to cross it, and Meares and the sledge of course followed with them, happily without going in; but for myself there was no alternative but to jump, and as it was too wide and with rotten edges I naturally went through with my legs and one of my finnesko got filled up with water, but I scrambled out and was not cold as it all froze up and kept the wind out. We then ran up a snow drift over the tide crack and on to the top of the Glacier Tongue and across it in a biting wind and drift—and then we saw that the sea ice had gone out and we were cut off from Cape Evans. So we turned and ran across the glacier and then down the same drift and over the same tide crack which gave us a terrific bump, and looking back I saw we had run over a crevasse which had let half the length of the sledge down in its run, only the dogs were going down hill so fast that it had come up again. Then we ran over the wide crack again, this time both on the sledge, trusting in Providence that we shouldn't go in the water—so we didn't. Then, not liking to camp so near the edge of the ice, which seemed only too likely to break up any time, we ran on south for about 5 miles and then camped with precious little snow on hard glossy sea ice— all that we could find. The wind and drift had been very bitter all day and all night while we were travelling and we had some trouble pitching our four-man tent with only the two of us to do it in the strong wind. But as soon as we had supped the wind dropped and then we had a comfortable night.

We turned out at 8 a.m. and as it was again blowing and bitterly cold we ran the **Wed 1 Feb** team right on with hardly a stop till we again reached the others at Safety Camp. There were enormous numbers of Weddell Seals along the pressure crack running out from Pram Point, and all along here were hollows full of blue sludgy ice and water through which the dogs rushed us helter-skelter in their excitement over the seals. We were at Safety Camp by noon and then I resumed the transport of stores from the Barrier edge with my own team. In the evening I had to decide whether Atkinson could come on with us or not—and I had to say no. He was frightfully disappointed and Crean was chosen to remain behind with him in Safety Camp until he could walk, and then they were to return to Hut Point—if possible to be picked up by the ship which was to come there and leave a note after landing the Eastern Party at King Edward's Land, and so be taken back to Cape Evans. As a matter of fact, though they went to Hut Point they got there after the ship had called and gone away again, and they therefore had to stay there until we returned in March. They put the time in very usefully by making a complete clearance of the living hut, so that when we got back it was all clean and tidy and quite habitable. Atkinson's foot was bad for about a week after we left him, but then gradually got well.

Safety Camp. Turned out 7 a.m. Packed my sledge with a big load for 11 dogs. **Thurs 2 Feb** We left everything here in a depot that we could dispense with just now. The horses all went first. Scott and Teddie Evans leading the two that Atkinson and Crean had been leading. Meares and I followed in 2 hours with our dog teams and caught the horse party up by lunch time having done 5 miles. It was decided that we should now travel by night time instead of by day as the surface, which was dreadfully soft for the horses, would be firmer in the lower night temperatures. Our lunch camp, therefore, became a night camp and our night camp a lunch camp. We are to turn out at 10 p.m. tonight and march through the night. The weather is fine and still and sunny but cold, and this morning we had a very biting wind in our faces at −4°F. Turned out at 10 p.m. and did 5 miles.

Fri 3 Feb Lunch Camp at 2 a.m. Very cold breeze. Ran the dog team from 4 a.m. to 6 a.m. then camped for the supper and turned in. Cold going and soft crusty surface. Turned out 10 p.m. Ponies got away after midnight.

Sat 4 Feb Ponies made 5½ miles from 1 a.m. to 4 a.m. Meares and I followed with the dogs. Lunch camp 4 a.m. to 6 a.m. After lunch the ponies made 5½ miles from 6 a.m. to 9 a.m. and again we followed with the dogs giving the ponies 1 to 1½ hours start. While we wait Meares and I build a large cairn to mark our camp site. Camped at 9 a.m. and turned in about noon. No wind during the march, warm sun though low in the south. Good surface on the whole, soft drifts alternating with smooth hard wind-swept sastrugi which gave splendid going in the second march both for dogs and horses. We broke into two crevasses in today's march, otherwise no excitements. Temperature from zero F. to +20° or more. We had a parhelion[3] with very bright iridescent clouds at midnight. During the day while we slept it came on to blow with drift and snow fall and an overcast sky. Our dogs are getting 1 lb of dog biscuit each a day. They get nothing on turning out—1 biscuit after the first march and 2 in the evening after the second march. The biscuits are Spratts and contain meat and codliver oil—but we have decided that 1 lb of these biscuits is too little for them. They are all thinning down very much.

Sun 5 Feb Lying up. Blowing and drifting and thick with snow. This is called Corner Camp because here we turn south on 169°E. longitude.

Mon 6 Feb Lying up all day. Warm and wet. Temperature +20° to +24°F. We lie in hollows where the sun melts out under our bags, but we are very comfortable. The horses have been looking very wretched in this snow storm and the dogs have been buried again and again. Wind force 6 to 7. The dogs are quite happy and the only trouble they give is from twisting up their harness into knots by turning round and round every time they get up, before lying down again.

Tues 7–Wed 8 Feb Now 2 p.m. and still blowing 3 to 4, but no more drift and the sun has appeared. We start marching again this evening at 8 p.m. Everyone busy taking sights and digging out sledges, and I sketching. We made 5 miles in our first march and 5 again in our second and camped and turned in about 8 a.m.

Thurs 9 Feb Got under way soon after midnight. We with dogs remained 2 hours behind and built a cairn. Made 10 miles in the day. Surface hard and good.

Breeze and overcast with low surface drift. Turned out 9 p.m. Broke camp 11 p.m. **Fri 10 Feb** Horses got away at midnight. Dogs got away 1½ hours later. Dogs arrived lunch camp about 4 a.m. Mended my sleeping bag which was split. Horses got away again about 5 a.m. Dogs about 6 a.m. and arrived at the IXth Camp at 8 a.m. Distance in the day 7 miles + 5 miles = 12. We had wind against us and a bad light so that we lost all trace of the horse party's tracks. Each member of our tent takes a week on as cook in turn.

Grey and overcast but no wind. The surface was excellent for the dogs all day. **Sat 11 Feb** There was a sunset light on the western mountains today for the first time warning us that the season is closing in. My dog team's pace with fair loads, not heavy ones, and a good surface, such as today's, was 5 miles in 50 minutes. We covered eleven miles in all today and of that I ran about 4 by the side of the sledge in spells of a few hundred yards at a time off and on all day. Splendid exercise.

Septuagesima Sunday. Overcast and not cold. We did 10 miles in the march. **Sun 12 Feb** Travelling with animals like this and being very careful not to overdo them we have long hours in our sleeping bags and time to read as well as to sleep.

Blizzardy storms off and on all Sunday and into the night with a good deal of **Mon 13 Feb** drift, but sun breaking through occasionally. This delayed our start until 1.30 a.m. when Scott, Oates, Bowers, Cherry-Garrard and Gran went on with 5 horses while Evans, Keohane and Forde returned with 3 rather worn out horses. My eleven dogs are now taking 100 lbs of Geelong horse fodder, 200 lbs of dog biscuits, a tank full of provisions, a tent, floorcloth and poles, a sleeping bag, an alpine rope and bo'sun's bag. I should think about 50 lbs a dog. After lunch Meares and I waited behind for an hour as usual after the horses, when a snow storm came on so thick that we decided it was impossible to follow them with any chance of finding them, so we remained where we were and had the tent to our two selves. The other 5 crowded into one tent for the night and were warm! The wind and drift dropped at 7 p.m. so we struck camp and followed the others up and had breakfast with them.

Cherry-Garrard has now joined our tent in place of Evans. We are now Scott, **Tues 14 Feb** Meares, Cherry and myself, 2 horse leaders and 2 dog drivers. Coming into camp today one of the ponies known as Weary Willie, led by Gran, foundered just as Meares with his team of dogs was passing. The whole team turned into wolves like a wink and made for the horse as it lay in the snow and were all on top of it in a moment notwithstanding all that Meares could do to check them. They knew at once, as they always do, that the horse was done and an easy prey, and they all knew it. Gran and Meares both broke their sticks promiscuously on the dogs' heads and the horse kicked and bit at them, and they were at last driven off, but not before the poor beast of a horse had been pretty severely bitten. I was behind Meares when his team took charge and my own dogs at once spotted what was going on and wanted to rush, but I was prepared for them and stopped where I was till the whole show was done and the horse on his legs and in camp again. The surface was soft and very heavy for the dogs after the snow storm yesterday. Weary Willie couldn't pull his load in the afternoon so we only managed 7½ miles in the whole day, 6½ of which were done in the first march. As this was Meares' birthday we had a special effort for the supper meal consisting of dry hoosh—i.e. biscuit crumbs fried with pemmican and cheese rind and curry powder—cocoa thickened with arrowroot and sultanas, biscuit and a piece of chocolate. One sleeps very well in this life. I slept from 10 a.m. to 10 p.m. with the exception of one hour's reading in my bag.

Wed 15 Feb Still and calm and clear sun. Temperature −4°F. We did 4 miles in the first march, starting soon after midnight, and 3 miles in the second march. The surface was generally good but here and there were heavy drifts of soft sand-like powdery snow. There were also innumerable subsidences of the surface, the breaking of crusts over air spaces under them, large areas dropping a quarter of an inch or so with a hushing sort of noise or muffled sort of report[4]. My leader Stareek, the nicest and wisest old dog in the whole of both teams, thought there was a rabbit under the crust every time one gave way close by him, and he would jump sideways with both feet on the spot and his nose in the snow. The action was like a flash and never checked the team—it was most amusing. I have another funny little dog, Mukaka, small but very game and a good worker. He is paired with a fat and lazy and very greedy black dog, Nugis by name, and in every march this sprightly little Mukaka will once or twice notice that Nugis isn't pulling and will jump over the trace, bite Nugis like a snap, and be back again in his own place before the fat dog knows what has happened. This occurs nearly every march. At our lunch camp the temperature went down to −15°F. and there was much mirage. While we were all asleep in the tents today one of the horses known as Uncle Bill first ate his hobble, then got to a bale of fodder, and then got to one of our canvas tanks[5] of biscuit and ate a lot of them. They are dreadfully hungry, poor beasts. I think their compressed fodder isn't very feeding for them. This horse eat a whole cloth puttee the other day and has eaten endless head ropes and his picketing line. Now he is on a steel wire.

Thurs 16 Feb We made 5 miles and 3½ in the two marches still always at night and camping for the day. This of course is to suit the horses as the surface is so much better when the sun is low in the south at night. Sunny and clear today, but −20°F. with a breeze. Nearly everyone got frost nipped—ears or cheeks or noses. I am hardly ever troubled in this way.

Fri 17 Feb We reached our final camp and made a large cairn and a depot of a ton of food for men, dogs and horses. It was very cold and windy, everyone getting frost nipped. The building up of this and the planting of a flag and 2 sledges and the sorting out of provisions took us all our time and we made no march. This is to be called One Ton Depot and it is in sight of the Bluff[6].

Sat 18 Feb Overcast, temp. −10°F. Marched nearly 11 miles before we camped for lunch. We have divided the party now for the homeward march. The 5 horses are to go

'Beaufort Island, Ross Sea. Jan.4.11. 1 a.m.'

S.P.R.I. 416

Delbridge Islands and the slopes of Mt. Erebus. 30 March 1911. 6.30 p.m.

S.P.R.I. 452

'Mt. Erebus from Hut Point. March 1911'

alone with Oates, Bowers and Gran, while Meares and I with our dog teams are to take Scott and Cherry-Garrard as passengers. We of course go much faster than the horses. We covered 23 miles in the day—or rather night—and then camped. I have Cherry on my sledge, and he and I take turns at running alongside.

We covered 25 miles in all after an overcast night with drift and some wind. All **Sun 19 Feb** plain and straightforward travelling, Cherry and I running alongside in turns. Our team was running a few hundred yards behind Meares who carries Captain Scott.

A beautiful night with a marvellous orange pink afterglow all night lighting up **Mon 20 Feb** Erebus and Terror. We covered 33 miles today and passed a snow cairn which Evans had built to mark a bale of fodder which he had depoted. We found out on meeting him that we had missed another cairn close by where he had buried one of his horses which died on the way back. He is still ahead of us with Forde and Keohane and 2 horses.

The light was bad today, but there was no wind happily. We got too near in **Tues 21 Feb** towards White Island and found ourselves running over irregular ice—snow drifts alternating with weathered blue ice surfaces, the sort of stuff that I knew would be crevassed. We however kept running as before and as I ran I knew from the noise and feel under foot that every now and then we were crossing rotten lidded crevasses. Once my foot went through and I leapt on to the sledge and saw my leading dog at the same moment scramble out of a crack into which he had broken with his hind feet—but the sledge was running fast and all the team and the sledge with Cherry and myself ran over all right. This sort of surface continued for a mile or a mile and a half and I was running my team abreast of Meares, but about 100 yds on his right, when I suddenly saw his whole team disappear, one dog after another, as they ran down a crevasse in the Barrier surface. Ten out of his 13 dogs disappeared as I watched. They looked exactly like rats running down a hole—only I saw no hole. They simply went into the white surface and disappeared. I saw Scott, who was running alongside, quickly jump on the sledge, and I saw Meares jam the brake on as I fixed my sledge and left Cherry with my dogs and ran over to see what had really happened. I found that they had been running *along* a lidded crevasse, about 6 to 8 ft wide, for quite a distance, and the loaded sledge was still standing on it, while in front was a great blue chasm in which hung the team of dogs in a festoon. The leader, Osman, a very powerful fine dog, had remained on the surface and the 2 dogs next the sledge were also still on the surface. The long trace hung in a long loop down the crevasse between these two rear dogs and the leader Osman, and from it hung the remainder of the team in their harnesses, whining and yapping and trying to get a foothold on each other and on the crumbly snow sides of the crevasse. Two of the dogs had slipped out of their harness and fallen 40 feet down to a snow ledge where they immediately curled up and went to sleep! The crevasse was 40 ft deep to this ledge and then blue holes went deeper here and there. The miracle was that the sledge hadn't followed the dogs with Meares and Captain Scott. We first got the sledge off the crevasse lid and then unpacked it in case it should be dragged in with our tent and sleeping bags while we were retrieving the dogs. We had one alpine rope, and having bridged the crevasse with our empty sledge we tied the rope to Meares and lowered him till he could reach the nearest two or three dogs which he cut out of their harness and hoisted out one by one. We, meanwhile, were hanging on also to the sledge end of the trace and saving Osman from being throttled, for the only reason that he did not go down with the rest was that the trace had cut into the edge of the crevasse edge and was using him as a sort of toggle, and as it had a turn round his chest it was all but choking him. We then got the alpine rope attached nearer to the weight of the remaining dogs on the trace and hauled until one by one the dogs came within reach and could be cut loose and hoisted up, and so by degrees we got all of them up, though it took about an hour and a half. There were still two more on the ledge at the bottom and after testing the length of the alpine rope we let Scott down at his request. We all wanted to go instead of him, but he insisted, and so we recovered all the dogs that went down. Several of them suffered a bit from their adventure having hung head down in their harnesses for a long time by a tight band round the hind-quarters. They showed signs of damage inside for some days, and one dog never got over it and died about a month later. We luckily had no wind all the time we were working at this business—it was cold for the hands as it was, holding on for an hour or two and hauling on thin taut rope. When we had all the dogs up they were of course loose—many in cut harness ends—and the first thing they did when we were not watching, was to wander over, one or two of them, to my team and start a fight and in a second the whole 24 dogs were all in a furious fighting, biting, barking, ravening heap, with my team's trace and harness tied up in knots that took me about an hour to unravel when they had finished, which they did pretty quickly with the four of us—no three of us, for Captain Scott was at the bottom of the crevasse at the moment and we had to leave him there till we stopped the dog fight—three of us hammering them promiscuously and dragging off the loose ones. One of my dogs was badly bitten all over, evidently had been the centre of attraction—it was the fat little black lazy one, but he soon recovered and was none the worse for his doing. We camped here and had lunch and then made another march on a bad surface, but without any more crevasse incidents, and then camped for the day.

Wed 22 Feb All day while we were camped it was clear brilliant sunshine, drying everything and making the tent so warm that we worked 2 or 3 hours after supper at sewing and writing. We turned out to a brilliant evening and got off at 10 p.m. with gorgeous sunset to the south behind White Island, and a glorious salmon red glow over Erebus and Terror. We lunched after 10 miles and after lunch came to Safety Camp in 4 miles where we found Teddie Evans with Forde and Keohane, who had now only one pony alive of the three they were bringing home. The other two had died on the way back completely worn out. We turned in at 7.15 a.m. and had sleep till 11 a.m. when we again turned out and started off on foot for Hut Point, now 6 miles off, since here we expected to find the last news which the ship could leave us before going north after having been to King Edward's Land with the

Eastern Party. Scott, Evans, Cherry-Garrard, Meares and I went there with a sledge. We expected also to find Atkinson and Crean there, or else a note to say that the ship had taken them to Cape Evans. We found neither—no Crean or Atkinson, no note to say where they had gone, and no message from the ship, although scrawled on the door was a line to say that we should find the ship's message and letters from Pennell in a bag hung on a certain nail in the hut. This bag was gone, and we could make nothing of it except the possible coincidence that on this very day Atkinson and Crean might have left the Hut to go and meet us with these letters at Safety Camp, and they *might* have gone by the sea ice round Cape Armitage instead of by the Gap[7] which was the way we came. So we might have missed them, and this was exactly what had happened, unlikely as it looked at the time. They got to Safety Camp before we did and there we heard the news which Pennell had left us before going north for good. Briefly, it was that after separating from us at Glacier Tongue he had taken the Eastern Party with two ponies, under Campbell, along the Barrier until held up by very heavy ice which prevented them from reaching King Edward's Land. They found no landing place at all possible and so they came back to the Bay of Whales[8] where they were surprised to find the *Fram* with Amundsen and a party of Norwegians in full swing, landing stores and a host of dogs on the Barrier ice, in what appears to us from their account to be a very unsafe position. Our party and the Norwegians exchanged courtesies and Amundsen suggested that Campbell should also land there, but Campbell preferred not, so they left and returned to Cape Evans, depositing the two ponies which Campbell thought would now be of more use to us than to him. Then having left notes and some supplies for us at Hut Point, they turned north with the intention of landing Campbell and his party somewhere in the neighbourhood of Cape Adare or Cape North, and this of course is the last we know of them at present. Campbell will very likely have landed at Cape Adare itself as it would give him a fine field for work which Borchgrevink never touched. As for Amundsen's prospects of reaching the Pole, I don't think they are very good, for I don't think his dogs—though he has so large a number, 116, and good drivers with lots of experience—I don't think he knows how bad an effect the monotony and the hard travelling surface of the Barrier is to animals[9]. Another mistake he seems to have made is in building his hut on sea ice below the Barrier surface instead of on the Barrier itself. It will be a fortunate thing for him if the whole hut doesn't float out into Ross Sea. There are 8 in his party. However, he may be fortunate and his dogs may be a success, in which case he will probably reach the Pole this year, earlier than we can, for not only will he travel much faster with dogs and expert ski runners than we shall with ponies, but he will be able also to start earlier than we can as we don't want to expose the ponies to any October temperatures[10]. The ship's message with this thrilling news was left at Hut Point on Feb. 8th. Atkinson, who had been laid up with a bad foot at Safety Camp, 6 miles off, didn't see them. His foot is now quite well, and he and Crean had spent their time making Hut Point habitable for our return. We were pretty well tired when we got back to Safety Camp as we had been on the go all night and all day with only an hour or two of sleep. We now once more began the day routine—sleeping at night and being up at day.

Thurs 23 Feb While the others prepared to make a man-haulage party to Corner Camp to meet Oates and Bowers and Gran, who were coming along with their 5 ponies, Meares and I went off with my dog team to get a supply of seal meat for the dogs, and for the camp. We killed and cut up 2 large Weddells out of a bunch of 13 that we found in a hollow under the Barrier edge and brought the meat back to camp. It was a horrible day, very cold and blowing and drifting all the while, and nearly everything was blotted out of sight, so that we had some little difficulty in getting back to our camp on the open Barrier. However, we were back by 5 and Cherry made us supper and we turned into our bags—the others had been lying up all the afternoon.

Fri 24 Feb Turned out at 5 a.m. Snowing flaky crystals and a very heavy rime and dense white fog. Scott, Cherry-Garrard and Keohane with one sledge, Atkinson, Evans and Forde with another, left on ski for Corner Camp. Meares and I remained in Safety Camp with our two dog teams which wanted rest and seal meat after their run home. We also had a lot of dog harness to mend and dog biscuit cases to bring in to this camp from the depot at the edge of the Barrier.

Sat 25 Feb We turned out at 6 a.m. Too thick to leave camp during the forenoon so we mended harness and built a long shelter wall[11] for the horses which we expected soon to arrive. They turned up at 10 p.m.—all right—with Oates, Bowers and Gran. In the afternoon I ran my team to the dog biscuit depot and brought in 3 cases.

Sun 26 Feb Quinquagesima Sunday. Blowing and drifting all day from the E. and N.E. We occupied ourselves building walls for the ponies and to shelter our own tents, otherwise lying up in our bags—happily with some good reading, as Atkinson had brought several old *Eclectic Magazines* into this camp from Hut Point.

Mon 27 Feb Lying up all day—Meares and I in our tent, Oates, Bowers and Gran in theirs. Very heavy drift and snow fall and high wind burying the ponies up to their bellies behind their shelter walls.

Tues 28 Feb Wind and drift dropping and sun appearing. Our sleeping bags and the tent cloth sopping wet. The Corner Camp party returned. Meares and I are now to take our dog teams to Hut Point with all our gear and the horse party will follow us. We had a somewhat lengthy discussion on the advisability of going there by the Gap or by the other way round Cape Armitage which meant round the large thaw pool off Cape Armitage. I was all for the Gap, for I didn't believe that the sea ice would still be safe the other way without making a very big détour round the Cape Armitage thaw pool—and this point I urged—but I was overruled to the extent of being told to go round Cape Armitage way if possible, but to feel quite independent and so far as the dog teams were concerned to be guided by my own judgment. As it turned out this freedom of movement saved Meares and myself from getting into great trouble with the two dog teams. With the ponies we had nothing to do, as Captain Scott was in charge when we left the camp and as we travel nearly three times as fast as the ponies we very soon left the camp behind, and before the ponies were ready to start we were getting on to the sea ice. Then began a remarkable chain of incidents which led to the loss of all the remaining ponies, except one, and very nearly to the loss of three lives, and I firmly believe that the whole train of what looked so like a series of petty mistakes and accidents was a beautiful prearranged plan in which each one of us took exactly the moves and no others that an Almighty hand intended each of us to take—and no others. Each of us, preyed upon by just those feelings that our particular pasts had made us open to, did just those things which were necessary to produce the required result and teach the necessary lessons. The whole thing was just a beautiful piece of education on a very impressive scale. At any rate there was no doubt about its having been impressive enough. Well, Meares and I led off with a dog team each, and leaving the Barrier we managed to negotiate the first long pressure ridge of the sea ice, where the seals all lie, without much trouble. The dogs were running well and fast and we kept on the old tracks, still visible, by which we had come out in January, heading a long way out to make a wide détour round the open water off Cape Armitage, from which a very wide extent of thick black fog, 'frost smoke'[12] as we call it, was rising on our right. This frost smoke completely obscured our view of the open water, and the only suggestion it gave me was that the thaw pool off the cape was much bigger than when we passed it in January and that we should probably have to make a détour of 3 or 4 miles round it to reach Hut Point instead of 1 or 2. I still thought it was not impossible to reach Hut Point this way so we went on, but before we had run two miles on the sea ice we noticed that we were coming on to an area broken up by fine thread-like cracks —evidently quite fresh—and as I ran along by the sledge I paced them and found they occurred regularly at every 30 paces which could only mean that they were caused by a swell. This suggested to me that the thaw pool off Cape Armitage was even bigger than I thought, and that we were getting on to ice which was breaking up to flow north into it; and we stopped to consider and found that the cracks in the ice we were on were actually working up and down about $\frac{1}{2}$ an inch with the rise and fall of a swell. Knowing that the ice might remain like this with each piece tight against the next only until the tide turned, I knew we must get off it at once in case the tide turned in the next half hour, when each crack would open up into a wide lead of open water and we should find ourselves on an isolated floe. So we at once turned and went back as fast as possible to the unbroken sea ice. Obviously it was unsafe now to go round to Hut Point by Cape Armitage, and we therefore made for the Gap. It was between 8 and 9 in the evening when we turned and we soon came in sight of the pony party led, as we thought, by Captain Scott. We were within $\frac{1}{2}$ a mile of them when we turned right across their bows and headed straight for the Gap, making a course more than a right angle off the course we had been on. There was the seals' pressure ridge of sea ice between us and them, but as I could see them all quite distinctly I had no doubt they could see us, and we were occupied more than once just then in beating the teams off stray seals, so that we didn't go by either very quickly or very silently. From here we ran into the Gap where there was some nasty pressed up ice to cross and large gaps and cracks by the ice foot, but with the alpine rope and a rush we got first one team over and then the other without mishap, on to the land ice, and were then practically at Hut Point. However, expecting that the pony party was following us, we ran our teams up on to level ice, picketed them and pitched our tent, deciding to remain there for the night as we had a half mile of rock to cross to reach the hut, and the sledges would have to be carried over this and the dogs led by hand in couples—a very long job. Having done this we returned to the ice-foot with a pick and shovel to improve the road up for the horse party, as they would have to come over the same bad ice we had found difficult with the dogs. But they were nowhere to be seen close at hand, as we had expected, for they were miles out, as we soon saw, still trying to reach Hut Point by the sea ice round the Cape Armitage thaw pool, and on the ice which was showing a working crack at every 30 paces. I couldn't understand how Scott could do such a thing, and it was only the next day that I found out that Scott had remained behind and had sent Bowers in charge of this pony party. Bowers having had no experience of the kind before didn't grasp the situation for some time, and as we watched him and his party—or as we thought, Captain Scott and his party of ponies—we saw them suddenly realise that they were getting into trouble, and the whole party turned back. But instead of coming back towards the Gap, as we had, we saw them go due south towards the Barrier edge and White Island. Then I thought they were all right, for I knew they would get on to safe ice and camp for the night. We therefore had our supper in the tent and were turning in between 11 and 12 midnight, when I had a last look to see where they were and found they had camped, as it appeared to me, on safe Barrier ice, the only safe thing they could have done. They were now about 6 miles away from us and it was lucky that I had my Goerz glasses with me so that we could follow their movements. Now, as everything looked all right, Meares and I turned in and slept. At 5 a.m. I awoke and as I felt uneasy about the party I went out and along the Gap to where we could see their camp, and I was horrified to see that the whole of the sea ice was now on the move and that it had broken up for miles further than when we turned in, and right back past where they had camped, and that the pony party was now, as we could see, adrift on a floe and separated by open water and a lot of drifting ice from the edge of the fast Barrier ice. We could see with the glasses that they were running the ponies and sledges over as quickly as possible from floe to floe whenever they could, trying to get near the safe Barrier ice again. The whole strait was now open water to the north of Cape Armitage with frost smoke rising everywhere from it, and full of pieces of floating ice, all going up north towards Ross Sea.

Wed 1 March Ash Wednesday. Now the question for us was whether we could do anything to help them. There was no boat anywhere and there was no one to consult with for everyone was on the floating floe as we believed, except Teddie Evans, Forde and Keohane, who with one pony were on their way back from Corner Camp. So we searched the Barrier for signs of their tent and then saw that there was a tent at Safety Camp, which meant evidently, to us, that they had just returned. The obvious thing was to join up with them and then go round to where the pony party was adrift and see if we could help them to reach the safe ice. So without waiting for breakfast we went off—6 miles—to this tent. We couldn't go now by the Gap,

'The rescue from the sea ice. March 1, 1911'

for the ice which we had reached land by yesterday was now broken up in every direction and all on the move to go out up the strait. We had no choice now but to cross up by Crater Hill and down by Pram Point and over the pressure ridges, and so on to the Barrier and off to Safety Camp. We couldn't possibly take a dog sledge this way so we walked, taking the alpine rope to cross the pressure ridges which are full of crevasses. We got to this tent soon after noon and were astonished to find that not Teddie Evans and his two seamen were here, but that Scott and Oates and Gran were in it, and no pony with them. Teddie Evans was still on his way back from Corner Camp on the Barrier and hadn't arrived. It was now for the first time that we understood how the accident had happened. When we had left Safety Camp yesterday with the dogs, the ponies began their march to follow us, but one of the ponies was so weak after the last blizzard and so obviously about to die, that Bowers, Cherry-Garrard, and Crean were sent on with the 4 capable ponies, while Scott, Oates and Gran remained at Safety Camp till the sick pony died, which happened, apparently, that night. He was dead and buried when we got there. We found that Scott had that morning seen the open water up to the Barrier edge and had been in a dreadful state of mind thinking that Meares and I, as well as the whole pony party, had all gone out into the strait on floating ice. He was, therefore, much relieved when we arrived there and learned for the first time where the pony party was trying to get to fast ice again. We were now given some food, which we badly wanted, and while we were eating we saw in the far distance a single man coming hurriedly along the edge of the Barrier ice from the direction of the catastrophe party and towards our camp. Gran went off on ski to meet him and when he arrived we found it was Crean, who had been sent off by Bowers with a note, unencumbered otherwise, to jump from one piece of floating ice to another until he reached the fast edge of the Barrier, in order to let Captain Scott know what had happened. This he did, of course, not knowing that we or anyone else had seen him go adrift, and being unable to leave the ponies and all his loaded sledges himself. Crean had considerable difficulty and ran a pretty good risk in doing this, but succeeded all right. There were now Scott, Oates, Crean, Gran, Meares, and myself here and only 3 sleeping bags, so the three first remained to see if they could help Bowers and Cherry-Garrard and the ponies, while Meares and Gran and I returned to look after our dogs at Hut Point. Here we had only 2 sleeping bags for the 3 of us, so we had to take turns and I remained up till 1 o'clock that night, while Gran had 6 hours in my bag. It was a bitterly cold job after a long day. We had been up at 5 with nothing to eat till 1 o'clock, and walked 14 miles. The nights are now almost dark.

Thurs 2 March There was a very bitter wind blowing and it was a cheerless job waiting for 6 hours to have a sleep in the bag. I walked down from our tent to the hut and watched whales blowing in the semi darkness out in the black water of the strait. When we turned out in the morning the pony party was still on floating ice, but not any further from the Barrier edge. By a merciful providence the current was taking them rather along the Barrier edge, where they went adrift, instead of straight out to sea. We could do nothing more for them so we set to our work with the dogs. It was blowing a bitter gale of wind from the S.E. with some drift and we made a number of journeys backwards and forwards between the Gap and the hut carrying our tent and camp equipment down and preparing a permanent picketing line for the dogs. As the ice had all gone out of the strait we were quite cut off from any return to Cape Evans until the sea should again freeze over, and this was not likely until the end of April. We rigged up a small fireplace in the hut and found some wood and made a fire for an hour or so at each meal, but as there was no coal, and not much wood, we felt we must be economical with the fuel and so also with matches and everything else, in case Bowers should lose his sledge loads which had most of the supplies for the whole party to last 12 men for 2 months. The weather had now become too thick for us to distinguish anything in the distance, and we remained in ignorance as to the party adrift until Saturday. I had also given my glasses to Captain Scott. This night I had the first go in the bag and turned out to shiver for 8 hours till breakfast. There was literally nothing in the hut that one could cover oneself with to keep warm, and we couldn't run to keeping the fire going. It was very cold work. There were heaps of biscuit cases there which we had left in *Discovery* days, and with these we built up a small inner hut to live in.

Spent the day transferring dogs in couples from the Gap camp to the hut. In the afternoon Teddie Evans and Atkinson turned up from over the hills having returned from their Corner Camp journey with one horse and 2 seamen, all of which they had left encamped at Castle Rock—3 miles off on the hills. They naturally expected to find Scott here and everyone else and had heard nothing of the pony party going adrift, but having found only open water ahead of them they turned back and came to land by Castle Rock slopes. We fed them and I walked half way back to Castle Rock with them. **Fri 3 March**

Meares, Gran and I walked up Ski Slope towards Castle Rock to meet Evans' party and pilot them and the pony safely to Hut Point, but half way we met Atkinson who told us that they had now been joined by Scott and all the catastrophe party who were safe, but who had lost all the ponies except one—a great blow. However, no lives were lost and the sledge loads and stores were saved, so Meares and I returned to Hut Point to make stables for the only 2 horses that now remained —both in wretched condition—of the 8 with which we started. Of the 4 that went adrift on the floe, one happened to be standing where the ice first cracked and fell through and disappeared at once under the floe. Two others were lost in jumping them from floe to floe—they fell in the water, and as they couldn't be got out they were pickaxed to save them from the Killer Whales which were hanging around in numbers all the time. In the evening Scott, Bowers, Cherry-Garrard and Atkinson joined us at the hut. We had then finished building a very comfortable stable for the 2 horses. It blew half a gale all day, bitterly cold, from the east and S.E. **Sat 4 March**

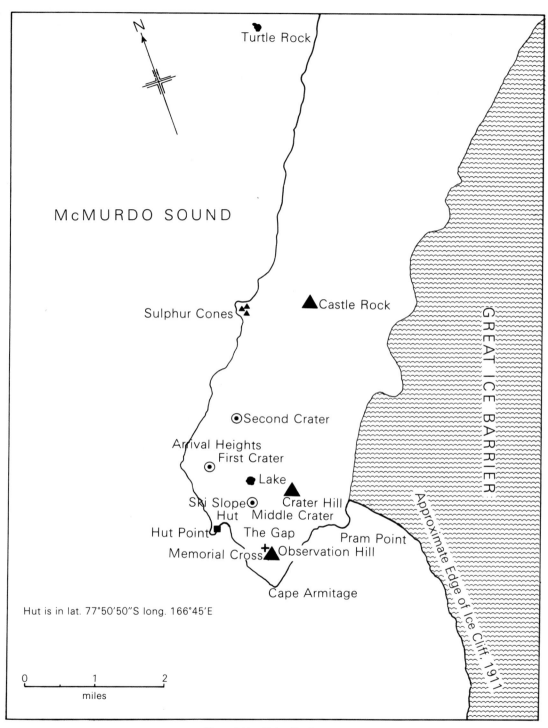

Turtle Rock

McMURDO SOUND

Sulphur Cones

Castle Rock

GREAT ICE BARRIER

⊙Second Crater

Arrival Heights
First Crater
⊙

●Lake

Ski Slope⊙   Crater Hill
Hut   Middle Crater

Hut Point■   The Gap   Pram Point

Memorial Cross+▲Observation Hill

Cape Armitage

Approximate Edge of Ice Cliff 1911

Hut is in lat. 77°50′50″S long. 166°45′E

0   1   2
        miles

Map of Hut Point Peninsula

9

LIFE AT HUT POINT

IRST Sunday in Lent. Bad weather, thick drift and threatening blizzard. We all went out to beyond Castle Rock along the hill tops to Evans' camp to fetch in the two ponies, and I had to act as guide taking them by a way which would be all on snow—no slippery ice—and then down by a very circuitous route to the hut[1], with steep slopes everywhere from 700 ft to sea level. It was no joke in thick weather when one could see very little ahead, but we got down without a slip. The 2 horses are stabled and the whole party now settled into our old hut with an improvised stove to burn seal blubber which is our only fuel for the next 2 months or so. We had an extensive view of the open water in the strait yesterday away to Cape Evans. We saw that the whole of the end of the Glacier Tongue was gone; evidently there was a very heavy swell and high seas when the ice in the strait was so suddenly broken up the other day. We wonder what our hut at Cape Evans may have suffered as it is built very low on a shelving northern beach and the swell seems to have been from the N. or N.E. A depot of provisions which Shackleton left on Glacier Tongue—and which we saw in passing—has now gone out to sea on one of the bergs. The first young ice of this season has appeared today—no—tomorrow.

It was a flat calm and the whole sea visible from Hut Point was covered with a thin film of ice. Captain Scott and I walked over Crater Hill to Pram Point where I killed a seal, and we both came home loaded with fresh meat, seal's liver and long strips of blubber for our new stove.

We had a long day sealing at Pram Point, fine and sunny but low temperature. Cherry, Gran, 3 seamen and myself killed 4 seals, and brought back 200 lbs of meat, 150 lbs of blubber and depoted 200 lbs more. Very heavy dragging this up hills 700 ft and then down again to Hut Point. We got back at 6 p.m.—very hungry. Forde got down a crevasse to his middle. There were lots of seals.

Up at 6 p.m. to help drag sledges and equipment up Ski Slope for a party which was going out for 3 days to pick up some gear left at Doleful Camp—where the pony catastrophe happened. Then with Titus Oates to the Gap to fetch in my dog sledge and a bale of fodder. After lunch worked round the hut cutting blubber into strips for firing, tending my dog team and preparing food for the party.

Thurs 9 March Walked to Castle Rock and climbed half way up to see if there is a feasible way over the slopes of Erebus to Cape Evans. There is a way, but it is crowded with crevasses and necessitates a climb to about 5,000 ft or more. It was not very attractive, and though Captain Scott kept Cherry and me at the hut waiting on the weather with a view to making the attempt, it never came off. The weather was too bad and it was too late in the season for such risky travelling in a bad light. It was a nice day today, however, and Castle Rock was warm to touch in the sunshine. There is still an intact bay of old sea ice in the corner between Glacier Tongue and Hutton Cliffs, but Turtle Rock is surrounded by water and so are the Delbridge Islands. We now have a roaring blubber stove going all day in the hut and it is getting more comfortable; the roof inside, however, is full of ice which must thaw out and drip itself dry.

Fri 10 March Meares away so I had all the dogs to snow down and clean up. A party went to Pram Point and brought in the blubber we depoted there the other day. The Doleful Camp party returned late in the evening.

Sat 11 March Make and mend. All our clothing wanted a lot of attention; finneskos² to patch. Meares and I had torn ours to pieces in crossing rocks so often with the dogs between the Gap and the hut. Also made shelter walls for the dogs as it looks like an approaching blizzard.

Sun 12 March Second Sunday in Lent. Blizzard came. Very thick drift and snow fall. We had Church in the forenoon. All the young sea ice has been blown to sea again, rough open black water everywhere. We all spent the day in the hut already very black from the blubber smoke and very greasy. Thawed out some old magazines and picture papers which were left here by the *Discovery* and gave us very good reading.

Mon 13 March Blizzard still all day—no one went out. Titus and I spent our time trying to make an acetylene gas plant as we found a case of carbide here. I knew it was a dangerous game and insisted on collecting a sample of the gas in a galley jar first. This exploded so promisingly when we lit it that no one suggested putting a light to the main plant, and it was passed bodily out into the blizzard! Several others tried the same thing on a small scale, happily with no success, or I am certain we should sooner or later have had a bad explosion. Gran, as it was, trying to make it in a tea tin, blew the thing up to the roof and across the hut, bursting the tin but happily hurting nobody. We have candles enough and can eke them out with blubber lamps which are quite efficient in a hut like this where we are all black and greasy anyhow.

Tues 14 March Weather improving. Went to top of Crater Hill with Cherry, Atch and Bowers. Saw the Western Party returning—Griff Taylor, Wright, Debenham and Seaman Evans. So we went to meet them and helped them in. They were all fit having been out 6 weeks and having had 5 weeks of good weather.

Wed 15 March A beautiful day—and a long and hard day's work. Cherry, Bowers, Atch and I, with 3 seamen, left after breakfast for Pram Point, killed and cut up 11 seals for meat and blubber. Scott and Evans brought us lunch with a tent at 2, and in the afternoon we hauled a very heavy sledge load of meat and blubber over Crater Hill and down to the hut, a heavy pull. New ice forming again on the strait. A number of small whales were blowing some way off.

A party left to bring in some provisions from Corner Camp. We all helped to lug the sledges up Ski Slope. Scott and I then went up Crater Hill. The new sea ice at Pram Point already bears a seal's weight. The new ice at Hut Point, however, again went out and left us open water. After noon I dug shelter holes for all my dogs and gave them dry gravel to bed on. **Thurs 16 March**

Bad weather again—a heavy snowstorm from the N. Went round later to a regular gale from the S. and by night a tremendous sea was running in on to the Hut Point ice foot and breaking over the Point. By midnight things looked very bad indeed for the dogs, and Meares and I turned out to let them loose from the picketing lines for they were getting frozen into solid jackets of sea water. It was a dreadful night and Meares and I were both coated from head to foot with frozen sea water before we had finished. The breakers were 20 and 30 ft high and the spindrift froze and rattled on the hut and blew right across the Hut Point promontory. The magnetic huts and even Vince's Cross[3], about 40 ft up on the hill, were an inch deep in frozen salt water by the morning. We got the dogs in under the lee of the hut where they were more sheltered, but they were in a pitiable condition of cold and wet. **Fri 17 March**

Cape Evans Hut. May.15.11′   S.P.R.I. 1802

pe Evans Hut. May. 15.11.

Sat 18 March Tending the dogs and building a much bigger shelter wall for them. All allowed loose today to run about and dry themselves except the 4 worst fighters. A pure white Giant Petrel flew over the hut today. Skuas still here also.

Sun 19 March Third Sunday in Lent. Blowing again very hard from the S. Reading, trimming seal skin, tending the dogs, cooking and cutting up meat and blubber. We take turns at cooking, which for one whole party requires 3—one to keep the blubber stove going, one to cook the meat hoosh, and one to cook the cocoa. We have large appetites here and require plenty, though the variety is small. For breakfast we have seal hoosh, cocoa, and biscuit. For lunch we have chupatties, made flat of flour and biscuit dust—we have no baking powder—and with them a piece of butter and some cocoa. For supper again seal hoosh, biscuit and cocoa. We live as in a sledge camp, sleeping in our reindeer sleeping bags on the floor, and of course no change of clothes and no possibility of a wash, a thing we haven't enjoyed since January.

Mon 20 March Bad weather—wind and drift. Walked up Ski Slope with Scott and the geologists to show them some boulders.

Tues 21 March Fine day. Went to top of Observation Hill with Scott and geologists to show them some very queer concentric weathering of trachyte[4] which looked like nests of pudding basins let into the ground.

Wed 22 March Two journeys to the Gap and brought in all the remainder of our camp equipment. Had a long talk with Gran who is fetching blubber from Pram Point every day.

Thurs 23 March Blowing and drifting again. The Corner Camp party returned having had $-42.7°$F. on the Barrier, their first experience of a low temperature. They were glad to get in as their kit was pretty solid with ice.

Fri 24 March Heavy soft snowfall. Went to Pram Point with Gran. At Pram Point the new ice is now 7 inches thick in one place, but $1\frac{1}{2}$ inches only further out. Temperature up to $+20°$F. and everything dripping water in the hut. No blizzard came, however.

Sat 25 March Went up Harbour and Arrival Heights and on to the Sulphur Cones[5] with Wright. Afterwards sketching—a beautiful evening with reflections and new young ice all over the strait. There were some Killer Whales in the strait.

Sun 26 March Fourth Sunday in Lent. Prayers read in the hut. Cooked a welsh rabbit for all hands for lunch. After lunch up Ski Slope with Oates and Taylor. A beautiful sunset and much young ice.

Mon 27 March Bad weather—wind and drift. Went to Gap with Wright and could see there was no drift on Barrier though it was blowing hard and drifting heavily here.

Tues 28 March Bad weather again, blowing and drifting with temperature at zero. Went up middle crater with Debenham. Sea all frozen—4 inches thick in our bay—from

Hut Point to Pram Point Bay. Open water all north of Hut Point and a large open pool off Cape Armitage. New Moon. Made seal rissoles for all hands.

Sketching along tide crack to Cape Armitage forenoon. Afternoon with Scott to **Wed 29 March** Harbour Heights. Whole strait now covered with young ice[6] but southerly breeze in the evening made large openings. The new ice bore Gran from Pram Point half way to the Gap and there were ice flowers on the new ice at Cape Armitage.

Out sketching afternoon—fiery orange sunset. Ice all out again to Hut Point. At **Thurs** Cape Armitage it is 8 inches thick. Two Antarctic rorquals are often seen just now **30 March** in the strait blowing at holes in the young ice 5 or 6 times running. Occasionally one saw one of them barge through it.

Blowing again. Out up Middle Crater forenoon and to top of Observation Hill **Fri 31 March** afternoon. Grand sunset 5.30–7. Sketched up there comfortably for an hour. Wright and Taylor walked from Pram Point to the Gap on sea ice today and found a number of small fish frozen on the surface—two sizes—and in one case the larger one had a little one in its mouth. Evidently they chase one another when the sea has a thin film of ice on the surface and breaking up through it they can't return, and get frozen on the top. One or two Emperor Penguins about.

Sketching from top of Observation Hill all afternoon till nearly dark at 7.30 p.m. **Sat 1 April** Walked over the bay ice today. Wright killed an Emperor Penguin which weighed 90 lbs. Scott walked on sea ice from Hut Point to Pram Point. The pool off Cape Armitage is still open. Two rorquals again playing in the pool off Hut Point—one appeared at surface, belly up once, quite white.

Fifth Sunday in Lent. Church at 11. The first aurora was seen here last night. **Sun 2 April** Afternoon went to top of Observation Hill. Sketching at −7°F. in a very cold wind was difficult but the sunset was beautiful. Got some unusually good augite crystals[7] out of an ash boulder. As we are getting the hut warmed the ice in the roof melts out and gives us a sort of snipe marsh to lie in at night.

Blowing and very cold. Spent forenoon skinning the Emperor—a male, very fat. **Mon 3 April** Half the breast and the liver was a substantial meal for 16 men with nothing else but some pease, cocoa and biscuit. We fried it in butter and it was excellent. Afternoon to Observation Hill with Debenham.

Bad weather day—no going out. Made a new blubber lamp and long talks. **Tues 4 April** Plenty [of] fun over a fry I made in my new penguin lard. It was quite a success— tasted like very bad sardine oil.

Fine aurora curtain across zenith. Perfect day, with glorious colour at daybreak. **Wed 5 April** Up Ski Slope skiing in forenoon. Afternoon on to sea ice round Harbour Heights with Scott and Wright examining ice flowers, there were at least 3 distinct kinds. New ice one inch. Older new ice 8 inches. Then went alone to top of Observation Hill and got 12 sketches as sun went down.

Thurs 6 April Fine waving curtain of aurora again last night, very bright straw yellow. A glorious day again and wonderful sunset like yesterday. Went to top of Observation Hill again, but a strong northerly breeze made it very difficult to sketch. The ice is apparently frozen everywhere over the strait and if the weather holds we are to try and get across it in 2 days.

Fri 7 April A grey sky—no wind. Sketched all forenoon on top of Observation Hill and with Cherry up the Middle Crater in the afternoon. Several people walked on sea ice to the Sulphur Cones today and Taylor went in through a thin ice lead.

Sat 8 April Blizzard blowing and no start possible. All the ice gone out to within half a mile of Hut Point and a wide crack open at Hut Point. Walked out to the Second Crater with Scott—much drift and frost smoke. Saw the last skuas today.

Sun 9 April Sunday next before Easter. Palm Sunday. Prayers were read. The weather was not good, but Cherry and I went up Arrival Heights to see the open water extent. All ice gone out except a small corner south of Glacier Tongue and the bay N. of Glacier Tongue inside the islands.

Mon 10 April The man party without animals was to have started for Cape Evans by land as far as Hutton Cliffs and then by sea ice, but it snowed thick all day and cleared only for a beautiful sunset when I went up Observation Hill and sketched until it was dark. The lights were wonderful and the silence and stillness were absolute.

Tues 11 April Weather very unsettled again—looks like snow—but Scott, Evans, Bowers, Taylor, Wright, Debenham, Seaman Evans, Crean and Gran started off for

Sketch for a watercolour of Hut Point, 7 April 1911

S.P.R.I. 1802

'New ice at Hut Point. Mar.29.11. noon'

'Hut Point from the top of Observation Hill. April 1.11. 5.30 p.m.'

Cape Evans. We helped them up Ski Slope and along the hill tops to Second Crater. They intended to get down to the sea ice at the Hutton Cliffs and so by Glacier Tongue to Cape Evans. After leaving them I went to the top of the Third Crater with Oates and Cherry—viewed the strait which is again getting a covering of thin ice. Snow again falling. After lunch Cherry and I again went to Second Crater top with glasses, but it was too thick to see anything of the party. On returning we killed and cut up a very large fat seal at Hut Point crack. The ice in our bay is now 16 inches thick, and in the crack which was open water on the 8th, 5 inches i.e. more than an inch a day. Our party is now reduced to Oates, Meares, Cherry, Atkinson, Keohane, Forde and myself to look after the dogs and horses and bring them along when the sea ice bears.

About 6 a.m. the wind broke on us in a blizzard with high drift and heavy squalls. **Wed 12 April** No one went out, and we hoped the other party had got in. As a matter of fact they got caught in a camp under Little Razorback Island and had to stay there till the blizzard stopped, with many fears as to whether the ice was going out or not. We had open water again right up to Hut Point.

Weather gradually recovered during the day. Darned socks all forenoon and **Thurs 13 April** after lunch went up Second Crater with Cherry to see what the ice had done and make sure that the other party hadn't been cut off anywhere. It was all right. We had arranged that they should fire coloured lights at 10 p.m. for 3 nights after their arrival, and sure enough this evening we saw their lights and we signalled back with a flare of paraffin and tarred felt. Here we have come to an end of our sugar today. We have also finished our flour so we can't make chupatties. We have also finished our oatmeal, but we have lots of seal meat and biscuit and cocoa. Butter is running out, but we can't starve! And we are a very happy party of bohemians. Our clothes are soaked in seal blubber and soot—black and greasy—and we are all bearded and very dirty.

This is Good Friday. No wind but heavily overcast and threatening blizzard. We **Fri 14 April** had to make a day's journey with a sledge out to the Barrier edge and fetch in some fodder bales for the 2 horses. Five of us went on ski with a sledge—left at 11, got there at 2, and back by 4.30. We went hard the whole way there and back without a halt except to load up at the depot, and we eat nothing. It was a good walk, all on sea ice about 11 miles. Coming round Cape Armitage we had the usual biting easterly wind, and several got frost-bitten pretty promptly. The step up from sea ice to the Barrier was still a cliff, except in one or two very isolated spots where the trend was sufficiently E. and W. to catch the southerly drift snow. Up one of these we got. Elsewhere there was ice cliff of 12 and 14 ft and seal holes at the foot in use. Cape Armitage thaw pool is now frozen over, but we didn't cross it.

Easter Even. Blowing a gale with drift and temperature −18.5°F. Some of our **Sat 15 April** severest weather when a blizzard comes on and the temperature remains so low. Spent the day in all of us, darning and sewing and reading. Our salt ran out and we have replaced our stock by boiling down brine collected off the top of young sea ice. No new clothes to put on tomorrow, I fear, but we have been saving up our only tin of milk, a thing we haven't tasted since the end of January. We also have 8 more meals of marmalade.

Sun 16 April Easter Sunday. Blowing and very cold and heavy drift. We enjoyed life in the hut. In the afternoon I had a quiet time reading and in the evening got notes for a magnificent stormy sunset.

Mon 17 April Same storm and snow drift at −22°F. We were getting short of blubber fuel, however, so Oates, Meares, Cherry, Forde and I took a sledge round to Pram Point for a seal. We couldn't find one, but we brought back blubber we had cached there some weeks ago. Saw a skua again today. The whole strait N. of Hut Point is again covered with new ice, except for an open lead along the coast 30 yards wide.

Tues 18 April A party came back with more food for us from Cape Evans. Scott and 7 others. They came by land as before they had gone to Cape Evans. Scott and I went to Pram Point in the afternoon—again no seal. Very cold and windy. A glorious evening of colour.

Wed 19 April Same colouring this morning. I have sketches enough to occupy me months when I get back to a paint box. This stay at Hut Point with so little to do has been a godsend to me at this time of the year when the colours are far the best, and most wonderful sunsets surprise one with some new light effect every day. Oates, Nelson and I went to Pram Point again today, but got no seal. The others, however, in other directions, got 3. After lunch it began to blow again with very high drift. Cherry and I went up the hills and got bushed for a time in a very thick bit of blizzard which froze both our faces. The whole strait is now ice-covered as far as the eye can see, but at 2 p.m. when it began to blow the whole of it at once broke up and got on the move, leaving big leads of open water all over the strait and a quarter of a mile of water all along the coast to Hut Point. The new ice has held between Tortoise [*sic* Turtle] Rock and Hutton Cliffs for the first time.

Thurs 20 April We were to have started back for Cape Evans today, but it was blowing a blizzard. I am to return this time as Demitri, the Russian dog driver, has come to take charge of my team and have a little taste of Hut Point. Cherry will also come back, and Atkinson, while Day and Nelson will remain with a couple of the seamen. Oates returns with us, too. Meares now remains in charge of Hut Point instead of me. All the forenoon we stayed indoors, but Nelson and I went out in the afternoon and it was just as bad as could be. We went round two small bergs off Cape Armitage and were soon back again.

Fri 21 April Weather improved a bit so we left Hut Point for Cape Evans. Two sledges and two tents. I was with Captain Scott, Atkinson and Crean. Bowers, Oates, Cherry-Garrard and Hooper were on the other. We had a lot of heavy pulling over the hills going along the top of the promontory to Hutton Cliffs and here we all went down a 20 ft ice cliff by rope on to the sea ice in a smother of snow as a small blizzard came on. We then also lowered the loaded sledges one by one, camped under the cliff, and had some tea 4 p.m. It was getting dark, but we crossed the bay to the Glacier Tongue, and then crossed the Glacier Tongue—a perfect maze of crevasses—when it was so dark that we were constantly putting our feet through. No one went in, but we had more difficulty in finding a way down again on the north side to the sea ice as we wanted to go down a sloping drift instead of over a 40 ft ice cliff and it was too dark to see anything. However, we were saved at last and then we plodded along over 6 miles of rubbly sea ice in the dark until at 9.30 p.m. we got to Cape Evans—dry clothes, and a supper, and some cleanliness after three months without a wash or getting one's clothes off. $17\frac{1}{2}$ miles of heavy pulling.

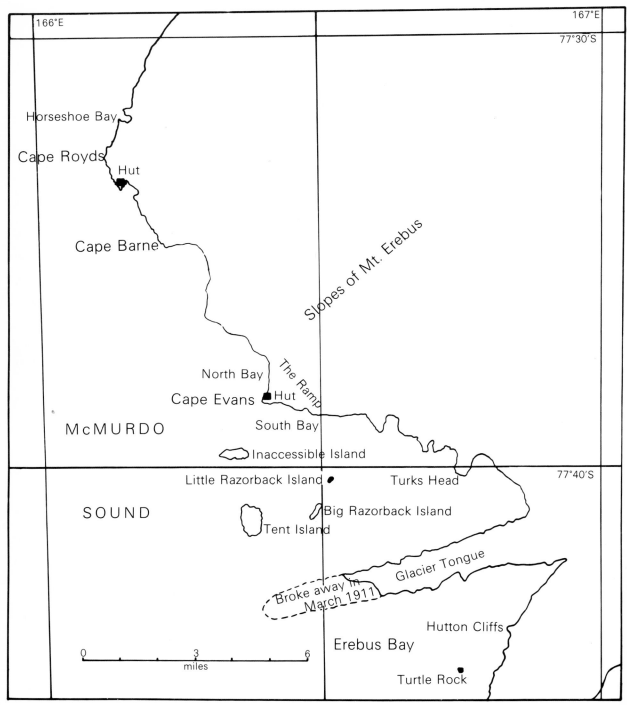

Map of part of the west coast of Ross Island

10

WINTER QUARTERS

IN comfort once more. The hut is a very different thing now to what it was **Sat 22 April** when we left it in January. Acetylene gas jets everywhere, stoves, clothes lines, clocks, telephones, electric gadgets, and scientific apparatus everywhere, all in full working order. Sunny Jim, Day and Nelson have been busy with their combined inventive genius, and they have made a first class job of things. Spent the day sorting gear and cleaning myself. Had a hot bath—shaved off my beard and moustache after Ponting had perpetuated them in a photo. Thoroughly enjoyed the gramophone. Everyone here very fit and well.

First Sunday after Easter. The last day on which we shall see the sun from here **Sun 23 April** until August 23rd, but it gave us a grand sunset to finish up with. Church at 10.30 and then I went over all the scientific arrangements in the hut and outside in the ice caves and magnetic hut. Afternoon painting sunsets.

All day painting at my Hut Point sketch notes, and it was my turn to be on watch **Mon 24 April** all night so I also painted all night, but on lantern slides for Ponting, who wanted me to try with some special colours he had got from Kodak, but they were not easy to manage. We take turns—all of us—at being night watchman, going out every hour to make a note on the weather and aurora and to keep the kitchen fire going and eat a box of sardines.

Ponting has a lot of beautiful Japanese lantern slides, and I spent the forenoon **Tues 25 April** looking over them. Many are painted by Japanese artists and are very beautiful. I painted sketches the rest of the day and turned in soon after supper.

Painting all day and finished 8. The temperature of the hut is between 55° and **Wed 26 April** 63°F. and very comfortable and the only trouble at all is the freezing of moisture in corners and against the walls. My pillow and mattress are both frozen hard with a collection of ice to the wall which they touch, and the steel spring mattresses, being low near the floor, condense a lot of moisture and keep one's mattress sopping wet on the under surface—but one feels nothing of it in the bunk.

All day painting again. We have made out a list of lectures for the winter—3 **Thurs 27 April** evenings a week. I am down for 5—Birds, Whales, Seals, Penguins and Sketching. Cherry-Garrard has been made editor of the S.P.T.[1] which we are going to continue. The first volume is to appear on Midwinter Day.

Fri 28 April Calm all day, and at noon we had for 3 hours the finest colour imaginable all over the sky. Out all the forenoon making sketches at temperature $-13°$F. Painting the remainder of the day. This evening we had one of the best auroras I have ever seen, very brilliant curtains and moving very rapidly—colour lemon green, and wherever the movement was most rapid the edges advancing—and the lower borders were crimson red. None of the photo plates which we have, though brought down as being specially sensitive for this purpose and the most rapid plates made—and though we have specially rapid lenses for the purpose—will give any result whatever when exposed even to very brilliant displays. The light of an aurora is monochromatic and yellow, and has no actinic rays in it worth mentioning. No one has ever got any results except one Norwegian[2] who was consulted before we left England, and whose advice in every respect has been taken. We are apparently doing exactly what he did yet we get no results at all here, while he published what appear to be extraordinary results from Lapland auroras in a weekly illustrated paper.

Sat 29 April Went with Scott to top of Inaccessible Island, 520 ft only, and then round the island on the ice foot where the sea spray thrown up by some of our last southerly gales has frozen in enormously bulky masses on the rocks up to 20 and 30 ft. We have 6 or 7 very fine icebergs stranded on shallow reefs round our winter quarters; they are in varying conditions of weathering, one quite a fresh tabular berg, one with a green ice tunnel through it which has made some lovely photos, and one had a fine high arch right through about 50 ft high, which I drew a rough sketch of a few days before the arch fell in with a mighty crash. These bergs are always dropping large masses from time to time, so one has to give them a wide berth. They also make weird noises on a still day, a sort of æolian humming and then a periodic creaking and groaning and singing and sighing—all made by the rubbing of the floe ice against the berg.

Sun 30 April Second Sunday after Easter. Calm weather. Prayers at 10–11, after which Scott and I went up the Ramp, a great moraine embankment on the lowest slopes of Erebus at the land end of Cape Evans. We went 600 ft up the glacier towards Erebus until we came to crevasses. From here we could see that part of the strait had been opened up again by yesterday's blow—a storm which came up in the afternoon. The strait is rapidly freezing over again, but the last 6 days' ice has been much broken up and large sheets have come up the centre of the strait. There is water now along the coast from Hut Point to Turtle Rock and up to the Glacier Tongue.

Mon 1 May Calm and fine, but daylight rapidly shortening. Spent the day preparing the lecture which I have to open the course with this evening—on Antarctic birds. Very moderately interesting I rather think, but I made it short.

Tues 2 May Calm again and a sky flecked with red over the glacier. Erebus' smoke rising in 5 jets to a large cloud lit brilliantly rose red on a pale blue sky. We had a game of football—association—on the floe. Painting.

Discussion of scientific work with Scott all the forenoon. After lunch ran a dog **Wed 3 May**
team over the floe for exercise. Then sketching. Cherry is building a stone hut
close to the main hut for seal skinning. Sunny Jim (i.e. Simpson) gave a lecture
on meteorology. Afterwards discussed our food with Scott and got a good many
doubtful things cut down and seal meat increased. For breakfast seal meat 3 days
a week. Tinned sausages cut off altogether. Lunch 2 days jam, 1 day honey, 1 day
cheese, 1 potted meats and 1 sardines. For dinner 1 day of cold meat, the rest
mutton and seal.

Drawing till 12.30, then football. After lunch drawing ice crystals for Silas (i.e. **Thurs 4 May**
Wright) which is cold work as one has to do it outside the hut and is detailed
drawing, taking time. After supper drawing, and almost every evening we have
the gramophone or pianola. The best thing on the gramophone is *A night hymn at
sea* by Clara Butt and K. Rumford, and *'Tis folly to run away from love* by Margaret
Cooper. But we have a lot of other good things.

Calm day again. Working at seal embryology all forenoon. Ran a dog team out **Fri 5 May**
for exercise. Heard the arched berg fall in with a roar today. In the evening had a
good lecture on physiography from Taylor.

Calm but snowing till noon. Football in which I strained the back of my leg, and **Sat 6 May**
I felt this for about 6 weeks. Oates did the same thing. Atkinson is using the fish
trap and got 40 notothenia[3] today in the morning and 41 in the evening—at least
3 species, but all very much alike, not as much flesh on 2 of them as there is on a
whiting. I painted 2 of them—one reddish orange, the other bluish brown. They
are full of parasites, protozoa, nematodes, trematodes and a copepod on the gill
covers. We eat them all the same, but I can't say they are nice.

Third Sunday after Easter. Church as usual and the rest of the day painting **Sun 7 May**
parasites for Atkinson. The catch of fish has now dropped to 12, 10, and so on,
night and morning, just as they used to drop at Hut Point. Deep red starfish crawl
into the trap, which is made of wire netting. Evening drawing and as it was my
night watch, I prepared my lecture on sketching, i.e. I read Ruskin's *Elements
of Drawing*, which I have here, and made my lecture on that.

Calm again. We are having an unusual spell of fine weather. Drawing and **Mon 8 May**
painting all day, parasites under the microscope first, and then pack ice pictures.
After supper we had a lecture from Scott on his plans for the summer's work and
the prospect of getting to the Pole. The most annoying thing is that the South
Pole party, if it gets there, cannot be back in time to catch the ship. This means
that the ship will have left before I have read my letters, and can send no answers,
and cannot return myself for a year, however urgent the need may be. Naturally
one wonders whether one is right to hope to be one of the final four for the Pole,
and I cannot help thinking that having come down for this journey chiefly one
must carry it through at this risk. It makes it difficult, for one imagines all sorts of
things that may have happened in the past year making it advisable for me to

come back, and I shall not know about them until it is too late to come. However, things always turn out for the best, and generally in a different way to what one expects.

Tues 9 May Calm and overcast. Helping Ponco (i.e. Ponting) with a flashlight photo of a fish. Then stone hut building with Cherry. After lunch up the Ramp to the thermo-meter screen which has been fixed there 250 ft up to compare with 3 others lower down by our hut and on the sea ice. The temperature is often very different—occasionally as much as 20 degrees, but usually only 2 or 3 degrees. After dinner painting.

Wed 10 May Forenoon discussing sledge rations with the Owner as Captain Scott is always called here. Afternoon drawing a fish with parasites on its gills. Then up the Ramp a short scrambling climb over rocks and ice and snow which takes one a short three quarters of an hour, but gives one a good breather as part of it is steep. In the evening Ponting showed us a beautiful set of lantern slides of Burmah—pagodas, Buddhas and Buddha caves.

Thurs 11 May Painted most of the day but made 2 journeys up the Ramp, first to explore and later to take temperatures.

Fri 12 May Blowing hard, nearly always from an easterly direction here E. or E.S.E., except in real blizzards when it blows from the S. Painting all day. Afternoon up the Ramp. Evening Debenham's lecture on petrology, which was good and interesting.

Sat 13 May Calm again and a brilliant moon and lunar halo and prismatic mock moons, which I painted. Forenoon chiefly went in discussing sledging arrangements with the Owner. At 5 p.m. up the Ramp. No ice has gone out in the last wind—the strait is frozen as far as the eye can see to the north. Meares and Demitri turned up today with the dog teams from Hut Point, and Nelson, Day, Lashly, Forde and Keohane with the 2 ponies, so now we are all at last together in the Cape Evans hut.

Sun 14 May Fourth Sunday after Easter. Calm and brilliant moonlight which is such a god-send in Antarctic winter. Church at 11 and much of the day preparing lecture on penguins for tomorrow. Also a walk to the Ramp and from there to the Inacces-sible Island screen in the S. Bay, and from there to N. Bay screen[4], and so back. Temperature −23°F. and breeze enough with it to make it pretty cold. There was today the finest double prismatic-coloured lunar corona[5] I have seen, which I sketched and afterwards painted. Spent the evening over penguins.

Mon 15 May Blowing from the north with drift. Spent the day at my lecture on penguins and got rid of it in the evening. Atkinson has been testing the alkalinity of everyone's blood[6]. All indicate good health, my own is as good as anyone here, N/30, but 2 are decidedly less good than the others. Most are N/40, but these two are N/50, which is not good.

'Barne Glacier from the Ramp. April 30.11. 1 p.m.'

'Corner of Barne Glacier. Sept. 1911'

Sunset. 10 April 1911. 6 p.m.

S.P.R.I. 438

'Parhelion from the Ramp. Sept.14.11'

'Berg off Cape Evans. April 23.11. Last day of the sun'

Still blowing hard from N., but in the afternoon turned and blew from the S. **Tues 16 May**
By the evening it was a thick blizzard. Painted all day except for a trot up the Ramp
in the blizzard. Our acetylene gas lighting is using too much carbide, so from
now all lights have to be out at 11 p.m. which is a good thing—though it would be
better if we had no candles. We are allowed 2 a week.

Dissected a dog that died this morning—so far as we could find out no reason but **Wed 17 May**
worms, of which it had very few. Went up Ramp with Wright in forenoon and
with Bowers in the afternoon. Lecture on management of horses from Titus Oates.

Calm but thick with snowfall. I find myself a very fairly reliable means of prognos- **Thurs 18 May**
ticating blizzards for I almost invariably get a sort of migraine headache 10 or
12 hours before the blizzard begins[7]. Today was the third time and again it was
right. Painted all day and up the Ramp and to N. Bay screen. Painted in the
evening some S.P.T. work.

Blizzard all night. Calm and clear by evening. Bright moon and corona. Out all **Fri 19 May**
forenoon looking for seals by Inaccessible Island, but couldn't find one. Painting
afternoon and then up the Ramp. Lecture on ice by Silas Wright. Still light enough
at midday to play football.

Painting for S.P.T. Ponting is taking a series of photos in the hut by flashlight— **Sat 20 May**
some are very good pictures, especially one taken of Oates and Meares smoking
over the blubber stove in the stables. Today he took me painting at my table. After
lunch painting again at S.P.T. work and at a fish parasite. Then up the Ramp
in a blizzard of wind and drift with temperature −25°F. and back with Bowers.
Both of us came into the hut with pieces of cheek frozen solid much to the amusement of everyone, for my face hardly ever gets caught and I didn't know it had
been this time. However, it was, for it soon began to scald and then blistered, but
it wasn't much.

Church as usual and then a long discussion on the old pinnacle ice of Koettlitz **Sun 21 May**
Glacier. Beautiful moonlight and calm. Out to N. Bay and up the Ramp with
Birdie (i.e. Bowers) and Cherry. In the evening all our measurements were taken
and I find I am heavier than ever before, namely 11 st 2 lbs in the Maude Allen[8]
or more so, altogether, costume.

Misty morning cleared to perfect moonlight. Six of us went off with our sleeping **Mon 22 May**
bags to spend a night at Shackleton's hut and see what stores there are there and
what state they are in. We didn't start till noon and got there very easily in a comfortable calm. There was no sign of open water until we reached Blackbeach at
Cape Royds itself, where the ice had evidently only quite recently formed and
wouldn't carry a man. There were seal tracks on the beach but no seals. The ice
was being pressed in on shore from the north making very weird noises. The
Owner and I walked on and round the moraine to Blue Lake, which we crossed,
and so back to the hut. We then supped and examined everything left in the hut.

It was a very cold place and my sleeping bag much too large to warm up. Moreover I rolled plump off the bench I was sleeping on, in the middle of the night, fast asleep. It was interesting to see the remains of this party's life here and their various corners in the hut. There were a lot of good men in their party—David, Day, Priestley and Mawson, and 'Puttyface' Marston[9] the artist, who must have been a great humorist. Mackay[10] must have been a good sort in his way. Day has told us much that is good about all these people, and the more one hears of them all the more one realises their difficulties. They had a rotten man as cook and Joyce[11], who was in the *Discovery*, was also a rotter.

Tues 23 May We overhauled all the stores remaining here and then had tea and biscuits and started back for Cape Evans. It began to blow strongly from the S. in our faces almost at once with a good deal of drift, and this lasted all the way back—about 6 miles. We were trying a new and very unsuccessful invention on wheels—a bedstead frame supported on four bicycle wheels with pneumatic tyres, specially invented for smooth sea ice. It was pretty rotten. Temperature was $-31.2°$F. at Cape Royds.

Wed 24 May Blowing from the N. all day with some snow. Drawing all day—partly for S.P.T. and partly for Atkinson who lectured on parasitology in the evening. Went up the Ramp—very dark—no moon—and blowing.

Thurs 25 May Ascension Day. Blowing a very heavy blizzard all day and very thick—the heaviest we have had as yet. No one out. All day at S.P.T. work.

Fri 26 May Discussing food values, and sledging rations all forenoon. At 5 p.m. up the Ramp. Evening a lecture on biology from Nelson, who is called indiscriminately 'Marie', 'Bronté' or 'Ducart'.

Sat 27 May Blowing again and high drift. All day painting S.P.T. work. Cherry typewriting at the same always now. Evening lecture from Bowers on sledge rations.

Sun 28 May Sunday after Ascension. Calm beautiful weather. Very little light at midday now. Church at 11. Painting and discussing Barrier problems with the Owner till lunch. Painting and the Ramp. Aurora every day now in the evenings and at night whenever it is clear. Last night I was awoken by banging and groaning in the stables which are built against the wall of our cubicle, so I called Oates and ran out to see what had happened and found that one of the ponies had fallen forward under its head ropes and had bent its neck right back on its shoulders so that it couldn't breathe. It was lucky that it kicked the wall where it did or it would have come to a bad end by the morning.

Mon 29 May Again hours discussing sledge rations and food values. I want an increase of fats and a reduction of carbohydrates. The Owner and Bowers and I went out on ski to Inaccessible Island. We found and killed a young Sea Leopard on the sea ice. I followed its tracks and found that it had come about a mile over the ice from the tide crack. This was a great piece of luck as we haven't had one before. After lunch skinned it with Cherry and buried it with the skeleton in the big drift behind the hut. In the evening Ponting gave us a lantern show of perfectly beautiful Japanese slides—many tinted.

Out with Birdie on ski to South Bay screen. Sun shining on some cirrus cloud to the N. shows it isn't gone away for ever tho' we shall see nothing of it till end of August. Calculation puts this cloud at 12 miles high. After lunch got a young Crabeater male on the tide crack by the hut. Killed, skinned and skeletoned it—and buried it. Atkinson got some parasites from it. Continual discussion on sledge foods, blubber lamps, etc. **Tues 30 May**

Again had a blizzard headache and the blizzard came right enough with gusts up to 72 miles an hour. Hurricane force is 75 for an hour. I was nearly blown off the roof when clearing the anemometer. Gave the day up to preparing my lecture for tonight on sketching and this came off all right. We have several people here who do a certain amount of drawing—Debenham, Taylor and Day—but none so good as Day who draws very neatly. Spent the whole night copying Lillie's caricatures for the S.P.T. as it was my night on watch. **Wed 31 May**

The blizzard blew all night and all day as well. At 5 p.m. went up the Ramp with Birdie and Gran. Painted and drew all day. **Thurs 1 June**

Blowing hard all day till 5 but no drift and temperature which has been up to 14°F. is again falling. High temperature is always typical of blizzards from the **Fri 2 June**

Cape Royds Hut, June 1911

S.P.R.I. 1802

'Our Bill'

south, winter and summer. Painting and drawing and discussing things all day. At 5 up the Ramp and to N. Bay screen. Spent the evening talking of Japan with Ponting.

Blowing a bit all day. Painting most of day. Went on ski to S. Bay screen, then **Sat 3 June** up the Ramp. Sunny Jim gave second lecture on meteorology.

Whitsuntide. Calm and beautiful day. Church at 11. Played at building an igloo— **Sun 4 June** with no success. After lunch out to bring in a Crabeater which Birdie and Cherry caught and killed in the forenoon. Painted rest of day and now have got 50 sketches done.

Snowing all day, little wind but high temperature up to $+16°$. Painting all day. **Mon 5 June** Up the Ramp at 5. Taylor gave us a lecture on the Beardmore Glacier in the evening. Blizzard warning again this morning, and it blizzed all right this evening and all night.

Scott's birthday, for which the cook made a magnificent cake and I painted his **Tues 6 June** sledge flag and a Union Jack, and all our flags were hung round the hut. The blizzard stopped about noon—brilliant moon all the afternoon and night. Up the Ramp and got some moonlight sketches. Ponting making fine photos by flashlight. All day painting, except for interruptions which are numerous.

Went on ski to S. Bay screen. Deep orange red moonrise on the way. Worked till **Wed 7 June** noon at S.P.T. and after lunch also. To Ramp with Bowers and Ponting who photoed us at the screen by flashlight. Evening, the Owner gave us a paper on the Barrier and Inland Ice Cap.

Out skiing in S. Bay and round Inaccessible Island and the icebergs. Up the Ramp **Thurs 8 June** afternoon. My night on watch—drawing for the S.P.T. part of the night and painting a new species of trematomus—fish. Fine lunar corona.

Out skinning a Weddell Seal for meat and blubber—the latter being used every **Fri 9 June** day for making soft food for the horses. Also visited Wright's ice cave where he is making experiments with ice crystals, ice grains etc. No lecture in the evening. Drawing with gramophone going.

Blowing hard all day with snow. Drawing all day at protozoal parasites— **Sat 10 June** biflagellate trypanosomes[12] from a fish—for Atkinson.

Trinity Sunday. Church, then skiing towards the Razorback Islands and to **Sun 11 June** Nelson's fish hole which he visits every day taking sea temperatures, samples of sea water, and making catches of plankton. Afternoon up the Ramp with Bowers and Sunny Jim—then painting till bed time. Full moon and flat calm.

Drawing all forenoon, then to S. Bay screen on ski with Atch. Afternoon drawing **Mon 12 June** and up the Ramp. Weather thick but not blowing. Erebus at breakfast time got the moonlight and looked like a vast 13,000 foot sugar mountain. Taylor and Wright walked to Cape Royds and back today. Cherry and Birdie have gone there today for the night. Teddie Evans' lecture on navigation, or rather surveying.

Tues 13 June Calm and brilliant moon. Drawing dolphins until noon then to S. Bay screen on ski. Very silent day—no sound but an occasional crack in the glaciers and twice a roar in the distance where a few tons of ice fell off the bergs or off the face of Barne Glacier. After lunch we got a Crabeater Seal at Atkinson's fish trap hole. To N. Bay screen on ski and to Ramp. Debenham and Gran have today returned from Hut Point where they have spent 4 or 5 days in the hut. They went to fetch geological specimens. One of the dogs, Mukaka, was lost a month ago, and they found him waiting there, thin, but covered by seal blood. Bowers and Cherry returned from Cape Royds, having seen no sign of open water. Evening drawing dolphins.

Wed 14 June Lunar halo and overcast. Drawing dolphins all forenoon. On ski to N. Bay screen, then up Ramp by 4, when it was blowing a stiff blizzard with a lot of drift. Lecture by Nelson on biological gear, water sample collecting bottles, reversing thermometers and current meters etc.

Thurs 15 June Blowing hard forenoon. Calm afternoon. Double lunar halo. Day went in preparing my clothing for Cape Crozier journey, on which we start upon at the end of this month. Also went to N. Bay screen and the Ramp in the afternoon with brilliant moonlight. Reading up halos and coronas etc. all the evening.

Fri 16 June Sewing at sledge gear. Then to S. Bay on ski. Cherry's stone hut is finished. 10 seal skins on the roof. After lunch sewing again, then up the Ramp. Lecture by Debenham on volcanoes.

Sat 17 June Stitching all day at sledge clothes. Up the Ramp with new form of crampons on finnesko. They are large canvas shoes with aluminium soles and spikes of iron which one binds over the fur finnesko with cords. They are good. Evening worked up the various methods of pickling Emperor Penguin embryos for microscope work.

Sun 18 June First Sunday after Trinity. Again had a blizzard headache in the night and though it was dead calm when we were at breakfast the blizzard came on with a whoop directly after and blew all day. Church at 11. Whole day reading Ponting's book on Japan *In Lotus Land Japan* which I think is beautiful in illustration and in the feeling of its writing. After supper had all our measures taken. Everyone is up to the mark well and good.

Mon 19 June Whole forenoon preparing apparatus for collecting and pickling embryos at Cape Crozier—the object being to get a series for cutting sections and microscopic work. Afternoon sewing sledge gear. Then to N. Bay and up the Ramp. The moon having gone for a bit now we tumble and trip over rocks and drifts all the way.

Evening—lecture by Day on the sledge motors. Ours have been badly damaged in the landing of gear from the ship. We had three. One went through the ice to the bottom of the sea. The other two were much used backwards and forwards on the hard blue ice, and the turning each time did the damage by bringing wood rollers against metal, and ripping pieces out each time—a thing which was not visible till the motors were overhauled at the end when the damage was done. No rollers having gone before only about 30 spares were brought, and some dozens are broken. Each chain contains 74 rollers, i.e. 296 in the 2 cars. We have no turning lathe with us, but later, in September, Day most cleverly improvised a turning lathe on the crank shaft of a small petrol engine used for driving a dynamo and succeeded in turning quite a number of oak and greenheart rollers to replace the damaged ones.

Tues 20 June Calm and low temperature —36°F. Erebus smoke in large volume. Various preparations for our sledge journey, amongst others a blubber cooking stove. We have arranged to have a Christmas tree as a surprise on Midwinter Night, the 22nd of June. Birdie has undertaken to make a tree of bamboo slips and skua feathers, and Constance's boxes of all sorts of extraordinary toys, gilguys[13] and gadgets are just the very thing. Birdie and I went up the Ramp. There was a beautiful lunar cross and small mock moons. The cross is a beautiful thing—vertical and horizontal shafts of light, with the moon as a centre, formed on thin cirro stratus which is not thick enough to dim the stars, so the cross looks as though set in a perfectly clear sky.

Wed 21 June Calm. —37°F., a low temperature for this place. Spent the whole day making preparations for the Crozier trip and for Christmas festivities tomorrow. The tree is a great erection behind a rug in Birdie's bunk. I made a fine sprig of holly with wire, bristol-board, green paint and sealing wax.

Thurs 22 June Our Midwinter Day and a general holiday. The forenoon I spent painting a large ménu for signatures which is to appear in the S.P.T. 2nd part of Vol. III. At lunch we had the hut decorated with all our sledge flags and a huge cake and then the S.P.T. first part was handed by the editor to the Owner who read it out loud amidst much amusement. All the afternoon went in preparing Birdie's Christmas tree with Con's knick knacks, crackers and candied fruits. It was a huge success when it was carried in after the dinner by some of the seamen. We had a huge dinner—so had the men and the whole party was photoed by Ponting by flashlight. Then there were speeches. Everyone was expected to say something, which was the silly thing it usually is. Then the Christmas tree and then a splendid show of lantern slides by Ponting—all new Antarctic ones. Then snapdragon and punch and gramophone. I was on night watch so didn't get to bed. Read Ponting's book on Japan. All night a fine aurora going, brighter and more coloured than I have seen it before.

Fri 23 June Breakfast late. Making preparations all day for Cape Crozier and a long interesting talk with Ponting on Japan. Up the Ramp at 5.30. Turned in directly after supper —very tired and sleepy.

Sat 24 June All day preparations for sledging. Blubber lamp cooker trials, and a lot of other things. Up the Ramp at 5.30. Photo tips from Ponco all the evening.

Sun 25 June Second Sunday after Trinity. Church as usual Cherry playing the piano for the 3 hymns which we always have. After lunch Scott and I went up the Ramp and had a long talk about future plans and the people of our party and also about arrangements for an exhibition with Ponting when we return. He also impressed upon me the necessity of bringing back my two companions unhurt from Cape Crozier for the southern journey.

Mon 26 June Fairly calm day. Preparations for Cape Crozier, weighing up and packing sledges makes our loads up to 250 odd lbs each with 6 weeks food. We start tomorrow. Never was such a collection of apparatus taken on a sledge journey, but then also never was anyone before so led to undertake such a journey in midwinter darkness on the Barrier. It is an experimental journey. Taylor lectured in the evening on their western journey.

MENU FOR
MIDWINTER DAY 1911.

CAPE EVANS
McMURDO SOUND

CONSOMME · SEAL
ROAST BEEF & YORKSHIRE PUDDING
HORSE RADISH SAUCE
POTATOES A LA MODE & BRUSSELS SPROUTS
PLUM PUDDING · MINCE PIES
CAVIARE ANTARCTIC
CRYSTALLISED FRUITS · CHOCOLATE BONBONS
BUTTER BONBONS · WALNUT TOFFEE
ALMONDS & RAISINS
WINES
SHERRY · CHAMPAGNE · BRANDY PUNCH · LIQUEUR
CIGARS · CIGARETTES & TOBACCO
SNAPDRAGON
PINE·APPLE CUSTARD · RASPBERRY JELLIES
BUSZARD'S CAKE

GOD SAVE THE KING.

'Menu for Midwinter Day 1911, Cape Evans, McMurdo Sound'

Midwinter Day dinner, 22 June 1911. *Left to right seated*: Debenham, Oates, Meares, Bowers, Cherry-Garrard, Scott, Wilson, Simpson, Nelson, Evans, Day. Taylor. *Standing*: *(left)* Wright, Atkinson, *(right)* Gran.

PAUL POPPER

The Cape Crozier party about to leave Cape Evans, 27 June 1911. *Left to right*: Bowers, Wilson, Cherry-Garrard.

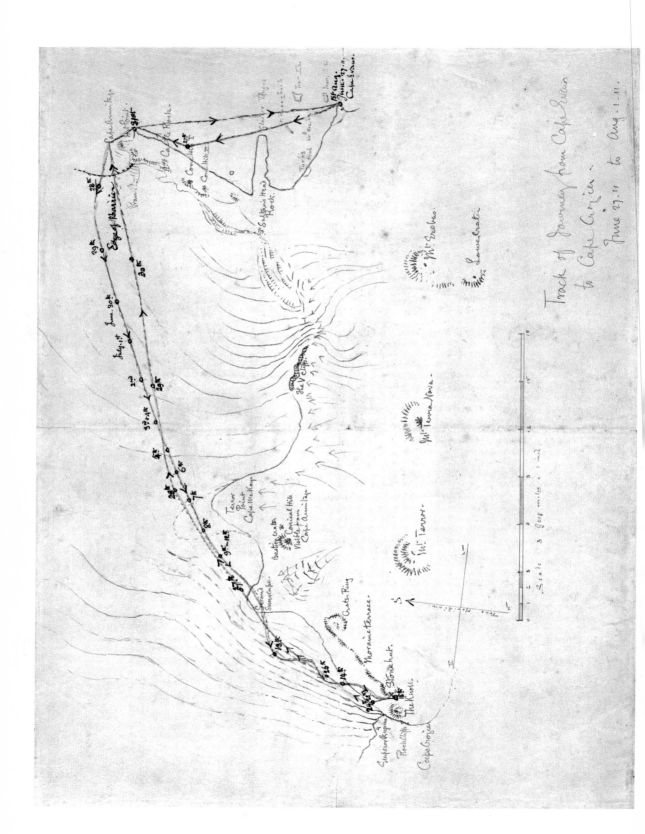

Track of Journey from Cape Evans
to Cape Crozier.
June 27.11 to Aug. 1. 11.

11

THE WINTER JOURNEY

LEAVING the Hut at Cape Evans a little before 11 in the morning after being photoed with our sledge in the dark by flashlight, Bowers, Cherry-Garrard and I started off for our first day's march, accompanied by Simpson, Meares, Griff Taylor, Nelson and Gran, who all helped us to drag our two sledges. A number of others came to see us off round the Cape. Nelson and Taylor left us when we had gone $3\frac{1}{2}$ miles. We continued with the other three. We made in to pass as close as possible to the end of Glacier Tongue where there were said to be fewer pressure ridges in the sea ice. It was so dark, however, that we never saw Glacier Tongue and we only knew we had passed it when we saw Turk's Head disappear. We then ran in to some very bad hummocky ice[1], and our rear sledge capsized. It was too dark to avoid them, so Meares, Simpson and Gran helped us on till we were again on smooth ice. At $5\frac{1}{4}$ miles they also left us, and returned to Cape Evans. The loads were heavy enough now, on sea ice even, to make us slow, though the surface was good. We camped for lunch at 2.30 at $6\frac{1}{3}$ miles from Cape Evans. We were using a lined tent which was an invention of Sverdrup's[2] in his last expedition, and we found it a great boon for it undoubtedly made one more comfortable in camp at the low temperatures we were to have this journey. It wants care and we made a point of brushing all the hoar frost off it every time we struck camp. The steam of the cooker otherwise gradually collects in the tent and ices the whole inside up. It was the duty of the cook for each day to see to this, and we were cooks each for one day at a time in turn. The lowest third of our tent, as a matter of fact, became badly iced up, but the upper parts we managed to keep clear of ice. Getting away at 4 we made for what we believed to be Hut Point, but in the dark got a good deal too close in to Castle Rock. Our pace was slow owing to the weights and we got into an E.S.E. wind which blew force 5 till we camped at 8 p.m. Then the wind dropped and we had a clear starlight night. We had purposely started several days before the moon would rise in order to have all our moonlight later when we got on to less well known country than this. The temperature for the day ranged from $-14\cdot5°$F. to $-15°$F. and the minimum for the night was $-26°$F. So ended our first day out, and perhaps I should say here why we had started on a sledge journey of such length. We hoped to be away 6 weeks in the darkest part of the whole year, instead of remaining comfortably in the hut, simply because the Emperor Penguins at Cape Crozier laid their eggs, as far as we could judge from what we found out in the *Discovery* days, in June and it was up to me to go and collect some of them to get early embryos—as I have said—for microscopic work. If vestiges of teeth are ever to be found in birds of the present day it will be in the embryos of penguins which are the most primitive birds living now, and the Emperor is quite the most interesting of them all, and the most difficult to get at, as will appear shortly from my account. Travelling with sledges in this way in mid-winter had not been done before, I believe, so it was an experiment of some interest. I had the pick of the whole party, Birdie Bowers and Cherry-Garrard, as my companions whom I had chosen and who were allowed to come by the Owner on condition I brought them back undamaged. They were the best of all our new sledging lot.

Wed 28 June Turned out 7.30 a.m. The going became heavy and we made little more than a mile an hour. Surface rough sea ice. We reached Hut Point at 1.30 and lunched there. After lunch made better going to Cape Armitage and then had the only really good 2 miles' going that we met with the whole of this journey, and soon reached the edge of the Barrier finding a good slope up and having no difficulty in hauling the sledges up one at a time. There was a snow covered crack at the top of the drift invisible until stepped into, but we knew it would be there and so had no difficulty. Coming down the slope of the Barrier was a steady stream of very cold air which we noticed only a few yards from the bottom and lost a few yards from the top. It was now 6.30 p.m. and we camped at 7, the last half hour being uphill on the Barrier and very heavy dragging compared with the sea ice we had just left. Temperature ranged from $-24.5°$F. in the morning to $-26.5°$F. at Hut Point, and $-47°$F. at the edge of the Barrier.

Thurs 29 June A cold night with temp. down to $-56.5°$F. and it was $-49°$F. when we turned out at 9 a.m. in pitch dark with a candle in the tent. But the day was fine and calm with occasional light easterly airs and aurora in curtains to the east both morning and evening covered the greater part of the sky. One of our chief pleasures on the march eastward was to watch these changing auroras for hour after hour ahead of us—almost always in the east and south east, and up to the zenith over our heads. The temperature remained at $-50°$F. all day, and we felt the cold a good deal in our feet on the march, Cherry getting his big toes frost bitten and I my heel and the sole of one foot. A good many of Cherry's finger tips also went last night and

Sketch panorama by Wilson of the south coast of Ross Island showing the route from Hut Point to Cape Crozier are blistered this morning, but he takes them all as a matter of course and says nothing about them. The surface all day very heavy and made our progress very slow.

The surface today was too heavy for us with both our sledges, so we relayed from **Fri 30 June** 11 a.m. to 3 p.m. by what little daylight there was, and from 4.30 to 7.45 by candle lamp. We thus took one sledge on at a time and came back for the other one. The surface was just like sand at these low temperatures. We made only 3¼ miles today in all, but walked about 10. The temp. ranged from −55° in the morning to −61·6° at lunch, and −66° on camping at night. Calm weather and aurora.

Turned out 7.30 a.m. From 10.45 till 3 we were able to do relay work by the **Sat 1 July** daylight. After lunch we continued with a candle lamp till 7.45 p.m. Surface like sand and the dragging so heavy that we could only just manage to pull one sledge by itself now. Subsidences in the crust were frequent all day. We made in all 2¼ miles today—very slow work. There was a fine aurora 5 to 7 p.m. Minimum temp. last night was −69° and today it ranged from −66·5° to −60·5° at 10 p.m.

Third Sunday after Trinity. Minimum for the night −65·2° with a breeze of **Sun 2 July** force 3 from S.S.E. with slight drift. Temperature during the day ran from −60° to −65° with calm and light airs which forced us to use our nose nips, for the slightest breeze with such low temperatures freezes any exposed part of one's face at once. We turned out at 7.30 a.m., relayed 11 to 3, then lunch and again relayed from 4.30 to 8 p.m., this time by moonlight, the rising moon giving us just enough light to go by. At one time it passed exactly behind the crater of Mount Erebus and looked like a magnificent eruption. We made only 2½ miles in the day—very heavy sandy snow.

Minimum temperature for the night −65°. Sky becoming overcast with some **Mon 3 July** storm clouds on Mount Terror—1½ miles by day glimmer and by moonlight after lunch. Temp. during the day ranged from −52° to −58·2°. We had a magnificent aurora in the evening when long swaying curtains almost covered the sky up to the zenith where they all became foreshortened, as though hanging right overhead, and swinging round from left to right in a rapidly moving whirl, constantly waxing and waning in brightness in different places, with bands of pale orange and emerald green and lemon yellow colour rippling along the borders of the curtains, and all fading upwards into the darkness of the sky as though they were curtains hanging from the roof of a vast dark cave stirred by some winds which didn't reach us on the surface. It was so very striking that we all three lay on our backs in the snow and watched it till we were too cold to watch it any longer, but we had a great part of it ahead of us as we marched. Our sleeping bags are beginning to get wet thanks to these low temperatures. One has to shut oneself right in all night to sleep at all and one's breath of course gradually makes the bag wetter and wetter. So all the sweat of seven or eight hours heavy hauling each day freezes in one's clothes and this also thaws into the bag every night. Cherry's bag is a large one. My own was a good fit on the small side—it became too small when it was really wet and frozen later on, and it broke at each end and nearly in two across the middle and gave me some beastly cold nights. Birdie's bag was the right size for him and lasted well. We also took with us eider down, or rather ducks' down, sleeping bag linings as a standby, in case our reindeer sleeping bags became impossibly wet and frozen. Cherry was so cold in his large bag last night that he began his down lining today. Birdie and I were as warm as we expected to be in our reindeer-skin bags. He has his with the hair outside. I have mine with the hair inside.

Tues 4 July Min. temp. for the night −65·4°, but we turned out at 7.20 to find the sky all overcast and snowing with a gusty southeasterly wind. At 9.30 a.m. the temp. had risen to −27·5° with a wind of force 4 from the N.E. Nothing could be seen by which to steer a course so we had breakfast and turned into our bags again to wait. We were fairly warm and comfortable all day and it began to clear as night came on. The min. temp. for the day was −44·5° and in the night it again fell to −54·6°. Clouds entirely obscure Erebus and Terror. This day in our bags has saturated our clothing and our bags so the moment we leave the tent we are frozen stiff into a sort of tin mail. It is difficult to realise how clumsy all one's movements become when all one's clothing is frozen stiff right down to the vest and shirt nearest the

skin. They are the only articles which one cannot shake a cloud of hoar frost out of when one returns to the hut after a cold journey at these temperatures. The clothing I was wearing on this journey was as follows: on my head a balaclava of close fitting woollen stuff with a windproof covering. A muffler—and these covered one's head and neck, only the face showing, nose, eyes, mouth and cheeks which could be further covered by a face guard buttoning across—but I only had to use mine twice the whole 5 weeks we were out. On my body I had a very thick woollen vest, a thin woollen shirt, a knitted cummerband reaching from the chest to the hips with canvas shoulder straps to keep it from slipping down. This is a splendid article—Ory made me several of them. Over this a grey woollen sweater and over all a wind-proof gaberdine blouse. On my legs a pair of thick pants—thick woollen pyjama trowsers—and over all windproof gaberdine trowsers. On my feet 3 or 4 pairs of socks and reindeer skin fur finnesko. On my hands half mits, leaving the fingers and thumb bare—these never came off—with short removable mits to cover the thumb and fingers, and a large pair of fur mits hung round the neck with lamp wick. With all this clothing wet and all frozen stiff it becomes difficult to move with one's customary agility and any climbing up ropes or out of crevasses becomes exceedingly difficult for anyone but an acrobat. Our feet have so far been warm except in the heavy soft surface snow on which we make such slow progress on the march. One's finnesko get frozen into stiff leather boots and lose all their value in giving the feet free play. So I had to keep a very watchful eye on 3 pairs of feet and continually when one asked if they were cold, it was only to be told they had been cold, but the owner didn't think they were frozen as they were most comfortable. I had to judge then whether they were really warmer or actually frozen, and sometimes it was exceedingly difficult to tell what was happening even with one's own feet. Happily we had no more than superficial frost bites on our toes and heels and soles, but every now and then we had to camp and have our lunch an hour earlier on account of this. We couldn't afford to risk getting anyone crippled in the feet above all else.

At 7 a.m. we turned out and the surface was the worst for pulling on that we had **Wed 5 July** yet had. We relayed for 8 hours and only advanced $1\frac{1}{2}$ miles in the day. The min.

temp. last night −54·8° and by the evening it fell to −60·1. We are surrounded now by white fog, but we can see Erebus and Terror and the moon with a halo and mock moons and vertical shafts of the lunar cross. We were hauling up hill all day crossing Terror Point, a long snow cape.

Thurs 6 July Calm and clear, though a heavy fog bank lies over the pressure ridges on our right and over the seaward area ahead of us. Relay work again for 7½ hours in which we made 1½ miles advance. The min. temp. for the night was −75·3°. At starting in the morning it was −70·2°. At noon it was −76·8°, and at 5.15 p.m. when we camped for lunch it was −77°. At midnight it rose again to −69° with some low lying mist. These are very low temperatures, about 10 degrees lower than any we got in *Discovery* sledging. This was the lowest we got −77° i.e. 109 degrees below freezing point Fahrenheit. Amundsen had lower temperatures in the north but it wasn't sledging as we are. I shall be very much surprised if he isn't beating all temperature records where he is now on the edge of the Barrier at the Bay of Whales.

Fri 7 July We got away late at noon in a thick white fog which made it impossible to see where we were going. We still had to relay though the surface was certainly improving. We had 4 hours between noon and 4, then camped for lunch and then went on till 9.45 p.m. when the fog was so thick that we couldn't see where we were going. We made only 1⅔ miles in the whole day. The min. temp. last night was −75·8°. At 2 p.m. −58·3° and at 7 p.m. −55·4° a rise for which we were grateful as it is distinctly easier to save one's feet from frost bite at −50 than at −70.

Sat 8 July A day of white fog and moonlight but no sign of land to steer a course by. We relayed again, 4 hours for 1¼ miles in the forenoon and 3 hours for 1 mile again after lunch. Surface improving as we get into a more windy area. Min. temp. for the night −59·8° and by the evening it had risen to −47°.

Sun 9 July 4th Sunday after Trinity. Relaying impossible owing to the fog and falling snow which covered our footprints and made it impossible to find the sledge load left behind. We found that we could drag the two sledges together, however, today. We couldn't see where we were going as everything was obscured by fog. Our chief difficulty now was to avoid running unwittingly up on to the

Terror slopes on the left where there are many patches of crevassed land ice, and into the Crozier pressure ridges on the right. No landmarks visible. We advanced about a mile in the forenoon march and ¾ mile after lunch—the moon invisible. In the after lunch march we ran into crevassed ground after having suspected we were pulling the sledges up and down over several rises. Pulling in the dark it is almost impossible to know whether the pulling is heavy because one is on a bad flat surface, or because one is pulling up hill. We expected some rises before reaching the second long snow cape beyond Terror Point, so we went on. The surface was again hard and icy in places with sometimes 6 inches of snow on it, as it was also yesterday. Our feet often went through the soft snow and slipped on the hard wind-swept sastrugi underneath. This was on the top of the ridges. In the hollows the snow was deep and soft. One could judge a good deal of the nature of the surface and the chance of running into cracks by the sound and by the pitch of the note which one's feet made on the more exposed snow—a much higher pitch than the lower note of deep and safer snow—and this in the dark without seeing what one was walking on at all. Occasionally the moonlit fog caught the edge of a snow ridge, but otherwise one saw nothing. We appear to be still out of the run of the main blizzard winds for which Cape Crozier is famous, and in an area of eddying winds, snowfall and fog. We call it Fog Bay. The moon became visible overhead but nothing else until just as we found ourselves going up a longer and steeper rise than usual we saw an irregular grey mountainous looking horizon ahead of us loom through the fog. It was evidently close up. So we unhitched from the sledges and tying ourselves together by our sledge harness traces we walked up a long hard snow slope to the top of our mountainous horizon and then found we were on one of the large Crozier pressure ridges with another appearing over the fog again. This was more certain to us when we stood still and heard the ice creaking and groaning ever so deep down under us and all around. This excursion from the sledges gave us our proper direction for safety, as we thought, but after retracing our steps and then turning more to the left, i.e. north, with our sledges, we again ran in amongst pretty big pressure ridges with cracks and crevasses in them, and so finding a hollow with deeper snow in it we camped for the night and decided to wait until we could see exactly where we had got to. The question of tide crack was in our minds all the time while we were crossing the long rounded snow capes which run out from Mount Terror into the Barrier, notably at Terror Point or at Cape Mackay, and the 'Second Cape' further on towards Cape Crozier. We certainly did cross several small cracks on these slopes which had the appearance of a certain amount of working, but they were inches only and if they are tidal they must take up very little of the tidal movement. Probably nine-tenths of the tidal action is taken up by the large pressure ridges. Today the temp. ranged from $-36\cdot7°$ up to $-27°$, with light airs. Some hours after midnight it began to blow and snow began to fall heavily while the min. temp. for the night was $-24\cdot5°$ up to noon of Monday,

Mon 10 July when a blizzard was blowing from S.S.W. force 6 to 8, and the air was as thick with snow as could be. This continued all day and we lay warm and wet in our bags listening to the periodic movements of the ice pressure underneath our tent and all around us.

Tues 11 July The temp. at 10 a.m. went up to $+7\cdot8°$, and at 8 p.m. was still $+6\cdot8°$. The lowest all day was $+3\cdot2°$. The wind was southwesterly force 5 to 9, very squally, and this continued all day with a heavy snowfall which packed our tent about $1\frac{1}{2}$ to 2 feet all round, as well as burying our sledges. Cherry sleeps in his down bag lining inside his fur bag. I turned my bag from fur inside to fur outside, the high temperature and the long lie in during this blizzard has steamed us and our bags into a very sodden wet condition. One wonders what they will be like when the temp. goes down again. We have discussed our respective rations and they have been revised somewhat as follows. To begin with we all three decided on simplicity, so we cut our foods down to biscuit, pemmican, butter, and tea—nothing else. We cut out sugar, chocolate, and cocoa, and all the etceteras, like raisins, pepper, curry powder. Further, we decided to make our rations experimental, so each of us had the 3 foods in varying proportion. I was all for increasing the fats because I am certain that every ounce of fat one can digest is worth more to one in heat and energy than an ounce of any other food. We therefore started with the following daily ration each. Birdie had 12 ozs of pemmican, 20 ozs of biscuit and no butter = 32 ozs. Cherry had 12 ozs pemmican, 20 ozs of biscuit and no butter. I had 12 ozs of pemmican, 12 ozs of biscuit and 8 ozs of butter. At the end of a week Cherry felt the need of more fat, but he increased his biscuit and for a time found that it did something towards satisfying him. We all kept to our 32 ozs of food per day, and when we settled down to a proper proportion we found we were eating all that we wanted and literally craved for nothing. We not one of us missed sugar, but I found I couldn't eat my extra half pound of butter a day—the most I could eat was 4 ozs. So Cherry and I made a bargain and I took 4 ozs of his superfluous biscuit and gave him 4 ozs of my butter. This made for each of us a perfect diet—4 ozs of butter, 12 ozs pemmican, and 16 ozs of biscuit = 32 ozs per day each. Birdie continued with his 16 ozs of biscuit and 16 ozs of pemmican, but he rarely eat more than 12 or 13 ozs of pemmican. The best diet was undoubtedly the one Cherry and I hit on, for Birdie allowed afterwards that he could have eaten butter when he couldn't eat more pemmican—but he wouldn't take it when we offered it to him. We rarely eat more than 2 or 3 ozs of our 4 ozs allowance of butter per day. Our ration, Cherry's and mine, compared with Birdie's gave $7345\cdot6$ foot pounds of energy instead of only [   ][3]. Towards evening the wind abated considerably but came on again during the night with snow and violent gusts, increasing at times to force 10. We couldn't march. The min. temp was −7·6°.

We had to remain in our bags all day. Wind force 10 from S.W. with much drift. **Wed 12 July** Temp. up to +2·9° again in the morning. Towards night the wind began to drop. Bowers turned his bag for the first time from hair outside to hair inside.

We dug out our sledges and tent, everything being deeply buried in snow. We got **Thurs 13 July** off a really good day's march on a decent surface 7½ miles in 7½ hours. During our march, in our efforts to avoid the pressure ridges on our right, we got too high up on to the land ice surfaces of Mount Terror and were held up by a very wide crevasse covered with a rotten, sunken looking lid which we caught sight of in a glint of moonlight just in time to avoid. We turned down its side and found it was one of many for we had run into a disturbed part of the névé running over a low mound of rock. We made east again and got on to the safer area below between the land ice and the pressure ridges. We camped at 8 p.m. There was a striking rosy glow of daylight in the north today behind the slopes of Terror. Min. temp. for last night −22·2° and by the evening it was −28·6°.

We made 5⅓ miles today, a good morning march, but the afternoon march was **Fri 14 July** cut short by a complete failure of light. After lunch we found we had again gone too far east and had run right into one of the big pressure ridges again. We turned north and soon encountered more crevasses, but by zigzagging and sounding with a pole we got away from them. In the bad and doubtful and absent light in which we were travelling continually it was most difficult to keep the middle way between the traps which lay on either side of us, or when we found ourselves caught in one of them, to know which it actually was. In daylight, in the *Discovery* days, we used to have but little difficulty here, but we were never here in the dark. It seemed in the fogs and darkness which lit our way now as though the pressure ridges had encroached on the land ice everywhere. The min. temp. for the night −35°. At 8.30 a.m. it was −17·4° and in the evening −24·6°.

The min. temp. for the night −34·5°, but at 10.30 a.m. it was −19·2° with a breeze **Sat 15 July** from S.S.W. We got a clear view this morning and after a short uphill 3 miles pull over very deep cut hard sastrugi, we reached the shelf of moraine where we had decided to build our stone hut. Rounding the lower end of this moraine we found ourselves in the Knoll Gap and pitched our tent in a large open smooth snow hollow, hard and wind swept on the surface, but in places not deeply cut. This camp was the last one on our outward journey for we had at last reached the place where our work lay. The camp lay about 150 yards below the ridge where we proposed to build our stone hut. We had originally intended building on the Adélie Penguin rookery, but our time had been so taken up in getting here and our supply of paraffin so short, that we decided it was better to build at once and as near to the Emperor Penguin rookery as possible. In the Adélie Penguin rookery we should have been sheltered from blizzards, but here we should be right in their track—only 5 miles nearer our work. On the ridge top above this snow

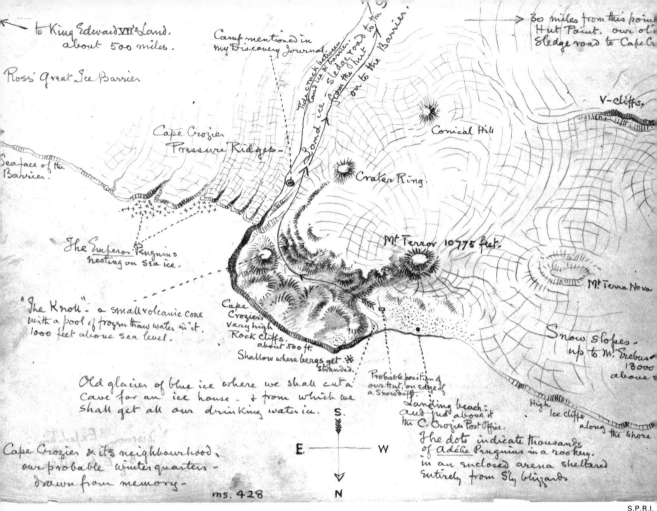

Sketch map of Cape Crozier. Probably drawn by Wilson in 1910 when he was preparing a report advocating this area as suitable winter quarters for the *Terra Nova*.

hollow where we camped was a low rough mass of rock in situ with a quantity of loose rock masses lying around and erratics of various kinds, some granite, some hard basalt, and some crumbly lava. There was also a lot of coarse gravel and plenty of hard snow which could be cut into slabs like paving stones.

So here we had all the material we wanted for building, and we chose a spot 6 or 8 yards on the lee side of the edge of the ridge, a position which we thought would be out of the actual wind force, but which we eventually found was all the more dangerous for that reason, as it was right in the spot where the upward suction was to be at its greatest.

At lunch time 4.15 p.m. we still had a wind of force 4 at −13° which we believed to be due to a more or less constant flow of air down the slopes of Terror. From this spot where we built our stone hut we had a magnificent outlook. To the E.

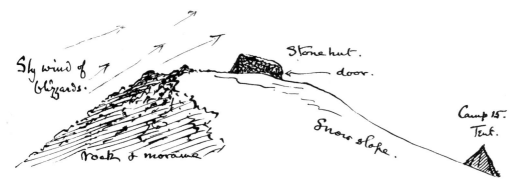

Sketch of the location of the stone hut at Cape Crozier S.P.R.I. MS. 505/1

and N.E. we looked over the whole of the Great Ice Barrier and Ross Sea, below us about 800 ft below was the whole range of great pressure ridges where the Barrier is moving along the shores of Ross Island. To the south we looked over the Barrier to White Island and the Bluff, and to the west we had the summit crater and all the slopes of Mount Terror, pile upon pile of snow and rock and glacier. Facing the door was the Knoll, a small extinct crater with the daylight in the north at noon behind it. Ross Sea was completely frozen over as far as we could see in the moonlight.

Sun 16 July Fifth Sunday after Trinity and an anniversary[4] not easily forgotten. We began the building of our stone hut, and I called it Oriana Hut, and the ridge on which it is built Oriana Ridge. We worked as long as there was light enough at midday and by the waning moon. Bowers and I collected the rocks and Cherry did the building. Then we piled up the out sides with snow slabs and gravel, two or three layers thick. We had a pick and a shovel with us. The hut was 8 feet across and about 12 feet long. The weather wall was a foot higher than the lee, and the entrance, in the lee wall, just allowed us to crawl in on all fours. We laid our 9 foot sledge across the walls as a ridge beam to support a strong canvas roof which had been prepared beforehand with long valance to build in all round.

Mon 17 July We continued building the hut and finished all but putting on the roof and door for which it was blowing too hard. Temp. −23·3° only.

Tues 18 July Temp. −27·3° and blowing too hard to finish the hut or do anything else. We therefore lay in our bags and were very cold for want of exercise.

Wed 19 July Turned out to be a calm day so we decided to make an effort to reach the Emperor Penguins' rookery and get some blubber for our stove, as our last can of oil but one was running very low and we couldn't afford to touch the last can, which we should want for the journey home. We made an early start and were away by 9.30 a.m. before any appearance of dawn. We took an alpine rope, ice axes, harnesses and skinning tools and a sledge. We had about a mile down snow slopes to the first pressure ridge, and our intention was to keep right in under the

151

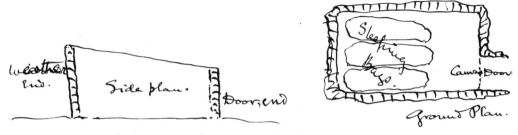

Profile and plan of stone hut at Cape Crozier   S.P.R.I. MS. 505/1

land ice cliffs, which are now very much more extensive than they were 10 years ago, and then on under the actual rock cliffs which had always been the best way before in the *Discovery* days. Somehow, in the bad light, we got down by a slope which led us into a valley between the first two pressure ridges and we afterwards found it impossible to get back in under the land ice cliffs. We tried again and again to work our way in to the left towards the spot where the land ice cliffs joined the rock cliffs, but though we made considerable headway between whiles along snow slopes and ridges by crossing the least tumbled parts of the pressure, yet we could not get a path through and the short midday light, which was absolutely essential here, was fast running out. We were working in a maze of crevasses all the while, roped together of course, and bridging the crevasses we couldn't cross with our sledge. It was quite exciting work but it grew very much more exciting as the light got worse and worse. All round us was a chaotic mass of tumbled blocks of ice with crevasses everywhere either gaping wide or else bridged with snow drift. We tried one opening after another and found them all impossible until at last we were faced by a small mountain of ice blocks shutting off any further progress and about 60 ft high all round us, we being in a drift-filled valley at

Sketch of the construction of the stone hut at Cape Crozier   S.P.R.I. MS. 505/1

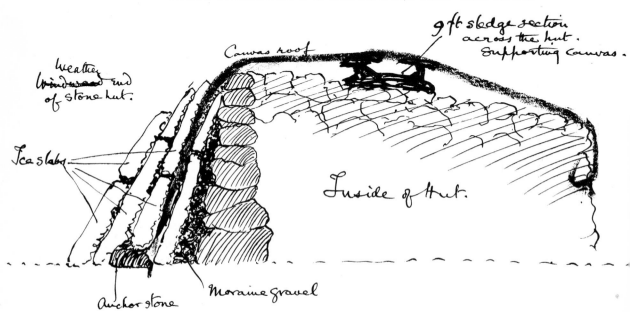

Emperor Penguins   S.P.R.I. 1462

'Erebus slopes and the Ramp from Cape Evans. 6.11. 6 p.m.'

the bottom. Here we had the mortification of hearing the distant cries of some of the Emperor Penguins echoed to us from the rock cliffs on our left. We were still, however, as far from the sea ice and the rookery as ever and more than two thirds of our daylight had gone. So we were forced to give up any further attempt that day and with great caution and much difficulty, owing to the failing light, we retraced the steps it had taken us three hours to make, and we were all but benighted before we reached safe ground after 5 hours clambering to no purpose. During the day a light southerly breeze had been blowing with a clear sky. The temp. had varied from −30° with southwesterly wind to −37°, which had been the minimum in the early morning between 3 a.m. and 9.30 a.m.

We turned out at 3 a.m. and got the canvas roof of our hut, with the door piece, **Thurs 20 July** fixed on and built in and made safe with blocks of snow and gravel and rocks anchoring it all round. It was a fine hut and would have made a top-hole living place in any other land. All that we wanted now was blubber for our stove, and as the weather was propitious we decided on another attempt to reach the rookery. We again made an early start before daylight broke. We took the same equipment and as before tied ourselves together and took crampons on our feet and ice axes. We had a tremendous clamber and reached the sea ice and the rookery. This time we found quite a different narrow snow slope off the land ice cliffs down into the first hollow. We had missed it yesterday when walking along the cliffs looking for a way down. Today we got it and it took us where we wanted to get, right in under the land ice cliffs, which show what wind can do. They are a hundred or more feet high and the whole face overhangs from having been scooped out into vast grooved hollows as though by a gigantic gouge. By following the foot of these cliffs one comes to places where the black basalt cliffs stand out of the ice at the foot of the Knoll on its eastern side and by a series of slides and climbs and scrambles between ice and rock and snow drifts one comes to where far loftier ice cliffs and rock cliffs take the pressure of the Barrier ice. It is at the foot of these cliffs, amongst rock débris and snow drifts and boulders which have fallen into the trough, that one comes to a possible path down to the sea ice. It is an extraordinary climb all the way, up and down in one cul de sac and over a wall into another. At one place we appeared again to be held up by an impasse, for we came to a spot where one of the biggest broken pressure ridges butted right into the rock cliff and the only way through was a man hole in the ice just big enough for each of us to squeeze through in turn. Here, therefore, we had to leave our sledge as it wouldn't come through. Once past this we were in a snow pit with almost vertical walls which required 15 steps to be cut before we could climb out. From this we again got into a series of drift troughs between the rock cliffs and the ice of the pressure ridges, and at last we got out on to the ice foot overlooking the sea ice, and there were the Emperor Penguins. There was a small but troublesome overhanging ice cliff of 10 or 12 ft which we could easily get down but couldn't so easily get up again. Everywhere else it rose to 20 or 30 ft and the edges corniced and overhanging. So we left Cherry on the top to help us up with the alpine rope and Birdie and I jumped down. The light was rapidly going and we had some very bad crevassed pieces of pressure ridge, as well as a lot of snow bridges and a razorback ridge with 30 or 40 ft to drop each side, to go back over on our way home. If we got benighted here we should have a nice long time to put in in the dark without food or shelter, something like 18 hours; that was why we were so careful *not* to get caught by the darkness. We rushed over the sea ice to where the Emperors were huddled together in a heap under the Barrier cliffs. There were, if anything, less than 100 instead of something like the 2,000 we found here in 1902. We saw at once that many of them had eggs on their feet because they moved along so very slowly and carefully while the others walked easily as usual. We collected 5 eggs, of which only 3 unfortunately reached camp intact, and these split when they froze on the way home[5]. We also, seeing that there were no seals on the ice here, quickly killed and skinned 3 Emperors and carried the skins home with the blubber on for our lamp. They were exceedingly fat, and the oil burned splendidly, even better than seal blubber oil. As we hustled the penguins to take some of their eggs we noticed an extraordinary thing. There were eggs dropped here and there on the ice, and as Birdie and I were collecting those we took, we both picked up lumps of rounded dirty ice the size and shape of eggs. We picked them up first thinking they *were* eggs and put them down when we found we were mistaken. While I was skinning one of the birds I saw an Emperor walk back close to me. It came across this lump of dirty ice and immediately proceeded to tuck it

Dirty ice eggs adopted by Emperor Penguins   S.P.R.I. MS. 505/1

in under its flap of feathers on its feet and incubate it! Seeing that there was a real egg getting cold close by I fetched it and put it down close by this bird, when it at once dropped the cold nest egg and came and incubated the real egg. We had to hurry away after this as it was all the while getting darker and darker. Then came a difficulty in getting up the little ice cliff. I got on Birdie's back and was soon up, but Cherry and I, hauling both as hard as we could, were unable to haul Birdie up, as the rope cut into the cliff the more we pulled and did nothing else. We got him an ice axe and then by hauling on him as he cut himself steps we at last got him up. On the sea ice Bowers unfortunately stepped through a crack and got one of his feet and legs wet through. They of course froze into a solid block, but he didn't get very cold. We had a difficult clamber back in the failing light and got in when it was quite dark—back to camp. On returning we at once flensed one of the Emperor skins, and cooked our supper on the blubber lamp, which gave out a furious heat and nearly choked us altogether. We soon got black and greasy. We slept that night for the first time in our stone hut, and it was a bad night for me for I got a spirt of burning oil in my eye and it gave me great pain for a good many hours. The temp. had not been below −28·3°. In the evening the wind freshened to force 6 from S.S.W.

Our first night in the hut was good save for my eye. The wind rose to force 8 and **Fri 21 July** had an effect on the canvas roof which we didn't quite like the look of. It made it quite taut at the same time just raising it off the supporting sledge rafter. We couldn't quite understand it and certainly didn't quite grasp the significance as we should have done. The wind dropped next day but looked unsettled. We spent the whole day in further packing every crack and crevice of our hut with snow, and we strengthened it in every way we could think of. Also put large slabs of icy snow on the canvas roof to counteract its tendency to 'lift' in the wind. We thought it was perfect when we had finished. Then we brought our tent up and pitched it under the lee of the hut quite close to the door for convenience, as we found it easier to warm the tent with our blubber lamp, concentrating the heat on wet socks and mits more than in the hut. We therefore decided to have our meals in the tent in future and to sleep in the hut until we could get seal skins to put over the canvas roof and keep the heat in. When we turned in the sky was overcast but there was no wind. We slept in the hut and my eye was very much better. The wind came on suddenly at 3 a.m. from the south and blew hard with little drift.

By 6.30 a.m. it was blowing 9 to 10 with heavy drift and very violent gusts, and **Sat 22 July** soon after this when Bowers looked out of the hut door he saw that the tent had been bodily blown away, legs, lining cover and all, leaving most of the gear we had left in it over night on the ground. The drift was very thick and the only thing to be done was to collect the gear and pass it all into the hut—which we quickly did. We found that two pieces of the cooker had been blown away—happily not the most essential parts, either of them. None of our finnesko had gone, happily, and a lot of mits and socks and such like small things, which might easily have followed the tent, were still there on the ground. My fur mits, however, were never seen again. Meanwhile in some inexplicable way the snowdrift was finding its way through every crack and crevice of our stone hut notwithstanding the canvas cover and sides and snow and gravel packing. It came in in such quantities that we and all our gear were soon inches deep in it, and later when the drift eased up we were layered down in fine black gravel dust which came in in the same way and smothered everything. We tried plugging the cracks with socks and mits but it wasn't any use. The wind was so strong and blew so hard over the roof of our hut that it sucked the canvas up and tried to lift it right off. It was sucked up as tight as a drum about 6 inches off the sledge which was supposed to be supporting it. This suction produced a sort of vacuum inside the hut and thus the snow dust and gravel dust was sucked in from outside, actually the stuff we had used for packing. So long as the large ice slabs, which we had put on the roof, remained there, there was no flapping or friction of the canvas on the stones, but before the next night was over they were all blown off. However, as the storm continued all day, we decided to cook a meal on the blubber stove. One comfort we felt was that we had 3 penguin skins for this purpose which would last us some days. Alas—we got the stove going, and after a few efforts it had nearly boiled the water for our meal when suddenly the heat unsoldered a feed pipe which ought to have been brazed, and the stove was at once useless. We poured the oil off into this for use on the way home in case of necessity, and then began to consider matters in the light of having only one remaining can of oil for the journey home and no tent. We still had a little oil in our last can but one—but it was obviously necessary for us to avoid touching our last can—and as soon as we are forced to we must go. It looked like coming to this very soon, for it would be very difficult now to improvise a stove without materials. As for a tent we believed we could improvise a shelter good enough to get home under with the canvas roof of our hut. Lying in our bags ruminating over these things in the hut, we were sopping wet and getting wetter every time we had to get in and out of our bags for anything, there was so much snow drift in the hut, but we were not cold, thanks to the rise of temperature with this blizzard. We finished our meal on the primus lamp when the blubber lamp gave out—and this was our last meal for a good many hours as it happened. The disappearance of the tent was a great surprise to us, for we had got a perfect spread and we had taken every possible precaution against wind. The valance was first buried in snow and then we added 4 or 5 rocks to the snow in each bay—and as a final precaution we slung a very heavy canvas tank of provisions and extra gear, so heavy that Birdie and I had to lift it together, on to the skirt. We can only think that the same lift acted on it and carried it away. Anyhow it was gone and out of sight, and we couldn't look for it till the blizzard stopped and a little daylight gave us a chance. Worse was to happen before this happened however.

Sun 23 July Sixth Sunday after Trinity and quite the funniest birthday I have ever spent. The wind was terrific. It blew almost continuously with storm force—there were slight lulls occasionally followed by squalls of very great violence, and at about noon the canvas roof of the hut carried away and we were left lying exposed in our sleeping bags without a tent or a roof. The storm continued all day with unabated vigour. There was no choice for us now—we had decided this before in the event of our roof being blown off—we had to remain lying there in our bags till the blizzard stopped. We had had two days of it, but here at Cape Crozier Royds in 1902 was laid up with his party for 5 days—and I with mine for 8 days out of 11. So we could only hope that this was not going to continue quite so long. If it did our best chance was to allow the snow drift to cover us up, which it was doing already, in order that we might at any rate keep warm. We could always eat biscuit and cold pemmican in our bags and we all had biscuit in our pockets. When the roof went Birdie and I were both out of our bags, for we were trying to stop the flap and the chafe of the canvas which began when the snow blocks were blown off the roof. The weakest spot was where the door came, but we had anchored it with very large stones. These stones the wind acting on the canvas joggled about like so much gravel and they gradually shifted out of place. We did all we could to jam them tight, but to no purpose, for while we were still at it the canvas ripped out all along the lee end of the hut with a noise like a battery of guns going off. In a second the canvas was ripped in about 10 places and it flapped to bits from end to end in a few minutes—leaving a ragged, flapping end attached to the weather wall which then went on bang, bang, banging for hours till the wind eventually dropped. The noise was most distressing, and we hardly noticed the rocks that fell in, or that the sledge was at once flapped off and fell in also across our three bags. We were at once in a perfect smother of drift when the canvas carried away, and Birdie and I bolted into our bags taking an enormous amount of snow in with our clothes to thaw out at leisure. We were not really so much disturbed as we might have thought, and we had time to think out a plan for getting home again now without our tent—in case we couldn't find it—and without the canvas roof of the hut which had gone down wind in shreds the size of a pocket handkerchief. We still had the floor cloth of the tent, and this we were lying on so it couldn't blow away. We could build a snow hut each night on the way home and put this over the top; or we could always dig a burrow in the Barrier big enough for the 3 of us, and make a very good roof with canvas flush with the surface—if there was wind it couldn't then be blown away. We had no doubts about getting back so long as this blizzard didn't last till we were all stiffened with the cold in our bags. The storm continued all day and on until midnight unabated.

At midnight the wind began to get more squally and dropped in force from 11 to 9 with short lulls. At 6.30 a.m. it had dropped to force 2. At 10 a.m. it was about force 3 and we waited for the moment when there would be light enough to go and look for the tent. While it was still dark we managed to cook up some pemmican, our first warm food for 48 hours. We did it by sitting up in our bags and drawing the floor cloth over our heads to protect the primus. When at last dawn came along it was by no means reassuring to see that in the south there was evidently a lot more blizzard still to come, so we lost no time in getting away down the slopes to leeward where our tent must have gone. Everywhere we found shreds of the roof canvas, and about a quarter of a mile round a corner of the hill Birdie found the tent—poles, cover and all hardly damaged. One of the poles was torn out of the cap, but that was nothing and soon remedied. We quickly brought it back, pitched it lower down the slope where it would be more sheltered, and then carried down our bags and the cooker and primus, and all the essentials and once more felt we were prepared for any amount of blizzard. It looked as though we shouldn't have long to wait. We then discussed our position and came to the conclusion that with one can of oil only we couldn't remain here and improvise a blubber stove for tent work, seeing, too, how very difficult the way down to the sea ice had become.

Mon 24 July

It was disappointing to have come all this way and to have done nothing worth mentioning of our work with the Emperor Penguins, but to remain now had become a practical impossibility. We had to own ourselves defeated by the Cape Crozier weather and by the darkness, which was really our greatest difficulty all through. We decided to put everything in order here today, to depot all that we could possibly leave that would be useful for [our] next visit here in the hut, and tomorrow to start back. We left the box of pickling solutions and all the apparatus I had brought for the penguin work. We also left a sledge, a pick, some bamboos, a variety of odd clothes and a down sleeping bag which was so solid with ice that nothing could be done with it. This was Cherry's. I also wrote and tied a note to the handle of the pick where it couldn't be missed, in a match box[6].

Tues 25 July Stiff breeze from the south. Temperature $-15\cdot3°$ with thick weather coming up, so we quickly made our final arrangements, and started off down towards the pressure ridges again with one sledge and our camp kit. We found that our sleeping bags were now so stiff with ice that rolling them up besides being difficult actually was a danger for the leather broke instead of bending. We therefore from now onwards laid them one on the other full length flat on the sledge. They were really about as bad as they could be and we were getting very little sleep in them at night. Cherry felt this most. Birdie slept most—I slept very little but didn't feel the loss of it much. I still kept my down lining in the bag though it was flat as sheet tin and about as warm and soft, but it held my reindeer skin bag together, which otherwise would have come in two pieces across the middle. My bag was broken at both ends as well as two big rents across the middle and the head eventually shrunk so hard and so immovably that I couldn't close the flap over. The journey home from here was by far the coldest experience I have ever had and by the time we got back to Hut Point we were all so short of sleep that not a meal passed without our having to wake each other up for fear of spilling the pemmican or falling into the cooker or the lamp. Well—we made a start home today but we hadn't gone more than a mile when it came on to blow so hard in our teeth that we had to camp again. We were then amongst very big, hard, icy sastrugi which made the tent pitching very difficult, but by anchoring the flap to a heavy case of biscuit we made it safe, and Birdie also tied himself in his sleeping bag to the tent poles, quite determined that if it blew away he would go with it and bring it back again. The gale continued and freshened to force 9, and lasted all night. Temperature during the day was from $-15\cdot3°$ to $-17°$ and the whole sky was overcast.

Wed 26 July The short midday light was all but gone when the wind dropped enough to allow us to start again. Leaving at 2 p.m. we then made $4\frac{1}{2}$ miles in $3\frac{1}{2}$ hours and once again got in amongst crevasses in the dark on smooth wind swept ice. We continued, however, feeling our way along by always keeping off hard ice slopes where the crevasses are bridged with rotten snow, and by keeping as far as possible to the crusty deeper snow which characterises the hollows of the pressure ridges which I believed we had again got foul of in the dark. We had no light and no landmarks to guide us except vague silhouetted slopes ahead which might be yards away from us or might be miles, but whose character it was impossible to judge. We travelled as much by ear and by the feel of the snow and ice under foot as by sight. We got to know very fairly well whether we could go ahead confidently or whether we were likely to fall through a lid. Probably my own feelings were quickened more than the others as I was on a long trace leading by about 10 or 15 ft ahead. The sky cleared when the wind fell and we had the temperature dropping from $-21\cdot5°$

at 11 a.m. to −45° at 9 p.m. We made our night camp among some pressure ridges on soft snow in one of the hollows.

We got away with the approach of daylight and found that we had camped, as **Thurs 27 July** we thought, right in amongst the larger pressure ridges and somehow, without crossing any large ridge yesterday, we had crossed several smaller ones safely in the dark and had then come on for a considerable distance between two very high ridges. Ahead of us was a safe and clear road along this hollow to the Barrier in the south, but our direction was S.W. and as the pressure ridge crevasses were so thinly bridged everywhere we hoped that by continuing along this hollow for a bit we might find some spot on the right where it would be low enough to cross more easily and so get on to the land ice again. We found no such dip, however, and after going some distance out of our course decided we must cross the ridge where we were. The whole thing was crevassed and one was so broad that we were all on the bridge with our sledge at once in crossing it. The next one I discovered by getting a leg down, but as I shouted a warning to the others I saw Birdie disappear down it, happily hanging by his sledge harness. He was quite helpless but with the alpine rope we gave him a loop for his foot and soon hauled him up again. After this we got on to better ground and soon reached safe land ice. We next got on to a very long upward slope and made good going till we had to camp, having covered 7½ miles in the day. The temp. varied from −45° to −47° during the day, but the weather was calm and what was more to the point, was clear enough latterly for us to see something of where we were going to in the dark.

We got away before daybreak and found ourselves still on the upward slope of a **Fri 28 July** very long gradient with a gentle breeze of cold air flowing down it. The Bastion Crater was on our right with the conical hill surmounting it, a landmark visible from Observation Hill. We went on and on up this slope until at last we found ourselves in a calm on the divide with a magnificent and encouraging view of the Western Range of mountains, Mount Discovery and Hut Point Peninsula, all showing like ghosts in the dim light. We then knew we were well over Terror Point and getting out of the blizzard area into the colder one. The surface all up this slope was good going. Over the divide we went down hill with the air stream on our backs. These local streams of cold air are typical of calm weather in this country; they occur on slopes. We soon got down on to the smooth soft Barrier surface again, our feet and the sledge runners both sinking in some inches. Subsidences also became frequent again.
Bright, fine weather—Erebus and Terror top showing all day. Temp. ranged from −47·2° in the morning to −38° in the evening. We made 6¾ miles in the day. Our sleeping bags are so wanting in any sort of attraction that we now cut our stay in them as short as possible, turning out at 5.30 a.m. and turning in about 10 p.m. We have dim daylight from about 10.30 a.m. when dawn begins, to about 2.30 or 3 p.m., but the sun is still so far from getting above the horizon at noon that it is only a sort of dim twilight all those hours at the best. The sun will not show himself at all above the horizon until August 23rd. However, even

this twilight is a great blessing now as we have no moon, and we arrange our marches to make use of it all before camping for lunch. After lunch we march in the dark. Our hands give us more pain with the cold than any other part—our feet are generally warm, but our hands are often dreadfully cold all night, soaking wet in wet mits the skin is sodden like a washerwoman's hands, and in this condition they get very easily frozen on turning out. Cherry's finger tips are all pretty badly blistered. I have only one bad thumb which blistered early and is now broken and very sore.

Sat 29 July Made $6\frac{1}{2}$ miles. Subsidences very frequent and at lunch the whole tent and the cook[er] and contents dropped suddenly with a bump and with so long and so loud a reverberation all round that we all stood and listened for some minutes. No wind today. Temp. from $-42°$ in the morning to $-45\cdot3°$ in the evening.

Sun 30 July Seventh Sunday after Trinity. We had fine weather again and did $7\frac{1}{2}$ miles in the day. Dawn on the horizon in the east is deep carmine running in a broad band along the Barrier horizon under a green sky. The temp. was low, $-55\cdot3°$ in the morning; $-63\cdot2°$ to $-61\cdot8°$ in the evening—pretty severe in our solid frozen wet sleeping bags. We have very poor nights and very little sleep. Fog banks were forming all along the Castle Rock ridge where the cold barrier air met the warmer air on the sea ice side of it.

Mon 31 July Turned out soon after 5 a.m. Calm weather again and we made $5\frac{1}{2}$ miles in $5\frac{1}{2}$ hours before stopping to lunch at the edge of the Barrier, $1\frac{1}{2}$ miles to the S. of Pram Point ridges. Here we ran down a drift slope on to the sea ice about 12 ft below. Temp. $-57°$ at this point where we lunched. After lunch $-43°$, and when we reached the hut at Hut Point it was up to $-27°$. We took very little time covering the $3\frac{1}{2}$ miles between the Barrier edge and Hut Point. Here we remained the night and decided to be up at 3 a.m. and get back to Cape Evans by dinner time.

Tues 1 Aug We slept where we sat in our tent which we pitched inside the hut, which was very cold indeed, but the tent we warmed up with a primus lamp as there was lots of oil here. We were in our bags for 3 hours, but at 3 a.m. it was blowing too hard to start and we remained dozing where we were until 10 o'clock. Then we had a meal and got away at 11 a.m. when the wind dropped. We marched on as long as there was any light and then camped for lunch off the Glacier Tongue. Then the new moon rose and we got away and were in at Cape Evans on the 36th day of our absence at about 10 o'clock in the evening. It was a great comfort to get off one's sopping and frozen garments and to turn into bed after a good supper of cocoa and bread and jam. We were pretty tired for want of sleep.

Wed 2 Aug Warm bath. Hair cut, shave—some extra sleep—and wandered round enjoying warmth and dry clothes. Feet, hands, nose and mouth all tingling and rather swollen and sore now that the reaction has set in. We have none of us lost much weight. Cherry only 1 lb, Birdie and I $3\frac{1}{2}$ lbs each.

Thurs 3 Aug

Enjoying comfort—with an enormous appetite. During our absence they have had two excitements. One was that Atkinson was very nearly lost in a blizzard. He was out 5 hours completely lost, and the whole party out in various directions looking for him. He came in eventually with his hands very badly frost bitten. The other excitement was that one of the ponies very nearly died of colic.

Emperor Penguin S.P.R.I. 67/1/4

12

PREPARATIONS FOR THE POLE

Fri 4 Aug WRITING up my report for the Owner of the Crozier sledge journey. Various discussions with the Owner over sledging matters. In the evening Sunny Jim gave us a lecture on meteorology—the most interesting point being the discussion of the 'fons et origo' of southerly blizzards. He is really getting at the root of it, I believe, and working it into a theory of Lockyer's[1] which has to do with the westerlies further north. My night on watch. I spent it writing up my report.

Sat 5 Aug Writing up my report again all day—22 hours on end at it, and nearly finished it in the rough.

Sun 6 Aug Eighth Sunday after Trinity. Church at 11. Spent most of the day writing my report again. Also had a sleep. My feet are feeling the reaction, so are Birdie's and Cherry's. They ache and are more or less numb and tingling to the toes.

Mon 7 Aug Writing report all day. Went up the Ramp at noon. Daylight was admitted to the hut windows today for the first time—it was just worth while and we removed the shutters. Ponting gave us a delightful show of Japanese lantern slides this evening.

Tues 8 Aug Report writing all day—copying out. Up the Ramp at noon. A perfect double lunar halo with mock moons and a lunar cross.

Wed 9 Aug Finished my report—40 pages of foolscap. Went up the Ramp. Temperature −33° and a breeze. Daylight increasing very rapidly. Afternoon read Roosevelt's *African game trails* and his chapter on Thayer's view of protective coloration[2]. Fine iridescent clouds all day over the slopes of Erebus; brilliant gleams of vivid orange and green and pink and silver in the curved slips of cloud.

Thurs 10 Aug Hands recovering, but still painful and the tips horny with no sensation. Thumb mending up fast. Feet still very numb and tingling; the sensation very slow in returning to normal in all three of us. Started painting again today and did a thing for Atch. Titus Oates gave us a second lecture on the management of horses and then we had a long discussion on horse snow shoes.

Blizzard blowing all night. Painted 5 sketches. **Fri 11 Aug**

Blizzard all yesterday and all night again. A beautiful day followed. Got 5 sketches **Sat 12 Aug** and finished 6 today. Began my snow baths again today. Birdie began his some days ago. Atch has had to drop his since he froze his hands. Feet still painful at night and tingling toes. Appetite completely out of hand. Birdie and Atch and I have had snow baths every morning all the winter—they are delightfully refreshing and with our shortage of water they keep one clean which is a great thing.

Ninth Sunday after Trinity. Church as usual. On ski to Cape Barne Glacier and **Sun 13 Aug** got a sketch. Sunny Jim sent a meteorological balloon up and got the instrument afterwards. Painted afternoon, 3 sketches.

Fine and calm. Erebus smoke voluminous and lit up with colour from the rapidly **Mon 14 Aug** approaching sun. In ten days we shall see him for a few minutes at noon. Mounts Lister and Huggins, which are over 13,000 ft, caught the sunlight on their tops today for the first time. Went out to S. Bay and Inaccessible Island and got some sketches. Finished 4 today. Wright lectured on radioactivity. Lassie produced a lot of pups.

Calm becoming overcast. Only got one sketch done. Went over all Ponting's **Tues 15 Aug** photos and discussed his ideas for an exhibition. He has got some very marvellous work done down here. He is really a master at getting pictures by photography.

We can read and write in the hut now by daylight for an appreciable time. The **Wed 16 Aug** whole day working at S.P.T. We want to get another number out by the middle of September. Lassie had 9 pups, and those she didn't lie on she trampled on, and those she didn't lie or trample on she left to die of cold—so the whole 9 are now dead. We got an Emperor Penguin today wandering round by itself with a wound on it, so we killed it for a specimen.

Calm and fine. Sun now striking Erebus smoke and summit. Painting all day **Thurs 17 Aug** parasites from the Emperor for Atch, S.P.T. pages and sketches of today's lights. Went for a ski run round the bergs at 4 p.m. They are most beautiful things in varying lights—sometimes emerald green, sometimes white, sometimes pure lilac or violet grey, and sometimes rose pink. Atkinson's lecture on scurvy.

Calm and fine. Painted most of the day S.P.T. and sketches and a sponge for **Fri 18 Aug** Nelson. Ski run round the bergs in the afternoon. We have daylight now from 9 a.m. to 5 p.m., but the sun below the horizon all the while still.

Blizzard all day and last night. Painting S.P.T. all day. The sun's upper limb is **Sat 19 Aug** theoretically visible today, but no one saw it.

Tenth Sunday after Trinity. Blowing still. Church. Spent the whole day reading **Sun 20 Aug** the *Confessio medici*[3] again. Also went up the Ramp. My night on watch.

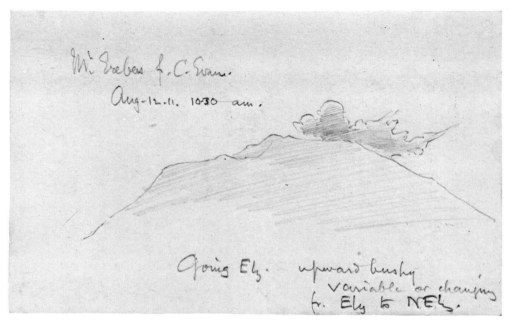

Steam cloud over Erebus, 12–14 August 1911

Mon 21 Aug Writing all night. Painting all forenoon and discussing ice problems. Went to glacier face with the Owner on ski. Slept after lunch till 5 p.m. then up the Ramp. After dinner a beautiful lot of lantern slides on India from Ponting.

Tues 22 Aug Blizzard again—very heavy gusts from 4 miles an hour to 80 miles an hour in one squall. Painting and drawing all day and S.P.T. work.

Aug. 13. 11.
2 pm.

Indefinite Mushroom with a lot of misty cirrus going to N. or NNW.

Aug. 14. 11 - 10 a.m.

Blue

Violet.

brown & grey

pale ochre

S.P.R.I. 1802

Very thick blizzard, the worst we have had down here, with tremendous drifts. **Wed 23 Aug**
No one out. All day painting S.P.T.

Blizzarding thick as ever. All day painting S.P.T. except for a long discussion on **Thurs 24 Aug**
making map of locality to be done conjointly by plane-tabling by Taylor,
Debenham and Wright under Teddie Evans, who is excellent at map drawing and

surveying. His map making and printing are wonderfully neat. Lecture on physiography by Taylor.

Fri 25 Aug   Still blizzarding. Smells and feels like a southwesterly gale at home today—warm and damp. S.P.T. work all the forenoon. All the afternoon rambling over the Ramp where the glacier butts on to the moraine. Splendid clouds today forming under Erebus and flowing N. to form the usual bank of cumulus over Cape Bird way.

Sat 26 Aug   A beautiful day with pink glow behind Erebus, even at 8.30 a.m. At 1.30 I saw the sun above the Barne Glacier clear and cloudless. Ponco photographed me at the sunshine recorder too on Wind Vane Hill, the first snap shot taken this season. Out all day over the morainic heaps of Cape Evans. Read *Kim* again for a change.

Sun 27 Aug   Eleventh Sunday after Trinity. Blowing hard again all day till 6 p.m. when I went up the Ramp with Birdie. Church at 10.30 as usual. Painting Antarctic birds all day and got a lot done. Julik, one of our dogs, has today come back after a month's absence, no one knows where. He may have been up north to Cape Royds and got carried away on floating ice for a time. Evidently hasn't been

Mount Erebus, 25 August 1911, 5 p.m.

feeding very full, but is covered with seal blood. The poor seals have a very wretched time here when there's an expedition on the go.

Painting birds all the forenoon. After lunch went with Silas to the Land's End **Mon 28 Aug** where we were in time for a magnificent afterglow of salmon pink and blue. Also went up the Ramp. After supper Meares gave us a lecture on his travels in central Thibet with Brooke who was killed there in the Lolo country.

Fine day. Meteorological balloon went up but the instrument was not recovered. **Tues 29 Aug** Drawing birds again all forenoon. Afternoon went over the cape and got a sketch or two—then drew birds again. A chess wave has struck the hut, and there are two or three sets played every evening.

Clear day but windy. Painting and drawing birds. Hunting over the bay ice and **Wed 30 Aug** the cape with Sunny Jim for one of his balloon instruments which was afterwards found in N. Bay. After dinner at birds again. Have been redrawing all the rough sketches I made of petrels, albatrosses and other sea birds which I got done on the voyage out.

Calm day but gradually overcasting and in the afternoon a blizzard suddenly **Thurs 31 Aug** sprung on us when nearly everyone was out. I was on the cape and up the Ramp

167

with the Owner hunting up points in connection with the glacier moraine. The Owner and Bowers are very deep in the working out of weights for the southern journey all these days. Preparations for spring sledge journeys are also going ahead.

Fri 1 Sept Had to start exercising my pony today—taking him out for 2 hours a day. My pony is Nobby, one of the 2 survivors of last season's depot journey. He is slow, but one of the quietest and most reliable of the lot. After lunch went out sketching and got drawings of our bergs. In the evening drawing.

Sat 2 Sept Bright daylight at 7 a.m. Pony exercising. Painting 11.30 to lunch. Skiing and sketching after noon, round Inaccessible Island. Heavy line of pressure there up north from the west end of the island, rising to 6 ft or more. Bowers' lecture after dinner on polar clothing history.

Sun 3 Sept Twelfth Sunday after Trinity. Dull and misty. Church as usual. Horse exercising. Went up the Ramp. Finished *Kim*.

Mon 4 Sept Blowing too hard for horse exercise. Spent a long time fixing my ski up for the southern journey. My night watch. Cherry stayed up too and finished off the S.P.T.

Tues 5 Sept Horses afternoon. Forenoon painting S.P.T. and a berg.

Wed 6 Sept Blizzard all day, heavy drift. No going out. Drawing all day, S.P.T. chiefly. Nelson was the only one who was out today; he visits his fishing hole whenever he can to break out the newly formed ice.

Thurs 7 Sept All the forenoon drawing pen and ink panorama sketches for Taylor. After lunch pony exercising. Glorious sunset. Erebus looking most beautiful. Earth shadows showing over Lister at 8 a.m. now. A week ago they were an hour later. The 2nd part of the S.P.T. was published today after dinner, when Ponting also gave us an exceedingly interesting show of lantern slides on China, Pekin and the Ming Tombs.

Fri 8 Sept Pony exercising forenoon. Wonderful earth shadows and a tremendous volume of steam from Erebus also throwing a shadow right across the sky. Painting most of the day and reading Sherlock Holmes, *The Memoirs* and *The Return*.

Sat 9 Sept Pony exercising forenoon. Remainder of day painting. Have now done just over 100 sketches. Went up the Ramp. Teddie Evans, Gran and Seaman Forde started on a sledge journey to Corner Camp to renew the cairn marking the depot.

Sun 10 Sept Thirteenth Sunday after Trinity. Church as usual. Horse exercising. Up the Ramp. Reading.

Mon 11 Sept Calm day but overcast. Whole forenoon at my clothing. Sorting out for the S. journey sledging. Pony exercising, always taking Nobby out with Cherry's horse

Aug. 8.11. 3 pm. Cape Evans. looking North.

Exercising the ponies. 8 August 1911

S.P.R.I. 527

Mount Erebus. 13 August 1911. 10 a.m.

Mᵗ Discovery + Inaccessible Iᵈ. Aug. 14. 11. 1 p.m.

'Mt. Discovery and Inaccessible Id. Aug.14.11. 1 p.m.'

'Iridescent clouds – looking north from the Ramp on Cape Evans. Aug.9.11'

Michael and Birdie's horse Victor. Up the Ramp. Evening lecture by Nelson on biology.

Calm day but threatening. Drift running on Erebus slopes. Horse exercising. Up **Tues 12 Sept** the Ramp with Taylor. Drawing pen and ink panorama. After dark I saw a red glow lighting up the smoke cloud of Erebus for 3 or 4 minutes, the light coming from glowing lava in the crater.

Horse exercising. Fine parhelion and mock suns well in front of the Ramp and **Wed 13 Sept** Erebus with a very broad and brilliant shaft of light below the sun. Up the Ramp. After lunch went out on ski to the seal crack where were 8 seals, 5 males and 3 cows. The Owner gave us an account of the programme for the southern journey.

Fine day, misty afternoon with snow crystals in the air and a very brilliant **Thurs 14 Sept** parhelion and mock suns which lasted right on into actual sunset. Sewing sledge kit all forenoon. Afternoon horses—then up the Ramp sketching for an hour or more. Evening Silas lectured on the constitution of matter.

Scott, Bowers, Simpson and Petty Officer Evans left, sledging for the west side **Fri 15 Sept** of the strait. Teddie Evans, Gran and Forde returned the same evening from Safety Camp and Corner Camp having been out 6 nights with −73° their lowest temperature on the Barrier. One march they made of 34 miles. Forde's fingers and thumb badly frost bitten. After lunch painted yesterday's sketches.

Exercised ponies and went up the Ramp and did a sketch there. Temperature **Sat 16 Sept** −2·7° on the Ramp and −21° on the floe, only 250 ft lower—and yet all this difference in temperature. Painting all remainder of day and began doing circular pictures, a shape that suits these sketches that one gets down here with so much horizon and horizontal skies and floes.

Fourteenth Sunday after Trinity. Turned out 5.30 a.m. Made tea and read and **Sun 17 Sept** wrote till breakfast. A very beautiful sunny day. Snow was seen melting on wood in the sun today—first time. Horse exercising. Up the Ramp and sketched there. Painting afternoon and evening.

Up at 5 a.m. to read and write—a new routine to get time for quiet; which is the **Mon 18 Sept** most impossible thing all day. Horses and up the Ramp forenoon. Painting all the rest of the day. My night watch. I spent it writing up a copy of my journal of which this is part. When Ory's birthday came I wrote to her.

✠Ory's birthday. Horse exercising and up the Ramp in the forenoon—and in the **Tues 19 Sept** afternoon lay down and slept as I was tired. After supper went on with my writing till bedtime.

Strong blizzard warning in the morning, turned out at 8 a.m. only. Horse **Wed 20 Sept** exercising and up the Ramp. Afternoon painting a siphonophore[4] for Nelson. Evening copied out the Owner's programme for southern journey.

Thurs 21 Sept Up at 6 to read and write. Blowing very hard from the S. No one out today except to roll the ponies on the beach. Ponting showed us some slips of the cinematograph pictures he has been taking—beautiful things many of them, especially of Erebus' smoke and of a seal playing along a rocky coast in and out of the water. Copied pictures of the Beardmore Glacier mtns. from Shackleton's book. Also read Wild's account of the journey up the glacier. Day has succeeded in making an impromptu turning lathe on the crank shaft of Sunny Jim's small petrol engine. This he uses for turning oak and greenheart rollers for the motor sledges. He finds many of the rollers have been spoiled by turning the sledges on hard sea ice when they were being used for landing things from the ship last January. Having only a few spares he has improvised this lathe and is making a lot of new ones. His cleverness with his fingers is always coming out. He has made most beautiful covers for the S.P.T. out of Venesta[5], stained and french polished and beautifully carved and fitted with sealskin bindings.

Fri 22 Sept Up at 5 a.m., read and wrote. Blowing hard. Spent forenoon sewing leather mits for horse leading. Nobby is just shedding his old coat; he is before all the others in doing this which looks well for him. Afternoon took him out. After that sewing till bed time. Cherry's horse ran a French nail into its hoof, left hind foot, today and it drew blood and was very tender when we got it out. He was all right, however, in a day or two.

Sat 23 Sept Up at 5 a.m., reading and writing. Made a map on tracing cloth of the southern journey route that we shall use on our journey. After lunch horse exercising and

'From the Ramp. Mt. Lister. Noon. Sept.17.11.'

S.P.R.I. 1802

then up the Ramp. Meares and Demitri have left with the two dog teams for Hut Point where they will be for some weeks making dog pemmican of seal meat. Evening after supper slept till 11 p.m. and then came on for night watch.

Fifteenth Sunday after Trinity. Whole night writing up my journal. Forenoon **Sun 24 Sept** exercising pony, then up Ramp with Silas and down the drift slope of Barne Glacier. Fog spreading thick over the strait from the west. Looking over snow goggles for the summer. They are as good a pattern as can be, everyone thinks, and Sharpe has managed the making of them excellently, but he mustn't say anything about them publicly, or in his shop window, until we all return! Slept for an hour and a half, very tired. After dinner painted a sketch of this morning's sunrise.

Up at 6 a.m. reading and writing. Weather thick and threatening. Exercised **Mon 25 Sept** horses and up the Ramp in forenoon. Painting afternoon and evening. Did 4 circular ones. Chess is played every evening. Dominoes had a spell but have been given up now. The seamen play cards.

Up at 5.15 a.m. Blizzarding very hard all day. Thick drift. No one out. All day **Tues 26 Sept** writing journal. Forde's finger and thumb are turning out badly—the frost bite has gone deeper than we thought. He may lose the end of the finger, and the thumb nail will be lost for good.

Up at 5 a.m. Blizzarding all day again—no one out. Very thick. All day copying **Wed 27 Sept** journal.

Up at 5.15 a.m. Blowing very hard still but the sky clearing and off and on no drift; **Thurs 28 Sept** but at 5 p.m. it came on as thick and as bad as ever. No one out, and I got my journal copy up to date for sending home. We have been expecting the Owner's party back for some days now—but probably they have been staying at Hut Point till the [blizzard] was over. They will have had a poor time if they started today. From now till we leave on the southern journey on November 1 I hope to write more about what the others have been doing all the winter and less of what I have done, but my short daily diary has not run to more than the important things that happened—and my own insignificant ways of spending my time. Just at present I am fed up with having written this journal for so many days on end. Every now and then I have had to go and play the pianola to work off my writer's cramp, mental chiefly. However, my early hours will be continued and I shall manage to get some account written of what has been going on. Our winter life has been very quiet as may be judged by the regularity of our horse exercising, my continual painting and drawing, and the lack of exciting incident to put into this old journal of mine. At 1.30 in the night, long after we had all turned in, except Day who was night watchman, the Owner's sledge party returned. They had been marching through the storm in order to avoid another camp on sea ice. Except for the last two days they had had exceptionally good weather and no temperature lower than $-43°$ which they had only once. They had been across from here to the Ferrar Glacier, then up the glacier a bit to a row of stakes planted there last year. These were again examined and a very definite movement was found to have taken place since February. They then came down the glacier again and went up the coast as far as Dunlop Island towards Granite Harbour. They found the end of our old Glacier Tongue stranded along the coast and intact with the depot which Shackleton had put there, and with our fodder and bamboo stakes and everything exactly as it had been when we left it—still attached to the Glacier Tongue in January—but now broken off and drifted away 50 miles across the strait. The most unexpected thing about it was that it was still intact, for the surface was a perfect maze of crevasses and many of them are deep— yet below the water line it must be solid ice.

Fri 29 Sept Didn't turn out till 8 a.m. after the interruption of the sledge party's return last night. Sunny Jim's face is a picture of frost bites, but none of them serious ones. No one has suffered any damage at all and they were not even very wet, having had such good weather. Today took horse out and a nuisance he was. Having had no exercise for 3 days and feeling the breeze very much with his new, and at present thin, coat, and wanting to go back every minute of the two hours he was out he played all sorts of pranks. His favourite game is first to violently shake his head when he thinks you are off your guard; this hits you either in the chest or in the face or in the stomach, and then he tries to rear, comes down with straight forelegs on your feet, which are by this time just in the right place, and then you see his heels somewhere over your left shoulder. The only thing to do is to hold him tight by his head with a stiff arm, so that one is out of reach of his head and his forelegs and his hind legs. If one punches him in the ribs, or still more if one pretends to use the end of the rope lead, he never jumps away from you but always towards you and up go his heels. Of course they can't reach you because you are at his shoulders, and knowing this he then tries to bite you in the leg! Take him all round on a breezy day with a cold wind which he hates, he keeps one pretty busy and one would hardly believe that he is one of the quietest of the whole lot on the march. One hasn't very much control over the animals really as they have no bits, and one merely hangs on to a halter or headstall. Some of them are much worse; they seem to have learned every trick a horse ever knew—the worst is striking with the forefeet which is difficult as one is always within reach by their heads. The comfort is that they all give up these tricks when they have been in harness with a loaded sledge on the Barrier for a few days. Their one idea is then to eat everything—they eat their hobbles, their picketing lines, their puttees, if they have any, and their head ropes, and if they get loose they go for a sack of oats on the sledge or else for our biscuits which they reach by getting through the canvas tank.

After horse exercising I went up the Ramp, and in the afternoon posed, or as we call it here, 'ponted'[6] for Ponting with several of the others as a foreground to the hut and Mount Erebus in the cinematograph. It is quite an amusing occupation— as good as amateur theatricals, and quite as difficult, for you have to try and be absolutely natural, and you have to completely ignore and forget the cinematograph. Ponting thinks the roll he got of this was as good as it could be. The individuals in it, besides myself, are Cherry-Garrard, Atkinson and the cook, Clissold. Some painting—some pottering over rocks they brought back from the west, the most interesting being some vein quartz with copper pyrites.

Exercised the horse and went up the Ramp with Birdie. Afternoon reading **Sat 30 Sept** medicine and then painting. My night watch so I slept from 9 till 11.30 p.m., when my watch began, and then I painted all night for the S.P.T.

Sixteenth Sunday after Trinity. The duties of night watchman include going out **Sun 1 Oct** every hour to observe the aurora and the clouds and the weather generally. Also looking after the galley fire which is kept in, banked, until about 6.30 a.m. when it is stoked up to warm very large baths of water for the horses' breakfast and large pots of water for our own. Then at 7 we have an early morning tea club— I make tea for Teddie Evans, Sunny Jim, Nelson and Day, not because they always turn out early, but because they all enjoy early morning tea. They bring me tea at 7 when I don't turn out also. Sunny Jim is up earlier than the others as he has to go out and see to his meteorological instruments every day at 8 o'clock before breakfast. His screens, anemometers, sunshine recorder etc., are all on the top of a little knoll about a couple of hundred yards from the hut—a knoll we call Wind Vane Hill. Evans turns out half an hour before breakfast every morning to wind the chronometers and take their rates. Nelson's uprising is very irregular, and Day only gets tea on fine mornings when he turns out for a ski run, so much of his day's work being in the hut, engineering work, and in the motor garage, that he has to get his air and exercise when he can. He is a hard worker and a very ingenious contriver with his hands. His motor garage is a house of stores built up with cases and covered with tarpaulin. He works here under difficulties as it gets full of snow drift every time it blows. Except for Gran, who is expert on ski, Day is the best of all of us and the keenest on ski, and is always trying slopes and turns. Today we had Church as usual at 10.30 a.m. Then out with the horses, and then up the Ramp where I got some very beautiful iridescent felspars in a piece of kenyte. Today we began breaking the horses into dragging sledges—an exciting game with some of the more lively ones. Painted a bit after lunch and then slept till dinner. Forde, who got his fingers and thumb badly frost bitten a short while ago, is gradually recovering, but one finger end still hangs in the balance—the damage is so deep that it may turn out that the bone is exposed. This remains to be seen.

Up at 5.30 to read and write. Very heavy blizzard blew all night and all today. **Mon 2 Oct** Very thick snow drift indeed—no one able to go out. Part of the day went in working for the S.P.T. and the rest in discussing plans for the coming season which are bound to be very complicated. The thing which most affects me and my movements is that we shall in all probability be so late in returning from our sledge journey to the Pole that we shall be too late to see the ship, for she is bound to leave fairly early in March. This means that whatever the urgency for a return home it will be impossible for another year—and perhaps the least pleasant part of this will be that we cannot possibly receive our letters until it is too late either to answer them or to act on them. This is the prospect and it is not what one can call a pleasant one. Still, I hope all will be right in the end. Obviously I cannot shirk the southern sledge journey on this account, having come down here to take part in it.

Tues 3 Oct The blizzard over. Up at 5. Ponies and up the Ramp after breakfast. S.P.T. work after lunch and in the evening.

Wed 4 Oct Up at 5. Pony exercising—with a sledge load. After this had to form one of a quartet in some amateur theatricals for the cinematograph. Captain Scott, Bowers, Seaman Evans and I went through all the stages of camp doings in a tent. We did it in sections—first we changed our footgear and lit the primus and hung up our socks and cooked the hoosh. Second, we opened up the steaming cooker and whacked it out in the pannikins, and had our meal. Third, we packed up the cooker, tied up the provision bag, put both out of the tent and then unrolled our sleeping bags. Fourth, we had our sleeping bags out and were sitting in them writing diary, winding watch, sewing, etc., and then all got inside the bags and went to sleep! This film is a splendid one, Ponting says, it has come out quite perfectly and will be kept as a special one for Scott's return—and lecture[7]. After lunch doing S.P.T. work all the afternoon and wrote up diary in the evening. Teddie Evans' party came in from Glacier Tongue today, weather too bad for surveying.

Thurs 5 Oct Pony exercise—up the Ramp and S.P.T. work with talks over the plans for the coming season occupied the day.

Fri 6 Oct Went in very much more strenuous fashion. Four of us, Oates, Cherry, Crean (seaman) and myself went with our four ponies and 4 sacks of oats and a sleeping bag each to Hut Point. It took us 5 hours and we had a nice day, 15 miles over sea ice, no halt on the way as Christopher, Oates' horse, kicks or tries to kick everything to bits whenever he stops. Meares and Demitri (the Russian dog-driving boy) were at Hut Point with the two dog teams, living there to make seal pemmican for the dogs in the summer travelling. We therefore came to a warm and comfortable hut and it was most pleasant. More than that we now have a telephone working between the Hut Point and Cape Evans. The wire is simply laid along the sea ice and the free end taken through a crack into the sea water for earth connection. It works well. We had a good supper and a comfortable night in our bags.

Sat 7 Oct We intended resting the horses here at Hut Point today, and so we were not much worried by the weather, though it blew hard and drifted all day. I found Conan Doyle's *Green Flag* book of stories and read comfortably all day long. The horses were quite comfortable in their stabling and Meares cooked us chupatties and seal liver.

Sun 8 Oct Seventeenth Sunday after Trinity. It was still blowing all the morning so that we didn't get off till 2.15 p.m. but then we had perfect weather for our 15 miles back, and the horses went a tremendous fast walk homeward and without loads. We got to Cape Evans by 6.15 p.m. Very nearly 4 miles an hour. We left Meares and Demitri at Hut Point with their dogs, one of which is sick. As we came just off the point of Cape Evans we were surprised to see 3 figures come off the land and go to one of the bergs near by, and then a party of men hurrying round the cape with a sledge and a sleeping bag. This could only mean an accident, so I gave Titus my horse to take in and went off to see. It turned out that Clissold the cook had been climbing up a small berg to help out a photo which was being taken of it, when he slipped and fell about 15 ft. When they came to him he was quite insensible, so they sent for a sledge and a sleeping bag. He soon came round, but had been badly shaken; he has concussion of the brain and he seems to have hurt his back though nothing is broken. We got him into the hut and to bed and there he will remain I fear for some time. The unfortunate thing is that he was to have been one of the Motor Party to start off in 3 weeks and it looks impossible for him now. So with seaman Forde, whose frost bitten fingers have been so bad, it hardly looks as though he would be able to start either. He was to have gone west with Griffith Taylor. And to make an evening of our home coming today, while we were at supper Wright came in and told us he had had to leave Griffith Taylor with whom he had been walking all day, as he, Taylor, was too done up to get back to the hut until someone brought him some food. He had been out most of the day trying to bicycle on the sea ice and had covered a good many miles, but the surface had been too much for him. However, as one can't sit down in this climate to rest without getting feet frost bitten, especially in a tired out condition like this, Scott sent out a sledge and a sleeping bag again to bring Taylor in! He wasn't really as bad as this, however, and he walked in on his own. He is a person who goes full bore at everything that interests him without a thought as to what has to be done after, or how he is going to get back; a trait which is good enough except for the half dozen people who have to go and nurse him home again.

Turned out at 5 to a fine morning. Atkinson had been up all night with Clissold **Mon 9 Oct** who had a good deal of pain in his back and chest and very short breathing. He had morphia and ice to suck, but slept very little. A. or I remained with him all day. Otherwise horse exercise and S.P.T. work.

I sat up the night with Clissold who still has a lot of pain and breathes badly. None **Tues 10 Oct** of his ribs are broken, though, and all his trouble is due to bruising and concussion. It was blowing a thick blizzard all night and drifting so much all today that horses didn't go out. S.P.T. drawing chiefly. Turned in soon after supper. It is extraordinary what a pandemonium one can sleep in here. I turn in now always at 10 p.m. and turn out early. But on days like this when I turn in at 8 or 9—soon after supper—when the pianola or the gramophone is full on and half a dozen people talking at the top of their voices, one puts one's head down almost in the midst of it all and is asleep in about two minutes and dead to the world so far as all ordinary noises are concerned until it is time to turn out. Sleep like this is a true godsend.

Wed 11 Oct Up at 6. We left Clissold to the night watchman, Ponting, who was to call Atkinson or me if anything was wanted; but he had a very good night and awoke much better. Exercised my horse in the forenoon and did S.P.T. work. Forde, who got his hand frost bitten, is still having it dressed morning and evening. There is still a doubt as to whether he will save the tip of one finger and a black slough has to come off before one can say if the bone is exposed. The nails of his thumb and middle finger came off today and as new nails are just reappearing at the root, the bite is not so deep here as it at first appeared. The effect of frost bite on nails is very unexpected sometimes. I had a superficial frost bite on one of my big toes at Cape Crozier in July and half the nail only was killed, so that now it has broken half across, half dead and half still growing.

Thurs 12 Oct Up at 5 writing and reading. Horse exercise and then up the Ramp and S.P.T. drawing the rest of the day. This just about finishes the S.P.T. for this third volume, and it is to be published on Sunday. It is a very poetical number—or rather versical—I am not sure that there is much poetry in any of the verses. I have even run to two verses myself[8]. Pathological I'm afraid—perhaps an early symptom of polar anæmia.

Fri 13 Oct Up at 5. Odd jobs all forenoon, arranging about the sending home of photograph negatives. Ponting is returning this coming season and he will take home all his own negatives and cinematograph films. Taylor also returns to N.Z. with him and will take all his negatives and print copies of them for his own use in writing up his physiographic report before sending them on to Ponting in England. The great danger is leakage of copies and their publication, so Taylor has undertaken to make his own prints and not to let any negative out of his own hands. Ponting is to have an agreement drawn up with whatever firm he chooses to deal with his negatives. It was a bit breezy early today but turned into a real hot sunny afternoon, temp. just about zero, but so hot that one had to take clothes off to enjoy walking, and one could thoroughly enjoy pottering about in the sun. The horses were all out in the afternoon and misbehaved themselves properly. They are all living high now and doing very little work—only enough to keep them fit, and the consequence is they get more mischievous every day. We have one brute, Christopher, who absolutely refuses to be harnessed to a sledge or to be taken out when once in. Anything within reach of his heels he tries to kick to pieces. Oates and the Russian stableman, Anton, deal with him and do their best to break him in, but it is a regular circus every day. The first thing is [to] strap up one of his forelegs before leaving the stable, and to get a bit and a twitch on. Then he leaves the stable on three legs and is brought down over the tide cracks on to the floe to the sledges. These are loaded with bales of fodder. He often succeeds in kicking out with his hind legs even though he has only the one foreleg to balance on, and so, since he learnt this, it has been necessary to bring him down on to his knees. He is never hit. None of the horses are ever hit whatever they do, and some of them are beginning to understand it a little for it is a change to them evidently. They all seem to have been ill treated all of their lives up to now. Christopher is brought to his knees by having a rope fastened round his remaining fore foot. This is then brought over

176

THE BARRIER SILENCE

THE Silence was deep with a breath like sleep
        As our sledge runners slid on the snow,
And the fate-full fall of our fur-clad feet
        Struck mute like a silent blow
On a questioning "hush", as the settling crust
        Shrank shivering over the floe;
And the sledge in its track sent a whisper back
        Which was lost in a white fog-bow.

AND this was the thought that the Silence wrought
        As it scorched and froze us through,
Though secrets hidden are all forbidden
        Till God means man to know,
We might be the men God meant should know
        The heart of the Barrier snow,
        In the heat of the sun, and the glow
        And the glare from the glistening floe,
As it scorched and froze us through and through
        With the bite of the drifting snow.

his shoulder and jerked up the first moment he lifts it off the ground. Then he is on his knees and can neither kick nor move, and his whole energies are spent in trying to bite. Then the sledge is drawn up to him and he is put into the traces. Now his forelegs are released—or one of them—while two men hang on to his head, and the moment he gets to his feet he rushes forward. If in this effort he kicks again, as he often does, he may again get his hind legs over the trace and the whole business has to be gone through again. I am glad we have such an excellent man as the Inniskilling Dragoon to manage these beasts. We should be in great trouble without him in the case of this horse. Today the brute suddenly bolted and got away alone with his loaded sledge on the floe, and there was great difficulty in getting hold of him again. For a long time he ran wild and then came up to where 2 or 3 others with sledges were standing, and when ever anyone tried to approach him he made a dash at him with his teeth and hind legs and there was a chance of someone being knocked off his legs by the following sledge. Cherry and I came up with our horses, which we were leading without sledges, and at this time there were four men on the loaded sledge all digging their heels into the snow to break it, and yet he was gaily trotting along and would allow no one to come near his head. Oates eventually got him and all was well. They are all more troublesome now than they will be when it comes to heavy and continuous work on the Barrier, but there will be some excitement during the first few days before they settle down. Ponting photographed me with my horse Nobby today, also Cherry-Garrard with Michael, and Crean with Bones. Bowers has Victor, Seaman Evans has Snippetts, Seaman Keohane has Jimmy Pigg, Atkinson has Jehu, Wright has Chinaman. Jehu probably won't start as he seems utterly unable to do anything. He was useless from the first and notwithstanding every care he has remained as weak as a cabhorse. All the others are pretty fit, but it is a pity they haven't all changed their coats early as Nobby did; he finished shedding his old winter coat a week ago and now looks fine. This evening Teddie Evans and Gran returned from Hut Point. They have been making a survey of the coast line of this island from here, Cape Evans to Hut Pt. It was only roughly done when we were here in the *Discovery*, and now in detail. I turned in at 10.

Sat 14 Oct Up at 5 to read and write. When I turn out the night watchman turns in. I make myself tea. At 6 I call Bowers who writes in his bunk. At 7 I call the cook and the sweeper and Anton the stableman. Also Sunny Jim to whom I take a cup of tea as he has to be out to his meteorological instruments and at work for an hour before breakfast. Day generally has a cup of tea at 7 and does an hour's work at his motors before breakfast. Up to 8 o'clock one has a very quiet time though, the only chance there is of a quiet time in the hut. One lives at such very close quarters and there are so many different jobs going on, and so few windows—and our window being the lightest generally has a crowd round it. Today was overcast and grey but no wind. Took ponies out with sledge loads, a two hours' walk round North Bay and then into S. Bay and then home. In places the sea ice is blue and windswept and slippery. Sometimes the ponies come down on it but they don't seem to mind much. Of course we keep them off this as much as possible and generally speaking the sea ice is good walking, covered with hard wind driven snow, or else crunchy and irregular like snow cobble. All the afternoon I spent fixing everyone up with snow goggles. Sharpe's leather goggles are tremendously popular, and the green glass is the most efficient I think. Sharpe shall have a pair or two of these goggles back if he likes with a letter, when I come home—but I can't send him one until then. They have been most successful. After supper painted a bit and turned in before 11.

Eighteenth Sunday after Trinity. Up at 5. Church at 10 as usual. 3 hymns, the **Sun 15 Oct** Psalms and morning prayer which Captain Scott reads. After that, though it was blowing pretty strong with surface drift, we took the ponies out, but the wind steadily increased and the ponies were so obstreperous that we didn't keep them out long. Snippetts has gone lame today—with a strained tendon. As we can't afford a single pony to go out of action now, this is unfortunate, but these old birds seem to go lame and get well again periodically for little reason, so we hope he will soon be all right. Jehu, Atkinson's pony, is almost certainly a non-starter—he is worn out. I am afraid the string of ponies which we have were not chosen under the best possible conditions at Vladivostok. The chooser was not very knowledgeable about horses and trusted too much to a dealer and a vet. He was rather handi-capped also by being told to get white ones if possible, which must have reduced his selection enormously. This preference for white ponies resulted from the fact that in Shackleton's lot down here the white ones survived longest and seemed hardiest, but I doubt whether there was enough in it to warrant the cutting down of a very much larger selection in the Vladivostok market. We really have very few decent horses amongst the whole lot, and several of them are as old as the hills and have passed a life of ill-treatment, hard work and poor food. Laminitis[9] is one of their troubles and general debility seems another. We lost the best of the whole lot last season—in fact 3 of the best— when the ice went out and Bowers got adrift on an ice floe. Now we shall do what we can with those that are left. If the motors work we ought to get to the Beardmore Glacier easily enough. The real hard work begins after getting there, first up the glacier, and then with low temperatures going fast by man haulage to the Pole and back on the summit. No one yet knows who will be on the summit party, it is to depend on condition and fitness when we get there. We are not going to depend on the dogs for anything except the laying of depots between this base and the Beardmore. Ponies of course can't be got up the Beardmore Glacier and so man haulage is the thing on the summit— and I think it can be done all right, though it will take time, and we shall certainly be late in returning to Hut Point. Hut Point is now provisioned for another period of waiting such as we had last year. This is in case the ice has gone out between it and Cape Evans. If, however, the ship is still waiting when we return she will pick us up at Hut Point and take us to Cape Evans. If not, we shall all wait at Hut Point as we did last year until the sea freezes over; then we return to Cape Evans and prepare for another winter. We have plenty of stores here and there are quite a number of stores at Shackleton's hut which we can get any day. Shackleton's hut is only half a day's walk over the sea ice or along the coast over the glacier ice where a way lies which is free from crevasses. Day and Gran walked there and back today. Day, who is our motor engineer, and Priestley who is with

Sketch for 'Cave berg off Cape Evans. Sept.1.11.5.30 p.m.' (see plate facing p. 184)

Campbell now somewhere north in Robertson Bay, are both former members of Shackleton's party at Cape Royds. Today the third volume of the S.P.T. was published, after lunch, and it caused great amusement. Some of the articles in it are decidedly funny to us in the light of all the humbug that goes on from day to day, but it will all have the same handicap that the old S.P.T. had, namely, that much of it will be unintelligible without explanation. However, it certainly creates a diversion down here so it is worth the time spent over it. The covers are beautifully done by Day—different each volume, but always made of Weddell Seal skin and Venesta board, partly plain and partly stained and polished. We really have great fun over these efforts and everyone takes the humbugging they get in the best spirit possible. Cherry-Garrard makes a splendid editor and we run the volume on very much the same lines as the old S.P.T. of the *Discovery*. Lillie's caricatures take the place of Michael Barnes'. Day always produces an illustration. Taylor is a real wit and writes very funny articles, and any number of them. This volume we have been flooded with poetic efforts. We are short of change and variety in the illustration, though we have three of Ponting's photos each number to relieve the monotony. I have been doing a series of silhouettes again and of black and white blizzard and sledging scenes and of sledge flags. The rest of my business is the illustration of articles and headlines. In the afternoon Meares rang us up from Hut Pt. on the telephone to say he had returned from Corner Camp with Demitri and the dog teams. I turned in at 9—sleepy.

Mon 16 Oct Up at 5.30. Writing and reading. Weather heavily overcast and threatening a blizzard which, however, didn't arrive though by telephone we learned from Meares that it was blowing a blizzard at Hut Point. Took ponies out in the forenoon—but only for an hour as the wind and snow increased from the N. This continued all day. Spent my time preparing kit for southern sledge journey. In the evening Ponting gave us another lantern lecture on Japan—the Kyoto temples and other things—most beautiful pictures, and after it was over he made a flashlight picture of the whole show from the back which has made rather an interesting picture.

Tues 17 Oct Up at 5.30 to a beautiful sunny morning, but by breakfast time the whole sky was overcast again. We took the horses out and the remainder of the day I spent sewing at my sledging gear. We are off now in less than a fortnight and there is a lot to see to before I go, for by the time I return the ship will not only have come but very possibly have gone too, so whatever message I have to send home next year must be sent now. It makes it difficult, for one can hardly realise the position. When I return too from this long sledge journey I shall find all the home letters waiting for me at Hut Point, and if the ship has already left for good it will be impossible for me to answer any questions in them. And worse still it will be impossible for me to alter plans however much I may be wanting to return—I shall have to stop for the year. I trust all will be well though. I don't see any other course open to me than to carry through the job I came here for, which was in the main this sledge journey for the Pole 'L'homme propose, mais le bon Dieu dispose' is an honest creed, and in this case l'homme hasn't decided to do anything from first to last that he wasn't convinced would be approved by his infinitely better half, and le bon Dieu will do the rest. Whatever of bad news there may be in the letters that are to come, believe me, if I can't act on them I shall be sorry indeed, but I shall not be unprepared for anything. Whatever happens, even if it's worse than anything one can bring oneself to imagine, there is no more to be said or done than this. This evening after supper the two motors were to have been brought out on to the sea ice from their garage on shore. They are to start off in a week from now. There was a good deal of difficulty, however, owing to the temperature, in getting them to start, and eventually when one was got under way it hadn't gone more than 30 yards when it did a side slip on some ice and the cogs rode up on to the rollers of the chain and the bumps which resulted cracked the axle casing, which is a great heavy piece of cast aluminium and a difficult thing to patch up. It looked at the time as though it would throw out this motor altogether and make it useless, and this was what Scott thought for the time. As a matter of fact two days later Day and Lashly had made what looked like an excellent job of it by bolting the whole together with long steel bolts—but it remains to be seen whether this is strong enough to stand the strain.

Wed 18 Oct A blizzard blowing hard all day—no going out—so spent the day in collecting notes from all my flock of science workers as to the work done during the past year and intentions for the year to come. Also spent some time over my sledging gear—devil of a lot of needlework.

Thurs 19 Oct The anniversary of our engagement day, and Oct. 19 1899 was a Thursday also. Turned out at 5. Blizzard as thick as a hedge all day—no going out, but a very happy day all the same—mainly needlework and discussing plans and the future with Captain Scott. If we return too late for the ship from this southern sledge journey, and if Amundsen reaches the Pole and goes home in the *Fram*, Ponting will not wait a year for our return but will make hay while the interest is alive and have his exhibition at once, and in that case we all here, i.e. Scott, Ponting, and I think it would be wise to have my sketches also exhibited with his photos, while the interest is alive and before we come home, only in this case the pictures would have to be sold outright, and that wouldn't do as they would then be lost for any further use. So after all they must be kept, and if Ponting has his exhibit in 1912, I will have mine, a separate one, in 1913, and take whatever interest remains. I don't want to sell any of my sketches much without keeping copies of them—besides I know some of them will be wanted for use. However, I will write finally to Ory about this and she will have the doing of anything there is to be done about them.

Fri 20 Oct Up at 5. Forenoon out with horses and writing an account of the scientific work of the past year, which is to go in to the press telegram returning with the ship in March. Afternoon dug out our medical stores and renovated all the sledging equipment—each party starting having a medical case of its own. In the evening we were all cinematographed playing football on the sea ice. Also a very good group was taken of the whole lot of us just outside the hut, and at dinner we had toasts to the success of starting parties as tomorrow will be the last day we are all together in this hut until April—no—the last time all together, for Ponting and Taylor are going home. The departures begin tomorrow with Meares and Demitri and the 2 dog teams who will leave tomorrow and spend the next two months laying depots from Hut Point and advancing loads from time to time. On Sunday the motor party leaves, Day and Lashly driving the two motors, Evans (Lieut.) and Hooper (domestic) going with them to make the course and assist. On Monday the western geological party is leaving, composed of Griff Taylor, Debenham, Gran and Forde (seaman). This party has been unlucky. Forde starts with a right hand almost crippled for the time being with frostbite, and Debenham has today hurt his knee pretty badly. I rather doubt if they will get away by Monday after all. Then we, the remainder, with Scott and all the ponies start off on Tuesday week, October 31. This leaves no one in the hut except Simpson, who remains to do his work all through the summer and to meet the ship. He remains in charge while we are away. Nelson also remains to do his work i.e. marine zoology. Clissold, who is still suffering from his fall and is in bed, but will be up before we leave—he remains as cook and domestic. Anton, the little Russian stableman, remains as he is to return in the ship. He is a delightful little study but hasn't been very happy down here as he is terribly superstitious and the winter darkness got on his nerves; he works like two men, but we think it best for him to go and he also wishes to return. Demitri, the Russian dog driver, is quite different, full of fun and mischief, absolutely fearless, and very quick in his mind and movements. He is the son of a Russian sent to Siberia, was born in its Far East, and drove the dog sledge mails in Petropavlosk. Ponting is going several shorter sledge journeys for photographic work, with Anton and Clissold, if he's fit for it, to help him. One journey will be across the strait and to Koettlitz Glacier—another up to Cape Royds to cinematograph the penguins. The main southern pony party consists of 3 tents—No. 1 contains Captain Scott, Major Oates, Petty Officer Evans and myself. No. 2 contains Lieut. Bowers, Cherry-Garrard and Seaman Keohane. No. 3 contains Surgeon Atkinson, C. S. Wright and Seaman Crean. So there are 16 men[10], 10 horses and about 24 dogs engaged in this southern journey —with 2 motors, and we hope to get somewhere—though there may be great difficulties in the way.

Up at 5.30. Sunny but blowing and it continued to blow all day. In the afternoon, **Sat 21 Oct** however, we took the horses out for a while. In less than a week we shall have the midnight sun with us—on the 27th—and then begins our summer of better weather for 4 months. Both the motors are now out on the sea ice with all the sledges packed ready for a start. The broken axle case of the one has been very satisfactorily patched up with steel bolts. Today I spent in getting various things done— writing report on the winter's work, finishing off my sledge gear, issuing medical cases for the sledge parties and so on. All goes well with our preparations except for the geological Western Party who are unfortunate; for Debenham's knee is as stiff as can be and he can't walk on it at all at present, and Forde's frost bitten fingers have not yet healed up quite, though they are doing very well.

Sun 22 Oct 19th Sunday after Trinity. A sunny morning and no wind. Up at 5.30. Writing and reading till breakfast. After church three of us with three horses and 22 cases of provision started off to sledge them over to the end of Glacier Tongue where Meares, with the dog team, is to pick them up from Hut Point. We had quite nice weather going out, and we made a pile of these boxes by the telephone wire about 7 miles out. Bowers had hold of the 3 horses' heads, Victor, Snatcher and Nobby, and Petty Officer Evans and I were busy with the sledge straps and cases, when Victor caught his nostril on the hames of Snatcher's harness and tore a piece of skin off. This frightened him so that he reared and frightened Snatcher who immediately plunged and broke away with his empty sledge and galloped off towards home. Nobby seeing Snatcher gallop off and Victor rearing and kicking, then jumped over Victor's sledge and galloped off also with his empty sledge dangling and swinging and flying about behind him. The only horse Bowers succeeded in holding was Victor with his nose torn. Evans immediately ran after his horse in the direction of home. I ran after Nobby who was running due west out into the middle of the strait. Both were thoroughly terrified by the empty sledges which kept jerking against their hind legs and frightening them as they galloped. Every now and then one saw them jump a pressure ridge of the sea ice and plunge into a snow drift, and then a cloud of snow would bury them for a second or two. But they went on and on, and then the wind came up and raised so much drift that I lost sight of Bowers and Evans and their horses and didn't dare stop running for fear of losing sight of mine, who evidently didn't know where his home lay, for he was going right away from it. I came up with him after running close upon three miles off the west end of Tent Island and he was walking along west. Happily I had a biscuit with me and I held it out to him a long way off, and he spotted it and allowed me to come up with it, and so I got hold of his head again. He was none the worse for his run and we then walked home. There was a very high wind and drift by this time but happily he was in a hurry to get back now and he didn't make a fuss. When I got in I found that Snatcher had come in alone with his sledge and in a lather of sweat having galloped all the 7 miles apparently. Evans got in shortly before me. Bowers came in with his horse about three quarters of an hour later, and then we doctored his horse's nose. So after all there wasn't much damage done, which was lucky as we can't afford to lose the use of a single horse now. After some tea I read and copied all Captain Scott's instructions to the various people who are in charge in different directions during the summer. Pennell in charge of the ship, Campbell in charge of the Robertson Bay Party, Meares the Dog Party, Taylor the Western Party, Simpson the Hut Party left at Cape Evans. Each one has been given written instructions which requires a great deal of forethought. Simpson and Nelson went to C. Royds and found that 3 Adélies had arrived there.

Mon 23 Oct Turned out at 5.30. Rather breezy but sunny. It is interesting that the first Adélie Penguins should have been seen at Cape Royds yesterday, because in 1902 the first Adélie was seen at Hut Point on exactly the same date. It was interesting to hear too from Nelson that today the collection of ice plate crystals, which have formed every day on his net lines all through the winter, were for the first

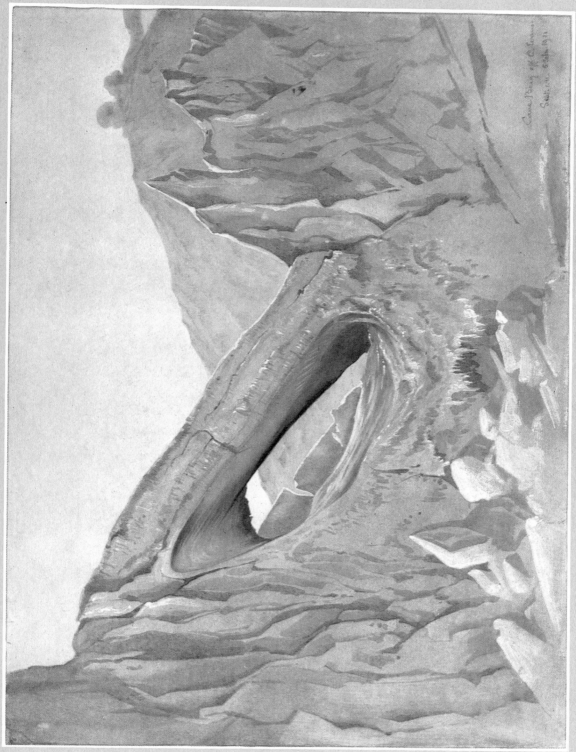

'Cave berg off C. Evans. Sept.1.11. 5.30 p.m.'

'Mt. Discovery and Inaccessible Id. from the Ramp. Sept.14.11. 5.30 p.m.'

time absent and that this absence coincided with a sudden large increase in the number of diatoms caught in the plankton net, and almost certainly with a rise in the temperature of the water. These water temps. are being taken with very extraordinary exactness nowadays, with thermometers which register to a thousandth of a degree centigrade[11]. Today also two baby seals were seen newly born at the large Razorback Island tide crack. Oates saw them when he was out there with his horses. All the forenoon went in trying to get the two motor cars off with their loads, but they wouldn't work well and kept stopping, though they were within an ace of being successful. So after spending half the day at one thing and another, it was decided to postpone the start till tomorrow. In the afternoon I was out with my horse, after that working at the taking of latitude sights— mathematics—which I hate—till bedtime. It will be wiser to know a little navigation on this southern sledge journey.

Up at 5. Sunny and clear. I have to write a note for the press telegram, which **Tues 24 Oct** Captain Scott is sending home, on the scientific work of the expedition up to date from the time of our arrival here. From January 22 when we left Cape Evans on the depot journey to April 22 when we returned there was practically no scientific work done by anyone, except by the Western Party (geological) consisting of Taylor, Wright and Debenham, and by the hut party consisting of Simpson, Nelson and Ponting. Atkinson and I were both on the sledge work as medicals. Therefore, to begin with, the hut work. Simpson's arrangements there for physical work of all kinds is the most important. He was given a good corner of the main hut with Wright, close by a window looking E.S.E. where he fixed up a working bench, a small writing table and a lot of shelves, his motor engine, his fan for the thermograph, his electric apparatus and various instruments. In this corner, without leaving the hut, he can read off recording instruments giving continuous records of the temperature outside, the barometer and (by standard barometer and 2 barographs), the wind force (by Dines' anemometer and by an anemograph which records miles per hour as well). In the hut porch he has another clockwork drum, which records the direction of the wind continuously. Then in his own corner he records continuously the potential gradient of the air. On the top of a small hill, about 300 yds from the hut, he has instruments for the following observations:– a sunshine recorder, which gives a continuous record— a glass globe which turns a line on a slip of card—also 2 Robinson's cup anemometers for wind velocity records. Further screen instruments for temperature to check those by the hut, and so on. To check these continuous records observations are taken independently every 4 hours and so also are observations on the nature and directions of motion of clouds, and on the weather and the direction of Erebus' smoke, which gives the wind direction at 13,000 ft. All through the winter hourly observations were made on the aurora, and as long as there was any absence of light these were continued by the night watchman. Measurements of atmospheric radioactivity were taken from May to August for winter values, and these will be repeated as opportunity offers for summer values. The upper atmosphere was from time to time investigated whenever weather conditions allowed a chance of recovering the instruments sent up, or of following the course of the balloon—first by balloons sent up without instruments, simply to give the direction of the upper currents, and secondly with instruments which recorded the height and the temperature in a regular curve on a minute plate of silvered metal. A still more important part of the work done by Simpson was observation of the magnetic elements continuously by Eschenhagen's magnetograph, while weekly observations of the absolute value of the dip, declination and horizontal force were also made. The cunning devices by which all the working out of these instruments with the electric lamps and periodic cut-offs, and the electric bells every hour, and alarm bells to go off when any recorder broke down, were extraordinarily good and well thought out. Simpson's ingenuity in this way overcame the absence of his special meteorological hut. Instead of it he has managed work with the corner given him in the main hut, and with a small asbestos sheeting hut and a good big cave hewn out of a small blue ice glacier not 100 yards from the main hut door. So much for Simpson's work which is all on the top line, as he knows well what he is about and spends his whole time at it. He has really worked hard and continuously ever since we came down here, and has managed to overcome innumerable difficulties.

Nelson also had the late summer months, or rather the 3 autumn months, for his work at the station while we were away, but he was handicapped by living on a moraine with no sea ice to work from. He got all his apparatus well into order for the winter work and all through the winter kept a good hole open in a shelter off the end of the cape which he visited and worked at every day over 100 fathoms of water. Here plankton samples were taken at short intervals with townets of various meshes. Quantitative samples have also been taken in 93 fathoms with international pattern nets. By dredging and traps larger material has been taken from the bottom as well as a good many fish. Nelson has also been doing hydrographic work at his hole in the ice. Water samples have been taken at intervals from a depth of 2 to 170 metres. Soundings have been made over a number of cracks in the sea ice. The purpose of the water samples is to obtain their salinity values, current measurements, velocity, and direction, throughout a period of 24 hours for spring and neap tides, and measurements of the amount of light at various depths beneath the ice are forming part of the spring programme. There is also interesting work to do in the various fresh water lakes and pools on Cape Evans itself, these being full of vegetable growth and minute life. The botanical work is limited, there being only a few lichens and seaweeds and mosses. As soon as the sea ice froze sufficiently a permanent tide gauge was erected and a continuous curve of the rise and fall obtained throughout the winter. No seiches have been observed, however.

While this work was going on at the main station at Cape Evans the Western Geological Party was doing good work on the west side of the sound. Physiography, geology, petrology and ice work with a good deal of surveying and amplification of existing *Discovery* surveys were all undertaken and brought very interesting results. Detailed maps have now been made of Dry Valley and its vicinity under the head of Ferrar Glacier. The west Koettlitz Glacier and its tributary valleys have also been mapped in detail. A number of districts here are forming—or have recently been forming—structural characteristics which are obviously comparable with those of other now ice free regions of the world. The Dry Valley, for example, has with its barriers and defiles its counterpart in similar characteristic valleys of the southern Alps. The opposed parallel glaciers, Ferrar and Taylor, suggest the northern arm of Ferrar Glacier as an illustration of the origin of the Lake of Lucerne. And again the wonderful series of cwm or cirque valleys of Mounts Lister, Hooker, Rücker and Huggins show the characteristic topography of the Rockies. The discovery of small volcanic craters on the glaciated shoulders of Dry Valley mark an interglacial period of volcanicity. Another point of interest is the existence of what appears to be a drainage area into Lake Bonney (4 miles long) below the Taylor Glacier and remote from the seashore; an inland drainage with no apparent exit to the sea. Dry Valley turned out to be a rich petrographic province with numerous quartz veins poor in minerals and unsuccessfully panned for gold. One of the most complete opportunities for the investigation of the sequential disintegration of a great glacier face lay in the 20 miles of the Koettlitz Glacier, and this was taken advantage of by most of this party. A general study of erosion throughout the district shows the comparatively large part played by wind and by water. The latter acting for only a short period at the height of summer has nevertheless very great power. The ice work done on this journey consisted of an accumulation of facts concerning the crystallography and growth of ice. The development of nivation glaciers from snow drifts is rapid and widespread here—numerous photos were taken and have turned out well. This sums up the work that was done up to about the end of April when all who had scientific work to do were again at Cape Evans. Simpson's subsequent work I have mentioned. Wright's work for the winter included ice in its various aspects, pendulum observations and the natural ionisation of water[12]. This summer it will include photometry, and later I hope to go through some experiments with him on feather and fur radiation and conductivity. But as regards his ice work, which is the most important for him, one cannot give the results. One can only say that a tremendous number of facts and photos and measurements are being collected and that results will eventuate. Glaciers, their various forms, indications of movement and structural details are all of paramount interest here when we have miles of a great glacier front at our hut door and some of the biggest glaciers in the world to work on within reach. The interest is increased as there is everywhere indication of a gradual diminution of the glaciation, and structural details of the rock beneath are being disclosed fresh from the hands of the sculpturing agent instead of time and weather-worn, as in so many other parts of the world where they occur. The sea ice is also getting full attention both as to its structure and growth, and it looks as though its growth depended largely on the deposition of fragile crystals on the under surface. The formation, ablation, and subsequent modification of surface ice by radiation, impurities and so on, and the deposition, structure, modifications due to wind, temperature etc., of surface snow are also going to give results, particularly interesting here, where ablation is often excessive and radiation is for months together unaffected by any heat from the sun direct. The temperature and conductivity of ice, and the formation of various ice crystals and their dependence on temperature and humidity, are things requiring experiment and observation extending over a length of time, and these are being fully dealt with photographically. Pendulum observations were made in the winter but will be repeated as there was considerable difficulty in getting suitable conditions in an ice cave at low temperatures, and in the hut there is difficulty in obtaining a satisfactory immovable pillar for the instrument. This is the same as was used down here in the *Discovery* and came from Potsdam, where it is in the keeping of Prof. Helmert. A set of observations was taken at Christchurch, New Zealand, on the way out and another will be taken on the way home as well as at Potsdam again when it returns. Testing of sea water for radioactivity has not yet been done down here, but samples of sea water are being sent home to Prof. Joly in Dublin as occasion offers. The apparatus has, however, been prepared here and in the coming winter experiments will be repeated on the spot by way of check.

Taylor's work and Debenham's since our return to Cape Evans has been mainly the examination of this coast, of Ross Island, and the working up of the results of the last season's journey west. They have with the help of Lieut. Evans and Wright made a very detailed plane table survey of the whole of our immediate neighbourhood, and this is the basis of Debenham's work on the petrology, Wright's work on ice distribution, and Taylor's on the physiography of the area. Debenham has made microscopic sections of a large number of rocks as well as a detailed petrographic survey. The rocks here are all volcanic heaps of lava and ash. The only outside elements being erratics and raised beaches. There are other pieces of work which have been under way during the winter. The tide has been recorded continuously by a series of levers acting on a drum. Seiche effects were rather expected but they have not been obtained. Coming to biological work, Nelson's has already been outlined and it continued through the winter, naturally hampered by darkness and bad weather, but he has got a good deal of collecting done as well as hydrographic work. Atkinson has been doing the parasitology and has examined the animals that were procurable in the winter months including the fish, 3 species of seal, viz, Weddell, Sea Leopard and Crabeater; the penguins, Emperors and Adélie, and the Skua Gull. From these he has a collection which includes ectoparasites, hirudines, and copepods; and endoparasites, cestodes, nematodes, trematodes, and echinorhynchi—as well as protozoa, trypanoplasma, gregarines and two others unrecognised. The bacteriology is postponed until nearer the time for departure as it is impossible to maintain cultures without loss of all characteristics over a lengthy period of time. They will, therefore, be collected at the last moment and taken home at once. My own work on the embryology of the Emperor Penguin, which entailed our winter sledge journey in June and July to Cape Crozier, proved to be an impossibility from here. But there was every reason for making the attempt. The only chance now of getting eggs of the Emperor for this work is in the case of an expedition wintering quite close to the Emperor rookery. We were lucky in securing several Crabeaters and one Sea Leopard during the winter, otherwise vertebrate zoology has been unsuccessful. The notes made on Antarctic whales last season are much more satisfactory than they were on the last occasion, though there was no possibility of making any attempt to kill or capture. The photographic work has been quite exceptional thanks to Ponting, both in plate work and cinematography. Colour is represented by over 100 of my sketches.

This completes all that can be called scientific work. I may take out these last 8 pages[13]. If I do it is because they contain other people's information which perhaps ought not to go home through me—as yet. I wrote it out more or less fully to give me an idea as to the relative importance of the various parts for this press telegram which is to go home. Now I must get to work with that and if it contains most of what I have written here I shall let these pages stand. Today, after about an hour's tinkering, the 2 motors got away on the road to Hut Point with their loads. By the evening they were beyond Razorback Islands and out of sight from here. We hope they will arrive there tomorrow. At present they are going very slow, but when the engines have tuned up a bit and when they get on to softer surface we hope the pace will improve. We ought to know today by telephone from Hut Point how they have been doing. I took Nobby out for exercise in the forenoon. Afternoon I spent in stowing away all my damageable goods for my long summer absence. We have very damp places in the hut and I had to make certain that all my drawing paper and drawing material, medical stores and surgical instruments, gun, and what not wouldn't be mildewed and rusted by the time we return in March—or even April. I'm afraid there is hardly any chance of my being back here in time to read my mails and send an answer back by the ship. She will almost certainly have gone home by the time we return from our southern journey. In the evening I did some writing.

Up at 5.30 and finished off the report on scientific work. Now that our cook, **Wed 25 Oct** Clissold, is on the sick list and Hooper, the wardroom servant, has gone off with the motors, we have to do the cooking and housework ourselves. Atkinson, with Keohane's help, has done the baking and cooking, while Bowers and Cherry-Garrard and others have done the sweeping, fire-lighting, table-laying and what not. Today it was blowing a gale of wind all the forenoon, and I finished off the boiling down of the scientific work report. Couldn't get any ponies out till the afternoon. The motors have not got to Hut Point yet as we can see with glasses from here, but they are more than halfway and probably were forced to lose most of today by the wind. This afternoon, later on, the sun came out and it was really quite pleasant. One saw the Irishmen sitting smoking on the provision cases outside the hut, as though outside their own shabeen in Kerry. Crean, Forde and Keohane are all Irishmen, but especially Crean who is a delightful creature. Simpson and Gran set off after dinner to Hut Point to see whether the telephone was in working order or the wire broken as we haven't been able to ring Meares up today. It may be that he is away to one of the depots with his dogs though.

Up at 5.30. Writing, and a fine calm sunny morning. We have the sun above the **Thurs 26 Oct** horizon all the 24 hours tomorrow and soon the weather should begin to settle down. We have had more than our share of wind and blizzard lately. We hear this morning from Hut Point that the motors have been having great difficulty with smooth blue sea ice and in places have only managed about a mile in five hours. So eight of us started off to help them over this ice by hauling. We took two tents and our sleeping bags and expected to find the motors off the Glacier

Tongue, i.e. in about 6 or 7 miles, but we actually overtook them in about 14 miles, i.e. about a mile off Hut Point, as they had got on to snow covered ice again and were once more going a very good speed, Day's car sometimes going well on its high gearing at 3 miles an hour with a ton and a half of stuff. Lashly is driving the other car, but can't go quite so fast. However, as they both over-heat and have to stop periodically to cool down, they keep together pretty easily. The great difficulty is to balance the overheating of the air cooled engines again[st] the cooling down of the carburetter. We camped and had lunch off Hut Point and then it came on to blow and drift so we saw both motors as far as Cape Armitage and then all our party and the motor party came in for the night to Hut Point where Meares and Demitri cooked us supper—and we spent a very comfortable time.

Fri 27 Oct A fine day—and we all started off after an early breakfast to see the two motors with their loads on to the Barrier, 6 miles from Hut Point, before we left them again to their own resources for success or failure. Lashly's car did the distance with only two stoppages—the surface was good hard snow—but he was then so overheated in his engines that he had to stop, and then Day, who had come with more stoppages for cooling on the way, also came up and passed him and ran easily up the snow slope on to the Barrier on his top gear and we bade him good-bye as he went off. Lashly, having cooled down, then followed him up and they were soon together again. We left them then and went back to Hut Point. Then we lunched there, packed up our sledges and started off for Cape Evans again. We camped once for tea on the way at the Great Razorback Island and got home by about 10 p.m. that night having done 27 miles since breakfast—15 with a sledge load. At the Great Razorback we were in the midst of a nursery of young Weddell Seals, all born within the last 4 or 5 days, and some only a day or so. They are jolly little woolly haired yellowish animals with great big black eyes. The old mothers took no notice of us, except one which lolloped in a great hurry after our sledge and viciously bit the end of it. I found one baby seal had got frozen into the ice—it was quite alive but lying in a pool of thaw water, so I freed it and put it back with its mother who continued to snooze a yard or two off and showed not the slightest interest. When I got back to the hut I found I had got a touch of snow glare, as I had marched without goggles, and I spent a lively night in consequence. Got to sleep about 4 a.m. and was all right again at breakfast. After Tuesday next, when we start for the south, I shall be in goggles for about 4 months on end—this bout has warned me just in time. The loss of these two days just when we wanted them most of all for letter writing and final arrangements has been rather a trial. A host of things have had to be left to the last moment and now it becomes a rush to get them done in time. However, this diary must supply my news and everyone must forgive me for not writing letters.

Sat 28 Oct Blowing all day so no going out with the horses. Spent the time getting things ready for our start on Tuesday. Packed up my sketches I am sending home to Ory in two packages—118 in all—addressed to Mrs. Ted Wilson, Westal, Cheltm., Engld. I shall get Drake to send them from Christchurch, N.Z. insured and registered or by express—so they ought to get home all right. In looking at them you must remember they were all done by artificial light—acetylene—and so they look queer by daylight—the blues and the yellows are apt to go wrong. We had our first Skua Gull back again here on Thursday last, and I saw one here myself today hovering round the hut.

Twentieth Sunday after Trinity. Up at 5 to write and read, and at 10 we had **Sun 29 Oct** Church service. After this I took Nobby out for exercise and then Captain Scott and Petty Officer Evans, Crean and I went through various sledging and camping scenes for Ponting on the cinematograph. We were at it for about two hours and he got 700 ft of film. We were taken first in harness drawing our sledge load between bergs. Then along another berg to a patch of snow where we unharnessed and pitched camp. We set the tent, filled the cooker, passed everything in to the tent and then got in ourselves. Then we had striking camp and packing up and getting under way and then we had finally a length of sledge hauling on ski. The whole series with the scenes in the tent, which we did the other day, ought to be awfully good, I think, as there is no humbug about them at all; they are all straight forward photos of what we do every day on trek, only they can't possibly be taken under those conditions. We were late in lunching after this, and then I worked out my three Emperor Penguin's eggs which had well formed chicks in them of three different sizes, fairly young, but a good deal older than I had ever expected, which is all the better for my work. I got these well pickled for future work. As they are quite unique and probably the most primitive embryos of this most primitive bird at present living on the earth they may turn out to be interesting. They were obtained under difficulties too, and won't be got again in a hurry, I think, unless Amundsen has an Emperor rookery in his Bay of Whales during the winter. Our departure on the southern journey is postponed for a day as the two days at Hut Point put everyone back in their final arrangements. So we start on Wednesday. I wrote a few letters in the evening and finished off the eggs.

Up at 5.30 to write and read. Took pony out after breakfast and then wrote letters **Mon 30 Oct** and finished up preparations for a start and had various confidential talks with various people who had confidences to bestow—while it blew a whole blizzard all the afternoon outside.

Up at 5, writing letters. Still blizzarding, but looks like clearing. Today will go **Tues 31 Oct** in completing preparations for tomorrow's start, I know, so I won't keep this book out any longer. Anything else I can send home will be in a few notes at odd times by returning parties on the Barrier—and these I expect will be short ones addressed to Ory. God bless you all. I wish I could have made this journal more interesting and less personal. Keep it from any chance of getting used for publications. I am just as fit as I have ever been in my life, and I hope with all my heart that all of you at home are getting along well and happily. God be with you all.

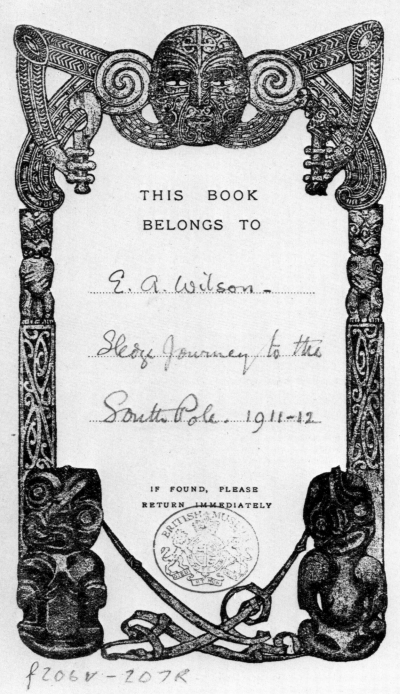

THIS BOOK
BELONGS TO

E. A. Wilson.

Sledge Journey to the

South Pole. 1911-12

IF FOUND, PLEASE
RETURN IMMEDIATELY

f.206v - 207R.

Title page of Wilson's sledging diary to the South Pole

60 1910—JUNE
22. ○ Full Moon 8.12 p.m.
24. Midsummer Day

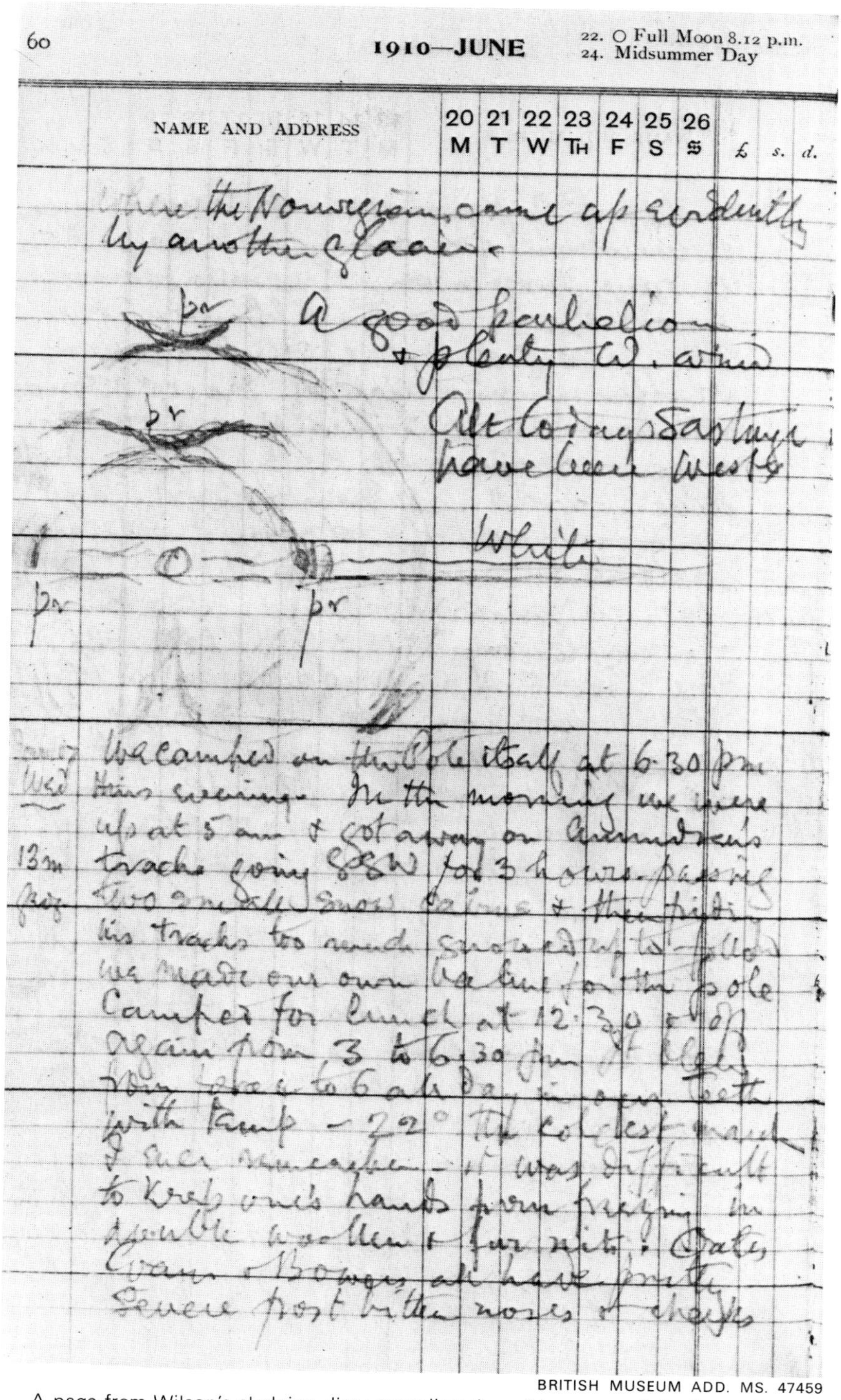

NAME AND ADDRESS	20 M	21 T	22 W	23 Th	24 F	25 S	26 S	£	s.	d.

where the Norwegians came up evidently by another glacier.

pr — A good parhelion & plenty of W. wind

pr — All coming sastrugi have been West

White

pr — pr

Jan 17 Wed — We camped on the Pole itself at 6.30 pm this evening. In the morning we were up at 5 am & got away on Amundsen's tracks going SSW for 3 hours passing two small snow cairns & then finding his tracks too much snowed up to follow we made our own bee line for the Pole. Camped for lunch at 12.30 & off again from 3 to 6.30 pm. It blew force 4 to 6 all day in our teeth with temp −22° the coldest march I ever remember. It was difficult to keep one's hands from freezing in double woollen & fur mitts. Oates, Evans & Bowers all have pretty severe frost bitten noses & cheeks

13 m

BRITISH MUSEUM ADD. MS. 47459

A page from Wilson's sledging diary recording the achievement of the South Pole, 17 January 1912

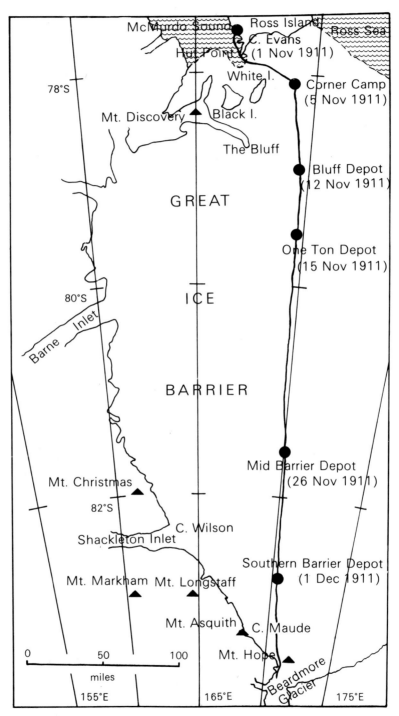

Map of the Pole Party's route from Ross Island to the Beardmore Glacier

13

SLEDGE JOURNEY TO THE SOUTH POLE
1 CAPE EVANS TO THE BEARDMORE GLACIER

LEFT Cape Evans. 10 horses. 10 men and loaded with some Hut Point provisions—about 11 a.m. Arrived about 3.30 p.m. **Wed 1 Nov** 12 m

Remained at Hut Point all day till 9 p.m. when Owner, Cherry and I with Snippetts, Michael and Nobby followed after an advanced unit composed of Atkinson, Wright and Keohane with Jehu, Chinaman and James Pigg—the three weakest ponies. They started 2 hours in advance of us. We caught them up at Safety Camp 6 miles—where we lunched. The other 4 ponies—Christopher, Bones, Victor and Snatcher came right through without stopping for lunch about an hour after us. With them were Oates, Crean, Bowers and Evans. After lunch we and the advanced unit went on again 6 miles where we all camped for the day. We were turned in about 6 a.m. Wind which has been cold from N. all night with a good deal of drift at Hut Pt. and C. Armitage now dropped. At 1 p.m. the horses were fed. Turned out to a glorious hot day for half an hour. So hot left the tent door open. Slept all night in which was really day. **Thurs 2–Fri 3 Nov** 12 m

We had breakfast at 8 p.m. Did $5\frac{1}{2}$ miles by lunch and $4\frac{1}{2}$ afterwards. All the horses went well. Surface pretty soft well up to [see marginal sketch] at every step the long hair spreading out round the fetlock on the snow. Here and there a crust hard enough to hold them up. Gradually overcast towards morning and soon after turning in some wind and a little drift. I am cook this week. **Fri 3–Sat 4 Nov** 10 m

Overcast day but warm and calm—turned in all day except at horse feed time 1 p.m. All day yesternight we were coming across derelict cans of petrol, lubricating oil and eventually Day's derelict car itself, with the 'big end' broken—part of the piston of one of the 4 cylinders. Also, a huge pit at another camp where the party had been blizzarded and the other car dug out. £1,000 by the wayside! We had 9 miles to go before reaching Corner Camp. Did 5 before lunch, 4 after and about a mile on the home side of Corner Camp 6 horses got their feet into crevasse cracks at one place. It must be a regular honeycomb on a line rather E. of between C. Crozier and the Bluff. At Corner Camp we spent another fine warm sunny day. Can see what looks very like the other motor about 4 miles S. From here we go due south. We load up a lot of stuff here from the depot. Nobby's load amounts to about 650 lbs. **Sat 4–Sun 5 Nov** 9 m

Sun 5–Tues
7 Nov
10 m

We had a good march the night thro' in 2 pieces, but shortly before camping for the following day it began to blow and from being overcast to the E. and W. only, became overcast everywhere, so we prepared for a blizz and it came.

We therefore lay in all Monday—and Monday night and all Tuesday, turning out at intervals to see to the horses which includes feeding, rebuilding parts of their walls which they knock down, digging out snow drift accumulations, and knocking the lumps off their hoofs. My beast is comfs [*sic*] enough, feeds well and eats plenty snow and takes interest all round. Some of the others look rather wretched. Meares and Demitri with the dog team came up with us early this morning and camped a quarter mile off. I have spent most of my two days and a night asleep. My capacity that way is enormous just now. On Sunday read H.C. and a chapter. On our Sunday night's march we passed the second car also

Food depot

derelict, and 2 sledge loads of gear, petrol, forage and 1 complete unit of man food for a week. This is buried in snow under after-end of car. Also one bag seal pemmican and 1 can of oil on the car. This car was also a big end break. And it was left about 1¼ miles S. of Corner Camp.

Tues 7–Wed
8 Nov
10 m

On Tuesday night the wind dropped a bit though it remained overcast—but about midnight we got under way and went along in two pieces for 10 miles as far as two cairns, one of which is Blossom's[1] grave—the northernmost—and has a wire and a bit of bunting on it, black. Meares and Demitri and the dogs came up with us here again and I went over and had a talk with him. All's well. The weather gradually cleared all night and wonderful wreaths of cir. str.[2] rose vertically under the sun east to flow S.W. in long swathes. We had a glorious sun to camp in and a glorious day for our night's rest all Wednesday.

Wed 8–Fri
10 Nov
8½ m

At 10 p.m. we again got away—still in 3 detachments, all horses going strong and well, and by 8 a.m. on Thursday we were camping again in sunshine—light breeze. Wind came up and we made two marches in blind white snowy weather against mod. breeze. We passed a last year's cairn about a mile on our left. We following Teddie Evans' tracks are too much to the west. We camped in the same weather and spent the day in sleep.

Fri 10–Sat
11 Nov
9½ m

Turned out at 9 p.m. to the same weather again on Friday evening and made 9½ miles in 2 pieces over an abominable surface. In the first 5 miles we passed a cairn made recently by Evans and an old cairn of last year's about a quarter mile N. of our lunch camp where we again built a cairn. There were no cairns between lunch and camping for the day's sleep, but tomorrow's march ought to bring us to Blucher's[3] cairn in about 2 miles and to the Bluff depot in 5 to 6 miles from where we are today Sat. Nov. 11.

Sat 11–Sun
12 Nov
10 m

We could see the mainland to the W. today beyond the Bluff. Much deep snow has fallen everywhere. We came on 10 miles in 2 stretches again during the night of Saturday to Sunday. Chinaman going very groggy indeed—Jehu rather surprisingly well. We passed Blucher's cairn with some wires and a bit of black bunting and then the Bluff depot cairn—no depot but a flag staff with a tin

196

biscuit box and cairn. Here was one of Teddie Evans' camps. The surface was of very deep soft snow and snow fell in light airs at various times of the day—much coming from the N.E.

Camped Sunday morning thus ———²——— ———⁴——— ——³⁺¹——

Sun 12–Mon 13 Nov

10 m

Cherry took over the cooking at the supper meal. Snowed most of the day. Read H.C. and other things. Still snowing all next night when we did 6 miles in the first piece passing a night camp cairn of Evans' at about 2 miles. Surface very deep soft snow. Parts of fine parhelion occasionally. Also passed some of last year's horse walls at about 5 miles. After lunch we did 4 miles passing a cairn on the way and camped for Monday in hot sunshine which blessed us for an hour or two. Temp. in tent $+51°$ quite warm and comfs [*sic*]. Surface 6 to 8 inches deep in soft flocculent snow like swan's down—large plate crystals. The clouds and light and shade effects have been very beautiful. Snowing off and on all day and still snowing these crystal plates all the night. We got in 2 marches, 6 miles and 4 miles, through very heavy surface passing a good cairn at about 5 miles and another at 8 or 9 miles, and camped this Tuesday morning.

Mon 13–Tues 14 Nov

10 m

We have another yet about a mile or two ahead of us. Camp arrangements of horse walls on the 13th was irregular.

Tues 14–Wed 15 Nov

7 m

———————⁴
——————— ————²
—————³⁺¹

Camping arrangement for 14th was, ——————— ——————— ———————
 ³⁺¹ ² ⁴

Fine hot sunshine after the snowy night. Dog teams both up with us. Surface 6 inches deep with swan's down fluff. Clouds have been radiating S.E. and N.W. all day. Got in another march in 2 pieces during the night and reached One Ton Depot on Wednesday morning. We passed a newly made 10 ft cairn of Evans' at about the 3rd mile of the first march of 6 miles and about a mile further on an old squat cairn of last year's. After lunch we had only a mile to go and we reached One Ton Depot with its main cairn and flagstaff and 2 sledges. We dug for oats but found none. There is a regular hill of drift from a W.S.W. wind.

One Ton Depot

0 m

Captain Scott and the members of the Pole Party, photographed at the start of the depot laying journey. Wilson and Bowers seated.

Some of his companions sketched by
Wilson on the way to the Pole:
Scott ('RFS'), Cherry-Garrard ('AC-G'),
Bowers ('B' and 'HRB'), Keohane ('PK')
and Oates ('TO') S.P.R.I. MS. 797/1

Our horse walls here are arranged

$$\overline{3+1} \quad \overset{S}{\underset{N}{2}} \quad \overline{4}$$

We had a magnificent show of solar corona 3–4 and even part of a 5th ring showing. They were best seen through snow goggles as the glare was excessive— but though there were more rings at mid night, the rings were more perfect as the sun got higher. The cause of them was wreaths of fog about 20 to 30 ft over our heads moving rapidly and visibly across beneath the sun. The main colour was in the orange red rings which were very distinct but in the two parts below the horizon emerald green was vivid and brilliant as well. The blue and violet was more of a blue grey than distinctive colour. We rested the ponies at One Ton Depot for a day and a night and a day. So on the night of Nov 15 we made no march. The dogs are here resting also. We find all our provisions intact and a note from Evans showing him to be gaining on us and now 5 days ahead. The minimum temp. for the winter as given by thermometer left here was −72°F. Our present temp. is −15, but was up to +7 yesterday.

Thurs 16–Fri 17 Nov

$7\frac{1}{2}$ m

We have a cold Sly wind blowing all day with snow crystals driving and now and again beautiful parhelion in a blue glittering sky. We see land which must be Mt. Markham[4] from here. Also Evans' next cairn due south. Nobby's load from here is made up to about 580 lbs, 8 biscuit boxes + 100 lbs oil + standing wts. We have depoted some seal's liver here. Slept pretty well all Thursday—temp. too low to be very pleasant outside. The 3 crocky ponies got away about 7 p.m. and we with the remainder all together at about 10.15 p.m. and marched $7\frac{1}{2}$ miles geog. when we camped and had lunch. We passed on the way 2 cairns made by Teddie Evans—the first at about $2\frac{1}{2}$ miles—the next at $5\frac{1}{2}$. We made twin cairns at our lunch camp. There was iridescence[5] in the flocculent looking sheet of small cir. clouds[6]—which was very uniformly thin over a large area—thicker over another part. The iridescence showed only where the sheet was thinner—and here it was universal within the 22° circlet right up to the sun's brilliance. After lunch we did six miles more and camped with a very cold breeze—surface drift and ice crystals in the air—with temp. down to −18°. It was therefore pretty cold.

Fri 17–Sun 19 Nov

6 m

A fine parhelion—all coloured except the horizontal band and the mock sun beneath on the horizon. Surface much better than last march two nights ago. We passed a night camp cairn of Evans' at 4 miles from our lunch camp. We made horse walls thus

and the 3+1 wall fell down in the middle making a big breach. We had a sunny day but some Sly breeze and drifting crystals. We got away at 10.30 p.m. and lunched at 2.30 a.m. passing on the way a lunch cairn of Evans'—and a night camp cairn also of his. His tracks are covered by an inch of snow crystals but quite visible. The surface today is better to look at—more of the original to see

reddish orange
grey blue
reddish orange.
grey blue.
reddish orange
very brilliant
Sun light
red orange
red orange.
red orange.

dull
pale
blue
hazy
sky

brilliant white   haze -
dark grey

About an hour later.
Nov. 14. 11 -

One of two sketches showing colours of parhelion, 14 November 1911

7 m but the runners seem heavy. The horses were rather slower today—much mirage, clearer sky, clouds only to the west but land visible. Can see Erebus and Terror now and then—looking small. Temp. at lunch camp −20°F. but no wind. After lunch we made another 6 miles with deep soft surface but the ponies went well. We passed an Evans' cairn at the end of the first mile—and then no other—

6 m but today where we camp there is another cairn close ahead of us. Our horse walls at this camp are

$$\overline{3+1} \quad \overline{4} \quad \overline{r}$$

Sun 19–Mon 20 Nov Read H.C. and other things. This is Sunday and here we are dumping a sack of oats. Jehu and Chinaman are to last only 4 more days. We had a fine day for sleep —clear, sunny and no wind—and got off about 10 p.m. The crock brigade of 3 ponies got off a couple of hours earlier. We passed a cairn of Evans' in a quarter

$7\frac{3}{4}$ m of a mile and the next which was a lunch camp dated Nov 12th at $5\frac{3}{4}$ miles. We then went on until we had made $7\frac{3}{4}$ miles and built twin cairns at our lunch camp. The surface was very deep and soft. From this camp we can see back to our last horse walls $7\frac{3}{4}$ miles geogl.[7] There were good iridescent thin filmy cr. st. slips all over and round the sun at lunch in which the colour was greenish blue and pinkish violet chiefly, more or less in rings suggesting a corona more than a halo, but gradually diminishing outwards in intensity so that at no point could one say there was an outer limit to the colours.

This was at 3.30 a.m. app. time. During the second march Nobby and I had a

$5\frac{1}{4}$ m disagreement and he lodged one of his objections on my heel—without hurting me. After this he went exceedingly well. We turned in on a glorious hot morning at 10.30 a.m. Our horse walls arranged thus

$$\overline{3+1} \quad \overline{4} \quad \overline{r}$$

We had passed a cairn of Evans' at $3\frac{3}{4}$ miles before camping here for the day.

Mon 20–Tues 21 Nov Turned out about 8 p.m. and got away at 11. Made $7\frac{1}{2}$ miles by lunch time passing a night camp cairn of Evans' at $1\frac{1}{2}$ miles and lunching at another of Evans'

$7\frac{1}{2}$ m cairns which we converted into a twin cairn. All this march the sky has been becoming overcast with radiating cir. str. streaky cloud forming gradually from the S.E. and overcasting us and then extending to our west. The land at the same time has again become brilliant and clear—whereas when we were having clear sky overhead the last two days the land to our west was overcast with dense stratus. The surface today has been a trifle better—patches of hard road-like crust which carries the horses appeared for the first time last a.m. march. This p.m. march they have again been with us. No wind—light var[iable] airs.

$5\frac{1}{2}$ m Sastrugi in the main E. and S.E. After lunch when we made a twin cairn— mentioned above—we had another $5\frac{1}{2}$ miles reaching a cairn of Evans' and just passing it before building our horse walls.

Clouds high cir. st. radiating S.S.W. and N.N.E. and being caught by an easterly high current north of us. Sastrugi here show pretty strong S.Ely wind lately. We are now turned in with gentle S.Wly breeze and sunshine. Temp. $+2°$. Hot sunny day.

Turned out about 8 p.m. and got in $7\frac{1}{2}$ miles before lunch, passing a camp of **Tues 21–** Evans' at $4\frac{3}{4}$ miles and building our twin cairns at lunch, we then could see Evans' **Wed 22 Nov** camp and an enormous cairn by it built at $80°31'$ which we reached soon after $7\frac{1}{2}$ m $2\frac{1}{2}$ miles after lunch. Theodolite and 2 boxes biscuits depoted here. We found the motor party, Evans, Day, Lashly, and Hooper all fit and well and very hungry indeed. They had been waiting here six days and had read Pickwick through. Day looks thin—the others not so thin. They came along and camped with us at the end of our $5\frac{1}{2}$ miles, where we built

The cairn Evans built at $80°31'$ was about 15 ft high—enormous—and has a flagstaff. Two boxes of biscuits depoted here. Jehu is to go on 3 more days and then beats the distance at which Shackleton's first horse was shot[8]. The motor party continue with us till then, and then Day and Hooper return. The dogs go on with us indefinitely towards the glacier foot. Cloud radiation today is still from S.S.W. to N.N.E., but is clearing away. Surface improving slightly, still very deep when the horses go through crust. Horses all going very solid and steady. Nobby is here given an extra box of biscuits. Sastrugi strongly marked S.S.E. or S.E. Hot day of sun and no wind for our sleep.

After a long confab in our tent, attended by Scott, Cherry, Bowers, Evans, Day **Wed 22–** and Titus, and Meares and myself, we got away about 10.30 p.m. and did $7\frac{1}{2}$ **Thurs 23 Nov** miles passing a cairn made by the advance piloting and crock pony party at $4\frac{1}{2}$ $7\frac{1}{2}$ m

'Besides the dog camp . . . Nov.22.11.'

'Besides the dog camp.
10 horses. 4 tents. 3 snow walls. 11 sledges.   Nov. 22. 11.'

miles, and then making a twin cairn at lunch. Clear hot sunny night with light
following airs from the N. All the ponies going well. Surface rather deep for them
but not very bad. The surface crusty with crystals which allow sledges to glide
well as soon as the sun gets on them—but at night they are sandy and sticky. In
$5\frac{1}{2}$ m the a.m. march we did $5\frac{1}{2}$ miles passing a cairn at $2\frac{3}{4}$ miles and making horse
walls at the final camp.

Thurs 23–   We made $7\frac{1}{2}$ miles in our p.m. march after a good sunny day's sleep, and the
Fri 24 Nov   advance guard built a cairn at 4 miles about and a twin cairn at lunch. After
$5\frac{1}{2}$ m lunch we did $5\frac{1}{2}$ m. passing a cairn at 3 miles and our horse walls went up

There was radiating cir. st. forming all night across from due E. to N.W. and
cloud banking up thick in the S. with a S.E. puff occasionally and a Sly breeze in
the morning when we turned in. We have had some fine iridescence of high cirr.
today and yesterday—lemon yellow broad band nearest the sun, with pink and
vivid turquoise sort of prussian emerald blue outside, contrasting in its greenness
with the French blue of the clear sky and the pure white cirrus. Again today we
had grey windy and radiating high cir. st. with a break here and there showing
still higher cirrus cloudlets beautifully iridescent with pink centres and green
borders (see sketch)[9].

Fri 24–   There was a strong appearance of approaching blizzard weather from the south
Sat 25 Nov   all night and complete overcast low stratus and a few falling snow flakes when we
$7\frac{1}{2}$ m started off in the evening. Made $7\frac{1}{2}$ miles, passing a halfway cairn and making
2 at lunch. We had good surface and all the ponies went well. Made $5\frac{1}{2}$ m. in the
morning march and Titus shot Jehu when we arrived in camp. Jehu is for the
dogs. $81°15'$ is our position today and the sky has completely cleared. Very hot
$5\frac{1}{2}$ m sun and blazing glare. Light Sly air. During our first march there was at first a
S.Ely breeze and then a S.Wly. Our course from $80°35'$ has been S. 9 E., or
N. 12 E. magnetic. Jehu has been brought along a good few miles further south
than the lat. where Shackleton shot his first pony. We have 9 left and all going well,
though Jimmie Pigg and Chinaman are slow. Considering that when we left Cape
Evans Atch was started off a day ahead to see whether Jehu could walk 15 miles
$7\frac{1}{2}$ m without dying, he hasn't done so badly. We got away and did $7\frac{1}{2}$ miles before
lunch, passing a midway cairn and making twin cairn at lunch. After starting on
our second march we had some white fog and an attempt at a fog bow—also very
fine solar corona[10] in 3 rings, reddish orange, greenish and bluish, then orange
greenish and blue again outside that and so on—formed by the low fog—and the
strange thing is that the iridescent high cirrus round the sun appear to be the
same to some extent colour, and the similar coronae irregularly arranged. There
was another phenomenon today which we called the *Garrard halo*—a sparkling
ring round the sun, but only a few feet from one's eyes formed amongst the glitter-
$5\frac{1}{2}$ m ing crystals amongst which we were walking with brighter mock suns as usual on
each side but with no colour and the discrete crystals all visible. The surface
today was very heavy and looked as though a profuse growth of bunches of crystal

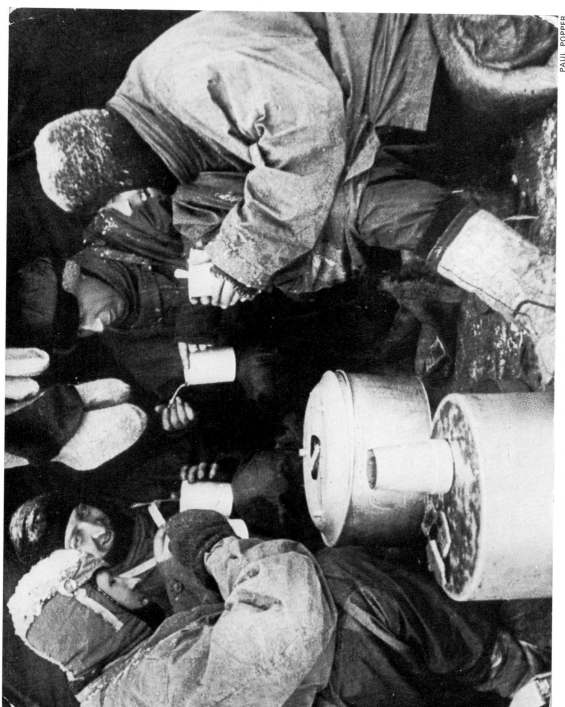

A hot meal on the march. *Left to right*: Evans, Bowers, Wilson, Scott.

points and plate points had grown on it. And on the N.E. side of the sastrugi everywhere there was 3 or 4 times the growth and the crystals were arranged in tiers. All the horses went well and Atch joined the man-hauling pilot party. Lashly joined our tent and we are now for the first time 3 units of 4 men each. 1. Scott, Cherry-Garrard, Lashly and myself. 2. Oates, Bowers, P.O. Evans and Crean. 3. Evans, Wright, Atkinson, and Keohane. Meares and Demitri follow us with the dogs. Jehu cut up into 4 days' rations for 20 dogs. Day and Hooper left us this day—no, yesterday evening, Nov. 24th—and turned home taking with them a letter from me to Ory. Turned in now about midday 25th to sleep.

Sun 26 Nov
7½ m

We start off later tonight by two hours, really at 1 o'clock on Sunday morning, so the marches are both a.m. of the same day now. We made 7½ miles with a midday cairn and at lunch depoted a week's provisions for 3 units in a large central cairn with bamboo and black flag and 2 small cairns one each side, not square with line of march. After lunch it became overcast and snowed and we did

5½ m

5½ miles making a midway cairn and horse walls as usual. Started my old depot finnesko today with holes in and got them full of snow and water. Surface not so bad. Horses going well all of them and loads lighter now by far. Nobby has now barely 500 lbs = 6 biscuit boxes + 100 lbs of oil + 99 lbs standing weight. Halo 42° today caused by stratus and corona with 2 rings caused by low fog against the stratus. No view at all. Read H.C. and other things in the bag.

Mon 27 Nov

Turned out to our breakfast meal at 1 a.m. Monday. Snowing more or less and a cold breeze chiefly S.E. Much windy cirrostratus overhead and later on overcast blind white weather. Soft surface, but horses went well. Did 7½ miles leaving

7½ m

a midway cairn and a twin lunch cairn. Capt. Scott took over the remainder of my week's cooking to save his foot which is painful. Chinaman is to be shot after tomorrow's march and then Lashly leaves our tent again and Keohane joins it.

5½ m

We had very heavy going for the second march. Snowing all the time could see nothing and the course was very erratic in consequence. We made a midway cairn and horse walls as usual. Still snowing and breezing from the S. when we turned in about 4 p.m. Capt. Scott cooking. We turned out this morning at 3 a.m. Tonight we turn out at 4 a.m. gradually working into day routine for the glacier which we should reach in a week and then finish with the ponies. Snowing pretty well all the time we were camped.

Tues 28 Nov

We turned out at 4 a.m. and got away at 6 a.m. Marched in a sort of summer blizzard with falling snow and some drift but no great force of wind—what there was was due S. and sometimes it blew a fresh breeze. Temp. +12°. Last camp it was +17°. The snow falling is damp and clogged the ski heavily when the pilot party tried them yesterday. Course today altered to due S. i.e. N. 20 E. again, as

7½ m

we are getting bad deep snow surface anyhow so we shouldn't gain much by keeping out. We can see nothing today—overcast everywhere and white. We did 7½ miles leaving a midway cairn and twin lunch cairns. Course has been very erratic yesterday—afternoon especially—and this first march today not so erratic.

5½ m

After lunch made 5½ miles and the surface was better, due to S.ly wind, but the march was in falling snow all the time often thick and warm, melting where it fell on the sledge. Shot Chinaman this camp and Cherry took on the 10 ft sledge, leaving his Michael's 12 ft sledge depoted here over the horse remains. Meares and the dogs are up now almost at same time as we are. Now that we have turned in the sky has cleared and the wind dropped, sun out and things look brighter. No land visible, though in the middle of the night Mt. Markham's 3 peaks and Mt. Longstaff[11] appeared fairly clear in places, but were obscured later and all next **Wed 29 Nov** day, though we had a good sunny march 7½ miles in the first half, then lunch and 7½ m then 5½ miles. The surface was deep, wettish snow into which the horses sank from 5½ m 8 or 10 inches to a foot very often and we ourselves had heavy walking. The horses all went well. Wright has now joined the manhauling party. There were once again continual settling crusts in the snow we were on today. They sometimes made a noise like 'hush' sometimes like ripping canvas and sometimes like thunder crackling and then rumbling—but of course not so loud. The cracks are quite visible rambling in circles round our line of march and the weight of the sledges cause[s] them. They occur generally when recent heavy drifts are stepped on—and today the snow on many parts has been heavy and wet packed.

We have today passed our previous furthest south and are now camped in 82°21′S. **Thurs 30 Nov** We could see Cape Wilson[12] from time to time. Glorious sunshine all day but often 7½ m a deep heavy surface into which the horses sank sometimes to their knees and almost up to their hocks. They are tired after it, especially Christopher, Victor, Snatcher and Michael. It was heavy walking for us too. After lunch we did 5½ miles and a little of the lower land showed, but nothing to sketch. Very hot. Tried 5½ m Nobby with snowshoes today, but they came off every time. Otherwise they would certainly be very useful in saving him from going in. We are in our bags now by 4 p.m., turn out about 2 a.m. Tomorrow the tents rearrange a bit. Titus comes into ours and Cherry goes into Bowers' tent.

Turned out at 11.30 p.m. and was sketching the coast which came out beautifully **Fri 1 Dec** clear until 2 a.m. when we had breakfast and got under way. We are about 40 miles out from Mt. Longstaff and can see Mt. Markham's peaks beyond and Christmas Mt. to the north and Cape Wilson and Capes Goldie and Lyttleton. Longstaff is a magnificent mass of mountain—not much rock showing and what there is of two kinds, the bulk of what shows from summit to base being very dark, almost black, while there was also a pale chocolate buff rock in vertical cliffs exactly as we saw this rock somewhere further N. by Christmas Height in 1902. There was this black rock both above it and below it and the two sides of the glacier coming down steeply from Mt. Longstaff has a 45° scarp on the N. side of the black rock and a similar snow covered scarp on the S. side where only this pale chocolate buff rock shows. This glacier is tremendously broken up like an icefall. This is the more northern of two glaciers coming down from Mt. Longstaff. The other one descends to the south of the mass of reddish cliffs. The whole range is a magnificent mass of mountains. We made 7½ miles in the first march. Nobby 7½ m on snowshoes for 5½ of them. They broke on the start of the afternoon march, so took all off. We then did 5½ miles and now are turned in. Overcast now after a 5½ m

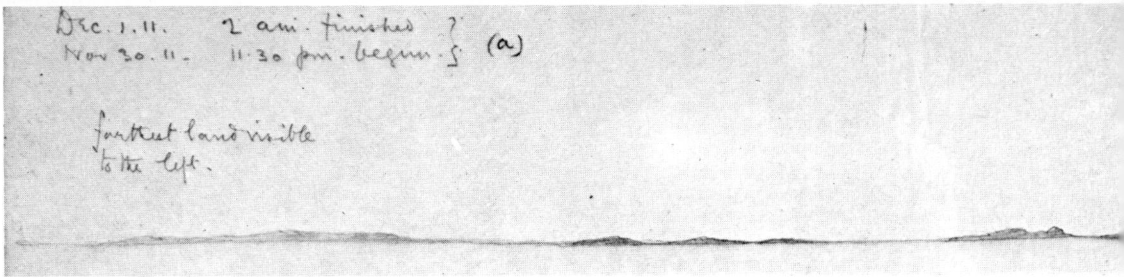

Dec. 1. 11.   2 a.m. finished ?
Nov 30. 11.   11·30 pm. begun. § (a)

furthest land visible
to the left.

Panorama of the landward approaches to the Beardmore Glacier sketched on the Barrier at 40 miles dist[ance]

Cape   Cape.

Mt. Longstaff

red cliff

Deep cut   Deep cut   Black rock.
gorge valley   glacier valley.   not red
rather narrow

Cwm
Distant v. high peaks   Snow   v. distant
Mt. Markham.   Cwm   v. high peak.

(i)

Cape Wilson

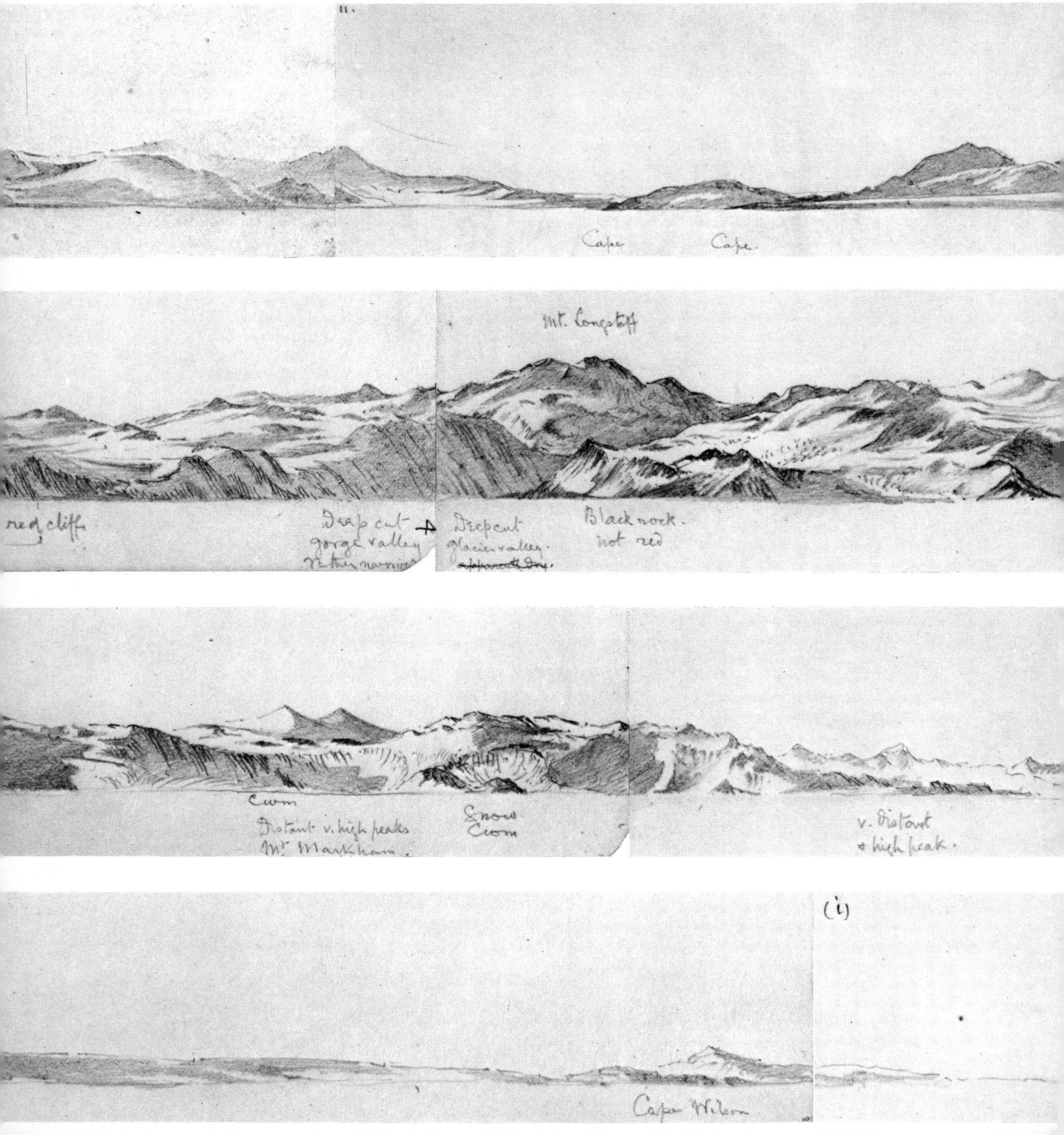

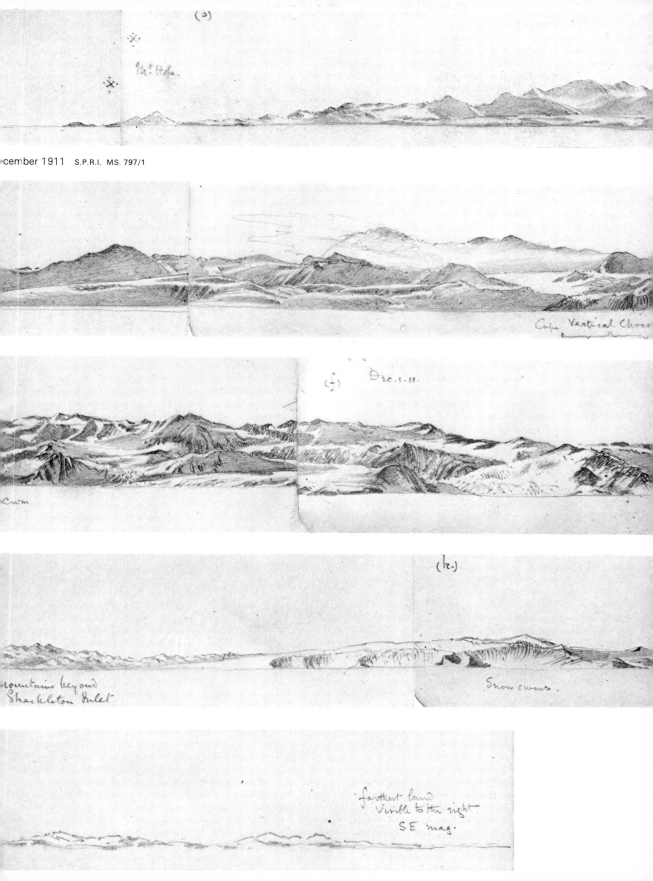

(a)

Mt. Hope.

cember 1911   S.P.R.I. MS. 797/1

Cape Vertical Chaos

(f)   Dec. 1. 11.

cwm

(h.)

mountains beyond
Shackleton Inlet

Snow cwms.

farthest land
visible to the right.
S.E mag.

very hot sunny day, the clouds having come from the S.E. All the sastrugi still from S.E. winds. No settlement of the crust today at all. Titus has come into our tent tonight and we have lost Cherry who has gone to Birdie's tent. Christopher shot tonight. We had some of Chinaman in our supper hoosh—and it was good like boiled beef—put in when water was cold in very small chips and boiled up with the pemmican. Here we are depoting a week's man food and a sledge and Christopher's bones.

Sat 2 Dec   Absolutely blind day, no land visible all day. Made $7\frac{1}{2}$ miles first march and $5\frac{1}{2}$
$7\frac{1}{2}$ m miles in the second and now turned in 7 p.m. In the evening Victor was shot and
$5\frac{1}{2}$ m cut up. We had a big meal of horse meat off Christopher tonight which was very good eating indeed, very tender and very slightly sweetish taste unless plenty of salt added, when it was just like beef to taste and sight. The surface all day was deep soft snow. The horses all started badly. It was very close and hot and snowing but when a light breeze which was Nly became Wly they went very well all the rest of the day. Still snowing and overcast and blind glare on turning in. No land visible. We are crossing undulations now without a doubt.
The snow is deeper and softer in the hollows than on the summit. I should say we crossed from one valley into the next in half a mile or less.

Sun 3 Dec   Advent Sunday. We awoke to a blizzard blowing from S.E. or S.S.E. Thick drift and heavy snowfall. We therefore lay in till noon when the sky cleared and we got off a march after lunch. We then saw Mt. Hope[13] and the Gap quite plainly but an hour after starting everything became obscured by low strat.[14] from the S.E. again
10 m and we walked 10 miles in deep, soft snow by 7 p.m. when we camped without having seen a shadow or any land at all. The course is therefore erratic. Scott and Bowers having no horses now went ahead on ski. Evans and the manhaulers camped at 6 miles. The dogs came up to us at 10 miles. Still blowing and snowing hard from N.W. when we turned in after a hoosh with plenty of Victor in it. The horses are going splendidly still, though their walking is very deep. The sledges pull light enough. Sastrugi not much marked, but all S.E. and today's N.W. wind is under cutting them into tongue shapes. Heavy banks of stratus in the S.E. here about seems the invariable sign of bad weather.

Mon 4 Dec   Blew all night and at 3 a.m. after about a quarter of an hour's lull the wind went round from the N.W. to the S.E. and by 7 a.m. we were having a regular thick blizzard. We lay in till 2 p.m. having built a new wall for the horses on the S.E. side. Heavy drifts of soft snow. We got away at 2 p.m. when the sky suddenly cleared and we could see the land ahead to the S., Mt. Hope and the glacier and all the land beautifully. There were several magnificent valleys with glacier icefalls
11 m coming down. We marched solidly on till after 8 p.m. when we had made 11 miles, then camped below a very big undulation 12 miles from Mt. Hope. We had the long line of pressure caused by the Beardmore Glacier in view on our port bow all the time and we crossed 3 or 4 big waves of undulations in the last two miles; they were very marked. While on our right we could see the dark lines of chasm splits toward the coast. This evening the wind seems again inclined to get up from the S.

and there are marked radiating clouds from the S.S.E. and N.N.W. beginning with high spidery cirrus, and now much lower with squally wind and surface drift. Michael was shot this evening. We are still eating Victor. One of the peaks on our starboard bow has bands of horizontally bedded rock at the top like Lister. There are fine craggy cliffs of a dark red rock—looks like granite to me but is said to be like Cathedral rocks which are of dolerite[15]. Three glaciers come down 3 valleys together on our starboard bow, all heavily crevassed and icefalls—no moraines showing anywhere but a heavy curved line of pressure always on the inner side. On our right beam is a part of the foothills where the ice appears to have first carved out scarps and ridges and later to have sheared the top of the ridges off into a plateau form.

It was midnight nearly when the first chance came to draw, and then not only was the sun due S. making everything in shadow and formless, but the wind drift got up.

By the morning we could see nothing. We were in a thick blizzard blowing very **Tues 5 Dec** hard at times and snowing very heavily, so that we had to lie up the whole day. It was +31 and very wet, indeed sopping in the tent. We turned out periodically o m to feed and dig out the horses who were nearly buried in drift. The wind is all from blizzd. the S. and S.S.E. and the blizzard was evidently coming down the glacier. Last night there were drift clouds off the tops and a white fog outlining all the upper heights making their outlines hazy, especially the rocky ones. Our sledges have been completely buried out of sight in some cases as we are in a depression.

Blizzarding like blazes all night and again all day making it impossible to proceed. **Wed 6 Dec** The horses are feeling it now—they are wet through, poor beasts, but they feed all right. Excessive drift, we have to dig them out every 4 or 5 hours. Our tent is more sopping than ever and our windproofs are soaked with water every time we go out as the temp. is +33° and the snow like heavy wet sleet. Bags getting pretty wet in consequence, so is all our gear. I sleep most of my time lying up between o m the meals and seeing to the horses. Also have read a good deal of Tennyson— blizzd. *The Princess, Maud*, etc.—in a volume I brought. Wind still from S. and S.E. Very wet and heavy snow.

Same weather all night though it lifted late yesterday evening enough for us to **Thurs 7 Dec** see some of the land. It still blew and snowed and this continued all night and all day today—no change in the wind and heavy soft snow driving all the while. Our wind clothes are absolutely soaking wet and we only put them on to go out, and take them off at once on turning in to the tent again. We have all begun our o m summit rations today—(a new box of biscuits and a new can of oil). We didn't blizzd. open one biscuit box until for the supper meal of the 7th today, but it was to weekly bag begin at lunch when we ate up our wet scraps. We filled our primus yesterday biscuit after breakfast, and still have a meal in it and a whole fill in the can which goes to Meares[16]. This can was used up during the blizzard. We didn't open the new oil can one on the 8th and breakfast of the 9th came out of the *old* one.

Fri 8 Dec We woke up to the same blizzard blowing from the S. and S.E. with warm wet snow +33°. All these three days frightfully deep and wet, and tremendous great drifts which have completely hidden several of the sledges and topped the pony walls. We turned out after breakfast but after digging out the sledges and all our gear, trying one of the horses on the deep surface and finding he went in up to his belly, and after trying weights on a 4 man sledge with and without ski, we decided to wait one more day for the weather. We then shifted all our tents and made a new camp to windward, had lunch and lay in all the afternoon while the weather very gradually improved—first the wind dropped and we had variable airs and gradually the snowfall began to break off and on, though the snow continued to fall all day and is still falling now from the N. and N.W. with a light breeze. Everything soaking wet, sleeping bags sodden, tent dripping, water everywhere till late this evening the temp. dropped to +29·7° and the snow began to diminish. It has been oppressively hot and steamy all day, making one sweat digging things out in a few minutes, have been living in pants only—windproofs all wringing wet, so also sleeping boots, socks, gloves, everything. Tobacco juice running brown out of Titus' private gear bag. It has been a phenomenal warm wet blizzard different to, and longer than, any I have seen before with excessive snowfall. Knee deep away from the camp and Nobby's belly touching the surface every step, poor beast. The 5 horses still living are on a very low ration, but it is mainly oilcake. I have kept Nobby my biscuits tonight as he is to try and do a march tomorrow and then happily he will be shot—and all of them as their food is quite done. We are just 12 miles from Mount Hope. Have been reading and re-reading Tennyson's *In Memoriam* this blizzard and have been realising what a perfect piece of faith and hope and religion it is, makes me feel that if the end comes to me here or hereabout there will be no great time for Ory to sorrow. All will be as it is meant to be, and Ory's faith and hope and trust will be to her what Tennyson's was to him. But *In Memoriam* is difficult reading, and the beauty of it wants pains to find, but it is splendid when found.

Sat 9 Dec A very long tiring and bad day though we got on the move at last and made 8 miles on the worst possible surface. We first of all started off the manhauling party to make a track in the deep soft snow for the ponies and then we tried to get the ponies on in this track with their loads. It was horrible work flogging them on, floundering belly deep as they were stiff from the 3 days' blizzard on low rations, very hungry and with a mere apology for a ration this morning, and no more
8 m food for the end of this march only a bullet for each. We marched solidly on with great difficulty and great exertion from 8 a.m. till 7 p.m. No stop and no food for ourselves, or the ponies. Nobby had all my 5 biscuits last night and this morning and by the time we camped I was just ravenously hungry. It was a close cloudy day with no air, and we were ploughing along knee deep alternately hammering and dragging and encouraging our poor beasts—for we couldn't have moved these loads ourselves on this surface. It was beastly work and the horses constantly collapsed and lay down and sank down, and eventually we could only get them on for 5 or 6 yards at a time—they were clean done. Then we camped. Shot them all and then before turning in had an hour or two of butcher's work cutting them

up and skinning them for dog food and for a depot for ourselves for our return journey. Thank God the horses are now all done with and we begin the heavier work ourselves. We left 4 sledges here, 3 10 foots and 1 12 foot on end, with some personal gear under the left most, as one goes home, and some meat under the next I believe. I left here my pyjama trowsers and my spare pants, some socks and mits and ski straps. Slept like a log in my still very wet bag and woke fit as a fiddle to a perfectly glorious hot morning.

S.P.R.I. MS. 797/1

Extract from Griffith Taylor's list of geological requirements from the Beardmore Glacier copied by Wilson into one of his sketchbooks

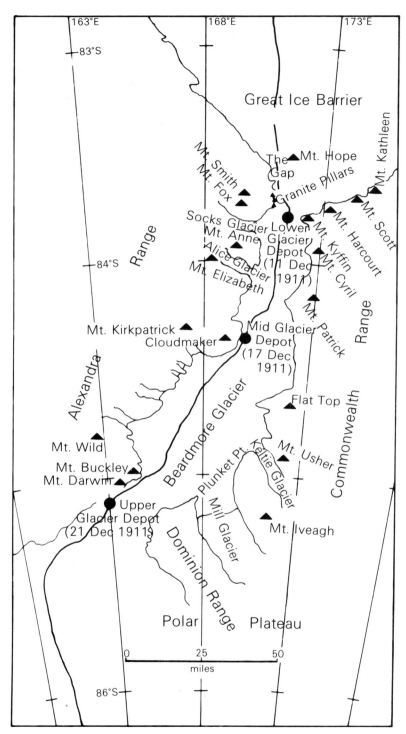

Map of the Pole Party's route up the Beardmore Glacier

14

SLEDGE JOURNEY TO THE SOUTH POLE
2 THE BEARDMORE GLACIER TO THE SUMMIT

BLAZING hot and only slight draughts now and then amongst the mountains. All yesterday we were approaching the Gap entrance gate to the Beardmore Glacier and Mount Hope on the left with Mt. Asquith[1] and Cape Maude and Cape Allen on our right. Magnificent ochreous reddish gneissic granite columnar crags and pillared mountains on both sides, the western end of Mt. Hope being low and rugged with the same nearly all in situ—not much scree anywhere and what angle the valley sides make is always about 45°. Enormous cwms on our right low down and full of snow with avalanches here and there and in one or two places the screes ended at the top in a sort of sheared off table-land of rock. The mountains of gneissic granite look almost like columnar basalt. They are weathering out vertically and their tops are flat at about 3,000 ft with a dip to the west about so much.

Mt. Hope is much rounded by glacier action and so is the smaller rocky foothill on the W. side of the glacier. However this is all yesterday's observation. About the pressure in the barrier ice—it is immense where the Beardmore exits east of Mt. Hope. Then comes our narrow entrance W. and then more pressure along the Maude Allen coast. We crossed some ridges and hollows all deeply snow covered and found only 3 or 4 crevasses, but Snippetts, one of the horses, very nearly disappeared in one of them—got all his hind quarters down. We unhitched the sledges and then flogged him out of it, and he scrambled out—but the crevasse would have taken any number. I made a circuit round and though Nobby must have crossed the same crevasse he didn't go through. This of course was on Dec. 9th, just before we shot them all.

Now for the 10th. Blazing hot. We made the top of the Gap slope partly on ski and partly on our feet—very heavy hauling. 600 lbs per sledge, 4 men each—3 sledges—very soft deep snow—and then lunched. Here Atch told me that Silas and Lashly are knocking up with the heavy work they have been doing. We ski-pulled all the afternoon and made 6 miles altogether and camped in a snow

215

hollow where we got caught in a very brisk drift storm—much dry soft powdery snow flying all round everywhere. We shall make a depot here of return food and go ahead tomorrow still taking the dogs for half a day further. We have come through the Gap now, and on both sides have had magnificent ochreous reddish columnar crags of gneissic granite weathering out like basalt vertically in columns. We are now camped with a view right up to the inland ice and down the glacier pressure to the Barrier, a fierce sight of pressure but wonderful and magnificent. As Meares returns tomorrow I must send a note to Ory by him.

Mon 11 Dec
7 m
approx

We made our Lower Glacier Depot in fine sunshine and raised a cairn and a flag on it, black bunting. Meares came on with us for the forenoon's march and we on ski in 3 parties made for the middle of the glacier in a line mainly for Mt. Kyffin[2]. We crossed some waves of pressure where the shiny blue ice showed up like combs here and there and P.O. Evans just behind me got into a crevasse with the whole of one leg and ski, the whole length of which broke through. We had 3 or 4 miles of this—not bad at all—and then the surface flattened out with very occasional irregularities only. We lunched and Meares and Demitri then started for home with my note[3]. Their dogs all very fit indeed. They ought to have a very easy journey. I sketched in the morning and after lunch and on the forenoon march visited a large boulder isolated in the pressure ridges and found it to be very coarse granite full of large quartz crystals an inch and a half square and white quartz veins, very full of mica and hornblende and quartz, and some isolated sort of inclusions of fine grain grey gneiss. We had full loads in the afternoon when Meares left us, 680 lbs or more. Scott tells me we are pulling close on 200 lbs each. We managed this better and better as we went on in the afternoon and eventually camped in very deep soft snow—up to our knees abeam of Pillar Rock. We had to dig down nearly 3 feet for hard snow for the cooker. Birdie's party came up soon after us. Teddie Evans' were still labouring up when we had our bags out, so Scott and I went and helped them up very late. Birdie, Teddie Evans, Keohane, Lashly and Titus Oates have all got pretty bad snow-glare. Both sides of the glacier at present all same reddish ochre rock—probably granite—in vertical column with bands of quartz. Kyffin side the same evidently, but below Kyffin is some blacker rock. Notice almost complete absence of screes of loose rock—all in situ. Also notice banded rock like Beacon Sandstone[4] top of high mountains to W.S.W. Also notice dip of flat top of red ochre rocks on our right to be so

E. NE apparently from middle of glacier

We had a very heavy forenoon's pulling on ski—the sledge constantly refusing to budge at all.

We turned out about 8 a.m. No crevasses, no ice—nothing but soft and softer **Tues 12 Dec** snow with an occasional mound where irregularities lay underneath. We were ?6 m going at first a bit towards Kyffin, but later towards Cloudmaker[5] and then even more to the right. See sketch made at lunch for detail of left side of our view. After lunch we got on much better—same soft surface though, and camped at 7, in snow up to our knees as we walked. Couldn't have gone a mile in this on foot hauling without ski. We are now abeam of? Socks Glacier[6], a basin outfall of ice on our right, while on our left we see the great disturbed ridge shot out just S. of Mt. Kyffin. Between us and it a huge névé hollow of soft smooth snow which we are avoiding. We can today see the Dominion Range at the very head of the glacier just above the horizon. We have passed the Pillar Rock and red cliffs. Both parties got on fairly well today, but the work was very heavy indeed. Now turned in 9 p.m.

Turned out 6 a.m. and had bad light to begin with but broiling sunshine by lunch **Wed 13 Dec** when we had done about 2 miles on the most awful surface. At lunch we fixed on the spare 10 ft runner and tried in the afternoon, but though the runners were a 3 m help the surface had got sticky and we did almost nothing—about a mile—the surface alternately excessively soft, and soft enough to just hold the sledge up one side only. It was killing work when the sledge hung up as it did every 20 to 30 yards. The other 2 sledges did relaying for the last bit—the first time. I had a grand 2 or 3 hours' sketching at the lunch camp, and did Mt. Elizabeth with Socks Glacier and Mt. Kyffin. Turned in a quarter to ten.

Turned out 5.30 a.m. and got in a real good day's travelling still on deep, soft **Thurs 14 Dec** snow, but the sledges went on it, all 3 of them. We still have our 10 ft runners ?10 m under the sledge and we exchanged sledges with Birdie's team to see whether they found ours heavier or lighter. We both thought ours was the heavier pulling, though the weights are identical, yet our team, Scott, Oates, P.O. Evans and myself—walked down both the other teams every time. The other teams are Teddie Evans, Atkinson, Wright and Lashly—and Bowers, Cherry, Crean and Keohane. We constantly struck blue hard ice with the points of our ski sticks covered by a few inches only of soft snow. The surface has improved a lot—much firmer. We rose 570 ft during the day now being 2,000 ft above the Barrier and at about Shackleton's position of $8\frac{1}{2}$[7]. We have passed Kyffin and Socks Glacier and are opening up more banded mountains ahead. The Cloudmaker shows its very carved out profile, hard and softer rock—very wet with a very hot march, now overcast. Northerly breeze. Turned in at 9 p.m. all satisfied. We began 8 biscuits a day today. Camped on soft snow but only a foot or so of it above hard blue ice and several crevasses—small ones stepped into camping. Got a sketch made at lunch time.

We had a good day's march—ski and all three sledges running well—but gradually **Fri 15 Dec** all land got overcast and we had to camp an hour before time as snow fell and hid 9 m everything for steering by. We passed Alice Glacier (see notes)[8] which I wish I could have sketched, but all became obscured. Surface getting much harder—

windier sastrugi and only a few inches to less than a foot of snow above the blue ice everywhere all day. Lips very cracked by sun—bleeding and sore—nose and face also blistered and scabby. Most of us are the same—but very fit and enjoying it. Have passed Alice Glacier opening now.

Sat 16 Dec We got away at 7 a.m. and though it had been overcast and snowing and a N.Ely
9½ m geog breeze the sky was clearing when we started. We got in a good 5 miles before lunch
11 m stat on ski, but after lunch there was a cold S.Ely breeze and the surface got so bad for ski that we took to hauling on foot—the snow being very trying only not deep above the blue ice—there was a very trying crust which gave way when you hauled on it. We found lots of crevasses with one leg, but nothing worse, and by 6.30 p.m. when we camped we were fairly well up to the great ridges of crevassed pressure caused by the Keltie Glacier running into the main glacier and in sight of the moraine running down from the Cloudmaker. The Cloudmaker has bands of black rock running across it. Got some sketches at lunch time. Now turned in 9 p.m. We are camped right up against bare ice pressure ridges.

Sun 17 Dec We made a good march over a long series of high pressure ridges to the westward,
10½ m all the forenoon tobogganing, then on crampons all the afternoon, on a hard surface with an infinite number of cracks and fissures into which we put our legs and feet. I had a rotten afternoon with snow glare, streaming eyes and at times
Mid Glacier nearly blind, but got through all right and had zinc sulphate in both eyes that
Depot night and as a consequence was awake for about 6 hours with pain. Got 2 or 3 hours in the early morning. Depot laid.

Mon 18 Dec We again had a fine hard rubbly ice surface with any number of fissures and
12 m cracks to step in, all bridged ones but many rotten. It was overcast and snow crystals falling. My eyes better but couldn't stand any light without green and brown goggles.

Tues 19 Dec We got on the same surface again to begin with and later in the forenoon on to
14½ m hard névé mixed with smooth blue ice and sastrugi; a transition from glacier ice to the summit surface. The rubbly blue wavelets in the blue ice lower down are here formed in opaque white ice. The sastrugi of size are all made by S.W. winds. We are now nearly up to Shackleton's 16th position and have Mt. Buckley ahead of us on the island which stands between Plunket Point on our left and Mt. [   ]⁹ on the right. The whole range on our right is magnificent series of stratified rocks terraced and carved by glacier, black and broad bands of paler yellowish rock. As we keep as far as possible in the middle of the glacier we get no chance of seeing rock or moraine. We made a long march on ice nearly all the way up 800 ft and covering over 20 statute miles.

Wed 20 Dec Starting 8 a.m. to 1 p.m. and from 3 p.m. to 7 p.m. we then camped on 85° lat.
17½ m geog —300 miles from the Pole just below a rise steep up to the main pressure here east of Mt. Buckley. Fine cliffs of banded rock. Crevasses of small size abounded all the day but not more than 6 in. to 6 ft across, running mainly S.E. to N.W. and at right angles to these old silt bands which had been jammed out of line and were

very much older than the crevasses. Much of the ice was marble smooth. Birdie and I at lunch hour walked about 3 miles to look for the sledge meter parts on the back track, but couldn't find it. We had fog rolling up from the N. at lunch, but it cleared again during afternoon when wind dropped. Rock stratification magnificent everywhere, but little chance of doing anything at it. Now abeam of Mt. Buckley[10] and turned in 10 p.m. The first supporting party returns tomorrow night—Wright, Atkinson, Cherry and Keohane.

Thurs 21 Dec

We had a very fine long hot day's march over much blue rugged ice and crevasses everywhere, in fact a regular day out, and as has happened the last several days we had a Nly breeze before noon which brought up a thick white fog and made it impossible to go on. We camped for lunch in a maze of crevasses and waited an hour or two till it cleared and then got in a very good finish to our march and reached a good place for the Upper Glacier Depot where we part with the first returning four. A flag was put up on the cairn of snow. All I depoted here was my sketch book—in an old pair of finnesko—and my crampons. Also a bottle of brandy to be picked up with a medicine chest by the second returning party. It was wretched parting with the others. Atch took my watch back as they were short and had only one. Silas took my sundial. Atch also took a letter from me for Ory[11].

Fri 22 Dec

We made a very good march—the two parties 4 each—in good weather and on a good surface, nearly all up hill and in a S.Wly direction with pressure ridges on our left beam and left bow all day. And the Dominion Range almost behind us on our port quarter. Sketched in the evening.

Sat 23 Dec
15½ m

We made a large and a small cairn and started away at 7.45 a.m. first down a flat, then up a slope over a ridge across another flat and up another ridge, and so on. I think we crossed about 5 of these ridges in all, today 3 and yesterday two. Camp tonight 7,700 ft above sea level. These ridges abut on the two pressure ridges formed by the movement of the summit ice down the glacier. We made over 8 m. in the 5 hours' forenoon march. Temp. about −5° and a hot sun with cool Sly breeze all day. We made 7½ m. more in the afternoon in 4 hours and are camped now on what certainly looks like the summit. Endless flat plains of snow lie before us to the S.S.W. and W. and just the tops of disappearing mountains behind us. On the ridges we have had a lot of nasty treacherous crevasses down which all of us put our legs in turn. Twice we had greenhouse ice[12] with a false bottom—very disagreeable to go over. We have also crossed many wide crevasses bridged well, but sunk and with very rotten lower edges this time, instead of upper edges as we had on the glacier below.

Sun 24 Dec
14 m geog

Christmas Eve. Fine and sunny with a good strong Sly or S.S.Ely breeze in our faces all day. Temp. −3°. We got in 14 miles in 9 hours marching and rose nearly 400 ft passing a few little ridges of pressure, but not a single crevasse and going due S. all day. Very promising—thoroughly enjoyed the afternoon march. Surface on top of the rises very white, smooth marble ice, otherwise flat crisp firm snow taking impressions well, but only a half to one inch deep, interspersed with pretty big hard sastrugi from S.S.E. Can still tonight see tops of one or two mounts especially Flat Top[13]—very high to the N.E. of us now.

Mon 25 Dec
15 m geog

Christmas Day and a real good and happy one with a very long march 17½ statute miles over two or 3 rises with any number of crevasses and greenhouse surface. Lashly had a straight drop the length of his harness. It was blowing 3–4 all day in our face—S.S.E. with surface drift—but otherwise was very bright and sunny with a clear blue sky which we get every day up here. Temp. −7. We have not risen much today, 250 ft, but in passing over one of the rises we were apparently passing over a mountain top and the highest point had a great bump of ice pressure with an enormous hole on the southern side. We had a magnificent lunch of 3 biscuits, 1½ pannikins of tea, a spoonful of raisins, a whack of butter, and a stick of chocolate. For supper we had a regular tightener. Started with pemmican and horse meat and onion powder and curry powder and biscuit dust hoosh— 1¼ pannikins. Then a pannikin of arrowroot, cocoa, sugar, biscuit dust and raisins, then a pannikin of good cocoa, then a large bit of plum pudding each, and then 5 caramels and 5 pieces of ginger and 1 biscuit each. We are now all in our bags—2 hoops[14]. Read H.C. and Christmas reading in bag.

Tues 26 Dec
13 m geog

Made 13 geographical miles on a steady going surface and rose 250 ft. We are now over 8,000 ft. We made 7½ miles in the forenoon and the rest in the afternoon. We had the same old south-southeasterly wind in our faces all day today with temperature −3° in the day and −7° to −10° in the evening, bright sunshine— quite pleasant. Worked off our Christmas feast all right. Still see patches of crevassed bumps here and there and still rising new horizons, but got on no crevasses today only on to sort of white marble ice with temperature cracks. No big sastrugi excepting such as are nearly buried in drifted snow.

Wed 27 Dec
13 m geog

We had another fine sunny day and good going except for one long stretch of crevasses on a rise where there was a lot of pressure and another great hole at the highest point. The crevasses were badly bridged in places and Titus and the Owner and I were all in at one time. We had less wind and it was hot in the bags in the night. I had a bad short go of snow-glare in the right eye all the afternoon while we were crossing the crevasses, but sleep cured it. Rose 300 ft Temp. −6.

Thurs 28 Dec
13 m geog

A long day. Camped at 7 p.m. Chopping and changing sledges—and pullers— all forenoon to find out what were causes of slowness of second sledge. After lunch we came on with the other sledge and found it infernally heavy. Did 8 miles before lunch and a bare 5 miles after lunch. Fine sunny weather, blue sky. Rose 100 ft only in the day. The other party found our sledge very easy pulling.

Fri 29 Dec
12 m geog

We had a long day pulling at times over a very heavy uphill sandy surface, twice going up a rise where the snow was all like sand. The surface all smooth more or less. No large sastrugi, and everywhere letting one in enough to spoil one's pull. The other sledge changed their loading and came on much more easily. We rose about 200 ft and passed an extensive valley on our right. Sky was well marked radiating cirrus all day E. to W.—first time really marked. Temp. —6° and cold Sly wind all day.

Sat 30 Dec

We had a good day but fairly heavy going. The other sledge fell back a very long way and came in in the evening three quarters of an hour later than we did. We had a short rise and bad surface to begin with in the morning and again a rise and bad soft surface late in the afternoon. Had a long talk with the other tent which is not at all satisfactory.

Sun 31 Dec
86°56′S., 165°6′.
7 m geog

We marched from about 8 a.m. to 1.30. The other sledge having depoted their ski at the last camp going ahead of us. We made about 7 miles and came up a very long rise all the way and then camped for lunch near the top and made a cairn with black flag on runner and dismantled the two twelve foot sledges and made up the two ten foot sledges. Evans, Crean and Lashly worked in one tent with the primus going. Scott, Evans, Bowers, Oates and I sat and did various mending jobs in the other tent. We bent the inner lining today for the first time. We had an extra pot of tea between lunch at 2 p.m. and our supper hoosh which was late—after 10 p.m.—as we waited till the 2 sledges were finished. We leave this depot tomorrow with 130 lbs per man without ski. Our unit still has ski which amount in 4 pairs with sticks and shoes to 70 odd pounds.

Mon 1 Jan
11 m geog

A fine day—we had our ski with the new 10 ft sledges and found they worked well—the load came easily. The other party have unfortunately depoted theirs. We are today in 87° 6′. Temp. —14°, but feel warmer than usual as there is little wind. We had difficulty in getting into our ski shoes, they were so flat and stiff and frozen. At lunch thawed them out. I got both soles blistered, but we had a pleasant day. Started running the [illegible] from this depot of last night's camp. We had only 6 hours sleep last night by a mistake, but I had mine solid in one piece actually waking in exactly the same position as I fell asleep in 6 hours before—never moved. Tonight being New Year's Day we had a piece of chocolate each. We have risen today about 150 ft. We are now 9,500 feet above the Barrier.

Tues 2 Jan
13 m geog

A splendid day, —17° last night —11° tonight, but no wind and the sky is now overcast from the S.E., the first time we have had any cloud worth mentioning. We were on ski all day—good surface and the other party on foot. We are still rising but very gradually. Surface surprisingly flat—very little evidence of high winds, at any rate lately. We are now about 87° 20′. We were surprised today by seeing a Skua gull flying over us evidently hungry but not weak. Its droppings however were clear mucus, nothing in them at all. It appeared in the afternoon and disappeared again about ½ hour after.

Jan. 2. 12. Obs. 87° 20′ 8″ S.
160° 40′ 58″ E.

Var. 180°

DR. 87° 19·8′ S.
160° 20′ E.

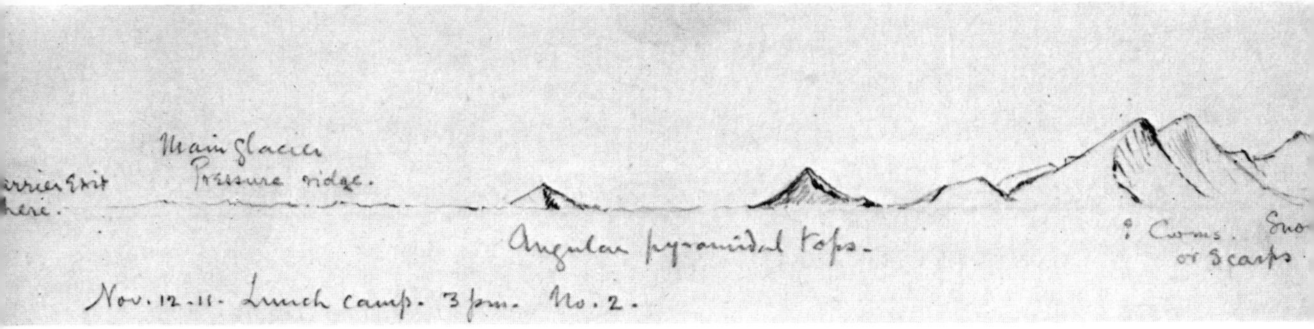

Barrier Exit here. — Main glacier Pressure ridge.

Angular pyramidal tops.

? Corms. Snow or Scarps

Nov. 12·11· Lunch camp· 3 pm· No·2·

Nov. 12·11· Lunch camp· 3 pm· No·3·
Dec.

Mt Harcourt·

Flat snow covered sloping top

Sno angular C...

Mt F. L. Smith
8367 ft
c'

d'

off plane top
dip, apparently to N.NW.
away from us.

Dec. 12·11·
looking NW.
No

The pillar rocks
rounded & Sno

Not so the re...
the precip...

a'

b'

? snow covered scarps
? more than 45°

Glacier surface

Kathleen

Mt. Scott.

Old Scarp
running away SE.

Ice fall

Seems a fair sized glacier
coming out here - long
pressure...into main.

Mt. Kyffin
5286 ft.

red ochre cliffs - same colour
as Pillar rock "b". the other side.
Vertical weathering - very
precipitous - probably
Granite or gneiss & slate!

Nov. 12 .11. Lunch Camp
3 pm. No. 4 -
Sketch
end

Commonwealth Range -

Disturbed glacier of considerable
size comes down here - Turned out to be a small one only

Panorama of the mountains bordering the east side of the Beardmore Glacier sketched at the lunch camp on 12 December 1911 S.P.R.I. MS. 797/2

Panorama of the mountains bordering the Beardmore Glacier, looking northwest, sketched on 12 December 1911 S.P.R.I. MS. 797/2

All red ochre crags & precipitous
rock faces. weathered in
vertical columns & pillars.

bare
Scooped
blue slate & red ochre
rock face

Ice fall

Dec. 13.11. 3 pm. Lunch Camp. No. 1.

Mt Elizabeth. 10761 ft.

Mount Elizabeth, 13 December 1911 S.P.R.I. MS. 797/2

Socks Glacier, 13 December 1911 S.P.R.I. MS. 797/2

Rock shows hardly anywhere but on the crests & tops

Dec. 13.11. 3 pm - No. 4 to 4.30 pm Lunch camp

Heavily crevassed

Very heavy ice fall

Dyke Combridge.

Socks glacier.

Mt. Kyffin. Dec. 13. 11. 2 pm.
Lunch camp.
Note red ochre rock crags show
out well beyond the black
rock scarps.

Mount Kyffin, 13 December 1911   S.P.R.I. MS. 797/2

Mount Patrick, a peak in the Commonwealth Range. 16 December 1911   S.P.R.I. MS. 797/2

Mt. Patrick. Dec. 16. 11. 2 pm.
Lunch Camp.
Rock face & talus slope
↓
really a different rock
black - not red like
the rest of the face
Cloudy tops.
ice falls
ice falls.
new rock
all
red
rock
black rock
scarp
(talus) & snow drift
heavily crevassed.

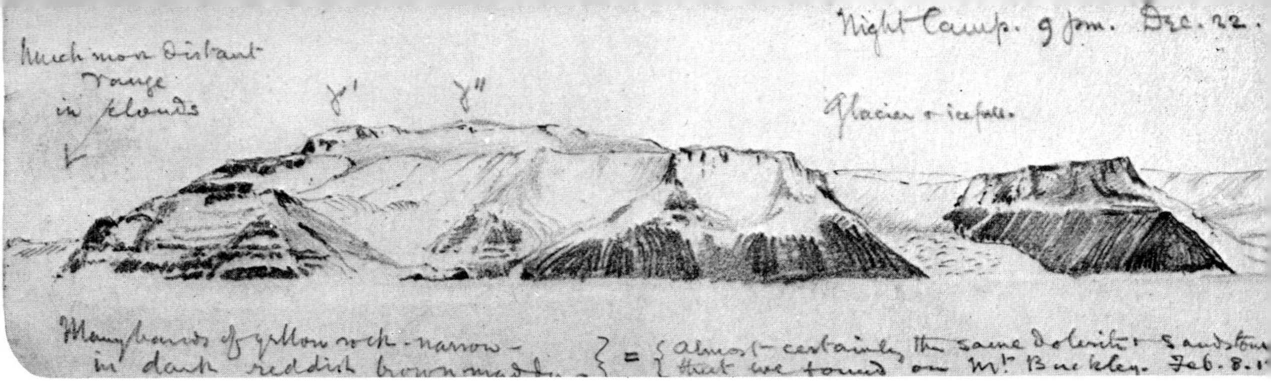

Much more distant
range
in clouds

γ' γ''

Glacier & icefalls.

Many bands of yellow rock - narrow -
in dark reddish brown mud.   } = { almost certainly the same dolerite & sandstone
that we found on Mt. Buckley. Feb. 8.

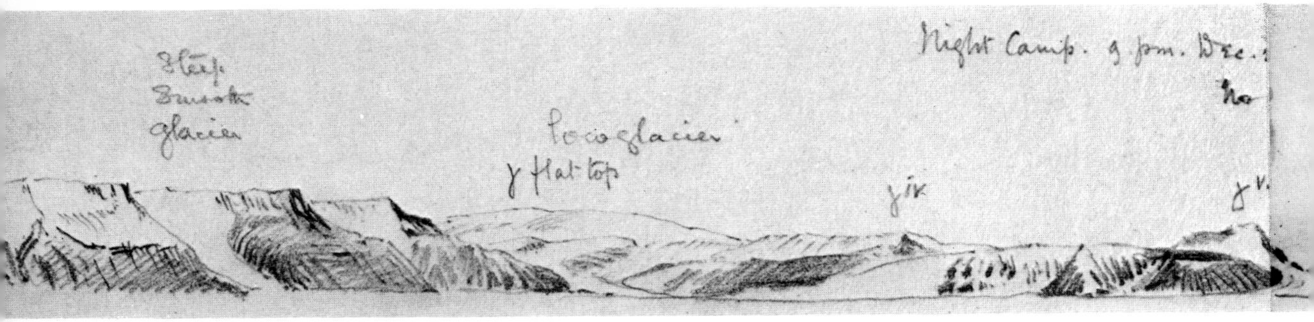

Steep
Smooth
glacier

Polar glacier
γ Flat top

γ ix   γ v

No.

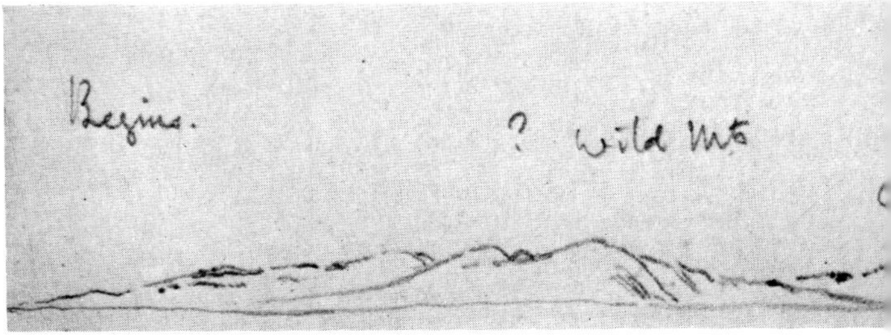

Begins.

? Wild Mts

No. 2

? Marshal Mts.

All snow covered this S. side

Mt.

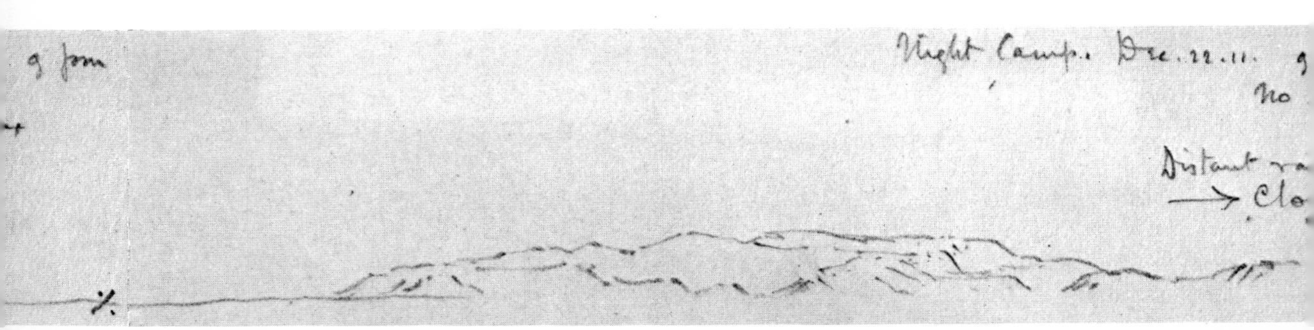

×

No.

9 pm

Distant ra
→ Clo

ight camp 9 pm Dec. 22.11.

No. 2

j'''   ice fall over line of cliff   Curtain
                                                                 gl.

Night Camp 9 pm. Dec. 22.11.

No. 4

Ends.

slope coming round from   .   .   Main pressure ridges.
gher level.

Night Camp. 9 pm. Dec. 22.11.   All snow covered this S side

No 1.   Clou

side almost wholly snow covered

mp. Dec. 22.11.   Night Camp. Dec. 2

No 3

                                    Birdie
                               Mt Buckley
arwin.

Mountain panorama near the summit of the Beardmore Glacier, 22 December 1911 S.P.R.I. MS. 797/1

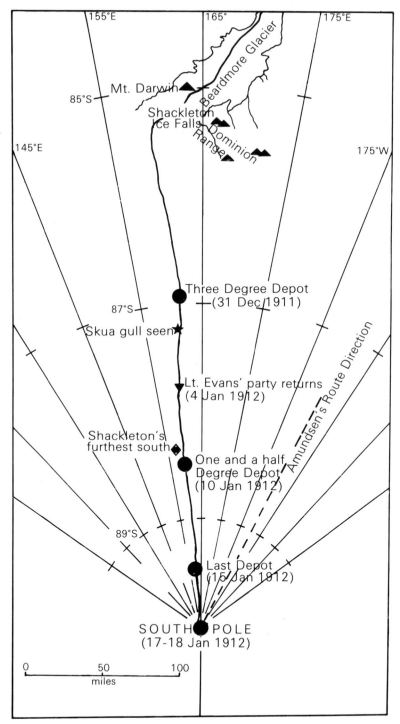

Map of the Pole Party's route from the top of the Beardmore Glacier to the South Pole

15

SLEDGE JOURNEY TO THE SOUTH POLE
3 THE SUMMIT TO THE SOUTH POLE

Blowing pretty hard from S.E. when we turned out and all day on our **Wed 3 Jan** march and pretty cold it was. We were on ski all day, the other party on foot. 12·3 m geog Last night Scott told us what the plans were for the South Pole. Scott, Oates, Bowers, Petty Officer Evans and I are to go to the Pole. Teddie Evans is to return from here tomorrow with Crean and Lashly. Scott finished his week's cooking tonight. I begin mine tomorrow. We have come up a hundred feet or so today. Surface very heavy in sandy drifts owing to the drift running all day. Looks windy but sky has few clouds. All fit and well. Writing last letter to go back to Ory tonight before we get back ourselves[1]. Position tonight should be 87° 32′ about 148 miles from the Pole.

We turned out as usual at 5.45 a.m. and there was some delay in getting off as **Thurs 4 Jan** Teddie Evans and his party of Crean and Lashly came along with us for a mile 12½ m geog before turning back to go home. I was very sorry for Teddie Evans as he has spent 2½ years in working for a place on this polar journey. We are now 5 and as we have only 4 pair of ski, Bowers has to go on foot just behind Scott and myself. 87° 45′

Our sledge is a pretty high pack. We had a perfect day without wind—calm and hot sun, but temp. −16·8° though so warm I took a bit of sun bath in the evening. The surface was bad, heavy sandy drifts and the sledge went heavy all the afternoon.

A fine calm day—light Nly and N.Wly airs all day with light but plenty of clouds **Fri 5 Jan** passing over us from N.W. Sun always visible. Sometimes crystals flying in the air 12½ geog and an effort at one of the brightly coloured parhelia in the forenoon. Pink and green iridescence in the clouds was frequent around the sun. Temperature −14·8°. No apparent rise. Surface heavy all day and sastrugi getting decidedly heavier and more abundant all from S.S.E. and Sly. We had 9 hours heavy pulling on ski—but it was very enjoyable with the following breeze. We sweat freely on these occasions. We ought to be at the Pole on the 15th.

We had very heavy pulling over the worst wind-cut sastrugi I have seen. All **Sat 6 Jan** S.S.E. or S. by E., rather and all covered with a growth of bunches of crystals exactly like gorse and best formed on the dagger-like ends of undercut sastrugi. Temp. −22. Last night −23·1, but no wind at all so quite hot in the sun. We 10½ geog

229

began the day on ski, but mid-forenoon took to foot and continued so all day. Tomorrow we leave our ski here as the surface is too much cut up for them and we think it continues so. We believe we came to the true summit late yesterday when we entered the wind cut area. Ice blink all round N., S.E. and W. We lost an hour today going back for a sleeping bag which dropped off, but we made 10 miles and a bit in 8 hours, very heavy work. We are now in 88° 7′, 113 miles from the Pole.

Sun 7 Jan
9 m geog

We were camped in a perfect sea of big sastrugi and so decided to leave our ski here as it looked like the same to the S., but after going a mile and a bit we got out of them, so we stopped and went back and fetched them and continued all day on ski. We thus lost an hour and only made 9·1 miles in the day. Surface very heavy but skiable. Very cold wind met us all the afternoon. Temp. −23. Last night was −27. We get our hairy faces and mouths dreadfully iced up on the march and often one's hands very cold indeed holding ski sticks. Evans who cut his knuckle some days ago at the last depot—a week ago—has a lot of pus in it tonight.

Mon 8 Jan
0 m

When we turned out a sort of thick mild blizzard was blowing from the S. or S. by E., with temp. −16, wind force from 4–6. We lay in all day as steering would have been very difficult and the going most uncomfortable.

Tues 9 Jan
6·5 m geog

We continued in our blizzard camp until noon by which time the wind had gone round to the east or E. by S. with temp. risen to −7 and later in the day to −3. We started off on ski after lunch and made 6·5 miles by 7.30 p.m. on a very good surface with very high deep cut sastrugi occasionally cropping up—all S.S.E. in direction. The whole sky today and yesterday has been overcast but never so as quite to obscure the sun. At this morning's breakfast a sad discrepancy of 26 minutes was discovered between the only two watches. Question is which has gone wrong.

Wed 10 Jan
10·5 m geog

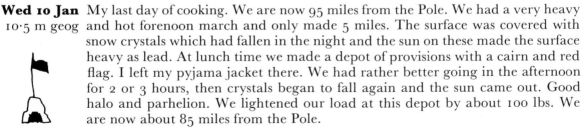

My last day of cooking. We are now 95 miles from the Pole. We had a very heavy and hot forenoon march and only made 5 miles. The surface was covered with snow crystals which had fallen in the night and the sun on these made the surface heavy as lead. At lunch time we made a depot of provisions with a cairn and red flag. I left my pyjama jacket there. We had rather better going in the afternoon for 2 or 3 hours, then crystals began to fall again and the sun came out. Good halo and parhelion. We lightened our load at this depot by about 100 lbs. We are now about 85 miles from the Pole.

Thurs 11 Jan
11·1 m geog

We had a very heavy surface all day—worse in the forenoon—but fine weather, misty to the horizon all round S. and E. and W. with glittering showers of ice crystals, but the sun out most of the day. Radiating cirrus from the S.E. to the zenith and in the evening windy, streaky cirrus in every direction above us, all thin and filmy and scrappy, but a generalized trend E.S.E. to N.W. We had well marked halos of 22° rad. several times but no elaboration. Our latitude tonight is 88° 46'. Temp. min. last night —14°, now —18°. Nothing but light airs today, some of them due south. We make a double cairn each night camp and a single one each lunch camp. For the 5 of us the evening meal takes $2\frac{1}{2}$ beakers of pemmican, 3 spoonfuls of onion powder and 5 pounded biscuits. This makes the hoosh. After that we have cocoa. For breakfast we have $2\frac{1}{2}$ beakers of pemmican and 3 biscuits and tea. For lunch butter and 3 biscuits and tea. The only extras we carry are curry powder, salt and pepper.

A poor surface but a very enjoyable day's march. Wly and S.Wly breeze came up **Fri 12 Jan** in the afternoon with overcast of strat. cum.[2] made it very cold in the evening, but temp. only —17·2. Surface was very free of sastrugi[3]—all deep soft crystalline non-coherent snow with no crusts. Min. [temp.] last night —26. Horizon clouds all being wafted to and fro a very characteristic effect hereabout.　　10·7 m geog

Slight breeze all day from the S. and Sly E. with sunshine and intermittent snow **Sat 13 Jan** crystals. Mouths get dreadfully iced up on the march. We did nine hours getting 11·2 geog in amongst sastrugi again early in the day and remaining amongst them all day. Sky blue with white thin wind-blown cirrus overhead and a white low mist of snow crystals all round the horizon. Sastrugi very mixed, the deepest cut being S.S.E. all the while. Temp. —22°. We are now in S.lat. 89° 8'—52 miles from the C65[4] Pole.

A very cold grey thick day with a persistent breeze from the S.S.E. which we all **Sun 14 Jan** felt considerably, but temp. was only —18 at lunch and —15 in the evening. 11·7 m geog Now just over 40 miles from the Pole in 89° 20' about. The surface was not much marked by sastrugi anywhere today and was uniform deep crystalline snow without crusts.　　C66

Heavy surface all forenoon, but the thick weather of yesterday and the wind are **Mon 15 Jan** both gone and the sun is out and warm again with temp. down to —25°. We 12·3 m geog made 6·1 miles in the forenoon and 6·2 miles in the afternoon—9 hours going. Calm all day except light Wly air in late afternoon and evening. Not a cloud in the sky. Sun about 22° high night and day. We are now 89° 32' about 28 miles from the Pole. We made a depot of provisions at lunch time and went on for our last lap with 9 days' provisions. We went much more easily in the afternoon, and on till 7.30 p.m. The surface was a funny mixture of smooth snow and sudden Cairn $66\frac{1}{2}$ patches of sastrugi, and we occasionally appear to be on a very gradual down gradient and on a slope down from W. to east.

We got away at 8 a.m. and made 7·5 miles by 1·15. Lunched and then in 5·3 **Tues 16 Jan** miles came on a black flag and the Norwegians' sledge, ski and dog tracks 13 m geog running about N.E. and S.W. both ways. The flag was of black bunting tied with string to a fore-and-after which had evidently been taken off a finished-up sledge. The age of the tracks was hard to guess—but probably a couple of weeks, or three or more. The flag was fairly well frayed at the edges. We camped here and examined the tracks and discussed things. The surface was fairly good in the forenoon— —23 temp. and all the afternoon we were coming down hill with again a rise to the W. and a fall and a scoop to the east where the Norwegians came up evidently by another glacier. A good parhelion and plenty W. wind. All today sastrugi have been westerly.

Wed 17 Jan
13 m geog
We camped on the Pole itself at 6.30 p.m. this evening. In the morning we were up at 5 a.m. and got away on Amundsen's tracks going S.S.W. for 3 hours, passing two small snow cairns and then finding his tracks too much snowed up to follow we made our own bee line for the Pole, camped for lunch at 12.30 and off again from 3 to 6.30 p.m. It blew force 4–6 all day in our teeth with temp. —22°, the coldest march I ever remember. It was difficult to keep one's hands from freezing in double woollen and fur mits. Oates, Evans, and Bowers all have pretty severe frost-bitten noses and cheeks, and we had to camp early for lunch on account of Evans' hands. It was a very bitter day. Sun was out now and again—observations taken at lunch and before and after supper and at night at 7 p.m. and at 2 a.m. by our time. The weather was not clear, the air was full of crystals driving towards us as we came south making the horizon grey and thick and hazy. We could see no sign of cairn or flag and from Amundsen's direction of tracks this morning he has probably hit a point about 3 miles off. We hope for clear weather tomorrow, but in any case are all agreed that he can claim prior right to the Pole itself. He has beaten us in so far as he made a race of it. We have done what we came for all the same and as our programme was made out. From his tracks we think there were only 2 men on ski with plenty of dogs on rather low diet. They seem to have had an oval tent. We sleep one night at the Pole and have had a double hoosh with some last bits of chocolate, and Ber's⁵ cigarettes have been much appreciated by Scott and Oates and Evans. A tiring day—now turning in to a somewhat starchy frozen bag. Tomorrow we start for home and shall do our utmost to get back in time to send the news to the ship.

Thurs 18 Jan
3¾ m geog
Sights were taken in the night and at about 5 a.m. we turned out and marched from this night camp about 3¾ miles back in a S.Ely direction to a spot which we judged from last night's sights to be the Pole. Here we lunched camp—built a cairn—took photos, flew the Queen Mother's Union Jack and all our own flags. We call this the Pole, though as a matter of fact we went half a mile further on in a S.Ely direction after taking further sights to the actual final spot and here we left the Union Jack flying. During the forenoon we passed the Norwegians' last southerly camp. They called it Polheim and left here a small tent with Norwegian and *Fram* flags flying and a considerable amount of gear in the tent, half reindeer sleeping bags, sleeping socks, reinskin trowsers 2 pair, a sextant and artificial horizon, a hypsometer with all the thermometers broken etc. I took away the spirit lamp of it which I have wanted for sterilizing and making disinfectant lotion of snow. There were also letters there. One from Amundsen to King Haakon with a request that Scott should send it to him. There was also a list of the 5 men who made up their party, but no news as to what they had done. I made some sketches here but it was blowing very cold —22. Birdie took some photos. We found no sledge there though they said there was one. It may have

been buried in drift. The tent was a funny little thing for 2 men, pegged out with white line and tent pegs of yellow wood. I took some strips of blue grey silk off the tent seams. It was perished. The Norskies had got to the Pole on December 16 and were here from 15th to 17th. At our lunch South Pole camp we saw a sledge runner with a black flag about half a mile away bearing from it. Scott sent me on ski to fetch it and I found a note tied to it showing that this was the Norskies actual final Pole position. I was given the flag and the note with Amundsen's signature and I got a piece of the sledge runner as well. The small chart[6] of our wanderings shows best how all these things lie. After lunch we made 6·2 miles from the Pole camp to the north again—and here we are camped for the night. 6·2 m geog

'Amundsen's South Pole mark, Jan.18,1912.' S.P.R.I. 546

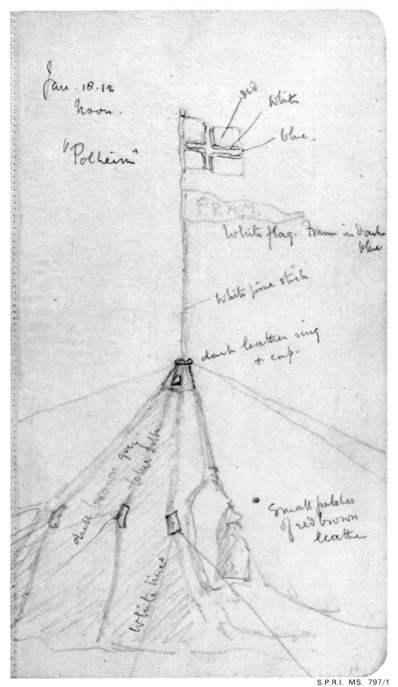

Jan. 18. 12
noon.

"Polheim"

red   White
blue.

FRAM.
White flag. Drawn in dark blue

White pine stick

dark leather ring
+ cap.

dull brown grey blue felt

Small patches
of red brown
leather

White line

Amundsen's tent at the South Pole, 18 January 1911

At the South Pole. *Standing:* Wilson, Scott, Bowers. *Seated:* Evans, Oates.

16

SLEDGE JOURNEY TO THE SOUTH POLE
4 RETURN TO THE BARRIER

Fri 19 Jan   WE followed this course till we struck the small cairn where we lost Amundsen's tracks—here we picked up our own and his and followed them N.E. till we reached his next small cairn and then the black flag camp our 68th outward camp. We went on due N. from here—taking his stick and flag—and lunched at 1 having done 8·1 miles. We have the floorcloth spread as a sail on the tent poles and inner tent as a mast. We had a splendid wind right behind us most of the afternoon and went well until about 6 p.m. when the sun came out and we had an awful grind until 7.30 when we camped. The sun comes out on sandy drifts all on the move in the wind and temp. −20° and gives us an absolutely awful surface with no glide at all for ski or sledge and just like fine sand. The weather all day has been more or less overcast with white broken alt. str.¹ and for 3 degrees above the horizon there is a grey belt looking like a blizzard of drift, but this in reality is caused by a constant fall of minute snow crystals—*very* minute—sometimes instead of crystal plates the fall is of minute agglomerate spicules like tiny sea urchins. The plates glitter in the sun as though of some size, but [you] can only just see them as pin points on your burberry. So the spicule collections are also only just visible. Our hands are never warm enough in camp to do any neat work now the weather is always uncomfortably cold and windy about −23, but after lunch today I got a bit of drawing done. Sastrugi today definitely S.Wly and S.Ely. Our old tracks are already covered in places by 1 foot old looking sastrugi—all fresh, many deeply cut, but not hard. We passed 67½ camp this afternoon and are now 9 miles from the last outward depot which is 66½ camp.

Sat 20 Jan   Blowing 4–5 from the S.S.W. and from time to time overcast but too much
16·1 m geog   sun and moving sandy drifts at this temp. for good going—they refused to allow the ski to glide at all. One had to shove them over. The going was irregular and uncomfortable but we made 9·3 miles by lunch in 5 hours, 10 minutes, when we reached 66½ camp where we had left a depot 'The last depot'. We passed camp 67 in the forenoon march. This afternoon we ought to pass camp 66 at about 7 miles from this depot. Snow was falling all forenoon again in minute little collections of spicules, but made a very grey mist all round and gave a complete double 22° halo. The lower edge of the inner ring just touching the horizon. One has to wear snow goggles always up here especially now that we are walking into the sun. We picked up a bamboo here used as our depot flag and discarded

236

Amundsen's 'Pole'—from which I took a number of hickory splinters. We go on from this depot with just 7 days' provision for the next 50 miles when we pick up our 1½ degree depot. In the afternoon we had a very heavy pull until 7.30 passing camp 66 shortly before halting. The weather very thick with a great quantity of drifting surface sandy snow which made drifts that clung to our ski like glue. Camp 66=night of 14th Jan. The wind all day has been S.S.W. and a fine double halo all day with horns as before. Bags and gear getting a bit wet and frozen up. No chance to dry things for some time now and temperature low, −28 last night, −18 this evening, always drift and snow crystals and wind and not much sun. Evans has got 4 or 5 of his finger tips badly blistered by the cold. Titus also his nose and cheeks—so Evans and Bowers.

Sun 21 Jan
5·5 m

We had a blizzard −18 to −11 and so thick that we had to lie up for the forenoon. It blew about 6, and it would have been impossible to follow the tracks, but after lunch the sun came out and it suddenly cleared and the wind died down blowing from S. by W. We got away at a quarter to 4 and marched till 7.45 and did 5·5 miles passing one cairn no. 65½. We are now about 89° 14′ S. and have 6 days food in hand to next depot. The cairn we passed was built of large single blocks of snow and had leaned down to 45° without any falling off.

Mon 22 Jan
14·5 m geog

Sun out and temp. as usual with clearing sky is dropping. Crystals in the air all the same but fewer and one could see cairn 65 about 1½ miles away today. We marched from 8 a.m. to 1 with a really heavy surface and very little breeze indeed. We made 8·3 miles geog. The S.S.E. sastrugi which we crossed coming over this march on our way S. are now all replaced by deep cut S. by Wly sastrugi in abundance. After lunch we made 6·2 miles and passed camp 64½ and went on from 3 p.m. to 7 p.m.—a very heavy drag and no wind but sun out. Temp. −21. We are apparently going over very gradual undulations, but the aneroid does not show much change. We are now 10,000 ft above sea level and the Pole 9,500. We have to rise to 10,500 before we begin going down the Beardmore. We are now 30 miles from our next depot and ought when we get there to have 10 days' food for the next 95 miles to the next depot.

Tues 23 Jan
15·5

We started for 2 miles in hot sun with no wind—then very heavy pulling—then wind came on much harder and drift, and we got off the tracks constantly. I wrote this at lunch and in the evening had a bad attack of snow blindness.

Wed 24 Jan
7 m

Blizzard in afternoon. We only got in a forenoon march. Couldn't see enough of the tracks to follow at all. My eyes didn't begin to bother me till tomorrow though it was the strain of tracking and the very cold drift which we had today that gave me this attack of snow glare.

Thurs 25 Jan
12·2 m

Marched on foot in the afternoon as my eyes were too bad to go on on ski. We had a lot of drift and wind and very cold. Had Zn SO$_4$ and cocaine in my eyes at night and didn't get to sleep at all for the pain—dozed about an hour in the morning only.

Fri 26 Jan
15·4 m
Marched on foot again all day as I couldn't see my way on ski at all. Birdie used my ski. Eyes still very painful and watering. Tired out by the evening—had a splendid night's sleep—and though very painful across forehead to light they are much better.

Sat 27 Jan
13·9 m
Very bad surface of deep cut sastrugi all day until late in the afternoon when we began to get out of them. We passed cairns 59 and 58½ and 58. One of these had curved into a semi-circle without dropping a block. Eyes better, was on ski all day again.

Sun 28 Jan
15·7 m geog
We had a fine day and a good march on very decent surface—a few isolated deep sastrugi, but otherwise nearly all surface wind marks like butterfly scales. Made sail as usual and had a brisk breeze most of the afternoon. Titus picked up his lost pipe at our camp tonight which was the lunch camp of Jan. 4th. It was just showing. We are camped at this cairn tonight. My eyes are well again and we are all on ski except Birdie. We are about 10,130 ft above s.l. We are now about 42 miles from our 3 degree depot, the next one, and when we get there we ought to have 3 days' food in hand to increase on. We are all pretty hungry—could eat twice what we have, especially at lunch and breakfast. Evans has a number of badly blistered finger ends which he got at the Pole. Titus' big toe is turning blue black. Lat. tonight about 87° 39′.

Mon 29 Jan
19·5 m geog
=22 miles
statute
We got in a very long march for 9 hours going over part good and part bad surface. There has been a lot of very glassy porcelain shell surface with raised footprints and sledge tracks on it and enormous snowdrifts and banks of hard crusted very deep cut sastrugi, awful for skiing over, but Scott and I were on ski the whole day —the other three on foot. I got a nasty bruise on the Tib. ant. which gave me great pain all the afternoon[2]. The sky radiating windy cirrus S.E. and N.W. and a stiff S.E. wind with low drift all day. Sky cleared at night. Temp. —25 with it made it very cold. We are now only 22 miles from our depot and 400 miles about to go before meeting the dogs with ship's news. Tonight about 87°20′. We passed the cairn of the last camp we had with the 2nd supporting party in the forenoon and from there onward had 3 sledge tracks to follow.

Tues 30 Jan
19·8 m geog
My left leg exceedingly painful all day so I gave Birdie my ski and hobbled along-side the sledge on foot. The whole of the Tibialis anticus is swollen and tight and full of tenosynovitis and the skin red and œdematous over the shin. But we made a very fine march with the help of a brisk breeze and a good going surface. Shell porcelain and very high deep cut sastrugi in patches under and over the old tracks.

Wed 31 Jan
13·5 m
Again walking by the sledge with swollen leg but not nearly so painful. We had 5·8 miles to go to reach our three degree depot, picked this up with a week's provision and a line from Evans and then for lunch an extra biscuit each, keeping 4 for lunch and $\frac{1}{10}$ whack of butter extra as well. Afternoon we passed cairn where Birdie's ski had been left. These we picked up and came on till 7.30 p.m. when the wind which had been very light all day dropped and in temp. —20 it felt delight-fully warm and sunny and clear. We have $\frac{1}{10}$ extra pemmican in the hoosh now

also. My leg pretty swollen again tonight. Evans' finger nails all coming off, very raw and sore. Surface is still biscuit porcelain with large sastrugi above and below the old tracks.

Cairns 2 in 6·5 and 5·5 miles were to be passed today, but we passed them and **Thurs 1 Feb** camped at the last having covered 15·7 miles. Temp. −20 in afternoon, a stiff 15·7 m breeze and porcelain eggshell china surface alternating with huge deep cut sastrugi. My leg much more comfortable—gave me no pain and I was able to pull all day holding on to the sledge. Still some œdema. We came down a hundred feet or so today on a fairly steep gradient.

We came down two slopes today. Scott had a nasty fall on the point of his shoulder. **Fri 2 Feb** We have not however seen a crevasse as yet on the way back but ought to to-morrow. We are still following our old tracks. I got through the day without any 7 m slips and no further damage to leg which is mending well. The surface was very largely eggshell porcelain, white and glistening like a woodpecker's egg and as thin—almost always gives way under foot. [In] some places there are 6 or 7 thin crusts in 2 or 3 inches depth of this snow. Wind was off and on today—very cold forenoon for me in the sail's shadow, but very warm afternoon march. Finished at 8 p.m. Very tired—sleep at once.

Sunny and breezy again. Came down a series of slopes and finished the day by **Sat 3 Feb** going up one. Enormous deep cut sastrugi and drifts and shiny eggshell surface. 16 m Wind all S.S.Ely. Today at about 11 p.m. we got our first sight again of mountain peaks on our eastern horizon almost abeam as we went N. about E. by N. or E.N.E. We had 9 hours of marching and finished at 8 p.m. Sunny and very little S.Ely breeze. We crossed the outmost line of crevassed ridge top today—the first on our return. Lost the old tracks and are now going due north—with still a week's food for about 65 miles to the Mt. Darwin depot.

We had 9 hours marching with a steady useful S.S.Ely breeze all day. All the **Sun 4 Feb** others went on ski in the afternoon but we all foot slogged all forenoon. Temp. −23. Clear cloudless blue sky—surface drift. During forenoon we came down 18·1 m gradual descent including 2 or 3 irregular terrace slopes on crest of one of which were a good many crevasses. Southernmost were just big enough for Scott and Evans to fall in to their waists—and very deceptively covered up. They ran east and west. Those nearer the crest were the ordinary broad street-like crevasses well lidded. In the afternoon we again came to a crest before descending with street crevasses and one we crossed had a huge hole where the lid had fallen in, big enough for a horse and cart to go down. We have a great number of mountain tops on our right and south of our beam as we go due north now. We are now camped just below a great crevassed mound on a mountain top evidently. The surface has been marble smooth on the crests with temperature cracks and on the south side rather softer butterfly scale. On the northern sides which are steeper the sastrugi are immense and deeply cut and often hard. Since the last depot we have been having extra food, making a week last 6 days, I believe, and we are grateful

239

for it, 4 biscuits for lunch and fat hooshes always now. Evans is feeling the cold a lot always getting frost bitten. Titus' toes are blackening and his nose and cheeks are dead yellow. Dressing Evans' fingers every other day with boric vaseline—they are quite sweet still.

Mon 5 Feb
18·2 m
We had a difficult day getting in among a frightful chaos of broad chasm-like crevasses. We kept too far east and had to wind in and out amongst them and cross a multitude of bridges. We then bore west a bit and got on better all the afternoon and got round a good deal of the upper disturbance of the falls here. We ought to have gone west of the big hump (see yesterday) and we should have missed all today's trouble. The weather was perfect—cloudless blue sky and sun [illegible] breeze most of the day and none at camping. We camped for the night on hard snow among crevasses. Evans' fingers suppurating, nose very bad and rotten looking. Land well in sight today. Mt. Darwin, Buckley, Dominion Range, Flat Tops, Kirkpatrick etc. The falls are all formed of large open crevasses.

Tues 6 Feb
15 m geog
We again had a forenoon of trying to cut corners. Got in amongst great chasms running E. and W. and had to come out again. We then again kept west and down hill over tremendous sastrugi with a slight breeze very cold—and afternoon continued bearing more and more towards Mt. Darwin. We got round one of the main lines of icefall and looked back up to it. We are now camped about 10 miles from the Upper Glacier Depot, but have seen none of our old tracks or cairns. We are on a terrace with another good drop ahead for tomorrow. Dominion Range has been looking very fine today—close enough to see some colour in the rock. The breeze rose again in the night Sly. Blew all day and fell calm −15 in the evening. Very cold march—many crevasses and walking by the sledge on foot found a good many—the others on ski. Weather last night became completely overcast with alto stratus, but all cleared quickly in the morning and we had a cloudless day of sunshine. Periodicity of Sly and S.Ely breezes seems possible—it often falls in the evening to nil and then feels real warm.

Wed 7 Feb
15·5 m
Clear day again and we made a tedious march in the forenoon along a flat or two and down a long slope and then in the afternoon we had a very fresh breeze and very fast run down last slopes covered with big sastrugi. It was a strenuous job steering and checking behind by the sledge. We reached the Upper Glacier Depot by 7.30 p.m. and found everything right which was satisfactory, after a breakfast which was given up to a discussion as to the absence of one day's biscuit. The colour of the Dominion Range rock is in the main all brown madder or dark reddish chocolate—but there are numerous narrow bands of yellow rock scattered amongst it. I think it is composed of dolerite and sandstone as on the W. side.

Thurs 8 Feb

Mt. Buckley
cliffs
A very busy day. We had a very cold forenoon march blowing like blazes from the S. Birdie detached and went on ski to Mt. Darwin and collected some dolerite, the only rock he could see on the nunatak[3] which was nearest. We got into a sort of crusted surface where the snow broke through nearly to our knees and the sledge runner also. I thought at first we were all on a thinly bridged crevasse. We

240

'Mt. Lister. Sept.16.1911. Evening'   S.P.R.I. 435

'May 13.11. 8 a.m. Paraselena. Cape Evans. McMurdo Sound'

'June 20.11. 10.30 a.m. Paraselena. McMurdo Sound'

Paraselena. Jan.15.11. 9.30 pm.
Cape Evans. McMurdo Sound.

'Paraselena. Jan.15.11. 9.30 p.m. Cape Evans. McMurdo Sound'

Buckley Id. (4).

As we travelled along the Cliff on the 9th we saw one or two seams of very genuine & really black coal. Some of the weathered blocks which we found on the moraine were of good burning shiny crystalline coal — but most of it was shaley, lignite or slaty, and much of it brownish black hard & devoid of anything like organic remains in appearance. There were to be found in many of the sandstone blocks twisted bands of coal — much contorted — & full of vegetable remains — These were yellow blocks with curly sheets of black coal — & the blocks split in curves with the contortions — These would be profitable for exam: But the best leaf impressions & the most obvious were in the rotten lumps of weathered coal which split up easily to sheath knife & hammer. Every layer of these gave abundant vegetable remains

S.P.R.I. MS. 797/2

Part of a page from Wilson's sketchbook with notes on the Mount Buckley coal measures
(9 February 1912)

then came on east a bit and gradually got worse and worse going over an icefall having great trouble to prevent sledge taking charge, but eventually got down and then made N.W. or N. into the land and camped right by the moraine under the great sandstone cliffs of Mt. Buckley, out of the wind and quite warm again— was a wonderful change. After lunch we all geologised until supper, and I was very late turning in, examining the moraine after supper. Socks all strewn over the rocks dried splendidly. Magnificent Beacon Sandstone cliffs. Masses of limestone in the moraine—and dolerite crags in various places. Coal seams at all heights in the sandstone cliffs and lumps of weathered coal with fossils, vegetable. Had a regular field day and got some splendid things in the short time[4].

We made our way along down the moraine and at the end of Mt. Buckley un- **Fri 9 Feb** hitched and had half an hour over the rocks and again got some good things Moraine written up in sketch book. We then left the moraine and made a very good march visit on rough blue ice all day with very small and scarce scraps of névé on one of which we camped for the night with a rather overcast foggy sky which cleared to bright sun in the night. We are all thoroughly enjoying temps. of +10 or thereabout now with no wind instead of the summit winds which are incessant with temp. —20.

Sat 10 Feb We made a very good forenoon march from 10 to 2.45 towards the Cloudmaker.
?16 m Weather overcast gradually obscured everything in snowfull fog, starting with crystals of large size—plate stars beautifully shaped and size of this—

changed to smaller of the same gradually by 7.30 p.m., when we camped, and after hoosh to minute agglomeration of spicules. We had to camp after 2½ hours afternoon march as it got too thick to see anything and we were going downhill on blue ice after crossing a few inches of névé. The snow in this névé is pitted in small cups on the east and S.E. but sastrugized with no pitting on the N. and N.W. This seems funny as the pitting is evidently due to the sun. An immense amount of rock dust is blown over the glacier and catches in sastrugi and in the cracks and snow-filled crevasses—gets stuck and makes the snow more sticky and goes on increasing so. Also water holes from these collections into the crevasses—but no water seen. These evidently form the silt bands—but there are bands of older dirty ice, possibly moraine sunk, which run down the glacier often at right angles to all the tension cracks and crevasses. These are old and planed off level with surface and often faulted. We are tonight about 20–25 miles from the Mid-glacier Depot and are making for the Cloudmaker. We have Wild Mt. and a glacier and Marshall Mt. on our left beam and have dropped Plunket Pt. today on our right quarter.

Mon 12 Feb We had a good night just outside the icefalls and disturbances and a small breakfast of tea, thin hoosh and biscuit, and began the forenoon by a decent bit of travelling on rubbly blue ice on crampons—then plunged into an icefall and wandered about in it absolutely lost for hours and hours.

Tues 13 Feb We had one biscuit and some tea after a night's sleep on very hard and irregular blue ice amongst the icefall crevasses—no snow on the tent, only ski etc. Got away at 10 a.m. and by 2 p.m. found the depot having had a good march over very hard rough blue ice, only half an hour in the disturbance of yesterday. The weather was very thick, snowing and overcast. Could only just see the points of bearing for depot. However we got there, tired and hungry, and camped, and had hoosh and tea and 3 biscuits each. Then away again with our 3½ days of food from this red flag depot and off down by the Cloudmaker moraine. We travelled about 4 hours on hard blue ice and I was allowed to geologise the last hour down the two outer lines of boulders. The outer are all dolerite and quartz rocks—the inner all dolerite and sandstone. The Cloudmaker has a huge bank of moraine terrace down half (lower) of its length, 700 ft above level of glacier. South of Cloudmaker is a glacier and S. of it another great cape of moraine.
We camped on the inner line of boulders—weather clearing all the afternoon.

Wed 14 Feb We made a good day's march along the ridge of a very long pressure ridge. I was on foot and the rest all on ski. We passed one boulder only, one of agglomerate sandstone made up of many coarse pebbles definitely waterworn of all sizes.

I got on ski again, first time since damaging my leg, and was on them all day for **Thurs 15 Feb** 9 hours. It was a bit painful and swelled by the evening and every night I put on $13\frac{3}{4}$ m geog [a] snow poultice. We are not yet abreast of Mt. Kyffin and much discussion how far we are from the Lower Glacier Depot—probably 18 to 20 miles—and we have to reduce food again, only one biscuit tonight with a thin hoosh of pemmican. Tomorrow we have to make one day's food which remains last over the two. The weather became heavily overcast during the afternoon and then began to snow and though we got in our 4 hours' march it was with difficulty—and we only made a bit over 5 miles. However, we are nearer the depot tonight.

Got a good start in fair weather after one biscuit and a thin breakfast and made **Fri 16 Feb** $7\frac{1}{2}$ miles in the forenoon. Again the weather became overcast and we lunched almost at our old bearing on Kyffin of lunch Dec. 15th. All the afternoon the $12\frac{1}{2}$ m geog weather became thicker and thicker and after $3\frac{1}{4}$ hours Evans collapsed—sick and giddy and unable to walk even by the sledge on ski, so we camped. Can see no land at all anywhere but we must be getting pretty near the Pillar Rock. Evans' collapse has much to do with the fact that he has never been sick in his life and is now helpless with his hands frost-bitten. We had thin meals for lunch and supper.

The weather cleared and we got away for a clear run to the depot, and had gone **Sat 17 Feb** a good part of the way when Evans found his ski shoes coming off. He was allowed to readjust and continue to pull, but it happened again and then again, so he was told to unhitch, get them right and follow on and catch us up. He lagged far behind till lunch and when we camped we had lunch and then went back for him as he had not come up. He had fallen and had his hands frost-bitten and we then returned for the sledge and brought it and skid him in on it, as he was rapidly losing the use of his legs. He was comatose when we got him into the tent and he died without recovering consciousness that night about 10 p.m. We had a short rest for an hour or two in our bags that night, then had a meal and came on through the pressure ridges about 4 miles further down and reached our Lower Glacier Depot. Here we camped at last, had a good meal and slept a good night's rest which we badly need. Our depot was all right.

We had only 5 hours' sleep. We had butter and biscuit and tea when we woke at **Sun 18 Feb** 2 p.m. then came over the gap entrance to the pony slaughter camp, visiting a rock moraine of Mt. Hope on the way.

Late in getting away after making up new 10 foot sledge and digging out pony **Mon 19 Feb** meat. We marched $5\frac{1}{2}$ miles was on very heavy surface indeed.

We got to the Blizzard Camp[5] by lunch time. **Tues 20 Feb**

We had a solid day's march and picked up one or two things—the horse walls of **Wed 21 Feb** Dec. 3, and an old tent ring and some ski tracks of returning parties. We had a very heavy surface of deep soft snow and we made $8\frac{1}{2}$ miles in the day on ski.

The Pillar Rock near where Petty Officer Evans died on 17 February 1912. Sketched on 11 December 1911.

Soon after starting it came on to blow and surface drift from the S.S.E. We were **Thurs 22 Feb** on ski and got the sail up and made 5½ miles in the forenoon. We failed to see anything of either the cairn of Dec. 2 or the horsewalls of Dec. 2, where Victor was 10½ m killed. We had a great pony hoosh in the evening. The wind lasted all day but fell in the evening.

Bad day off the tracks. We had thick weather and got no cairns. Lost much time **Fri 23 Feb** in discussing navigation. We were too far out and had to come well in. The drift and sunshine gave me very bad eyes.

Bad attack of snowglare—could hardly keep a chink of eye open in goggles to see **Sat 24 Feb** to the course. Fat pony hoosh.

My eyes much better. Started my week of cooking. No time for anything at any **Sun 25 Feb** meals. Very good day's going on ski. Took on job of pace maker and got sweated 11 m through—very cold night.

Good day's going on ski with little breeze from S.S.E. Fat pony hoosh. Temp. **Mon 26 Feb** down to −37 in the night. 11·5 m

Overcast all forenoon and cleared to splendid clear afternoon. Good march on **Tues 27 Feb** 12.2 m ski. Some fair breeze. Turned in at −37,

Here the diary ends. From this point onward conditions on the march for the Pole Party steadily worsened. When Mid Barrier Depot was reached on 1 March a critical shortage of fuel was discovered. On or about 16 March Oates, suffering terribly from frostbitten feet, walked out of the tent to his death.
The three survivors struggled on until 21 March when, after a nine day blizzard, they died in their tent, eleven miles from One Ton Depot and safety. Their bodies were discovered eight months later by a search party led by Surgeon Atkinson.

To Dr E. T. Wilson
Westal, Cheltenham

Dearest old Dad & Mother,
the end has come and with it an earnest looking forward to the day when we shall all meet together in the hereafter. Death has no terrors for me - I am only sorry for my beloved Ory & for all of you dear people. but it is God's will, and all is for the best. Our record is clean & we have struggled against very heavy odds to the bitter end - Two of the 5 officers are already dead, and the three are nearly done up. Scott's foot is badly frostbitten so that he can scarcely walk. Dear old home folk - how I love you all & how I have loved to think of you all. bless you. I have had a very happy life!

To Dr & Mrs E. T. Wilson   2
Westal Cheltenham
and I look forward to a very happy life hereafter when we shall all together again. God knows I have no fear in meeting Him - for He will be merciful to all of us. My poor Ory may or may not have long to wait - I am so sorry for her. However we have done all for the best believing in His guidance and we have both believed that whatever is, is His will - and in that faith I am prepared to meet Him & see all you loved ones in His care till His own time is fulfilled—

Now God be with you all.

Your own loving Ted

Appendix A

WILSON'S LAST LETTER
TO HIS FATHER AND MOTHER

Both Scott and Wilson as they lay in their tent close to death, with a Barrier blizzard howling about them, wrote letters home. These letters, with their message of fortitude in adversity and hope for the future, are a source of great inspiration. Wilson's letter to Mr. and Mrs. Reginald Smith and the two last letters to his wife have already been published in George Seaver's biography of Wilson. His last letter to his father and mother, written about 21 or 22 March 1912, is reproduced with the permission of his brother, the Reverend James Wilson, and the members of the family.

Dear old Dad and Mother,

    The end has come and with it an earnest looking forward to the day when we shall all meet together in the hereafter. Death has no terrors for me. I am only sorry for my beloved Ory and for all of you dear people, but it is God's will and all is for the best. Our record is clear and we have struggled against very heavy odds to the bitter end—two of the 5 of us are already dead and we three are nearly done up. Scott's foot is badly frostbitten so that he can scarcely walk. Dear old home folks how I love you all and how I have loved to think of you all—bless you. I have had a very happy life and I look forward to a very happy life hereafter when we shall all be together again. God knows I have no fear in meeting Him—for He will be merciful to all of us. My poor Ory may or may not have long to wait—I am so sorry for her. However we have done all for the best believing in His guidance and we have both believed that whatever is, is His will, and in that faith I am prepared to meet Him and leave all you loved ones in His care till His own time is fulfilled.

    Now God be with you all,

        Your own loving Ted.

Officers and crew of the *Terra Nova*. *Standing, below, left to right:* Taylor, Wright, Simpson, Nelson Levick, Oates, Evans, Bowers, Wilson, Scott, Campbell, Davies, Rennick, Priestley, Gran, Browning, Debenham, Day, Cherry-Garrard, Pennell, Meares, Drake, Bruce, Forde. *Standing, above, second from left.* Paton, *second from right.* Hooper.

Appendix B

BIOGRAPHICAL NOTES ON THE MEMBERS OF THE EXPEDITION

The brief biographical notes that follow are intended to supplement the information given by Wilson in his diary and by the editor in the references. The list is not intended to be definitive and includes only individuals mentioned by Wilson. A full list of expedition members will be found in *Scott's last expedition*, Vol. 1. pp. xix–xxi. The facts which form the basis of these notes have been culled from numerous published and unpublished sources in the library and archives of the Scott Polar Research Institute. The editor regrets that a number of notes are unavoidably incomplete owing to a lack of information.

George P. ABBOTT, *Petty Officer, R.N.*
Joined *Terra Nova* from H.M.S. *Excellent*. Subsequently served on the Northern Party under Victor Campbell.

Edward Leicester ATKINSON (1882–1929), *Surgeon, R.N.*
Known as 'Atch'. Educated at Forest School and St. Thomas's Hospital, London, qualifying in 1906. From 1908 to 1909 he was on the staff of the Royal Naval Hospital, Haslar and in 1910 he was appointed parasitologist and bacteriologist to the *Terra Nova* expedition. He was in command during the last year at Cape Evans and succeeded in the task of maintaining morale during the difficult time that followed the finding of the bodies of Scott and his companions. His fine character and qualities of leadership were afterwards displayed during his naval service in the First World War when he was awarded the Albert Medal for rescue work after an explosion on H.M.S. *Glatton*.

Henry Robertson BOWERS (1883–1912), *Lieutenant, Royal Indian Marine.*
Known as 'Birdie', on account of his beak-like nose, Bowers was described by Scott as 'the hardiest traveller that ever undertook a polar journey'. Born at Greenock. Entered as a cadet on H.M.S. *Worcester*. Listed midshipman, R.N.R., having served his indentures aboard a sailing barque to Australia. In 1905 he was appointed sub-lieutenant in the Royal Indian Marine serving in Burma and Ceylon. He took a keen interest in polar research, especially in Scott's *Discovery* expedition and Shackleton's voyage in the *Nimrod*, and was eventually introduced to Sir Clements Markham, President of the Royal Geographical Society, who introduced him to Scott while the latter was preparing for his second expedition. In March 1910 Scott telegraphed Bowers offering him a place on the expedition as storekeeper. Initially Bowers was a ship's officer only, but before *Terra Nova* had left New Zealand Scott was so impressed with Bowers's organisational ability that he decided to keep him with the Shore Party.

Frank V. BROWNING, *Petty Officer, R.N.*
A Devonshire man. Joined *Terra Nova* from H.M.S. *Talbot*. He was a member of the

Northern Party under Campbell. His diary of the expedition is in the Scott Polar Research Institute, Cambridge.

Wilfred Montagu BRUCE (1874–1953), *Lieutenant, R.N.R.*
Educated at Edinburgh Academy and on H.M.S. *Worcester*. On joining Scott's expedition in June 1910 he travelled independently overland to Vladivostok in eastern Russia to meet Meares and give assistance with the dogs and ponies. An entertaining and little-known account of this episode is given by Bruce in an article in the magazine *The Blue Peter*, June 1932. Bruce, whose sister Kathleen was married to Captain Scott, served on *Terra Nova* throughout the expedition. He served during the First World War on minesweepers. His diaries of the expedition are in the Scott Polar Research Institute, Cambridge.

Victor Lindsey Arbuthnot CAMPBELL (1875–1956), *Lieutenant, R.N.*
Known as 'The Mate'—sometimes 'The Wicked Mate'. He was First Officer on *Terra Nova* and in command of the Eastern (afterwards the Northern) Party which left Cape Evans on 25 January 1911 to set up a base in King Edward VII Land. After the meeting with Amundsen at the Bay of Whales plans were changed and it was decided to explore the coast west and south of Cape Adare. Campbell's party, which included Murray Levick, Priestley, Abbott, Browning and Dickason, was to have been brought back by *Terra Nova* to the main base before the winter of 1912 had set in, but gales and ice prevented the ship from reaching them. Campbell and his party spent seven winter months in a small cave on very short rations. On 30 September 1912 they set out on the 200-mile sledge journey to Cape Evans, arriving there on 5 November 1912. Campbell was promoted to the rank of commander for his part in the expedition. He fought in the Dardanelles during the First World War and in 1922 emigrated to Newfoundland.

Alfred B. CHEETHAM, *R.N.R., Boatswain.*
Described by Shackleton as 'the veteran of the Antarctic'. Served on the *Morning* when she relieved Scott's *Discovery* in 1903, as third officer and boatswain on Shackleton's *Nimrod* expedition, 1907–09, as boatswain on *Terra Nova*, 1910–13, and as third officer on Shackleton's *Endurance* expedition, 1914–16. He was drowned when his ship was torpedoed during the First World War in 1918.

Apsley George Benet CHERRY-GARRARD (1886–1959), *assistant zoologist.*
Known as 'Cherry'. Educated at Winchester and Oxford. In 1909 he was introduced to Scott by Wilson and recommended as potentially a very useful member of the expedition despite the fact that he was not a scientist. Quiet and unassuming, he shared every duty on board ship and took part in every major journey in the Antarctic, in spite of the fact that his sight was poor and he had to wear glasses for nearly all his activities. Cherry was involved in nearly every adventure—drifting out to sea on the pack ice, accompanying Wilson and Bowers on the midwinter journey and travelling with the Pole Party two-thirds of the way to the South Pole. During the winter at Cape Evans he edited the *South Polar Times*. In March 1912, with the Russian dog driver, Anton Omelchenko, he tried to meet Scott's returning party. His failure to do so, though no fault of his, preyed on his mind for the rest of his life. In 1922 he published his own account of the expedition, *The worst journey in the world*, probably the best polar book ever written.

Thomas C. CLISSOLD, *Artificer, R.N.*
Joined *Terra Nova* from H.M.S. *Harrier*. His expertise as cook was highly praised by Scott: 'We had some seal rissoles today so extraordinarily well cooked that it was impossible

to distinguish them from the best beef rissoles . . . our cook . . . really is excellent.' His unfortunate accident while posing for Ponting on an iceberg prevented him from joining the Southern motor party, but he was one of a party of four which hauled extra provisions to One Ton Depot in December 1911 and January 1912. After the First World War Clissold emigrated to New Zealand where he became a vehicle inspector at Napier.

Thomas CREAN, *Petty Officer, R.N.*
A native of County Kerry, Ireland. Joined *Terra Nova* from H.M.S. *Bulwark*. Had previously served on Scott's *Discovery* expedition as able seaman. Later served as second officer on Shackleton's *Endurance* in 1914–16 and was a member of the *James Caird* boat party from Elephant Island to South Georgia. Died in 1938.

Bernard C. DAY, *motor engineer.*
Before joining Scott's expedition to take care of the motor sledges Day had been to the Antarctic in 1907–09 and had gained experience with the Arrol-Johnston motor used on that expedition. It was Day who in his spare time made the venesta covers for the *South Polar Times*. He was also a competent amateur artist and a number of his watercolours painted both during and after his visits to Antarctica are recorded.

Frank DEBENHAM (1883–1965), *geologist.*
Known as 'Deb'. Born at Bowral, New South Wales, Australia. Graduated from Sydney University and was shortly afterwards selected to join Scott's expedition. During the summer of 1911–12 he accompanied the Western Party as geologist and the experience he gained here in mapping gave him an interest in cartography and survey which was very much to influence his later career. After service in Salonika during the First World War he went to Cambridge where he became a Fellow of Gonville and Caius College and lecturer in cartography. In 1920 he established the Scott Polar Research Institute, with the help of James Wordie and Raymond Priestley. He was its first director until his retirement in 1946. Debenham was also responsible for developing the Department of Geography in the university and was appointed its first professor in 1931.

Harry DICKASON, *Able Seaman, R.N.*
A Londoner. Joined *Terra Nova* from H.M.S. *Defiance*. He was a member of the Northern Party under Campbell.

Francis R. H. DRAKE, *Assistant Paymaster, R.N.*
Known as 'Franky'. He was expedition secretary and meteorologist on *Terra Nova*.

Edgar EVANS (1876–1912), *Petty Officer, R.N.*
Known as 'Taff'. Born at Rhossili, Wales. Joined the Royal Navy in 1891 and in 1901 volunteered for service with Scott's *Discovery* expedition. On his return to England he became a gunnery instructor. Though Evans occasionally fell from grace Scott thought the world of him: 'A giant worker with a really remarkable headpiece.'

Edward Ratcliffe Garth Russell EVANS, *afterwards* **LORD MOUNTEVANS** (1881–1957), *Lieutenant, R.N.*
Known as 'Teddy' or 'Skipper'. Educated at Merchant Taylors School and on H.M.S. *Worcester*. Joined the Royal Navy in 1896. As a sub-lieutenant on the *Morning*, took part in the relief of Scott's *Discovery* expedition in 1902. In 1910 he joined the *Terra Nova* expedition as navigator and second-in-command. In the Antarctic he was leader of the

last supporting party to leave Scott on the journey to the South Pole. During the return journey he suffered acutely from scurvy and would have died had it not been for the efforts of his two companions William Lashly and Thomas Crean (q.v.) to sledge him back to base. He was invalided home in 1912 but returned in *Terra Nova* in January 1913 to take charge during the last few weeks of the expedition. During the First World War he gained distinction when in command of the *Broke*. He was made a peer in 1945. His account of Scott's last expedition was published in 1921 as *South with Scott*.

Robert FORDE (1877–1959), *Petty Officer, R.N.*
Forde took part in two depot laying journeys and was sledge master during the Western Journey led by Griffith Taylor in 1911. He died at Cobh, Co. Cork, Ireland.

Demitri GEROF (1888–?1932), *dog driver.*
His full name correctly spelt was Dmitriy Semenovich Girev and he was born in Sakhalin, eastern Siberia. When Cecil Meares (q.v.) came to Nikolayevsk to purchase dogs for the *Terra Nova* expedition Demitri was recommended to him as an experienced dog-driver, and indeed it was he who helped Meares to choose the thirty-odd sledge dogs from various villages in the lower Amur River region. After the expedition Demitri went to England and then to New Zealand. Eventually he returned to Nikolayevsk and worked in the gold mines.

Tryggve GRAN (b.1889), *Sub-Lieutenant, Norwegian N.R. Ski expert.*
A native of Bergen, Norway. Gran was at twenty-one probably one of the most travelled members of the *Terra Nova* expedition. He was educated in Switzerland, entered naval college in 1907 and graduated in the spring of 1910. In March 1910 he was introduced by Fridtjof Nansen to Scott who was testing a motor tractor at Fefor, Norway. Here Gran, who was a prize skier, demonstrated the correct techniques of skiing for Scott who promptly engaged him to join *Terra Nova*, though Gran at the time was making plans for his own Antarctic expedition which then had to be abandoned. His skiing prowess and his general versatility and willingness to help others made him a very popular member of the expedition. He was one of the first to sight Scott's tent in November 1912. After the expedition he joined the Norwegian Flying Corps and later signed on as a captain in the Royal Flying Corps where he was mentioned in dispatches. He later rejoined the Norwegian Air Force and after the fall of Norway in the Second World War was for a short time a prisoner of war. He now lives in retirement at Grimstad, Norway.

William L. HEALD, *Petty Officer, R.N.*
Born at York. Served as an Able Seaman on Scott's *Discovery* expedition.

Frederick J. HOOPER (1891–1955), *some time Steward, R.N.*
Joined the *Terra Nova* expedition as a steward but was transferred to the Shore Party where he proved a valuable member of the expedition. He was a member of the search party which discovered the bodies of Scott and his companions on 12 November 1912.

Patrick KEOHANE, *Petty Officer, R.N.*
An Irishman from County Cork. Joined *Terra Nova* from H.M.S. *Repulse*. With Wright, Atkinson and Cherry-Garrard he was a member of Scott's supporting party which turned back at the top of the Beardmore Glacier on 21 December 1911. His field diary for this period is in the archives of the Scott Polar Research Institute.

R. F. Scott

C. S. Wright

T. Griffith Taylor

C. H. Meares

H. G. Ponting

Silhouettes of expedition members from the *South Polar Times*   BRITISH MUSEUM ADD. MSS. 51039-41

William LASHLY, *Chief Stoker, R.N.*

Born at Hambledon, Hampshire. Joined Scott's *Discovery* expedition from H.M.S. *Duke of Wellington.* Before joining *Terra Nova* served as an instructor at the Royal Naval College, Osborne. In the Antarctic he was usually selected for all the most difficult journeys and it was he, assisted by Crean, who successfully sledged Lieutenant Evans back to base after Evans succumbed to scurvy on the return of the last supporting party. In later life Lashly served as a custom's officer at Cardiff. His diary, now in the Scott Polar Research Institute, was published in 1969 as *Under Scott's command; Lashly's Antarctic diaries, edited by A. R. Ellis.* He died in 1940.

George Murray LEVICK (1877–1956), *Surgeon, R.N.*

Known as 'Toffer', 'Tofferino' or 'The Old Sport'. Qualified at St. Bartholomew's Hospital, London, 1902 and later joined the Royal Navy. In 1910 he was given leave of absence to accompany the *Terra Nova* expedition. He served as medical officer on Victor Campbell's Northern Party. Though not a scientist he was a careful and patient observer of the Adélie Penguins amongst which his party lived whilst at Cape Adare and his book *Antarctic penguins* (1914) was for a long time the standard work on the subject. In 1932 he founded the British Schools Exploring Society.

Dennis G. LILLIE (1884–1963), *biologist with ship's party.*

Known *inter alia* as 'Ooze'. Was largely concerned with collecting deep sea organisms, or 'benthos', during the various cruises of the *Terra Nova.* He also made observations on the whales and was responsible for the expedition's official report on this subject, making use of Wilson's own observations. Lillie made a number of penetrating caricatures of the expedition members while on board ship, some of which were later redrawn by Wilson for the *South Polar Times.*

Cecil H. MEARES.

Was responsible for purchasing the dogs for the *Terra Nova* expedition in the villages of the lower Amur River in Siberia. He was helped in this task by the dog driver Demitri Gerof (q.v.) who he met in Nikolayevsk and who also was recruited for the expedition. Meares was in charge of the dogs in the Antarctic and accompanied the Pole Party as far as the Beardmore Glacier. He was a wanderer at heart. Wilson in his diary refers to Meares's enthralling accounts of his adventures among the wild Lolo tribes of Tibet. He died in Canada in 1937.

Edward W. NELSON, *biologist.*

Known as 'Marie' or 'Bronté'. A Londoner. Educated at Clifton, Tonbridge and Cambridge. Joined the *Terra Nova* expedition from the Plymouth Laboratory as an invertebrate zoologist and also carried out tidal observations while at Cape Evans.

Lawrence Edward Grace OATES (1880–1912), *Captain, 6th Inniskilling Dragoons.*

Known as 'Titus', or sometimes as 'The Soldier'. Joined the 6th Inniskilling Dragoons in 1900 and served as a subaltern during the Boer War. Later saw service in Egypt and India. On hearing of Scott's proposed expedition Oates volunteered to take charge of the dogs and ponies and came home on leave in order to attend the interview. The War Office finally sanctioned an arrangement for his special extra-regimental employ with the British Antarctic Expedition, towards the costs of which Oates contributed a handsome sum. Scott undoubtedly selected him purely on his own merits. The famous picture by J. C. Dollman of Oates going to meet his death in the blizzard—'A very gallant gentleman'— now hangs in the Cavalry Club in London.

Anton Lukich OMELCHENKO (1883–1932), *groom.*
Born in Bat'ki, Russia, the seventh son of a poor farmer. At the age of ten he worked as a herd boy on the estate of a certain Mikhail Pekhovskiy who gave him a job looking after horses. He learned how to handle thoroughbreds and then trained as a jockey, a vocation in which he excelled. Later he travelled to race meetings abroad, including Europe. In 1909, while working as a jockey at Vladivostok, he met Scott's agent, Wilfred Bruce (q.v.), and travelled with him to Harbin to buy Manchurian ponies. After fighting in the First World War Anton joined the Red Army and was later involved in helping to set up a kolkhoz, or collective farm, at Bat'ki. He was killed by a lightning stroke in 1932.

James PATON, *Able Seaman, R.N.*
A Scotsman living in Lyttelton, New Zealand. Had served on Shackleton's *Nimrod* expedition and was boatswain on the *Aurora* during the relief of Shackleton's Ross Sea party in 1916–17.

Harry L. L. PENNELL (1882–1916), *Commander, R.N.*
Known as 'Penelope' or 'Pennylope'. Pennell was navigator of the *Terra Nova* and in charge of the magnetic work. He was probably one of the most competent members of the entire expedition and had a passion for hard work. As well as being a skilled navigator he was also a very competent naturalist and helped both Wilson and Lillie in the careful logging of birds and whales. Pennell was lost with his ship, the cruiser *Queen Mary*, during the Battle of Jutland, 31 May 1916.

Herbert George PONTING (1870–1935), *camera artist.*
Known as 'Ponco'. Spent his early years in a number of occupations and took to photography after a period of agriculture and mining in the western United States. He rapidly made a name for himself through the quality of his photographs taken during his travels in China and Japan. On Scott's expedition Ponting, who preferred the title 'camera artist' to photographer, set himself a high standard of work; all negatives that did not come up to his standard he would destroy. His still pictures and films were at that time well in advance of anything done by any previous traveller. After the expedition he indulged in a number of business ventures in the field of photography, mostly unsuccessful. He suffered deeply from the loss of Scott and Wilson and devoted himself for many years to the task of perpetuating their memory by public exhibitions of his incomparable photographs and his film *90° South.*

Raymond Edward PRIESTLEY (b. 1886), *geologist.*
Known as 'Ray'. Educated at Tewkesbury Grammar School and Bristol University. Began by studying botany but ended up as a geologist, in which capacity he joined Shackleton's *Nimrod* expedition of 1907–09. While in the Antarctic he learned much from Professor Edgeworth David and afterwards worked under him on the rocks of Victoria Land at the University of Sydney. When the New Zealand geologist, Allan Thomson, whom Scott had chosen to accompany him south in 1910, fell ill, Priestley filled the gap at very short notice. Priestley became a member of the six-man party under Victor Campbell that sailed on *Terra Nova* to Edward VII Land as the Eastern Party, but after the encounter with Amundsen in the Bay of Whales went to Cape Adare as the Northern Party. It was during this period that he spent the winter of 1911 in a cave scooped out of the snow on Inexpressible Island, the story of which has been told in his book *Northern adventure* (1914). The information he gained on glaciers in the Antarctic earned him a B.A. (Research) degree at Cambridge after the war. Then followed a distinguished academic and adminis-

trative career; he became in turn Vice-Chancellor of Melbourne University, Vice-Chancellor of the University of Birmingham, Chairman of the Royal Commission on the Civil Service (1953) and Deputy Director of the former Falkland Islands Scientific Bureau. With Sir Charles Wright (q.v.) he is author of the volume on glaciology in the scientific reports of the *Terra Nova* expedition. He was knighted in 1949.

Henry E. De P. RENNICK, *Lieutenant, R.N.*

Known as 'Parny'. Joined *Terra Nova* from H.M.S. *Dryad*. He was in charge of the hydrographical survey work and deep-sea sounding. Unfortunately he was unable to join the shore party for medical reasons.

Robert Falcon SCOTT (1868–1912), *Captain, R.N.*

Called 'The Owner'. Educated at Stubbington House, Fareham and joined the training ship *Britannia* at the age of thirteen. Between 1883 and 1887 served as a midshipman on *Boadicea*, *Lion*, *Monarch* and *Rover*. In 1887 was commissioned sub-lieutenant and posted to H.M.S. *Amphion*. In 1899, while serving on H.M.S. *Majestic*, he was informed by Sir Clements Markham, Director of the Royal Geographical Society, of his plans for an Antarctic expedition. Scott applied for its command and was promptly appointed. In August 1901 he sailed south on *Discovery*, returning to England in 1904 having successfully carried out the first extensive land exploration of the Antarctic continent. In the same year Scott was promoted to the rank of captain. After completing the expedition narrative, *The voyage of the Discovery*, he served on several ships, eventually securing a staff appointment at the Admiralty. In September 1908 he married Kathleen Bruce by whom he had one son, Peter Markham. In 1913 Kathleen Scott was granted the same rank, style and precedence as if her husband had been nominated a Knight Commander of the Bath.

George Clarke SIMPSON (1878–1965), *meteorologist*.

Known as 'Sunny Jim' (after the trademark on the 'Force' breakfast food packet). Educated at Owens College, Manchester. For a time he worked at the Meteorological Office before joining the Indian Meteorological Service at Simla in 1906. In 1909 Captain Scott invited Simpson to go as meteorologist with him to the Antarctic. Simpson's meteorological records at Cape Evans were a model of their kind and were subsequently published with the expedition's scientific reports. Simpson was recalled to Simla a year earlier than he had expected. After service in the First World War he succeeded Sir Napier Shaw as Director of the Meteorological Office where he remained until 1938. Simpson was knighted in 1935.

Thomas Griffith TAYLOR (1880–1964), *geologist*.

Known as 'Griff'. Born at Walthamstow, Essex. He emigrated with his family to Australia and graduated in science at the University of Sydney in 1904. In 1907 he went to Cambridge to continue his studies. At the time of joining Scott's expedition he was working as a physiographer for the Australian Weather Service. In 1915 his account of the expedition was published as *With Scott: the silver lining*. Afterwards he enjoyed a distinguished academic career. He was in turn Associate Professor of Geography in the University of Sydney, Senior Professor of Geography in the University of Chicago and Professor of Geography at Toronto University. He married a sister of Sir Raymond Priestley (q.v.).

William WILLIAMS, *Chief Engine-room Artificer, R.N.*

Born at Bristol. Joined *Terra Nova* from H.M.S. *Indomitable*.

256

Charles Seymour WRIGHT (b. 1887), *physicist.*

Known as 'Silas' (after Silas K. Hocking, an American novelist). Born in Toronto, Canada and educated at Upper Canada College. Was an undergraduate at Gonville and Caius College, Cambridge and did research at the Cavendish Laboratory between 1908 and 1910. After a distinguished career in the First World War, during which he gained a Military Cross and an O.B.E., he became in turn Director of the Admiralty Research Laboratory and Director of Scientific Research at the Admiralty. With the formation of the Royal Naval Scientific Service in 1946 he was appointed first chief of the Service. He was knighted the same year. He then returned to North America to continue his own research, working at the Scripps Institute of Oceanography, the Defence Research Board of Canada's Pacific Naval Laboratory and the University of British Columbia. He now lives in retirement with his daughter on Saltspring Island, near Vancouver, British Columbia. His report on the glaciological work of the *Terra Nova* expedition, written jointly with Sir Raymond Priestley (q.v.) and published in 1922, became a classic in its field. Like his fellow Antarctic scientist Griffith Taylor he was married to a sister of Raymond Priestley.

The *Terra Nova*

Plan of the *Terra Nova*

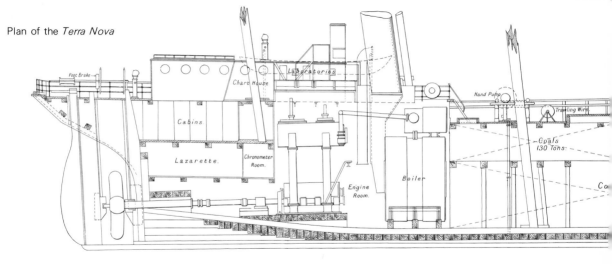

Foot Brake

Chart House

Laboratories

Hand Pump

Trawling Wire

Cabins

Coals
130 Tons·

Lazarette.

Chronometer
Room.

Engine
Room.

Boiler

Co

Appendix C

THE 'TERRA NOVA'

The *Terra Nova* was built in 1884 at Dundee for the Arctic whale fishery and was considered to be one of the finest ships of her class launched from that port, a claim that was to be justified by her subsequent history. After serving on the Jackson-Harmsworth Arctic expedition 1894–7 she sailed to the Antarctic in 1903, with the *Morning*, to relieve Captain Scott's *Discovery* expedition. In 1909 she was purchased from her owners, Messrs. C. T. Bowring and Co., for £12,500 and underwent an extensive refitting and cleansing, for she was, as Surgeon-Commander E. L. Atkinson remarked in a subsequent report, 'decidedly smelly from the storage of whale oil'. A number of additions were also made on the upper deck. These included an ice-house to be used for the cold-storage of meat. Despite its lining of four thicknesses of boarding and a layer of zinc this amenity was not an unqualified success. 'The temperature was not constant', observed Atkinson, 'and there was a great deal of decomposition amongst the carcasses, so much so, that several of them had to be got rid of.' Other improvements, in addition to a new galley, included extensions to the saloon, or wardroom, to enable it to sit the 24 officers and scientific staff. Various cabin doors opened off the wardroom, including a large cabin on the port side designed to sleep 4 seamen but on this occasion housing 6 scientists. These latter being the youngest on the expedition, the cabin was appropriately referred to as 'The Nursery'. Below decks the vessel was reinforced from bow to stern with a seven-foot thickness of oaken beams to take the strain of a prolonged encounter with the Antarctic pack-ice.

OVA.

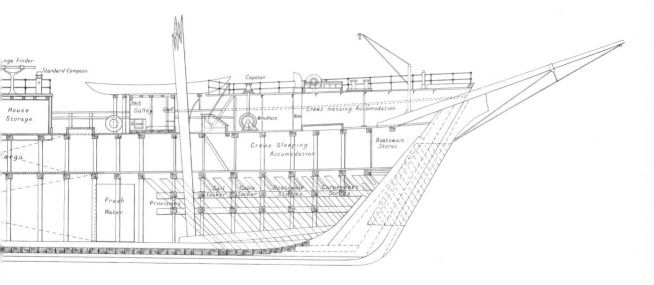

Terra Nova's motive power was provided by both sail and steam. She was barque rigged with square sail on the fore and main masts and fore-and-aft sail on the mizzen mast. Her steam engines were rated at 140 horse-power, though their 60 revolutions a minute (subsequently, thanks to the ingenuity of engineer Williams, increased to 89) were barely adequate to provide the required propulsion. Steam from the boilers was available not only to provide power for the pumps but to melt ice, in two iron tanks, to provide fresh water. The agonies suffered by those required to maintain this head of steam are vividly expressed by Wilson himself.

Despite two mysterious leaks, not traced till the ship's overhaul in New Zealand, and the near disastrous choking of the pumps by a mixture of oil and coal dust, *Terra Nova* gave remarkably little trouble. 'The ship behaved splendidly', wrote Cherry-Garrard. 'No other ship, not even the *Discovery*, would have come through as well.'

After the return of the expedition *Terra Nova* was bought back by her former owners, Messrs. Bowring, and was engaged in the Newfoundland seal fishery for many years. She sprang a leak and sank on 13 September 1943, while returning from a voyage to Greenland, the crew being rescued by a United States Coastguard cutter.

Appendix D

LIST OF BOOKS FOR FURTHER READING

The following list of books about the *Terra Nova* expedition does not include the published scientific reports. A much fuller list, including scientific papers, will be found in the book by Brian Roberts listed below.

CHERRY-GARRARD, Apsley George Benet. *The worst journey in the world; Antarctic 1910–13. Vols. 1 and 2.* London, Constable, 1922. (Other London editions by Chatto & Windus, 1923, 1937, 1950, 1951, 1965.)

DEBENHAM, Frank. *In the Antarctic; stories of Scott's 'last expedition'.* London, John Murray, 1952.

EVANS, Edward Ratcliffe Garth Russell. *South with Scott.* London, Collins, 1921.

GRAN, Tryggve. *Hvor sydlyset flammer; leir- og ekspeditionsliv paa antarktis . . .* Kristiania og København, 1915.

GRAN, Tryggve. *Kampen om Sydpolen.* Oslo, Ernst G. Mortensens Forlag, 1961.

LEVICK, George Murray. *Antarctic penguins; a study of their social habits.* London, Heinemann, c. 1914.

PONTING, Herbert George. *The great white south; being an account of experiences with Captain Scott's South Pole expedition . . .* London, Duckworth, 1921.

POUND, Reginald. *Scott of the Antarctic.* London, Cassell, 1966.

PRIESTLEY, Raymond Edward. *Antarctic adventure; Scott's northern party.* London, T. Fisher Unwin, 1914.

ROBERTS, Brian Birley. *Edward Wilson's birds of the Antarctic, edited by Brian Roberts. From the original illustrations in the Scott Polar Research Institute, Cambridge.* London, Blandford Press, 1967.

SCOTT, Robert Falcon. *Scott's last expedition. Vols. 1 and 2. Arranged by L. Huxley.* London, Smith, Elder, 1913.

SEAVER, George. *Edward Wilson of the Antarctic. Naturalist and friend.* London, John Murray, 1966. (Paperback edition containing a memoir of Oriana Wilson.)

SEAVER, George. *Edward Wilson: nature-lover.* London, John Murray, 1937.

SEAVER, George. *The faith of Edward Wilson.* London, John Murray, 1937.

SOUTH POLAR TIMES. Vol. III. London, Smith, Elder, 1914.

TAYLOR, Thomas Griffith. *With Scott: the silver lining.* London, Smith, Elder, 1916.

WILSON, Edward Adrian. *Diary of the Discovery expedition to the Antarctic regions 1901–1904. Edited from the original mss. in the Scott Polar Research Institute, Cambridge, by Ann Savours.* London, Blandford Press, 1966.

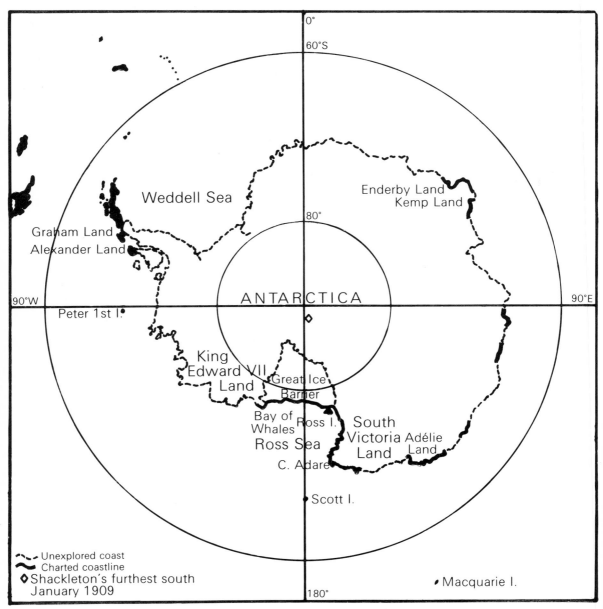

Antarctica in 1910

REFERENCES

CHAPTER 1

1 Oriana Wilson (1875–1945). Eldest of the five children of the Rev. F. A. Souper. She and Wilson were married on 16 July 1901 a few weeks before Wilson left on Scott's first Antarctic expedition on board *Discovery*.

2 Also known as the Pilot Whale or Blackfish, *Globicephala melaena* (Traill). Dr. F. C. Fraser of the British Museum (Nat. Hist.) associates the term 'caa'ing' with 'ca'' which can mean both 'call' and 'drive'. It is not clear, he says, whether the word refers to the herding habits of these whales or to the method by which they are driven shoreward for slaughter. Personally he inclines to the latter explanation.

3 Admiral Sir Leopold McClintock (1819–1907), Arctic explorer who discovered the fate of Sir John Franklin and was a pioneer of sledging and polar survival technique.

4 Edward W. Nelson, biologist on Scott's *Terra Nova* expedition.

5 William Eagle Clarke, editor of Yarell's *History of British Birds* which Wilson illustrated but which was never published.

6 Alex Lange.

7 The firm of Chr. Salvesen and Co. The partners at this time were the founder, Christian, and his three sons (not brothers) Theodore, Fred and Tom. The stations mentioned were all owned by the firm, not, as stated by Wilson, by individual family members.

8 Identification of whales referred to on p. 4
Bottle-nose Whale =*Hyperoodon ampullatus* Forster
Finner = Common Rorqual or Fin Whale *Balaenoptera physalus* (Linn.)
Seihval = Sei Whale or Rudolph's Rorqual *Balaenoptera borealis* Lesson
Humpback = *Megaptera novaeangliae* (Borowski)
Blue Whale and Sibbald's Rorqual are two names for the same species *Balaenoptera musculus* —the distinction implied in the text is not clear. Atlantic or Southern Right Whale. Atlantic= North Atlantic Right Whale, *Balaena glacialis*, Southern Right Whale = *B. australis*. Wilson's alternatives are understandable. The conspecificity of the northern and southern forms is dubious still.

9 Founded as Hvalfangeri Alexandra in 1904, the name was changed to Alexandra Whaling Co. Ltd. in 1907. The company was taken over by Chr. Salvesen and Co. in 1916.

10 Shetland Co. Properly Shetland Hvalfangerselskab, whose chief whaler was Anders Bernsten —probably the 'Capt. Bernstein' referred to in the journal.

11 Should read 'Norrøna'.

12 Founded by Chr. Salvesen as the Olna Whaling Co. in 1904. The factory equipment and manager, Henrik N. Henriksen, had been transferred from Iceland. It was the largest of the four Shetland stations and accounted for about 50 per cent of their total production.

13 Should read 'Herlofsen'.

14 R. C. Haldane, zoologist and whale observer.

15 In 1905 Wilson began a series of illustrations for Bell's *History of British mammals*, edited by Gerald Barrett-Hamilton and published in twenty-one parts between 1910 and 1921.

16 Dr. F. C. Fraser writes: 'The vernacular name Northern Rorqual for *B. borealis* is unfamiliar to me. It is not included in *Hershkovitz's Catalog of living whales* (Bulletin of the Smithsonian Inst. 246) which includes a comprehensive glossary of cetacean vernacular names.'

17 *Balaenoptera acutorostrata.*

18 *Balaena mysticetus* (Linn.)

19 A. S. Leslie, Secretary of the Board of Agriculture's Commission on the investigation of Grouse Disease in Scotland. Wilson was at this time hastening to complete his own contribution to the final report.

20 W. Berry, a colleague of Wilson's during the Grouse Commission investigations.

21 The Wilsons' house at Cheltenham.

22 William Sharpe and Sons, then at Colonnade House, Cheltenham, who manufactured the snow goggles used in the Antarctic. The firm ceased business about 1950.

23 St. Philip's Church, about a mile from Westal, where the Wilson family worshipped.

24 Ida and Biddy (Elsie), Wilson's sisters.

25 Wilson's family on his mother's side. She was born Mary Agnes Whishaw.

26 The changes of plumage in the Red Grouse (*Lagopus scoticus* Lath.) in health and disease. *Proceedings of the Zoological Society of London*, 1910, p. 1000–33.

27 William Robert Ogilvie-Grant (1863–1924), ornithologist at the British Museum (Nat. Hist.) who after the return of the *Terra Nova* took charge of Wilson's bird notes and specimens.

28 Gerald Edwin Hamilton Barrett-Hamilton (1871–1914), a friend of Wilson's since his undergraduate days at Cambridge and author of *A History of British mammals* which Wilson illustrated.

29 Presumably Charles Edward Fagan (1855–1921), ornithologist and conservationist, at this time Assistant Secretary of the British Museum (Nat. Hist.).

30 Reginald John Smith, K.C. (1867–1916), head of the publishing house of Smith, Elder and Co., who, with his wife, was an intimate friend of the Wilsons.

31 Aneroid barometer later to be used on the polar plateau.

32 Sir Clements Markham (1830–1916), President of the Royal Geographical Society and 'father' of Scott's *Discovery* and *Terra Nova* expeditions.

33 T. V. Hodgson (1864–1926), biologist on Scott's *Discovery* expedition, 1901–4, and Curator of Plymouth Museum.

CHAPTER 2

1 Originally referred to the hands who worked the after sails and who frequently berthed aft. Later this became synonymous with the officers, for the same reasons.

2 Ship designed for operation in polar waters and built for Scott's Antarctic expedition of 1901–4.

3 Converted sealer which relieved Scott's *Discovery* expedition in February 1903 and again, with the *Terra Nova*, in January 1904.

4 Now called the British Storm Petrel, *Hydrobates pelagicus*. But some of these birds were probably Wilson's Petrels, *Oceanites oceanicus*.

5 A marine animal belonging to the Tunicates.

6 Presumably the Basking Shark *Cotorhinus maximus*, whose Norwegian common name is Brugde.

7 *Orcinus orca* (Linn.).

8 *Oceanodroma leucorhoa.*

9 This was a preliminary report on the changes of plumage in the Red Grouse (see chapter 1, note 26). J. G. Millais and W. R. Ogilvie-Grant had both made special studies of this subject. Wilson acknowledged the comprehensive nature of their investigations but was himself able to give a more complete account, based on his collection for the grouse disease inquiry of some 600 skins, representing every age, phase and change of plumage.

10 *Stercorarius pomarinus.*

11 Michael Barne (1877–1961), Second Lieutenant on board *Discovery*, 1901–4.

12 Now called *Gygis alba.*

13 Probably the white-bellied Storm Petrel, now called *Fregetta grallaria.*

14 Cf. Cherry-Garrard, *The worst journey in the world*, p. 11. 'At other times we played the most childish games—there was one called "The Priest of the Parish has lost his Cap", over which we laughed till we cried, and much money was added to the wine fund.'

15 Ilha da Trinidade, an island about 750 miles off the coast of Brazil in lat. 20°29′S., long. 29°20′W.

16 Probably the Red-footed Booby, *Sula sula.*

17 *Puffinus gravis.*

18 The British passenger liner *Waratah* bound from Durban to London had disappeared without trace in July 1909.

19 Two species are known from the island: *Fregata minor* and *F. ariel*.

20 As Wilson suspected, the three forms described proved to be polymorphic, with several colour phases, now all united under the name *Pterodroma arminjoniana*.

21 Now called *Pterodroma mollis*.

22 *Diomedea exulans*.

23 Probably *Diomedea chrysostoma*, but at that time there was much confusion about the field identification of albatrosses.

24 See chapter 10, note 1.

25 Wilson evidently did not distinguish between the Sooty Albatross, *Phoebetria fusca*, and the Light-mantled Sooty Albatross, *P. palpebrata*.

26 *Macronectes giganteus*.

27 For an explanation of this term see entry for 19 October 1910.

28 Admiral Sir George Egerton (1852–1940), who had served as a lieutenant on the *Alert* during the British Arctic Expedition of 1875–6. He was Commander-in-Chief, Cape of Good Hope, 1908–10.

CHAPTER 3

1 Sir Arthur Everett Shipley (1861–1927), invertebrate zoologist, at this time Reader in Zoology at the University of Cambridge. He was a personal friend of Wilson and worked with him in the preparation of the grouse disease report.

2 Constance Souper, who had accompanied her sister Oriana Wilson to South Africa to await the arrival of the *Terra Nova*.

3 This station (lat. 33°S., long. 18°E.) was opened in 1910, the year of Wilson's visit.

4 Admiral Sir Arthur William Moore (1847–1934).

5 John Ruskin (1819–1900), whose artistic and social principles Wilson admired so enormously.

6 A relative of Wilson's.

7 Professor Sir Tannatt William Edgeworth David (1858–1934). In 1907, at the age of fifty, while Professor of Geology at Sydney University, he joined Shackleton's *Nimrod* expedition, taking with him the young Douglas Mawson

(see note 23 in this chapter). He organised and led the first ascent of Mount Erebus and without dogs or ponies achieved a journey to the South Magnetic Pole, a distance of over 1,300 miles. Among David's students were Griffith Taylor, Frank Debenham and Raymond Priestley, all three of whom travelled south with Scott on *Terra Nova*.

8 From a letter from Oriana Wilson dated 28 August 1910 and reproduced in the Wilson family's typed version of the diary (S.P.R.I. ms. 715/2).

9 Black-footed Penguin, *Spheniscus demersus*.

10 Several species of cormorant occur here, mostly *Phalacrocorax capensis*.

11 *Larus dominicanus*.

12 Grey-beaked Gull, *Larus cirrocephalus*.

13 *Haematopus moquini*.

14 Cape Gannet, *Morsus bassanus*.

15 Fridtjof Nansen (1861–1930), the Norwegian explorer who in 1893 unsuccessfully attempted to reach the North Pole by letting his ship *Fram* freeze in the ice and drift with the Arctic Ocean current. He eventually left the *Fram* and with one companion made a remarkable journey across the frozen seas to Franz Josef Land.

16 On 6 April 1909 the American explorer Robert E. Peary, with Matthew Henson and four Eskimoes, claimed to have reached the North Geographical Pole. The priority, however, was challenged by another American, Dr. Frederick A. Cook, who claimed to have reached it on 21 April 1908.

17 Properly *Balaenoptera musculus*.

18 More likely the Southern Right Whale *Balaena australis*.

19 = Sperm Whale *Physeter catodon*.

20 Minke Whale or Lesser Rorqual=*Balaenoptera acutorostrata*. Dr. F. C. Fraser writes: 'I cannot find a reference to *B. rudolphi*. The generic name *Rudolphius* Gray 1866 has as type species *Sibbaldius laticeps* Gray=*Balaenoptera borealis* Lesson.'

21 Dr. F. C. Fraser writes: 'The observation on the differences between the whalebone obtained from North Sea Sei Whales and West African Sei Whales is interesting in view of the fact that in 1912 the West African form with the inferior baleen was distinguished as a separate species *Balaenoptera brydei* Olsen.'

22 The price quoted was for Greenland Right Whale baleen.

23 Sir Douglas Mawson (1882–1958), Antarctic explorer and geologist. In 1907, while a lecturer at Adelaide University, he was chosen to accompany Sir Edgeworth David on Shackleton's *Nimrod* expedition to the Antarctic. Such was the quality of his work and his experience in man-hauling that Scott would have welcomed him on the *Terra Nova* expedition. Mawson, however, decided to head his own expedition in 1911–13, the first of a series culminating in a permanent Australian presence in Antarctica.

24 Sir Ernest Henry Shackleton (1874–1922), who had accompanied Scott on the *Discovery* expedition to the Antarctic in 1901–4 and had been invalided home with scurvy. In 1907–9 he led his own expedition to Antarctica on the *Nimrod*, discovered and ascended the Beardmore Glacier, and got to within 100 miles of the South Pole.

25 The Rev. W. H. Fitchett, who at the time of Wilson's visit to Australia was principal of the Methodist Ladies College, Hawthorn, Melbourne.

CHAPTER 4

1 Relatives of Wilson.

2 Rt. Hon. Andrew Fisher (1862–1928).

3 Frank and Mabel Wilson were cousins of Wilson.

4 Sir Thomas Gibson-Carmichael (1859–1926), later Lord Skirling, Governor of Victoria, Australia, 1908–11.

5 Sir John (later Lord) Forrest (1847–1918), Australian explorer, surveyor and politician. Treasurer of the Commonwealth of Australia 1909–10.

6 Son of Frank and Mabel Wilson.

7 Wilson's elder brother.

8 Sir Walter Baldwin Spencer (1860–1929), Professor of Biology, University of Melbourne, 1887–1919. One of Scott's most helpful sponsors in Australia.

9 Samuel Hordern, head of a large Sydney department store.

10 *Fregetta tropica*.

11 *Pachyptila desolata* subsp.

12 *Daption capensis*.

13 *Diomedea melanophris*.

14 James Wilson, Wilson's younger brother.

15 *Pelecanoides* sp.

16 Sir Joseph James Kinsey (1852–1936), head of Kinsey and Co., shipping agents, of Christchurch, New Zealand, and Scott's friend and trusted agent.

17 Wife of the Hon. Charles Christopher Bowen (1830–1917), an active business man and politician, at this period Speaker of the New Zealand Legislative Council. He was an old friend of Sir Clements Markham, President of the Royal Geographical Society, and threw himself heart and soul into the preparations in New Zealand for the Scott expedition.

18 Presumably the family of Sir Henry Francis Wigram (1857–1934), a public figure in Christchurch.

19 James Dennistoun joined *Terra Nova* in October 1911 in charge of the mules sent from India to replace the ponies.

20 Probably the daughter of C. A. C. Hardy, who owned a store at Rakaia. He was a member of the New Zealand House of Representatives from 1899 to 1911 and then a member of the Legislative Council from 1913 till his death in 1922.

21 William Benham, Professor of Zoology at Otago University and Curator of the Otago Museum.

CHAPTER 5

1 The Beaufort notation of the force of the wind is not supplied by Wilson. In an abbreviated form it is:

Force				Description
0	..	..	..	Calm
1–2	..	..	..	Light airs
3	..	..	..	Light breeze
4–5	..	..	..	Moderate breeze
6–7	..	..	..	Strong wind
8–9	..	..	..	Gale
10–11	..	..	..	Storm
12	..	..	..	Hurricane

2 Horizontal rail at ship's side carrying belaying pins.

3 Dr. F. C. Fraser writes: 'At the time of Wilson's writing the Fin Whale's specific name was *Balaenoptera musculus* and the Blue Whale's *B. sibbaldi*. The specific names now accepted are for the Fin Whale *B. physalus* and for the Blue Whale *B. musculus*.'

4 See the plate in Wilson's *Diary of the 'Discovery' Expedition* facing page 96, which illustrates these. Dr. F. C. Fraser has identified them, with reservations, as *Lagenorhynchus cruciger*.

5 The White-headed Petrel, *Pterodroma lessoni*.

6 The eastern extremity of Ross Island. It was discovered and named in 1841 by Sir James Clark Ross for his second in command, Commander Francis Crozier, captain of the *Terror*. It is only 3 miles from the junction with the ice shelf or 'Barrier', and close to a large Emperor Penguin rookery.

7 A cape forming the western extremity of Ross Island. It was discovered by Scott's *Discovery* expedition, 1901–4, and named for Lieutenant Charles Rawson Royds (see note 9 below).

8 The 'Great Ice Barrier' was so named by its discoverer Sir James Clark Ross during his Antarctic voyage of 1839–43. It is now known as the Ross Ice Shelf and is an extension of the continental ice-sheet floating on the sea. Its total area of 310,000 square miles is rather larger than that of France.

9 Admiral Sir Charles W. Rawson Royds (1876–1931). Accompanied Scott's *Discovery* expedition 1901–4 as First Lieutenant R.N. in charge of the meteorological work.

10 A small promontory lying N.W. of Cape Armitage at the southern end of Hut Point Peninsula on Ross Island. It was discovered and named by Scott's *Discovery* expedition 1901–4, which built a hut at this point, and was used as an advance base of Shackleton's *Nimrod* expedition of 1907–9.

11 Now called *Fulmarus glacialoides*.

12 Now called *Macronectes giganteus*.

CHAPTER 6

1 *Aptenodytes forsteri*.

2 *Pagodroma nivea*.

3 *Thallasoica antarctica*.

4 *Fulmaris glacialoides*.

5 *Oceanites oceanicus*.

6 *Pygoscelis adeliae*.

7 Leopard seal *Hydrurga leptonyx*.

8 Sobriquet for Dr. George Murray Levick, also known as 'Tofferino'.

9 Navigable passages through the pack ice.

10 In November 1908, J. W. Brooke, the explorer, accompanied by Meares, was on his way to India via Lolo Land, a wild central Asian land nominally tributary to Lhasa, when he was killed by lawless tribesmen.

11 *Catharacta skua*.

12 A flag bearing the arms of Caius College, Cambridge presented to Wilson by Mrs. Roberts, wife of the Master, Dr. E. S. Roberts, and later carried to the Pole.

13 Wife of John Poynder Dickson-Poynder, 1st Baron Islington (1866–1936), Governor of New Zealand (1910–12).

CHAPTER 7

1 A non-existent range of mountains which Sir James Clark Ross thought he saw in January 1841 to the east of Ross Island and running south of Cape Crozier, named for Sir William Edward Parry.

2 Petty Officer Jacob Cross R.N. and stoker Thomas Whitfield, of Scott's *Discovery* expedition 1901–4.

3 Refers to the rough surface of the ablation area on the Barrier in the McMurdo Sound region west of long. 166°E., varying in height from a few inches to 60 feet.

4 Explored for the first time on Scott's *Discovery* expedition 1901–4 when it was known as 'Discovery Glacier'. Named for Reginald Koettlitz (1861–1916), surgeon on this expedition.

5 The Wolseley motor sledges were powered by a four-cylinder air-cooled engine with gears giving speeds up to 2 or 3 m.p.h. They had neither steering nor brakes and were designed for use on snow. Despite previous tests in Switzerland and Norway they failed owing to

overheating and failure of the big ends. Nevertheless, they marked the first attempt to use track-laying transport in Antarctica and were the forerunners of the tank in the war of 1914–18.

6 One of seven major valley glaciers draining into the ice shelf, 100 miles long and 12 miles wide on average. It was discovered by Shackleton's *Nimrod* expedition in December 1908 and named by Shackleton for his patron Sir William Beardmore, later Lord Invernairn.

CHAPTER 8

1 For a note on this and other sledge dogs on Scott's last expedition see F. Debenham's article 'Stareek: the story of a sledge dog'. *Polar Record*, Vol. 4, No. 25, 1943, pp. 19–24.

2 Not Russian. Probably some local dialect of the upper Amur River or Sakhalin Island from which regions most of the dogs were selected by Meares.

3 Sometimes called 'mock suns', parhelia are images of the sun, coloured or white, appearing at the same elevation and on both sides of the sun. They are caused by the refraction of sunlight within hexagonal ice crystals.

4 Cf. Wilson's poem 'The Barrier Silence', p. 177.

5 A 'tank' was a large canvas holdall for use on a sledge.

6 Properly Minna Bluff, a narrow peninsula projecting S.E. from Mount Discovery into the N.W. portion of the Barrier. It was discovered on Scott's 1901–4 expedition and named for Lady Minna Markham, wife of Sir Clements Markham.

7 i.e. a gap between Crater Hill and Observation Hill serving as a back-door approach to Hut Point from the Barrier North of Pram Point, on occasions when there was no direct approach over sea ice.

8 A natural harbour in the Barrier about 330 miles E. of Cape Crozier. The area had previously been visited by C. E. Borchgrevink in February 1900, by the *Discovery* expedition in 1902 and then by Shackleton in January 1908, who named it because of the large number of whales to be found there.

9 The construction of this sentence is at fault, but it is reproduced as written in the original diary.

10 Amundsen, with four companions and thirteen dogs pulling four sledges, left his base 'Framheim' on the Bay of Whales on 19 October 1911. By 17 December they had reached the South Pole and by 25 January had returned safely to base, having thus covered a total of 1,860 miles in 99 days.

11 Snow walls were necessary to protect the ponies from wind and drifting snow. The ponies suffered considerably from cold during the early depot laying days because of their thin coats.

12 Fog-like clouds caused by the contact of cold air with relatively warm water.

CHAPTER 9

1 This was the hut built on Scott's *Discovery* expedition to be used as a workroom and refuge in case of shipwreck.

2 Finnesko (or finsko) means 'Lappshoe' in Norwegian and is a winter boot used by Lapps and Scandinavians living in the far north. The shoe was made of reindeer skin and lined with 'sennegraes' (dried sedge) to absorb moisture and insulate the feet.

3 A cross erected on the summit of Hut Point to commemorate Able Seaman George Thomas Vince, of the *Discovery* expedition, who drowned after slipping down a steep ice slope during a blizzard, March 1902.

4 A fine-grained igneous rock.

5 Volcanic features to the west of Castle Rock.

6 Floating ice in the transition stage between new ice and first-year ice about 4 inches to 1 foot in thickness.

7 Commonest of the pyroxene family of rock-forming minerals.

CHAPTER 10

1 The *South Polar Times*, the expedition magazine, started on the *Discovery* expedition with Shackle-

ton as editor, and continued on the *Terra Nova* expedition under Cherry-Garrard's editorship. Contributions (anonymous) were placed in a box nailed to the wall of the hut; a selection was made and the articles were typed. Wilson settled what illustrations he would paint and spaces were left for them where he wanted. The original is now in the British Museum but a limited facsimile edition of 350 copies was published by Smith, Elder in 1914.

2 Carl Størmer (1874–1957), an eminent astrophysicist, Professor of Pure Mathematics at Oslo University. He made a special study of aurora and devised a method of determining the heights and positions of aurora by means of photography.

3 A group of fish common in Antarctic waters.

4 Two of the three thermometer screens from which daily readings were taken. The third screen was sited on the Ramp.

5 A series of coloured rings surrounding the moon, produced by diffraction of the light by water drops.

6 At this period the condition of scurvy was attributed, wrongly, to increased acidity of the blood—acid intoxication—caused by bacterial action ('ptomaine' poisoning from canned foods, for example). Hence the practice of testing blood for its alkalinity, expressed as normal 'N'. Blood is normally on the alkaline side and can therefore be expressed chemically as the equivalent alkaline solution, an increase in acidity making the blood a weaker alkali. The true cause of scurvy as a vitamin disease was generally not accepted until after the First World War.

7 Dr. J. D. Gomershall writes: 'The most likely explanation for Dr. Wilson's experience . . . is an increase in positive ionisation in the atmosphere which precedes the wind. Dr. F. G. Sulman, Director of the Institute of Pharmacology, Hebrew University, Jerusalem, has found such ions in the atmosphere 24–48 hours before the wind called the Sharar which blows over the eastern Mediterranean from time to time. A similar effect has been found in central Europe before the wind known as the Foehn. The positive ions appear to enter the body via the lungs and cause the release of serotonin from the thrombocytes in the blood. This substance

and similar ones appear to affect the cranial blood vessels, causing the constriction followed by painful dilation characteristic of migraine. This response of the body to a build-up of positive ions may take several hours and the time of 10–12 hours preceding the blizzard would probably be the time in which one would expect symptoms.'

8 An actress of the period who allowed herself a degree of *déshabille* on stage which was considered to be well in advance of convention.

9 George Edward Marston (1882–1940), artist on Shackleton's *Nimrod* and *Endurance* expeditions of 1907–9 and 1914–16.

10 Alistair Forbes Mackay (1878–1914), biologist and surgeon on Shackleton's *Nimrod* expedition, 1907–9.

11 William Roberts (1872–?) and Ernest Mills Joyce (1875–1940). Joyce was a member of both Shackleton's *Nimrod* and Scott's *Discovery* expeditions. Sir Raymond Priestley, who knew both men well, writes: 'I should not have described either of the two men as being "rotters". . . . As regards Joyce, Wilson's opinion must, I think, stem from some incident on the *Discovery* expedition when the crew of the *Discovery*, not selected for that particular life, were compelled to spend two winters in the Antarctic through the ship being frozen in.'

12 Primitive family of the protozoa containing many parasites of man and animal.

13 'Gilguy—a gadget, especially used by sailors.' (*Webster's Third New International Dictionary*.)

CHAPTER 11

1 Now termed 'hummocked ice', this is a form of floating ice which has been squeezed together and in places forced upwards to form an uneven surface.

2 Presumably refers to Otto Sverdrup's expedition to the Canadian Arctic in the *Fram*, 1898–1902.

3 No figure given. Nowadays ration values are calculated in 'calories' or more properly 'kilocalories' and not in foot pounds of energy. The editor is obliged to Dr. Allan Rogers for the following note on the Pole ration: 'Scott's

barrier ration gave 4,250 Kcals per man per day. The summit ration used from the foot of the Beardmore Glacier onwards and for the whole of the return journey gave 4,600 Kcals a day. The summit ration gave protein 257 grams, fat 210 grams, carbohydrate 417 grams a day. It contained absolutely no vitamin "C" at all. It had an inadequate vitamin "A" and "D" content and only small quantities of the other vitamins such as the "B" group. Scott probably needed half as many calories again.'

4 His wedding anniversary.

5 For the subsequent history of the eggs see A. Cherry-Garrard's *The worst journey in the world*, 1965 ed., pp. 299–300 and 300A–D. Dr. C. W. Parsons of the British Museum (Nat. Hist.), who examined the embryos, wrote of them in his official report entitled 'Penguin embryos' in *British Antarctic ('Terra Nova') Expedition 1910–13. Natural History Reports. Zoology*, Vol. 4, No. 7, 1934, pp. 253–62. 'Taking a broad view of the facts as they have been adduced, both from a consideration of the unique group of three Emperor Penguin embryos and of the series of Adélie embryos, it must be stated that neither has added greatly to our knowledge of penguin embryology. . . .'

6 The site of the stone hut was visited as recently as January 1971 by Dr. and Mrs. D. Müller-Schwarze of Utah State University. Photographs sent to the editor by Dr. Müller-Schwarze show that the rectangular base of the hut is still more or less intact together with the opening or 'door'.

CHAPTER 12

1 Sir Norman Lockyer (1836–1920), distinguished astronomer, then Director of the Solar Physics Observatory, London. Lockyer's paper 'Southern hemisphere surface air circulation', 1910, is discussed by Simpson in *British Antarctic ('Terra Nova') Expedition 1910–1913 Meteorology*, Vol. 1, 1919, pp. 206–47.

2 Theodore Roosevelt (1858–1919), President of the United States of America (1901–8), included an appendix on protective coloration in his book *African game trails: an account of the African wanderings of an American hunter-naturalist* (London, 1910). Abbott H. Thayer was an over-zealous supporter of protective coloration in nature who tried to make it cover almost every type of coloration in the animal kingdom. He published a paper 'Concealing coloration: an answer to Theodore Roosevelt'. *Bulletin of the American Museum of Natural History*, Vol. 39, 1912, pp. 313–21.

3 An anonymous volume of essays by Stephen Paget, F.R.C.S. *Confessio medici. By the writer of 'The young people'* (London, 1908).

4 A primitive form of marine life.

5 Venesta board—plywood composed of three layers of wood cemented by a patent process and noted for its strength and waterproof properties. It was manufactured by Venesta Ltd. of London who supplied packing cases of this material to Scott's and Shackleton's expeditions.

6 Cecil Meares contributed a verse on this theme to the *South Polar Times*, the refrain of which ran as follows:

'Then pont, Ponko, pont and long may Ponko pont;
With his finger on the trigger of his 'gadget'.
For whenever he's around, we're sure to hear the sound
Of his high speed cinematographic ratchet.'

7 Under the title *90° South* and with a sound track added in later years by Ponting, this film has become a classic of its kind.

8 This poem, 'The Barrier Silence', was published in the *South Polar Times*, October 1911, p. 151, and is reproduced in facsimile on p. 177. It was 'his first and only poem' according to Wilson's biographer, George Seaver. In *With Scott: the silver lining* Griffith Taylor relates (p. 313) how Wilson came to him with the poem and asked him to type it so that Cherry-Garrard, editor of the *S.P.T.*, would not recognise it. 'He wanted it to be perfectly anonymous, for he knew anything of Bill's would go in from our admiration of the writer. I saw that he had copied my footnote (so as to puzzle Cherry further) asking that an illustration be appended by the artist on the staff!' A few days later Cherry congratulated Griffith Taylor on the authorship which the latter was compelled to disclaim. He then asked Griffith

Taylor to clear up two of the lines; this 'Griff' declined to do but suggested showing it to Wilson, as artist, declaring that anything he agreed to would satisfy the author!

9 Inflammation of a horse's hoof.

10 Organised as follows:
   Motor party: Lt. Evans, Day, Lashly, Hooper.
   Pony party: Scott, Wilson, Oates, Bowers, Wright, Atkinson, Cherry-Garrard, P.O. Evans, Crean, Keohane.
   Dog party: Meares, Demitri.

11 Sir Charles Wright comments: 'Marie Nelson's thermometer did not *register* to 1/1000th °C. but could be *estimated* to 1/1000th °C.'

12 Sir Charles Wright points out that this sentence should read 'pendulum observations and the natural ionisation of the atmosphere (over land, water and near islands).'

13 These pages are in fact lacking in Wilson's original manuscript (S.P.R.I. ms. 234/3) but they are included in the Wilson family's typed version of the diary (S.P.R.I. ms. 715/2) and are accordingly reproduced here.

CHAPTER 13

1 One of the ponies who had died during depot laying operations the previous February.

2 Cirrostratus—transparent, whitish cloud veil of fibrous (hair-like) or smooth appearance, totally or partly covering the sky.

3 Blucher—one of the ponies.

4 A triple-peaked massif (15,100 ft.) standing prominently above the surrounding lesser peaks S.W. of Shackleton Inlet along the western edge of the Barrier. It was discovered by Scott's southern party on 27 December 1902 and named for Sir Clements Markham, President of the Royal Geographical Society.

5 Tinted patches of red and green, sometimes of blue and yellow, occasionally observed in high clouds, generally within 30° of the sun, the boundaries of the tints tending to follow the outline of the cloud.

6 Cirrus clouds—detached clouds in the form of white, delicate filaments, or white or mostly white patches or narrow bands, having a fibrous appearance, or a silky sheen, or both.

7 Geographical miles (1 mile geographical = 1·15 statute miles).

8 On 21 November 1908, just south of the 81st parallel.

9 This sketch appears in one of Wilson's two field notebooks (S.P.R.I. ms. 797/1). Unfortunately, for technical reasons, it has not been practical to reproduce it here.

10 A series of coloured rings surrounding the sun produced by diffraction of the light by water drops.

11 Twin-peaked mountain (10,350 ft.) on the west side of the Barrier. Discovered by Scott's southern party on 26 December 1902 and named for Llewellyn Longstaff, principal contributor to the *Discovery* expedition.

12 A snow-covered rocky cape on the western edge of the Barrier discovered by Scott's southern party in 1902 and named for E. A. Wilson.

13 An isolated nunatak (2,758 ft.) projecting through the ice east of the western portal of the Beardmore Glacier. It was discovered and climbed by Shackleton's South Pole party on 3 December 1908 and so named because from its summit could be seen the Beardmore Glacier stretching south-westward to the polar plateau. The Gap, or 'Gateway' as Shackleton's party termed it, is the passage between Mount Hope and the mainland leading to the glacier.

14 Stratus—generally grey cloud layer with a fairly uniform base, which may give drizzle, ice prisms or snow grains.

15 An igneous rock.

16 Following this sentence Wilson originally wrote: 'So we shall begin our *new can* tomorrow 8th for breakfast instead of for lunch today 7th. This was used up during the blizzard. We opened the new one on the 7th and breakfast of the 8th came out of the old one.' The first sentence was afterwards crossed out and the third amended to that in the text.

CHAPTER 14

1 Discovered and named by Shackleton's 1907–9 expedition for Lord Oxford and Asquith.

2 A mountain (5,836 ft.) in the Commonwealth Range rising precipitously above the Beardmore Glacier about 22 miles up from its outlet. Discovered by Shackleton's expedition in 1908 and named for an Australian newspaper proprietor, Evan Kyffin-Thomas.

3 Published in George Seaver's *Edward Wilson of the Antarctic*, 1933, pp. 273–4. Meares and Demitri reached Hut Point on 4 January 1912.

4 A stratigraphical term referring to a distinctive group of fossil-bearing sedimentary formations discovered during Scott's *Discovery* expedition.

5 A mountain 9,971 ft. high forming the most conspicuous landmark along the west side of the Beardmore Glacier. It was discovered in December 1908 by Shackleton's southern party and so named because a cloud, usually appearing near the summit, provided a useful landmark.

6 A small glacier entering the west side of the Beardmore Glacier about 18 miles up the glacier from the Barrier. Discovered by Shackleton's southern party in December 1908 and named for the pony Socks who disappeared in a nearby crevasse.

7 Shackleton's position at midday on 8 December 1908.

8 This glacier is provisionally identified and described with a memory sketch in Wilson's sketchbook (S.P.R.I. ms. 797/2).

9 Left blank in the ms. Mount Wild (11,200 ft.) seems the most probable landmark. Discovered by Shackleton's southern party in December 1908, it was named for Frank Wild, one of the four men who marched to within 97 miles of the South Pole.

10 Also referred to as Buckley Island, an isolated peak (nunatak) 8,384 ft. high lying on the western side of the head of the Beardmore Glacier. Discovered by Shackleton's southern party in December 1908 and named for George Buckley, a New Zealand sheep farmer.

11 Published in part in George Seaver's *Edward Wilson of the Antarctic*, 1933, pp. 274–5. The First Supporting Party reached Hut Point on 26 January 1912.

12 Possibly the same as the 'glass-house' ice described by Griffith Taylor in his chapter 'The Western Journey', *Scott's last expedition*, 1913, Vol. 2, p. 205. On the lower reaches of the Koettlitz Glacier the party found '. . . . great curved platforms often thirty feet wide, which threw us all together in the middle and then dropped us several feet through the "glass" into a pool of water beneath.' On the higher reaches of the Beardmore there would have been no melt water beneath the ice surface.

13 A flat-topped mountain or ridge (13,300 ft.), the highest point in the Commonwealth Range.

14 Two hoops!—a topical phrase expressing a superlative degree. Cf. 'first rate'.

CHAPTER 15

1 An extract from this letter is published in George Seaver's *Edward Wilson of the Antarctic*, 1933, pp. 276–7. The Last Supporting Party reached Hut Point on 22 February 1912.

2 Strat cum.=stratocumulus—grey or whitish or both grey and whitish patch, sheet or layer of cloud which almost always has dark parts composed of tessellations, rounded masses, rolls, etc.

3 Sharp, irregular ridges formed on a snow surface by wind erosion and deposition. The ridges are parallel to the direction of the prevailing wind.

4 With this entry Wilson occasionally writes the camp number in the margin of the diary. Camp 1 was Hut Point.

5 Presumably Wilson's brother, Bernard.

6 There is no chart drawn in Wilson's diary or in either of his two sketchbooks. For a detailed account of the astronomical observations made by Scott and Amundsen's parties at the Pole see A. R. Hinks: 'The observations of Amundsen and Scott at the South Pole'. *Geographical Journal*, Vol. 103, No. 4, 1944, pp. 160–80.

CHAPTER 16

1 Alto str=altostratus—greyish or bluish cloud sheet of striated, fibrous or uniform appearance, totally or partly covering the sky, and having

parts thin enough to reveal the sun at least vaguely, as through ground glass.

2 For a conjectural diagnosis of Wilson's leg condition see Bernard J. Freedman: 'Dr. Edward Wilson of the Antarctic. A biographical sketch followed by an inquiry into the nature of his last illness.' *Proceedings of the Royal Society of Medicine*, Vol. 47, No. 3, 1954, pp. 183–9.

3 A rocky crag or small mountain projecting from a glacier or ice sheet.

4 Wilson's notes on this visit to Mount Buckley occupy six pages of detailed notes and sketches in one of his two sketchbooks (S.P.R.I. ms. 797/2).

5 i.e. Camp of 5–8 December 1911.

INDEX